# CANCER **RIGHTS** LAW

**SECOND EDITION**

## A Tool for Effective Navigation

MONICA FAWZY BRYANT AND
JOANNA FAWZY DORAN

ABA
AMERICAN BAR ASSOCIATION
Health Law Section

TRIAGE CANCER

Cover design by Mary Anne Kulchawik/ABA Design



Printed in the United States of America.

29 28 27 26 25     5 4 3 2 1

A catalog record for this book is available from the Library of Congress.

*To the hundreds of thousands of people who have been touched by cancer and have touched our lives over the past 30 years . . .*

*To those who have shared their stories of success and struggle . . .*

*To those who have sought a path toward knowledge and self-empowerment . . .*

*To those still searching for a guide through the maze of cancer-related legal issues . . .*

*To those who have donned the mantle of advocacy to help others . . .*

*We dedicate this book to you.*

# Contents

**CHAPTER FOUR**



**CHAPTER FIVE**

## CHAPTER SEVEN

# Preface

As of January 1, 2022, there were more than 18 million cancer survivors alive in the United States.[1] The number of cancer survivors is projected to grow to 26 million by 2040.[2] In 2024 alone, a little more than two million people will have been diagnosed with cancer.[3] In the United States, an estimated 42 out of 100 men, and 40 out of 100 women, will develop cancer during their lifetime.[4] Given the prevalence of cancer diagnoses, it is unusual to find someone who has not been touched by cancer in some way.

Our primary goals in writing this book are (1) to generate more awareness of the legal issues that often arise as a result of a cancer diagnosis; and (2) to cultivate more advocates to assist individuals diagnosed with cancer and their families, friends, and caregivers in navigating those issues.

## What Is Cancer Rights Law?

Cancer rights law is a colliding amalgamation of a number of separate areas of law, including employment, insurance, government benefits, consumer rights, and estate planning.

Some of the topics discussed in this book are not even thought of as legal issues by a lay audience, such as health insurance. However, the availability of health insurance coverage, consumer protections in the use of coverage, and the right to appeal denials of coverage are all routed in laws. And, this lack of awareness of the law and failure to recognize its power to help people has been a barrier to people getting their needs met.

---

1. American Cancer Society, Cancer Facts & Figures 2024 (2024), https://www.cancer.org/content/dam/cancer-org/research/cancer-facts-and-statistics/annual-cancer-facts-and-figures/2024/2024-cancer-facts-and-figures-acs.pdf.

2. American Cancer Society, Cancer Treatment & Survivorship Facts & Figures 2022–2024 (2022), https://www.cancer.org/content/dam/cancer-org/research/cancer-facts-and-statistics/cancer-treatment-and-survivorship-facts-and-figures/2022-cancer-treatment-and-survivorship-fandf-acs.pdf.

3. American Cancer Society, *supra* note 1.

4. *Id.*

In the context of a cancer diagnosis, an understanding of your rights can mean the difference between losing your job, your health insurance, or even your home. And in its most extreme case, it can be the difference between getting access to care or losing your life.

This is the first book of its kind to address these legal topics through the lens of cancer diagnosis.

# Foreword

## Joanna Doran: An Unexpected Path

When I started college, I was an international relations major on my way to an international law degree, with dreams of working at the United Nations or The Hague. During my senior year of high school, I started working as an administrative assistant for the John Wayne Cancer Institute's (JWCI's) Psychosocial Care Program. Within JWCI was the Positive Appearance Center, a first-of-its-kind, on-site boutique offering items to deal with the comfort and cosmetic side effects of cancer care. At various times during my eight years at JWCI, I managed operations at the Positive Appearance Center, including fitting patients with mastectomy bras and prostheses and billing insurance companies for those items.

When I started at Loyola Law School in Los Angeles, I learned that there was a course on Cancer Rights Law, the only class of its kind in the country. It was the first elective course I chose to take. I was surprised to learn that it was really a survey course, providing brief exposure to many areas of the law that may become an issue after a cancer diagnosis. I was also surprised to learn that I did not have to purchase a very expensive, four-inch-thick casebook to read for the class. No such casebook on cancer rights law existed. While relieved at the time, when I became the professor for this class eight years later, I realized what a challenge it posed in developing lesson plans. And the idea of writing a book started to form.

While taking the Cancer Rights Law class, I learned about the Women's Health and Cancer Rights Act (WHCRA). It was not a long law, unlike the Patient Protection and Affordable Care Act, but it had a huge impact. An estimated 313,510 women and men will have been diagnosed with breast cancer in 2024.[5] Forty-two percent of women with breast cancer undergo reconstructive surgery.[6]

5. *Id.*

6. Monica Morrow et al., Access to Breast Reconstruction after Mastectomy and Patient Perspectives on Reconstruction Decision Making, 149 JAMA Surgery 1015 (2014), http://jamanetwork.com/journals/jamasurgery/fullarticle/1893807.

WHCRA requires health insurance companies to cover the costs of reconstructive surgery following a mastectomy for breast cancer or breast prostheses to "achieve symmetry," if the plan covers the mastectomy.[7] Prior to the law, insurance companies would often deny reconstructive surgery or the prostheses, claiming that they were cosmetic and not medically necessary. The law also required coverage for reconstructive surgery on the breast where breast cancer was not found, in order to achieve a symmetrical appearance in both breasts.

One day, while working at the Positive Appearance Center, I was reviewing the insurance billing and realized that a patient had been denied coverage for her prosthesis. Breast prostheses are not inexpensive and I knew that it would be a hardship for the patient if she were going to have to pay for it out of her own pocket. So, I called the insurance company and was told that the claim was denied because it was not covered under her plan. After a series of questions, I was still at a loss for why she would have been denied coverage. Finally, I asked, "Wouldn't WHCRA apply to her policy, meaning that her prosthesis must be covered?" There was silence on the other end of the line. After a few moments, the claims representative quietly said, "Yes, I suppose you are right. Please resubmit the claim and we will approve it."

At first, I felt happiness at being able to get the issue resolved for the patient and then a bit of relief that I would not have to tell her that the insurance company would not pay for her prosthesis. But, as the afternoon wore on, the phone conversation kept gnawing at me. I kept wondering what would have happened if I had not mentioned WHCRA. Very few people are aware of such an obscure law, except, apparently, insurance companies. Yet, despite their knowledge of their obligation under WHCRA, it seemed as if their policy was to deny coverage and hope that no one noticed. And the worst thing that could happen is that someone like me could notice, and then they would just approve the claim.

The whole experience made me realize how important it is for all of us to know about and understand our rights and the options that are available to each of us, so that we can make educated decisions about our lives and get access to the benefits and protections to which we are entitled under the law. Advocating for laws that create protections and benefits is only the first step to advocacy. Educating people about those laws is the crucial next step.

That guiding principle led me to a career in advocating on behalf of others, focused on educating people about the rights and options afforded to them under the law. And, it has continued to drive my work in the cancer community for more than 30 years. I look forward to a day where advocates, like myself, are no longer needed.

7. 29 U.S.C. § 1185b (1998).

## Monica Bryant: A Winding Road

While my career path has been anything but straight, the common theme throughout has been a desire to fight for justice and fairness. As long as I can remember, I have had an interest in the law and how it can both oppress and empower people. The law touches almost every aspect of our lives and individuals have to use the law as a tool to become their own advocates. As an undergraduate law and society major, my studies focused on how the law intersected with other disciplines, such as sociology, psychology, anthropology, and biology. Having had the privilege to attend the George Washington School of Law in Washington, D.C., a whole new set of opportunities to interact with the law, in and out of the classroom, were presented. While in law school, and then after graduation, I witnessed and, in some small way, was able to help formulate public policy on a national level. As Legislative Counsel for Congresswoman Linda T. Sánchez, I frequently observed that lobbyists and large interest groups lead the conversation on policy, rather than the people who were going to be most affected by the policies being debated. It continues to amaze me that the average American tends to be unaware of the power they have to effect change using our legislative process.

When I left my job in Congress, I struggled to find a career where I could use my knowledge of the law and the legislative process, as well as my desire to help people find their voices. The stars aligned and my career shifted to that of a cancer rights attorney. Since then, I have found that providing individuals with even the most basic information about the law, in an understandable manner, can change their lives. Over the years, I have had a front-row seat to watch people go from despair over the seemingly unavoidable financial devastation caused by cancer treatment, to elation over finding out that their insurance companies were required to cover a particular treatment. Or that an employer did not have the right to fire them because they needed time off for treatment. It is somewhat of a joke among family and friends that I will never step off my soapbox of encouraging advocacy in its many forms. However, providing that glimmer of hope, in what is often the worst time in someone's life, continues to drive my work.

This book is simply another tool to help people find their voices as advocates.

# About the Authors

**Monica Fawzy Bryant, Esq.**, is a cancer rights attorney, speaker, and author dedicated to improving access to quality information on health care-related issues. She is the co-founder and Chief Operating Officer for Triage Cancer, a national nonprofit organization that provides education on the practical and legal issues that may impact individuals diagnosed with cancer and their caregivers.

In 2022, Ms. Bryant was named as one of Cancer Health 25, an annual list that honors individuals who have made a difference in the lives of people with cancer. In 2019, she received a 40 Under 40 in Cancer Award, and in 2015, was awarded the Legacy Advocate Award by a leading young adult cancer organization. She is an Adjunct Law Professor at the University of Illinois at Chicago School of Law, teaching a class on Cancer Rights. Throughout her career, she has provided nearly 1,000 educational seminars for individuals who have been diagnosed with cancer, their caregivers, lawyers, advocates, health care professionals, elected officials, and the general public.

She regularly shares her expertise through written book chapters, articles, and blogs, and appears on television, radio, and podcast shows. In 2023, she co-wrote an article for *CA: A Cancer Journal for Clinicians* entitled "Cancer Diagnosis and Treatment in Working-Age Adults: Implications for Employment, Health Insurance Coverage, and Financial Hardship in the United States"; and in 2020, she co-wrote the chapter "Cancer-Related Legal Issues" for the Oncology Nursing Society's book *Oncology Nurse Navigation: Delivering Patient-Centered Care across the Continuum*. Ms. Bryant provides expert review for a variety of national organizations, including the Social Security Administration, the American Cancer Society, the Leukemia and Lymphoma Society, Cancer Support Community, Cancer and Careers, National Brain Tumor Foundation, and Livestrong.

Previously, Ms. Bryant was Midwest Regional Director for a national disability rights organization where she forged relationships with cancer organizations, hospitals, law firms, members of underserved communities, and other community partners, to introduce them to the field of Cancer Rights Law. Prior to relocating to Chicago, she served as Legislative Counsel for U.S. Congresswoman Linda T. Sánchez and Law

Clerk for U.S. Senator Dianne Feinstein. During her time in Congress, she worked on health, justice, civil rights, and women's issues.

Ms. Bryant is a member of the American Bar Association's Cancer Legal Advocacy Interest Group, the Coalition to Protect Parenthood after Cancer, the National Cancer Legal Services Network, and many other legal and cancer community initiatives.

She earned a Bachelor of Arts degree in law and society, with an emphasis in criminal justice, and psychology, from the University of California, Santa Barbara and her law degree from the George Washington University Law School. She is a member of both the California and Illinois State Bars.

**Joanna Fawzy Doran, Esq.**, is a cancer rights attorney, author, speaker, and Chief Executive Officer of Triage Cancer, a national, nonprofit organization providing free education on practical and legal issues that may impact individuals coping with cancer and their caregivers, through events, materials, and resources.

Ms. Doran has spent more than 30 years working on behalf of individuals with cancer, including five as an Adjunct Professor of Law at Loyola Law School, teaching a seminar in Cancer Rights Law, and eight at the John Wayne Cancer Institute's Psychosocial Care Program and Positive Appearance Center. She has also taught a Community Advocacy Clinic, as an Adjunct Professor of Law at Wayne State University Law School.

Ms. Doran co-authored the book *Cancer Rights Law* for the American Bar Association—the first and only book of its kind. In 2020, she wrote a chapter, "Cancer-Related Legal Issues," for the Oncology Nursing Society's book *Oncology Nurse Navigation: Delivering Patient-Centered Care Across the Continuum*. In 2017, she wrote "Preventing or Minimizing Financial Toxicity across the Continuum of Cancer Care," a chapter for the Oncology Nursing Society's book *Cancer Survivorship: Transdisciplinary, Patient-Centered Approaches to the Season of Survival*. In 2009, she also contributed to a book entitled *Work and Cancer Survivors*. And, her work has appeared in a variety of other publications, such as *Psycho-Oncology*, *Heal*, *Cure*, *Coping with Cancer*, *Women*, and *Ability Magazine*.

Ms. Doran has presented more than 1,000 educational seminars on employment, insurance, health care, and advocacy issues throughout the country for individuals diagnosed with cancer, caregivers, health care professionals, advocates, lawyers, employers, and the general public.

In addition, she has served on numerous cancer community committees and boards, including as Chair of the Board of Directors for the California Division of the American Cancer Society, ZERO Prostate Cancer's Medical Advisory Board, and the Executive Committee of the American Bar Association's Breast Cancer Task Force.

Ms. Doran has received several awards and recognition for her service to the cancer community and her work in the area of legislative advocacy, including the 2009

Susan G. Komen for the Cure® Public Policy Advocate of the Year and the 2015 Legacy Advocate Award from Stupid Cancer. In 2010, she was recognized by the *Los Angeles Daily Journal* as one of the Top 20 Attorneys in California Under the Age of 40. In 2023, she was one of Cancer Health's 25 Champions of Health Equity.

Ms. Doran earned a Bachelor of Arts in political science with an emphasis in international relations from the University of California, Los Angeles and a Juris Doctor from Loyola Law School Los Angeles. She is a member of the California State Bar.

# About Triage Cancer

Triage Cancer is a national, nonprofit organization that provides free education on the legal and practical issues that may impact individuals diagnosed with cancer and their caregivers, through events, materials, and resources. In 2023, Triage Cancer reached more than one million people through educational materials, TriageCancer.org, CancerFinances.org, educational blog (https://triagecancer.org/blog), and newsletters. Additionally, from 2012–2023, Triage Cancer has provided more than 468,000 people with legal and practical knowledge through more than 1,416 online and in-person educational events held in all 50 states, D.C., Guam, and Canada. Triage Cancer's free programs and resources include:

## Educational Events

Triage Cancer hosts an average of 30 educational events a year, in a variety of formats and locations, to try to reach as many people as possible with critical information about cancer-related legal and practical issues. Triage Cancer offers free continuing education for nurses, social workers, patient advocates, physicians, lawyers, human resources professionals, and others through its educational programs. Triage Cancer also participates in more than 150 other events, across the country, each year.

- **Triage Cancer Conferences.** Events for patients, survivors, caregivers, advocates, and health care professionals that provide information about navigating practical cancer survivorship issues, such as self-advocacy, choosing and using health insurance, estate planning and medical decision-making, finances, employment, and disability insurance
- **Triage Cancer Webinar Series.** Monthly webinars on a wide variety of practical, cancer-related topics to help those coping with cancer navigate issues throughout the continuum of care
- **Insurance and Finance Intensive.** Accredited training for oncology health care professionals and advocates to learn crucial details about effectively navigating individual, employer, and government-sponsored health insurance options, as

well as work, disability insurance, and finances, to mitigate financial toxicity and improve access to care and quality of life

- **Community Health Worker Training.** Training for community health workers to learn about navigating communities through issues related to health insurance coverage, access to care, employment rights, and finances

**Legal & Financial Navigation Program (LFN).** The LFN provides individuals diagnosed with cancer, caregivers, and health care professionals with free one-on-one help, to get answers to questions about cancer-related legal issues.

## Materials and Resources

- **CancerFinances.org.** An online tool designed to be a comprehensive source of reliable information for individuals trying to navigate finances after a cancer diagnosis. After answering simple, relevant questions pertaining to their situations, individuals with any type of cancer will be presented with personalized and actionable information. Topics include health insurance, disability insurance, managing medical bills, estate planning, education, finances, and financial assistance programs.
- **Quick Guides, Checklists, Worksheets, and Practical Guides to Cancer Rights.** Educational materials on various cancer-related topics such as employment, health insurance, access to care, estate planning, finances, disability insurance, disclosure, housing, education, and much more
- **Educational blog.** Educational articles about cancer-related legal, financial, and other survivorship issues, including late-breaking news impacting the cancer community and cancer community educational events and resources
- **State information and laws.** Information for state-specific resources and charts of state laws relevant to those coping with cancer

**Triage Health.** As an acknowledgement that many cancer-related legal issues are not specific to the cancer community, Triage Cancer has made the information available through a program called Triage Health, providing free education on legal and practical issues that can be useful to anyone, including those with a serious or chronic health condition.

**Detailed information about these programs and services can be found at https://triagecancer.org.**

*All figures not otherwise cited in this book are the copyrighted works of Triage Cancer, used with permission.

# Acknowledgments

It is always a challenge to find a way to thank those who have made contributions to our work. Everything we do is grounded in a recognition of the importance of collaboration and we thank all of our partners in the cancer community and those individuals who improved this book by reviewing content and providing feedback.

We must also take this opportunity to thank those invaluable people in our lives who have helped lay a foundation for, and allowed us to thrive in, our careers. In particular, our parents, who are a never-ending source of inspiration, support, and encouragement, and our husbands, Patrick and Thomas, who stand by our sides, each day, supporting and grounding us. Finally, Eleanor and Evan, thank you for being a constant reminder of our "why" as we work towards change.

# Introduction

## Case Study: Maria

*After college, Maria worked as an assistant at a large company for four years. At the age of 42, she was diagnosed with cancer. After talking with her health care team, she decided her best course of action was to initially take four months off work to undergo treatment. When she shared her diagnosis with her employer, and expressed a need to take time off, she was told that she would be let go. At the time, she felt like she was being treated unfairly, but she could only focus on getting through her treatment.*

*Before Maria was let go from her job, her co-worker, and close personal friend, set up an online fundraiser for her and promoted the fundraiser through various social media platforms, tagging Maria in the posts.*

*Maria took coverage under the Consolidated Omnibus Budget Reconciliation Act (COBRA) to keep her health insurance, but her 18 months of COBRA are up and she is concerned about how to get health insurance coverage with a preexisting condition.*

*Maria is now 44 and is ready to get back into the workforce, especially since she has student loans to pay back, and a pile of outstanding medical bills. She also has a large amount of debt, as she used credit cards to pay some bills and feels weighed down by her financial situation.*

*She is not sure how to deal with the gap on her resume, and how to address it in an interview. Or if she even needs to discuss it.*

*Maria also has monthly medical appointments and has been experiencing "chemo brain." She is worried this will keep her from getting a job.*

*At the time of her diagnosis, she was told she may have a hereditary cancer, but she opted not to take a genetic test. Now that her cancer treatment is behind her, she is considering getting tested but is concerned about her privacy and whether or not her health insurance will cover the test.*

*Maria is particularly worried about disclosing her diagnosis to any future employers because she does not want it to affect her ability to get a job or to affect her two sisters who work in the same field.*

*Maria has also not made any estate planning or medical decision-making arrangements. When she went through her initial treatment, she experienced a complication and was admitted to the hospital for two weeks while in a medically induced coma. During that time, her rent was due, but she had not given financial power of attorney to her sisters to access her bank account, so they were unable to pay her rent for her. Fortunately, her landlord was understanding, but Maria wants to make sure that things are taken care of, if she is unable to care for or make decisions for herself in the future.*

*Finally, while Maria does not have any significant assets, she does have a few family heirlooms that she wants to make sure are passed to her family members in the event of her death.*

This book is about the intersection of law and health, or, more specifically, cancer. And Maria's case demonstrates the plethora of legal issues that may arise for someone diagnosed with cancer. A discussion of Maria's legal issues can be found in Chapter 7.

## What Is Cancer?

Cancer is a disease in which abnormal cells divide without control and can invade nearby tissues.[8] Cancer is actually a group of many diseases.

Carcinoma is a cancer that begins in the skin or in tissues that line or cover internal organs. Sarcoma is a cancer that begins in bone, cartilage, fat, muscle, blood vessels, or other connective or supportive tissue. Leukemia is a cancer that starts in blood-forming tissue, such as the bone marrow, and causes large numbers of abnormal blood cells to be produced and enter the blood. Lymphoma and multiple myeloma are cancers that begin in the cells of the immune system. Central nervous system cancers are cancers that begin in the tissues of the brain and spinal cord.[9]

As cancer is actually many different diseases, there are many different forms of treatment for a diagnosis of cancer, including surgery, chemotherapy, radiation therapy, hormone therapy, immunotherapy, and other targeted therapies.[10] Even within a type of treatment, such as chemotherapy, there are a plethora of different drugs

8. *NCI Dictionary of Cancer Terms*, NAT'L CANCER INST., https://www.cancer.gov/publications/dictionaries/cancer-terms (last visited Nov. 20, 2024).

9. *Id.*

10. *Cancer Treatment*, NAT'L CANCER INST., https://www.cancer.gov/about-cancer/treatment (last visited Nov. 20, 2024).

and drug combinations that are used to treat different types of cancer.[11] Each treatment may cause patients to experience a wide range of physical and psychological side effects.[12] Some side effects are termed long- or late-term side effects, as they can appear or last long beyond the point when treatment is completed.[13] And each patient may react differently to the same treatment.

Cancer does not discriminate. It affects people of all ages, races, ethnicities, and socioeconomic statuses.[14] While cancer most commonly develops in older populations, with 88 percent of diagnoses in people 50 years of age or older, cancer also has an impact on younger populations.[15] An estimated 9,620 children (ages 0 to 14) will have been diagnosed with cancer in 2024.[16] And about 86,000 adolescents and young adults (ages 15–39) were estimated to be diagnosed with cancer in the United States in 2023.[17]

An estimated 2,001,140 people will have been diagnosed with cancer in 2024.[18] However, the number of cancer survivors is increasing, as early detection methods and treatments improve. By 2040, the number of cancer survivors is projected to increase to 26 million.[19] Each of those cancer survivors may experience cancer-related legal issues.

## Who Is a Cancer Survivor?

In this book, we adopt the National Cancer Institute's definition of "cancer survivors" as individuals who have a history of cancer, from the moment of diagnosis, throughout their lives. It includes patients who are still receiving cancer treatment, as well as those who have completed treatment. We acknowledge that not everyone with a history of a cancer diagnosis identifies with the word "survivor."

## What Are Cancer-Related Legal Issues?

Cancer-related legal issues are any legal issues that arise as a result of a cancer diagnosis. A 2007 study identified the various legal needs of cancer patients, the extent to

---

11. *How Chemotherapy Drugs Work*, Am. Cancer Soc'y, https://www.cancer.org/treatment/treatments-and-side-effects/treatment-types/chemotherapy/how-chemotherapy-drugs-work.html (last revised Nov. 22, 2019).

12. *Side Effects of Cancer Treatment*, Nat'l Cancer Inst., https://www.cancer.gov/about-cancer/treatment/side-effects (last visited Nov. 20, 2024).

13. *Cancer Survivors: Late Effects of Cancer Treatment*, Mayo Clinic (Nov. 4, 2022), https://www.mayoclinic.org/diseases-conditions/cancer/in-depth/cancer-survivor/art-20045524.

14. American Cancer Society, *supra* note 1.

15. *Id.* at 4.

16. *Id.* at 14.

17. *Adolescents and Young Adults with Cancer*, Nat'l Cancer Inst., https://www.cancer.gov/types/aya (last reviewed June 6, 2024).

18. American Cancer Society, *supra* note 1.

19. American Cancer Society, *supra* note 2.

which these needs were being addressed in cancer care, and the impact of the needs on a patient's quality of life.[20] The study identified 30 medically related legal needs and categorized them under health care-related needs, estate-related needs, employment-related needs, and financial needs. Study participants rated these legal needs as having a significant impact on their quality of life and stated that their needs were not being met by their medical or supportive care teams.

Take the category of financial needs, for example; cancer survivors may need to understand their consumer rights and options for filing for bankruptcy when facing insurmountable medical debt as a result of their cancer care.

In 2001, the President's Cancer Panel released a report in which they stated that "[n]o person in America with cancer should go untreated, experience insurance-related diagnosis or treatment delays that jeopardize survival, or be bankrupted by a cancer diagnosis."[21]

Despite the attention on the increasing cost of cancer care, a 2009 study found that 62 percent of all bankruptcies in the United States in 2007 were based on medical debt. Even more significantly, 78 percent of those who had to file bankruptcy as a result of their medical debt actually had health insurance coverage, demonstrating a major failure of our health insurance system.[22] A 2014 report issued by the Consumer Financial Protection Bureau found that medical debts account for 52 percent of all debt collection actions, suggesting some improvement, which may or may not have to do with the health insurance consumer protections contained in the Patient Protection and Affordable Care Act.[23]

Bankruptcy is not the only impact of expensive cancer care. "Financial toxicity" is also linked with health outcomes, including quality of life,[24] compliance with prescribed treatment protocols,[25] and symptom burden.[26] One study reported that bankrupt cancer patients are nearly 80 percent more likely to die than patients who

---

20. Michael A. Zevon et al., *Medically Related Legal Needs and Quality of Life in Cancer Care*, 109 Cancer 2600 (2007).

21. President's Cancer Panel, National Institutes of Health, Voices of a Broken System: Real People, Real Problems—Report of the Chairman 2000–2001, at 11 (2001), https://deainfo.nci.nih.gov/advisory/pcp/archive/pcp00-01rpt/PCPvideo/voices_files/PDFfiles/PCPbook.pdf.

22. David U. Himmelstein et al., *Medical Bankruptcy in the United States, 2007: Results of a National Study*, 122 Am. J. Med. 741 (2009), http://www.amjmed.com/article/S0002-9343(09)00404-5/pdf.

23. Consumer Financial Protection Bureau, Consumer Credit Reports: A Study of Medical and Non-Medical Debts (2014), http://files.consumerfinance.gov/f/201412_cfpb_reports_consumer-credit-medical-and-non-medical-collections.pdf.

24. S. Yousuf Zafar et al., *Population-Based Assessment of Cancer Survivors' Financial Burden and Quality of Life: A Prospective Cohort Study*, 11 J. Oncology Prac. 145 (2015).

25. Alfred I. Neugut et al., *Association between Prescription Co-Payment Amount and Compliance with Adjuvant Hormonal Therapy in Women with Early-Stage Breast Cancer*, 29 J. Clinical Oncology 2534 (2011).

26. C.S. Lathan, *Association of Financial Strain with Symptom Burden and Quality of Life for Patients with Lung or Colorectal Cancer*, 34 J. Clinical Oncology 1732 (2016).

do not file for bankruptcy.[27] According to a survey by the Association of Oncology Social Workers, 66 percent of cancer patients with major financial challenges suffer from depression or anxiety.[28] Sixty-three percent of oncology social workers surveyed in that same study reported that financial issues reduce patients' compliance with their cancer treatment even though that treatment is key to their recovery.[29] Additionally, 40 percent of patients reported depleting their savings, nearly 30 percent reported dealing with bill collectors, and 54 percent of those handling a major/catastrophic financial burden said it had become more difficult in the past year to afford treatment.[30]

Financial challenges associated with cancer care are also exacerbated by low socioeconomic status and poverty. One report indicated:

> If poverty were treated as a "disease" then its "symptoms" or manifestations—absence of insurance, inability to afford co-pays for health care, limited access to primary health care providers . . . [and] the inability to take time off from work to access health care . . . must be dealt with in the context of improving the ability of poor . . . to receive . . . cancer screening, diagnosis, and treatment.[31]

To put these feelings about financial challenges in perspective, the Cancer Support Community found that "the trauma experienced by cancer patients due to the financial burden of cancer is on par with the level of trauma experienced by African Americans during and after Hurricane Katrina and individuals who witnessed and were present in lower Manhattan on 9/11."[32] And a 2016 study found that cancer survivors with cancer-related financial burdens have a 1.95 times higher likelihood of a depressed mood.[33]

The costs associated with cancer care have continued to rise and pose a serious challenge to those diagnosed with cancer and to their families.[34] Educating people about their rights and options under the law (e.g., access to reasonable

---

27. Scott D. Ramsey et al., *Financial Insolvency as a Risk Factor for Early Mortality among Patients with Cancer*, 34 J. Clinical Oncology 980 (2016).

28. Jennifer Mellace, The Financial Burden of Cancer Care, 10 Soc. Work Today 14 (2010), http://www.socialworktoday.com/archive/032210p14.shtml.

29. *Id.*

30. *Id.*

31. Susan G. Komen for the Cure, Executive Summary—Breast Cancer Mortality Report: Closing the Gaps in Eight Communities 3 (2007), https://www.komen.org/uploadedFiles/Downloadable_Files/071126_komen_sobc_2007.pdf.

32. Cancer Support Community, Understanding Challenges and Barriers to Financial Support for Cancer Treatment (2010), *discussed at* https://www.medscape.com/viewarticle/720643.

33. *Financial Toxicity and Cancer Treatment (PDQ®)—Health Professional Version*, Nat'l Cancer Inst., https://www.cancer.gov/about-cancer/managing-care/track-care-costs/financial-toxicity-hp-pdq (last updated May 29, 2022).

34. Julie Appleby, *Insurers Push Back against Growing Cost of Cancer Treatments*, KFF Health News (June 17, 2014), https://kaiserhealthnews.org/news/insurers-push-against-cancer-treatment-cost.

accommodations, paid leave options, disability insurance benefits, health insurance options, health insurance appeals, etc.) may assist in alleviating some of these financial challenges.

## An Effective Tool for Navigation

The integrated nature of how these issues play out in real life, instead of just a textbook, is why we chose to take an interdisciplinary approach to this book. Its audience includes all those professionals who may be in a position to come in contact with someone touched by cancer, be it a patient, caregiver, co-worker, employer, health care professional, or attorney. This book's audience also includes patient advocates, navigators, community health workers, individuals who have been diagnosed with cancer, and caregivers who want a better understanding of cancer-related legal issues.

This book presents each area of the law through relevant research, federal and state statutes and regulations, and case law. Each chapter includes case studies, exercises, and discussion questions for use in classrooms across a variety of disciplines, including law, medicine, psychiatry, psychology, social work, nursing, patient advocacy, patient navigation, case management, and others.

We have also chosen to present these issues to an interdisciplinary audience because research has shown that these legal issues do not occur in a vacuum. In 2007, the Institute of Medicine released a report entitled *Cancer Care for the Whole Patient: Meeting Psychosocial Health Needs*.[35] This report concluded that cancer care for patients must also address the *psychological and social problems created or exacerbated by cancer*, including *lack of information* or skills needed to manage the illness; *lack of transportation or other resources*; and *disruptions in work, school, and family life*, or patients may experience "additional suffering, weakened adherence to prescribed treatments, and a threatened return to health."[36]

The need to focus on these cancer-related legal and practical issues also extends past a patient's active cancer treatment, into post-treatment cancer survivorship. In 2005, the Institute of Medicine released the report *From Cancer Patient to Cancer Survivor: Lost in Transition*.[37] The report stated that patients completing treatment should be provided with a comprehensive care summary and follow-up plan that "would summarize critical information needed for the survivor's long-term care:

- Cancer type, treatments received, and their potential consequences

35. Institute of Medicine, Cancer Care for the Whole Patient: Meeting Psychosocial Health Needs (2008), https://nap.nationalacademies.org/catalog/11993/cancer-care-for-the-whole-patient-meeting-psychosocial-health-needs.

36. *Id.* at 1.

37. Institute of Medicine, From Cancer Patient to Cancer Survivor: Lost in Transition (2006), https://nap.nationalacademies.org/catalog/11468/from-cancer-patient-to-cancer-survivor-lost-in-transition.

- Specific information about the timing and content of recommended follow-up;
- Recommendations regarding preventive practices and how to maintain health and well-being;
- Information on legal protections regarding employment and access to health insurance; and
- The availability of psychosocial services in the community."[38]

Health care professionals are well-positioned to educate and navigate patients through these issues, which have foundations in the law, and occur throughout the continuum of cancer care. Many of these issues are difficult for patients to talk about and their health care team can serve as a trusted source of information. Patients may also not ask questions because they don't know what they don't know, so they do not know what to ask; are overwhelmed; do not think that their health care team can help with these issues; are concerned about their privacy; or are embarrassed by financial issues. However, health care professionals can effectively point patients toward valuable information and resources.

For instance, when a physician is discussing treatment options with a newly diagnosed patient, including when and where treatment may occur, such a discussion should also include the potential impact on other areas of a patient's life and may need to include other members of the patient's treatment team. Questions for discussion could include:

- Does the patient work (or is the patient in school)? What does the patient do at work? What schedule does the patient work? How does the patient get to work? Does the patient want to work through treatment? Is it possible to schedule treatment around work? What options does the patient have to take time off work? How will taking time off work affect the patient's finances?
- Does the patient have health insurance? How good is the coverage? Are the providers within network? What are the out-of-pocket expenses that the patient will have to pay in order to get treatment? What is the out-of-pocket maximum for the patient's health insurance plan? If the patient does not have health insurance, how does the patient figure out what health insurance options might be available? Are there financial assistance options available to pay for the out-of-pocket expenses?
- Does the patient have access to transportation to get to and from treatment if the patient is not able to take public transportation or drive? Given the frequency of treatment, is there an added expense to getting care? How much does parking cost at the health care facility? Does the patient have to travel out of the local area to get treatment?

---

38. *Id.* at 151.

- Does the patient have a family? Does the patient have children to care for? Does the patient have aging parents or parents-in-law to care for? Does the patient have a support system? Does the patient prefer to schedule treatment around family obligations rather than work?
- Does the patient have concerns about sharing the diagnosis with their family, at work, or at school?

These are just some of the questions that patients should get answers to, before they can make educated decisions about treatment options, but rarely do discussions take place at that depth and many of these issues never get addressed.

Unfortunately, a 2010 Livestrong survey found that while 98 percent of cancer survivors experienced the physical (i.e., pain), emotional (i.e., emotional distress), and practical (e.g., financial) concerns of post-treatment survivorship, *only 20 percent of survey respondents received help with their practical concerns.*[39]

In order to effectively begin to address this significant need in the cancer community, in addition to health care professionals, we hope to reach a greater audience of potential advocates, including patient navigators, patient advocates, and community health workers. We also want to reach attorneys who may work in one area of the law (e.g., employment law), and may encounter a client with a cancer diagnosis—to give them a more complete understanding of what their client may be experiencing in other areas of their lives, to help them identify other cancer-related legal issues that may be posing a problem for their client, to point their client in the direction of relevant resources, or to encourage those attorneys to provide pro bono legal assistance to the cancer community.

## The Law through a Cancer Lens

The legal topics presented in each chapter will be presented through a cancer lens. This book will focus on the areas that arise most often for individuals diagnosed with cancer and their caregivers and that pose the most challenges in navigation: health insurance, employment, genetics, disability insurance, estate planning and medical decision-making, and finances.

We understand that there are greater aspects of the laws that we discuss in this book, but our focus is to demonstrate how these issues may arise at each stage of the continuum of cancer care and how they may provide benefits, protections, and other rights for those touched by cancer. We acknowledge that the law is ever-changing, particularly in the areas of health insurance and even employment. Throughout the

39. Ruth Rechis et al., LIVESTRONG, "I Learned to Live with It" Is Not Good Enough: Challenges Reported by Post-Treatment Cancer Survivors in the LIVESTRONG Surveys (2010), https://triagecancer.org/wp-content/uploads/2012/12/LSSurvivorSurveyReport_final.pdf.

book we have pointed to places where readers can access additional and the most up-to-date information.

We also understand that many of the legal issues presented are not only a problem for individuals facing a cancer diagnosis, but also apply to those with many other types of serious medical conditions. We assert that the information herein can be applied in other settings, which drove the creation of Triage Health.

We strongly believe that the key to resolving these issues may be a greater understanding of the law and exercising of rights, but not necessarily through the use of litigation. Most people who are dealing with cancer-related legal issues need assistance with navigating these issues and the related systems in a timely manner. Litigation can be lengthy and may impose a burden on a person diagnosed with cancer. Our hope is that this book provides a greater understanding of the law and serves as a tool to help people exercise their legal rights.

Whether you teach a class, run a clinic, are interested in forming a medical-legal partnership, want to provide pro bono services in the community, are responsible for navigating patients through their cancer experience, or are coping with your own cancer diagnosis or a family member's or friend's, we hope this book will provide you with perspective, valuable information, and practical resources to effectively navigate cancer-related legal issues.

* Professors who are using this book in a classroom setting may email the authors for answers to case studies at the end of certain chapters, at info@triagecancer.org.

# CHAPTER ONE

# Health Insurance

## *Case Study: Samantha*

*Samantha is 44 years old and has been working as an accountant for the past ten years at a small firm, with 25 employees. When diagnosed with cancer, she had surgery and chemotherapy treatment. She is still experiencing some fatigue, "chemo brain," and some neuropathy in her feet. Due to these ongoing side effects, Samantha thinks that she may need to stop working. She is particularly concerned about what she is going to do for health insurance if she does take time off work since she has a preexisting condition. She is also worried about how she will afford to pay for her policy without a steady income.*

## I. Introduction

Health care spending accounted for 17.3 percent of the United States' gross domestic product (GDP) in 2022.[1] That number is expected to rise to 19.6 percent by 2031—totaling one-fifth of our nation's GDP.[2] Almost half of total U.S. health care spending is financed by the federal government through programs such as Medicare, Medicaid, and the financial assistance that is available to some individuals to purchase private health insurance. However, just having health insurance is not always sufficient to protect individuals from the often-devastating financial impact of a cancer diagnosis.

1. *NHE Fact Sheet*, Ctrs. for Medicare & Medicaid Servs., https://www.cms.gov/data-research/statistics-trends-and-reports/national-health-expenditure-data/nhe-fact-sheet (last modified Sept. 10, 2024).
2. Centers for Medicare and Medicaid Services, National Health Expenditure Projections 2023–2032, https://www.cms.gov/files/document/nhe-projections-forecast-summary.pdf.

One way to help mitigate the potential financial burden is for individuals to have adequate health insurance, to understand what is covered by their health insurance policies, and to know how their policies work.

Unfortunately, a vast number of Americans do not understand their health insurance policies. In 2018, a survey found that 96 percent of Americans could not define the four key terms used in health insurance.[3] In a 2023 survey, about half of consumers reported they do not understand their health insurance coverage, including about one-third who do not understand what their plan covers or what their out-of-pocket costs will be.[4] And, about six in ten insured adults reported that they had a problem with their health insurance in the past year, including lack of coverage, narrow provider networks, and higher than expected out-of-pocket costs.[5]

Needless to say, health insurance in this country is complex and multifaceted. Individuals diagnosed with cancer are typically thrown into a maze of issues, often left feeling as if there is no way out. The National Comprehensive Cancer Network states that psychosocial distress brought on by lack of information about cancer-related financial, legal, and practical issues should be recognized, monitored, documented, and treated promptly at all stages of the disease.[6] Patients and caregivers are faced with navigating a complex health care system, which is often changing, and with maintaining health insurance coverage that is typically needed to access quality health care.

Having access to adequate health insurance is not only a financial issue; lacking coverage or being underinsured can have significant health-related consequences. For example, uninsured individuals have significantly increased likelihoods of advanced stage diagnoses and worse survival rates, compared to those individuals with private health insurance.[7] The Institute of Medicine warned that failing to address employment, health insurance, and financial concerns may cause "additional suffering and threaten a patient's return to optimum health."[8]

---

3. *4 Basic Health Insurance Terms 96% of Americans Don't Understand*, POLICYGENIUS (JAN. 24, 2018), https://www.policygenius.com/health-insurance/health-insurance-literacy-survey/.

4. Larry Levitt & Drew Altman, *Complexity in the US Health Care System Is the Enemy of Access and Affordability*, 4 JAMA HEALTH F. E234430 (2023), https://jamanetwork.com/journals/jama-health-forum/fullarticle/2811354.

5. Karen Pollitz et al., *KFF Survey of Consumer Experiences with Health Insurance*, KFF (June 15, 2023), https://www.kff.org/private-insurance/poll-finding/kff-survey-of-consumer-experiences-with-health-insurance.

6. MICHELLE B. RIBA ET AL., *Distress Management, Version 2.2023*, 21 JNCCN 451 (2023), https://doi.org/10.6004/jnccn.2023.0026.

7. Jingxuan Zhao, *Health Insurance Status and Cancer Stage at Diagnosis and Survival in the United States*, 72 CA: CANCER J. FOR CLINICIANS 542 (2022), https://acsjournals.onlinelibrary.wiley.com/doi/10.3322/caac.21732.

8. INSTITUTE OF MEDICINE, CANCER CARE FOR THE WHOLE PATIENT: MEETING PSYCHOSOCIAL HEALTH NEEDS (Nancy E. Adler & Ann E.K. Page eds., 2008), http://nationalacademies.org/hmd/reports/2007/cancer-care-for-the-whole-patient-meeting-psychosocial-health-needs.aspx.

On March 23, 2010, President Barack Obama signed the Patient Protection and Affordable Care Act (ACA), also widely known as "Obamacare" or the Affordable Care Act.[9] The ACA has two overarching goals: (1) to increase the number of Americans covered by health insurance; and (2) to decrease the cost of health care. This landmark law sought to improve the affordability and quality of health care in this country. Although every American benefits from the changes in the ACA, those with serious medical conditions, like cancer, experienced the most significant impact.[10]

The ACA is a behemoth law stretching almost 1,000 pages itself, not including the regulations and guidance put out by various federal agencies. There were four main federal agencies involved in implementing the provisions of the ACA: the U.S. Department of Health and Human Services (HHS), the U.S. Department of Labor (DOL), the U.S. Department of the Treasury, and the Internal Revenue Service (IRS). These agencies have issued thousands of pages of regulations to date, related to the ACA. Additionally, each state has taken a different route in implementing the ACA and has passed state laws, issued state executive orders, and released state agency regulations. The ACA made changes to many areas of the health care system—from payments to consumer protection. The political opposition to the ACA has been significant since its passage. Congress has tried 70 times to repeal or curb all or part of the ACA. And, there have been a number of court cases, some still ongoing at the time of publication, to eliminate all or part of the ACA.[11]

While the ACA brought some much needed, and widespread, changes to the U.S. health care system, improvements can still be made. This chapter seeks to explore the common health insurance topics that individuals coping with cancer face and to guide them to additional resources to help navigate their health insurance options, rights, and benefits.

## II. Health Insurance Terms

The health care system in the United States has its own lexicon that can be very confusing to consumers. Health insurance policies will use specific terms to explain the coverage and costs they provide. Understanding these terms is critical for individuals to make the most of their policies.

---

9. For the purposes of this book, all references to the ACA actually refer to two separate pieces of legislation: the Patient Protection and Affordable Care Act (Pub. L. No. 111-148) and the Health Care and Education Reconciliation Act of 2010 (Pub. L. No. 111-152).

10. Jingxuan Zhao et al., *The Affordable Care Act and Access to Care across the Cancer Control Continuum: A Review at 10 Years*, 70 CA: Cancer J. for Clinicians 165 (2020), https://doi.org/10.3322/caac.21604.

11. Laurie Sobel et al., *Explaining Litigation Challenging the ACA's Preventive Services Requirements: Braidwood Management Inc. v. Becerra*, KFF (May 15, 2023), https://www.kff.org/womens-health-policy/issue-brief/explaining-litigation-challenging-the-acas-preventive-services-requirements-braidwood-management-inc-v-becerra/.

## A. Terms: Plan-Provider Contracts

- **Provider network.** Most insurance plans have a specific network of providers, doctors, hospitals, pharmacies, and other health care professionals from which individuals can receive care. In exchange for being part of the network, the provider has agreed to a certain payment rate from the insurance company. This payment rate is referred to as the allowed amount or contracted amount. Individuals who receive care from a provider in their insurance company's network will be charged the allowed amount. If individuals receive care from providers outside their insurance company network, the insurance company will cover less or none of that care, depending on whether the plan covers any out-of-network care.

It can also be important for consumers to know when their plan began:

- **Grandfathered plan.** A health insurance policy that was in existence on or before March 23, 2010. Plans will lose their grandfathered status at any time if they make substantial changes to the plan, such as significantly cutting benefits or increasing out-of-pocket spending for policyholders. Practically, the only grandfathered plans still in existence are large group-sponsored plans (e.g., plans for hospital employees). One reason it is important to know if a plan is grandfathered is that some consumer protections will not apply to grandfathered plans.

## B. Terms: Costs

There are some key terms that individuals should understand related to the costs of a health insurance plan:

- **Premium.** The monthly payment to have health insurance coverage. Individuals will pay this amount each month to have coverage, even if they never receive health care. It is similar to paying for car insurance all year, but never getting into an accident.
- **Deductible.** A fixed dollar amount that individuals are responsible for paying before their health insurance policy begins to pay for their health care. The amount of the deductible will depend on the plan, varying from a $0 deductible to a $5,000 or more deductible. For example, if Rachel's deductible is $1,000, her plan will not pay for her covered medical expenses until she has paid $1,000 for covered health care services subject to the deductible. This is also referred to as "meeting the deductible." However, it is important to note that deductibles may not apply to all services (e.g., some preventative services) and that not all out-of-pocket payments will count towards a deductible (e.g., some plans do not apply co-payments towards the deductible).
- **Coinsurance or cost-share.** The difference in what the insurance company will pay for an individual's medical expenses and what the individual pays for the medical expenses. For example, Ross has an 80/20 plan that has an allowed

amount for an office visit of $100. If Ross has met his deductible, his coinsurance payment of 20 percent would be $20. The health insurance plan pays the remaining 80 percent.

- **Co-payment.** A fixed dollar amount individuals pay for a covered health care service, usually at the time of service (e.g., visit the doctor or obtain a prescription drug from a pharmacy). The amount can vary by the type of covered health care service.
- **Out-of-pocket maximum.** A fixed dollar amount that caps how much individuals are responsible for paying out of pocket during a policy period (usually one year). After individuals reach that cap, the health insurance policy pays 100 percent for covered services for the rest of the year. The types of payments that count towards the out-of-pocket maximum depend on the type of plan. For example, for plans sold in the State Health Insurance Marketplaces, the limit includes deductibles, coinsurance, and co-payments made towards in-network, covered services. This limit does not include premiums, balance billing amounts for non-network providers, or other out-of-network cost-sharing. With some limited exceptions, the maximum out-of-pocket cost limit for any Health Insurance Marketplace plan for 2025 could be no more than $9,200 for an individual plan and $18,400 for a family plan. Employer plans may choose to carve out some payments from the out-of-pocket maximum (e.g., deductibles). Some types of health insurance policies are not required to have an out-of-pocket maximum, including short-term health plans, Original Medicare (i.e., Parts A and B), and grandfathered health plans.

### Out-of-Pocket Maximum Example

Simone falls off a ladder and spends a week in the hospital that is in her policy's network. She ends up with a $102,000 hospital bill. How much of that bill is Simone actually responsible for?

Simone's health insurance plan has a deductible of $2,000 and an 80/20 cost-share. The plan has an out-of-pocket maximum of $4,000.

First, Simone must pay her deductible of $2,000. She is now left with a $100,000 balance.

Because Simone has met her deductible, the insurance company will pay 80 percent of the bill and she is responsible for 20 percent—or $20,000.

However, Simone's plan has an out-of-pocket maximum of $4,000. Remember, she has already paid $2,000 in deductibles, which means that she will only have to pay another $2,000 out of pocket. The health insurance company will have to pay the remaining balance.

## C. Terms: Prescription Drugs

There are a few other concepts that are helpful for individuals to understand as they are shopping for and using their health insurance coverage.

- **Brand-name drug.** A prescription drug with a specific name from the company that sells the drug. At a point in the future, usually after a patent expires, a generic version of a drug may be available and sold by other companies.
- **Generic drug.** A prescription drug that contains the same chemical substance as a brand-name drug.
- **Specialty drugs.** Prescription drugs that have a high cost, high complexity, and/or require a high touch. Many drugs for cancer are considered specialty drugs.
- **Prescription drug formulary.** The list of prescription drugs that a health plan will cover and for how much. Understanding and using a plan's formulary will help individuals save money on their medications. With some formularies, individuals will pay the same amount regardless of the drug they receive. However, some plans have formularies with two or more cost levels, or tiers. The highest tier on most formularies is the "specialty" tier, which includes many cancer drugs. The higher the tier, the more the drug costs the individual. Generic drugs typically cost less than brand-name drugs, some brand-name drugs may cost more than others, and some are not on the formulary at all.
- **Exception requests.** Generally, if a drug is not on the formulary, the insurance company will not cover it. However, an individual may be able to file an appeal called an exception request. There are different types of exception requests:
  1. **Non-formulary drug exception.** A request to cover a non-formulary drug.
  2. **Tier exception.** A request to treat a drug as if it were in a lower tier, reducing out-of-pocket costs.
  3. **Brand exception.** A request to cover a higher-cost brand-name drug even if a generic is available.

  It is important for individuals to work with their health care team to show that taking a specific drug is medically necessary and why the insurance company should make an exception to their process.
- **Step therapy.** When an insurance company requires patients to try a generic or lower-cost drug before getting a brand-name or more expensive drug. If the lower-cost drug does not work or causes a bad reaction, the patient would be allowed to "step up" to another medicine. If an insurance company uses step therapy, individuals can file an exception request to try to get access to the drug prescribed by their health care team.

## D. Terms: Types of Health Insurance Plans

There are two main health care payment systems in the United States:

1. **Fee-for-service (FFS).** A health care provider is paid a fee for each service provided.[12] With these plans, individuals can go to any provider willing to see them. These are the types of plans that primarily existed before the rise of health maintenance organizations (HMOs) and preferred provider organizations (PPOs). With FFS plans, the individual pays a predetermined percentage of the cost of health care services, and the insurance company (or self-insured employer) pays the other percentage. For example, an individual might pay 30 percent for services and the insurance company pays 70 percent. The fees for services are defined by the providers and vary from physician to physician. While FFS plans offer individuals the freedom to choose their health care providers, over the course of a long treatment for an illness like cancer, these separate charges can lead to a significant expense.[13]
2. **Managed care.** Health care providers contract with a health insurance company to be a part of its network. If individuals go to a provider in the network, the provider has agreed to a certain payment rate for treating them (i.e., allowed amount). Regardless of what the provider bills, it is that "allowed amount" that will determine the patient's final cost. The patient typically pays a portion of the allowed amount, depending on the plan.

The most common types of managed care plans are HMOs and PPOs. Both types of plans use a network of providers to offer the highest quality care. However, there are a couple key differences between HMOs and PPOs.

- **HMO.** A type of health plan that employs or contracts with health care professionals, such as doctors and hospitals, to create a network of participating providers. There are two main types of HMOs:[14] (1) an HMO facility (e.g., Kaiser) and (2) an HMO plan, where individuals pick a primary care physician, who acts as a "gatekeeper." In other words, all of the individual's health care services go through that doctor. Generally, that means that individuals need a referral before they can see any other health care professional, except in an emergency. Visits to health care professionals outside of the HMO's network are typically not covered or covered at a very low rate. For example, if Janet has a skin rash, she would not go straight to a dermatologist. First, Janet would see her primary care physician. If that physician cannot help Janet, she will get a referral to a trusted dermatologist in her network. The benefits of coordinating your health care through a primary care physician are less paperwork and lower health care costs for everyone. However, in exchange for a lower cost, an HMO typically offers less choice in providers and less control.

---

12. U.S. Bureau of Labor Statistics, Definitions of Health Insurance Terms, https://www.bls.gov/ebs/additional-resources/definition-of-health-insurance-terms.pdf (last visited Nov. 4, 2024).
13. *Indemnity Health Plan*, Healthinsurance.org, https://www.healthinsurance.org/glossary/indemnity-health-plan (last visited Nov. 4, 2024).
14. *Glossary*, HealthCare.gov, https://www.healthcare.gov/glossary (last visited Nov. 4, 2024).

- **PPO.** A type of health plan that contracts with health care providers, such as hospitals and doctors, to create a network of participating providers. Policyholders pay less if they use providers that belong to the plan's network. However, they may have the option to use doctors, hospitals, and providers outside of the PPO's network for an additional cost. For example, a PPO plan may have an 80/20 cost-share for in-network care, but a 50/50 cost-share for any care received out of network. With a PPO, individuals are not required to have a primary care physician and they can see any health care professional, even specialists, without a referral. Typically, PPOs have higher monthly premiums than HMOs. However, individuals may need fewer appointments to get the care they need in that they do not need to visit a primary care physician first and there is more choice with respect to providers.
- **Exclusive provider organization (EPO).** A plan that is similar to a PPO, where individuals have a network of doctors and hospitals to choose from. However, unlike with some PPOs, an EPO will not pay for any services obtained outside of the network. In other words, there are no out-of-network benefits.

There are also some types of plans that are connected to savings accounts, to help individuals pay for out-of-pocket expenses:

- **High-deductible health plans (HDHPs).** Plans that had a minimum deductible of $1,650 per year for individual coverage and $3,300 for family coverage in 2025.[15] These plans allow individuals to also have health savings accounts (HSAs).
- **HSAs.** A type of savings account where the money in the account is used to pay for certain health care costs. This plan was created in 2003 for adults under the age of 65 who are covered by an HDHP. Individuals can use their HSAs to pay bills until they reach their deductible or use the funds to pay for co-pays and other health care expenses. Individuals are able to establish an HSA through a financial institution, or their employer may offer an option for an HSA. The money deposited in the account is not taxed. It is important to note that in order to use HSAs, the HDHP must be the individual's only health insurance plan. However, having vision, dental, disability, or long-term care insurance does not preclude individuals from establishing an HSA. In 2025, the maximum amount individuals could contribute to an HSA is $4,300 or for a family policy up to $8,550.[16] Unlike a flexible spending account (FSA), funds contributed to HSAs roll over and accumulate year to year if they are not spent.

  To determine whether an HSA would be beneficial, individuals should consider their budgets and potential health care needs for the upcoming year. Some

---

15. IRS Regulations, 26 C.F.R. § 601.602: Tax forms and instructions, https://www.irs.gov/pub/irs-drop/rp-24-25.pdf (last visited Jan. 29, 2025).
16. *Id.*

advantages of HSAs are that individuals are able to determine the amount of money to set aside for health care costs, they control how the HSA money is spent, and they are not required to pay taxes on money contributed to an HSA. However, the disadvantages to HSAs are that it is hard for individuals to predict when they will get sick, many individuals do not have extra funds to contribute to an HSA, and if money is withdrawn for nonmedical expenses, individuals will be taxed. For more information on HSAs, visit https://www.healthcare.gov/high-deductible-health-plan.

In addition to HSAs, there are also FSAs:

- **FSAs.** Savings accounts where the money in the account is used to pay for health care expenses such as deductibles, drugs, and other out-of-pocket costs.[17] FSAs are only available with employer-sponsored health insurance policies. If an employer offers an FSA, employees are able to set aside a portion of their salary to fund the FSA, and the money contributed to an FSA is not taxed. Employees can choose how much they want to contribute each pay period, up to a maximum of $3,300 per year in 2025.[18] Generally, money that is contributed to an FSA must be spent on qualified health care costs that year. However, in 2025, employees are able to carry over up to $660 per year to use in the next year. Alternatively, employers have the option to offer a "grace period" of up to 2.5 extra months to allow individuals to spend any remaining funds in the FSA. After the grace period or year, individuals forfeit any money left unspent in the FSA. However, FSA funds cannot be used to pay insurance premiums.

  There are several advantages to FSAs. For instance, the account is prefunded, so individuals have immediate access to the funds for that calendar year. In other words, if an individual has a large medical bill at the beginning of the year, the FSA will cover it even if the individual has not contributed that amount yet. Additionally, dependents can be covered under a Dependent Care FSA, and money contributed to the FSA by the parent is not taxed. Some disadvantages of FSAs include losing unused money remaining in an FSA account at the end of the year, having difficulty in estimating how much money to put into an FSA, and needing to keep track of all FSA-eligible expenses in order to be reimbursed from an FSA.

Another type of health insurance plan is a *short-term health insurance plan.* These are plans that last less than a calendar year. While these plans may have a lower monthly premium, individuals should be very wary of these plans. They are not required to comply with the consumer protections included in the ACA and they are

---

17. IRS, Publication 502: Medical and Dental Expenses (2023), https://www.irs.gov/pub/irs-pdf/p502.pdf.

18. *IRS: Healthcare FSA Reminder: Employees Can Contribute Up to $3,300 in 2025; Must Elect Every Year*, IRS, https://www.irs.gov/newsroom/irs-healthcare-fsa-reminder-employees-can-contribute-up-to-3300-in-2025-must-elect-every-year (last updated Nov. 25, 2024).

able to deny selling to individuals and exclude treatments for preexisting conditions, like cancer. Additionally, many of them have very high out-of-pocket costs for minimal coverage, costing individuals more in the long run. These plans are also not considered credible coverage since they are not required to renew coverage. This means that if these plans end midyear, then it does not trigger a special enrollment period (SEP) to buy a Marketplace plan, which may leave some uninsured.

Understanding these health care terms and concepts can help individuals when purchasing the most appropriate policy for their needs, as well as effectively utilizing their coverage when getting medical care.

## III. Sources of Health Insurance

There are three main places from which individuals obtain health insurance in the United States: from an employer; directly from a health insurance company; and from the government, primarily through Medicare, Medicaid, and the military, as illustrated in the following figure.

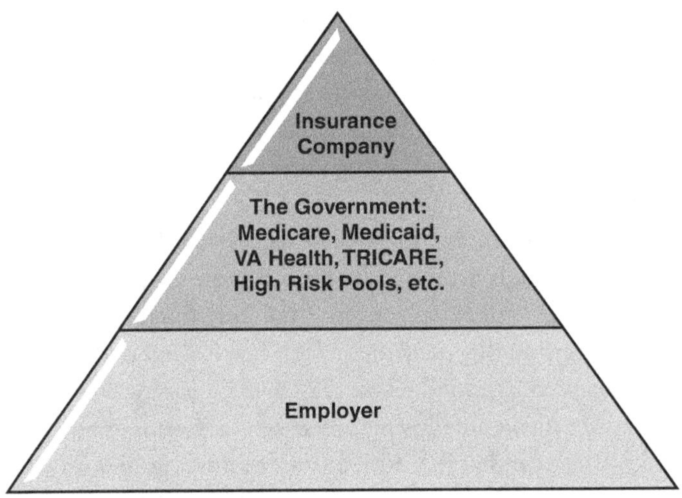


Group health insurance is typically provided through an employer or another group that individuals belong to (e.g., a union). Individual insurance is purchased through a State Health Insurance Marketplace or directly from an insurance company. Although it is called individual insurance, these plans can also be purchased for a family. Government-sponsored health insurance plans in the United States include Medicare, Medicaid, and plans offered to current and former military members. Some states and local entities also offer some options for health insurance coverage.

## A. Employer-Sponsored Health Insurance

In 2022, approximately 54.8 percent of Americans got their health insurance through their employer.[19] Some employers pay for health insurance coverage for their employees completely, while others require that the employee cover a portion of the monthly premiums.[20] There are two types of group health insurance plans: *funded* and *self-funded*. These are also referred to as *insured* and *self-insured*. An insured plan is one in which an employer purchases health insurance policies for its employees from a health insurance company. A self-insured plan is one in which the employer pays directly for the employee's health care costs. The employee may also contribute toward these costs. Often, an employer will contract with a third-party administrator to manage its self-insured plan. Typically, these third-party administrators are health insurance companies, so it can be confusing to consumers who may think that they actually have insurance from the third-party administrator. It is important for individuals to understand what type of plan they have, because the laws may apply differently. If individuals are unsure of what type of plan they have through their employer, they can contact the plan administrator or call the phone number on the back of their health insurance card for more information.

Health insurance that is available through employers can be very similar to options in the individual market; however, there are specific laws that may regulate employer-sponsored health insurance.

### 1. Employee Retirement Income Security Act of 1974

The Employee Retirement Income Security Act (ERISA)[21] was enacted to address public concerns that funds of private pension plans were being mismanaged and abused by employers. Although ERISA's primary purpose was not the regulation of private employer health care plans, today, it is the primary piece of legislation that does just that.

ERISA is divided into four sections:

- Title I applies to any employee benefit plan *maintained by an employer or employee organization* whose activities affect interstate commerce. Title I contains the benefit participant protections, such as reporting and disclosure requirements, minimum participation, vesting, benefit accrual and funding requirements (only applies to pension plans), fiduciary responsibilities, and

19. Congressional Research Service, U.S. Health Care Coverage and Spending (2024), https://sgp.fas.org/crs/misc/IF10830.pdf.

20. *Table 4. Medical Plans: Share of Premiums Paid by Employer and Employee for Family Coverage*, U.S. Bureau Lab. Stat., https://www.bls.gov/news.release/ebs2.t04.htm (last modified Sept. 19, 2024).

21. Pub. L. No. 93-406, 88 Stat. 829.

Consolidated Omnibus Budget Reconciliation Act (COBRA) and Health Insurance Portability and Accountability Act (HIPAA) protections.

- Title II amends the Internal Revenue Code to reflect participation, vesting, and benefit accrual provisions contained in title I of ERISA.
- Title III deals with which agencies are responsible for administration and enforcement of ERISA. Today, the administration of ERISA is divided amongst the DOL, the IRS, and the Pension Benefit Guaranty Corporation (PBGC)—the DOL oversees the reporting, disclosure, and fiduciary requirements; and the IRS oversees participation, vesting, and funding (with some limited overlap).[22]
- Title IV is primarily concerned with inadequate benefit plan funding and is administered by the PBGC.[23]

Title I is most relevant to individuals with employer-sponsored health insurance, as it provides the majority of rights and benefits available to employees. For example, under ERISA, individuals have the right to access certain documents (e.g., updated summary plan descriptions, bargaining agreements, contracts, etc.) within 30 days of a written request.[24] This means that employees are entitled to a copy of their health insurance policy or employment contracts.

Section 514(a) of ERISA preempts all state laws that relate to any employee benefit plan. In other words, ERISA limits states' ability to enforce health care legislation if it would have a substantial impact on employer-sponsored health plans. The rationale behind this clause was to try to create national uniformity in rules for employee benefits programs. However, section 514(b)(2)(A) of ERISA saves "any law of any State which regulates insurance, banking, or securities" from preemption. This is commonly referred to as the savings clause. The savings clause has been interpreted to allow states to regulate the activities of traditional insurance companies (e.g., mandating the types of benefits that an insurance company must provide). Yet, section 514(b)(2)(B) says that no self-funded plan "shall be deemed to be an insurance company . . . for purposes of [applying state insurance law]." This provision, commonly referred to as the deemer clause, prohibits state insurance regulations from being imposed on self-funded plans.[25]

The practical effect of ERISA is that state laws requiring coverage for certain benefits, like mastectomies, do not apply to any plans that are self-insured. It is useful for individuals to understand how ERISA may or may not impact their health insurance coverage, particularly with respect to state insurance mandates (e.g., coverage for oral chemotherapy, clinical trials, fertility preservation, etc.) and for rights to appeal any denials of coverage.

---

22. *History of EBSA and ERISA*, DOL Emp. Benefits Sec. Admin., https://www.dol.gov/agencies/ebsa/about-ebsa/about-us/history-of-ebsa-and-erisa (last visited Nov. 4, 2024).
23. *Id.*
24. ERISA § 104(b)(4).
25. Metro. Life Ins. Co. v. Massachusetts, 471 U.S. 724 (1985).

## B. Individual Insurance

Although many individuals obtain health insurance through their employers, some employers do not offer health insurance coverage as a benefit of employment. It is estimated that 10.2 percent of individuals in the United States have private individual health insurance.[26]

### 1. State Health Insurance Marketplaces

The ACA created a new way for individuals, families, and small businesses to get private health insurance: the State Health Insurance Marketplace. These Marketplaces are also referred to as exchanges. The Marketplace is like a health insurance shopping mall where individuals can buy a plan from a private health insurance company, or can get help determining if they are eligible for Medicaid in their state.

Whether an individual is uninsured or just wants to explore new options, the Marketplace is designed to give consumers more choice and control over their health insurance coverage by helping them find health insurance that fits their budget, with less confusion and hassle. Every health insurance plan in the Marketplace must offer comprehensive coverage of essential health benefits (EHBs). EHBs include items and services in the following categories: ambulatory patient services; emergency services; hospitalization; maternity and newborn care; mental health and substance use disorder services, including behavioral health treatment; prescription drugs; rehabilitative and habilitative[27] services and devices; laboratory services; preventive and wellness services; chronic disease management; and pediatric services, including oral and vision care.

The Marketplace helps individuals compare their insurance options based on price, benefits, and other features that may be important, in plain language, so they will get a clear picture of what they will pay and what they will get before they make a choice. For example, all plans must show that information in a document called the summary of benefits and coverage (SBC), an easy-to-read, standardized chart that explains the key information for each health insurance plan. The theory behind the standardized SBCs is that since every plan will provide its information in the same format, it will be easier for individuals to compare health insurance choices.[28]

Almost all individuals without insurance through an employer can use the Health Insurance Marketplace to explore health insurance options. There are only three requirements to get insurance through the Marketplace:

---

26. Katherine Keisler-Starkey & Lisa N. Bunch, U.S. Census Bureau, Health Insurance Coverage in the United States: 2023 (2024), https://www2.census.gov/library/publications/2024/demo/p60-284.pdf.

27. Habilitative services, like rehabilitative services, generally include occupational and physical therapy. However, habilitative services help people acquire, maintain, or improve skills and functioning.

28. *Summary of Benefits and Coverage*, HealthCare.gov, https://www.healthcare.gov/health-care-law-protections/summary-of-benefits-and-coverage/ (last visited Nov. 4, 2024).

- Individuals must live in the United States.
- Individuals must be U.S. citizens or nationals (or lawfully present).[29]
- Individuals cannot be currently incarcerated.[30]

In many cases, individuals will have a choice between purchasing several different plans in these Marketplaces. However, all health insurance companies that want to sell their plans through the Marketplace must offer plans using the following standardized plan levels: platinum, gold, silver, bronze, and catastrophic. The difference between these plan levels is the amount of money that individuals pay out of pocket for their health care costs (i.e., cost-share). For example:

- **Platinum.** Plan pays 90 percent; individual pays 10 percent.
- **Gold.** Plan pays 80 percent; individual pays 20 percent.
- **Silver.** Plan pays 70 percent; individual pays 30 percent.[31]
- **Bronze.** Plan pays 60 percent; individual pays 40 percent.
- **Catastrophic.** These plans are only available to be purchased by individuals younger than 30 years old.[32]

Every state has a Marketplace, but each state's Marketplace may operate differently. Depending on the model the state has chosen, different entities are responsible for operating the Marketplace (see the table following the bulleted list).

- **State Marketplace.** States are responsible for all Marketplace functions. Therefore, in these states, individuals as well as small employers and their employees apply for and enroll in coverage through Marketplace websites maintained by the states.
- **Federally facilitated Marketplace.** HHS is responsible for all Marketplace functions. Therefore, in these states, individuals as well as small employers and their employees apply for and enroll in coverage through https://www.healthcare.gov.
- **State-based Marketplace federal platform.** States are responsible for most Marketplace functions, except for the technology aspects. Therefore, in these states, individuals as well as small employers and their employees apply for and enroll in coverage through https://www.healthcare.gov.

---

29. Note: As of the date of publication, two states, Colorado and Washington, allow individuals who are undocumented to purchase health insurance through their state-run Marketplaces. These individuals are not eligible for federal Marketplace financial assistance options.

30. *Are You Eligible to Use the Marketplace?*, HEALTHCARE.GOV, https://www.healthcare.gov/quick-guide/eligibility/ (last visited Nov. 4, 2024).

31. 82 Fed. Reg. 98,346 (Apr. 18, 2017). Note: Under the Centers for Medicare and Medicaid Services (CMS) final "Market Stabilization Rule," the actuarial value of the silver plans may be as low as 66 percent.

32. *Health Plan Categories: Bronze, Silver, Gold & Platinum*, HEALTHCARE.GOV, https://www.healthcare.gov/choose-a-plan/plans-categories/ (last visited Nov. 4, 2024).

| State Marketplace* 19 | Federally Facilitated Marketplace HealthCare.gov 30 | State-Based Marketplace Federal Platform HealthCare.gov 3 |
|---|---|---|
| CA, CO, CT, DC, ID, KY, MA, MD, ME, MN, NJ, NM, NV, NY, PA, RI, VA, VT, WA | AK, AL, AZ, DE, FL, HI, IA, IL, IN, KS, LA, MI, MO, MS, MT, NC, ND, NE, NH, OH, OK, PA, SC, SD, TN, TX, UT, WI, WV, WY | AR, GA, OR |

* Updated December 10, 2024.

For up-to-date information on which states are running their own Marketplaces, which have Marketplaces run by the federal government, and which are partnering with the federal government, visit https://triagecancer.org/marketplaces.

## 2. Purchasing Insurance through a Marketplace

Each year, there is a period of time when individuals can shop for and purchase health insurance in the Marketplace. This is referred to as open enrollment. The open enrollment period typically runs from November 1 through January 15. During open enrollment, individuals can "window shop," compare options, renew coverage, switch plans, or opt out of purchasing insurance all together. For individuals who would like their plan to begin on January 1, they need to enroll in coverage by December 15.[33] The rationale behind having a set open enrollment period each year is to avoid situations where individuals wait until they get sick to purchase health insurance coverage. However, life changes do not always happen during a specific time of year. Therefore, there is a SEP available for individuals who experience certain "qualifying events," such as losing health insurance through a job, aging out of a parent's policy, or exhausting COBRA coverage. SEPs also provide the opportunity to add or remove family members to a policy after a marriage, divorce, birth, adoption, or death.[34] A SEP is also available when an individual has a change in residence, including:

- Moving to a new home in a new ZIP code or county
- A student moving to or from the place they attend school
- A seasonal worker moving to or from the place they both live and work
- Moving to or from a shelter or other transitional housing
- Moving to the United States from a foreign country or U.S. territory

Generally, during a SEP, individuals who have a change in their residence or in their family, have 60 days to shop for, and buy, new health insurance coverage in the

33. Press Release, CMS, HHS Finalizes Policies to Make Marketplace Coverage More Accessible and Expand Essential Health Benefits (Apr. 2, 2024), https://www.cms.gov/newsroom/press-releases/hhs-finalizes-policies-make-marketplace-coverage-more-accessible-and-expand-essential-health.

34. *Special Enrollment Periods*, HealthCare.gov, https://www.healthcare.gov/coverage-outside-open-enrollment/special-enrollment-period (last visited Nov. 4, 2024).

Marketplace, but there are some exceptions to this rule. It should be noted that moving for medical treatment or vacation will not trigger a SEP.

As discussed, individuals may qualify for a SEP if they or anyone in their household lost qualifying health coverage in the past 60 days, or expects to lose coverage in the next 60 days. It is important in maintaining insurance coverage to carefully time choosing the new plan. For example, if coverage is going to end in the middle of the month, and an individual picks a plan before the first of the month in which the coverage ends, then the new plan will be effective the first day of the month in which the coverage ends. For example, if coverage will end on May 15, and an individual picks a Marketplace plan on April 29, then the plan will begin on May 1. But, if that individual waits until June 5 to pick a Marketplace plan, then the plan would begin on July 1.

There are some additional SEPs that may be available based on special circumstances. For example, as of January 1, 2024, when an individual is losing Medicaid or Children's Health Insurance Program (CHIP) coverage in the next 60 days or up to 90 days after the loss of coverage, they will have a SEP to buy a Marketplace plan. State Marketplaces choose to offer this SEP.

Another example is the monthly low-income SEP. This is available in states that use HealthCare.gov for their Marketplace. It is optional for state-run Marketplaces. This SEP applies to individuals who are eligible for premium tax credits and have an income level at or below 150 percent of the federal poverty level (FPL) ($23,475 for an individual in 2025). Effectively, this means that individuals who meet these requirements and are uninsured can enroll in a Marketplace plan year-round. It also allows current enrollees to switch to a silver plan during the year—or if enrolled in a silver plan, they can switch silver plans, but they cannot switch to another plan tier. For this SEP, the coverage will start the first day of the month following their plan selection.[35]

## 3. Marketplace Financial Assistance: Tax Credits and Subsidies

In 2020, the average family in America spent 11.6 percent of the family's income just on health insurance premiums and deductibles.[36] It is therefore unsurprising that many Americans need financial assistance to purchase health insurance coverage. The ACA made financial assistance available for individuals who buy health insurance in the Marketplace, based on their income level. There are two different types of financial assistance in the Marketplace:

- **Premium tax credits**, which reduce the amount that individuals pay for their monthly premiums to have health insurance

35. Press Release, CMS, *supra* note 33.

36. Percentage of Median Income Spent on Premium Contribution and Deductible by U.S. Employees from 2008–2020, Statista, https://www.statista.com/statistics/631987/percent-of-income-spent-on-health-plan-by-us-employees (last visited Nov. 4, 2024).

- **Cost-sharing subsidies**, also known as cost-sharing reductions, which help to lower deductibles, co-payments, and coinsurance

As of January 1, 2014, tax credits have been available to U.S. citizens, and those who are lawfully present in the United States, who purchase a health insurance policy through their state's Health Insurance Marketplace and who have an income up to 400 percent of the FPL ($60,240 for an individual or $124,800 for a family of four for 2025 plans).[37] For purposes of the premium tax credit, eligibility for a certain year is based on the most recently published set of poverty guidelines at the time of the first day of the annual open enrollment period. Because open enrollment for 2025 began on November 1, 2024, the federally facilitated Marketplace used the 2024 FPL.[38]

To receive a premium tax credit, individuals cannot be eligible for government coverage (e.g., Medicaid or Medicare) or have access to health insurance through their employer. The only exception is if the individual's employer plan does not cover at least 60 percent of health care costs or if the portion that the employee has to pay for the employer-sponsored health insurance policy is more than 9.02 percent of their household income (in 2025).[39]

When individuals complete an application to purchase a health insurance policy in the Marketplace, they are required to include information about their families and finances so the Marketplace can determine if they are eligible for any of these financial assistance options. Further, individuals must project their income for the coming year. If they end up making more than they anticipated, they may be required to pay back some, or all, of the financial assistance they received from the Marketplace. Conversely, if they made less than expected, they may receive a lump-sum credit with their tax refund. Individuals are encouraged to report any changes in household size, income level, or offers of other creditable health insurance coverage to the Marketplace within 30 days. This can be useful to an individual who has lost a job and whose income level has dropped. If the change in income is reported immediately, then the individual's financial assistance to access health insurance would be increased.

The amount of the premium tax credits individuals can receive will depend on their income. Tax credits are provided on a sliding scale. Individuals with lower incomes will receive a larger credit. The tax credits are designed so that individuals will not pay more for their monthly premiums than a certain percentage of their income. Tax credits reduce the amount that individuals pay monthly for their health insurance premiums. For example, an individual who qualifies for a premium tax credit may choose a policy that is $242 a month, but based on income, they receive a $202 tax credit, meaning the individual only has to pay $40 for the monthly

37. Except in Alaska and Hawaii, which have different FPLs.

38. *Eligibility for the Premium Tax Credit*, IRS, https://www.irs.gov/affordable-care-act/individuals-and-families/eligibility-for-the-premium-tax-credit (last updated Aug. 22, 2024).

39. *Affordable Coverage*, HEALTHCARE.GOV, https://www.healthcare.gov/glossary/affordable-coverage/ (last visited Nov. 4, 2024).

premium. Individuals have the option to have the amount of their tax credit sent to the health insurance company monthly, or they can pay the full premium price monthly and receive the full tax credit amount included with their tax refund.[40]

Individuals who have incomes between 138 percent and 250 percent of the FPL (in 2025, $21,597 and $37,650, respectively, for an individual) may also be eligible for cost-sharing subsidies. These subsidies, also known as cost-sharing reductions, will reduce the cost of health care expenses an individual or family has to pay at the time of medical care (e.g., reducing the co-payment made when visiting a doctor's office). These subsidies are only available to individuals who purchase a silver level plan. The way that cost-sharing subsides work is that the insurance company reduces what they charge individuals and, in turn, the insurance companies are reimbursed by the federal government. Individuals living in a state that has not expanded Medicaid will be eligible for cost-sharing subsidies if their incomes are between 100 percent and 250 percent of the FPL.

The validity of the cost-sharing subsidies was called into question and ultimately upheld by the U.S. Supreme Court in *King v. Burwell*.[41] In *King*, the plaintiff argued that individuals who buy health insurance from a federally facilitated Health Insurance Marketplace should not be entitled to financial help to buy insurance plans. The case hinged on how the Supreme Court interpreted one sentence in the ACA, which says that the financial assistance will be available for people enrolled in an insurance plan through an exchange *established by the state*.[42] In the majority opinion, Chief Justice Roberts wrote:

> Congress passed the Affordable Care Act to improve health insurance markets, not to destroy them. If at all possible, we must interpret the Act in a way that is consistent with the former, and avoids the latter. Section 36B can fairly be read consistent with what we see as Congress's plan, and that's the reading we adopt.[43]

Therefore, eligible individuals in every state were able to continue receiving cost-sharing subsidies for insurance coverage purchased through a Marketplace.

## 4. Open Health Insurance Market

Health insurance is also sold outside of the ACA Health Insurance Marketplace. Individuals can go directly to insurance companies, agents, brokers, and online health insurance sellers to purchase these health insurance plans. There are several reasons that individuals may choose to purchase a plan outside of the Marketplace.

---

40. *Questions and Answers on the Premium Tax Credit*, IRS, https://www.irs.gov/affordable-care-act/individuals-and-families/questions-and-answers-on-the-premium-tax-credit (last updated Sept. 24, 2024).

41. 135 S. Ct. 2480 (2015).

42. *Id.* at 2496.

43. *Id.*

For example, in some states, the plans sold through the Marketplace have limited networks of providers. For some individuals diagnosed with cancer, having the ability to see a wider network of providers is necessary. Furthermore, in some states, the Marketplace does not offer higher level policies (i.e., gold or platinum). So, for individuals seeking a policy that provides a higher-level cost-share, purchasing plans in the open market may be a preferred option. Most plans sold in the open health insurance market still have to follow the consumer protections included in the ACA. However, individuals should keep in mind that if they purchase a policy outside of the Marketplace, they will not be eligible for financial assistance. In 2022, there were an estimated 1.2 million people paying full price for their health insurance policies in the open market.[44] It can be in the best interests of individuals to, at a minimum, check the policies available to them through their state Marketplace, before purchasing a policy in the open market. Additionally, individuals should be savvy consumers when shopping for health insurance in the open market. Some brokers may try to sell individuals short-term policies, which are often referred to as "junk insurance." These plans often exclude coverage for any care related to a preexisting condition (e.g., cancer), essentially making the insurance useless.[45] Furthermore, there have been several reports of scams in recent years. To protect themselves, individuals should check with their state's department of insurance to ensure that the company is properly licensed and that the plan goes through the calendar year.

As of 2022, more than 46 million Americans purchased individual insurance, a significant increase from 13.8 million in 2013.[46] The main reason for this increase is the implementation of the ACA provisions protecting those with preexisting conditions and creating the Health Insurance Marketplaces. The individual health insurance market will continue to be an important aspect of health insurance options in the United States, particularly for those who do not have employer-sponsored health insurance.

## 5. Individual Mandate

The ACA imposed a requirement to have health insurance or pay a penalty. The requirement to have health insurance coverage is often referred to as the individual mandate. The goal behind the individual mandate was not simply to penalize, but

44. Jared Ortaliza et al., *As ACA Marketplace Enrollment Reaches Record High, Fewer Are Buying Individual Market Coverage Elsewhere*, KFF (Sept. 7, 2023), https://www.kff.org/private-insurance/issue-brief/as-aca-marketplace-enrollment-reaches-record-high-fewer-are-buying-individual-market-coverage-elsewhere.

45. *Dirt-Cheap "Junk Insurance" Plans, Wiped Out by ACA, Could Reappear under GOP Health Bill*, KFF Health News (May 31, 2017), http://khn.org/morning-breakout/dirt-cheap-junk-insurance-plans-wiped-out-by-aca-could-reappear-under-gop-health-bill/.

46. *Table 4. Medical Plans: Share of Premiums Paid by Employer and Employee for Family Coverage*, *supra* note 20.

rather to encourage people to buy health insurance coverage.[47] Because individuals continued to receive coverage from employer plans, individual insurance policies, Medicare, Medicaid, Veterans Health Administration plans, and other types of coverage, most people did not feel the impact of the individual mandate.

The penalty for not having health insurance first went into effect in 2014 and increased each year until 2018, when individuals who did not have health insurance, and were not exempt from the mandate, paid $695 per person or 2.5 percent of the household income, whichever amount was *more*.[48] In December 2017, Congress passed tax legislation, which included a change to the individual mandate. As of January 1, 2019, the penalty for not having creditable health insurance coverage was reduced to $0. In response, these states passed laws that reinstated the individual mandate at the state level: California, Massachusetts, New Jersey, Rhode Island, Vermont, and Washington, D.C.

## C. Government-Sponsored Health Insurance

The government, at both state and federal levels, finances health care in many different forms: government agencies provide health insurance benefits to individuals with low incomes and seniors as well as to their own employees; counties and local governments provide health care through local hospitals and clinics; and the penal system finances health care programs for prisoners, the only group of Americans *constitutionally* entitled to government-funded health care.[49] The largest government-sponsored health care programs are Medicare and Medicaid. On July 30, 1965, President Lyndon Johnson signed Medicaid and Medicare into law at a ceremony in Independence, Missouri. Congress passed the Social Security Amendments of 1965, after three previous presidents had fought for the creation of a national health plan.

President Harry Truman was issued the very first Medicare card during the signing ceremony. Nineteen million Americans signed up for Medicare during its first year. At the time, these two federal programs were a groundbreaking way to provide basic insurance options for Americans without health insurance. Over the years, these government health insurance programs have continued to change, covering more Americans and providing additional benefits. For example:

- In 1972, President Richard Nixon expanded the coverage of Medicare to people under the age of 65 with long-term disabilities.
- In 2003, President George W. Bush signed the Medicare Prescription Drug, Improvement, and Modernization Act, which created Medicare prescription drug coverage.

47. Lawrence O. Gostin & Elenora E. Connors, *Health Care Reform in Transition: Incremental Insurance Reform without an Individual Mandate*, 303 JAMA 1188, 1188 (2010).

48. Internal Revenue Serv., *2018 Instructions for Form 8965* at 16, https://www.irs.gov/pub/irs-prior/i8965--2018.pdf (last visited Jan. 29, 2025).

49. Stuart Klein, *Prisoners' Rights to Physical and Mental Health Care: A Modern Expansion of the Eighth Amendment's Cruel and Unusual Punishment Clause*, 7 Fordham Urb. L.J. 1 (1978).

- In 2010, President Barack Obama signed the ACA, which expanded Medicare to cover free preventive and wellness services and improve prescription drug coverage.

As of October 2024, of the 334 million people in the United States, nearly 66 million Americans received health insurance coverage through Medicare. More than 79 million Americans have health insurance coverage through Medicaid.[50]

## 1. Medicare

Medicare is a government-sponsored program seeking to provide health insurance to individuals age 65 and older, regardless of income or medical history, and to individuals under the age of 65 who have certain disabilities.[51] To be eligible for Medicare, individuals must be U.S. citizens, or legal residents. Legal residents must live in the United States for at least five years in a row, including the five years just before applying for Medicare. In addition, to be eligible for Medicare, individuals must fall into one of three categories:

1. Be 65 or older and eligible for Social Security retirement benefits
2. Be younger than 65 years old, have certain disabilities, and have received Social Security Disability Insurance (SSDI) benefits for 24 months
3. Have end-stage renal disease or amyotrophic lateral sclerosis (ALS), commonly known as Lou Gehrig's Disease

**Parts of Medicare**

Part A: Hospital Insurance

Part B: Medical Insurance

Part C: Medicare Advantage

Part D: Prescription Drug Coverage

### *a. Parts of Medicare*

Medicare has four parts (A–D), each providing its own benefits and services.

#### *i. Part A—Hospital Insurance*

Part A pays for hospital care and inpatient care, including a semi-private room, hospital meals, skilled nursing services, care in special units (e.g., intensive care), drugs, medical supplies and equipment, lab tests and x-rays, operating room and recovery

50. *August 2024 Medicaid & CHIP Enrollment Data Highlights*, Medicaid.gov, https://www.medicaid.gov/medicaid/program-information/medicaid-and-chip-enrollment-data/report-highlights/index.html (last visited Nov. 4, 2024).

51. 42 U.S.C. §§ 1395–1395ccc.

room services, and some blood transfusions. It also covers rehabilitation services after a qualified inpatient stay; part-time, skilled care for individuals who are homebound; and hospice care.

Typically, eligible individuals will be automatically enrolled in Parts A and B after turning 65. For most individuals, there is no charge for Part A. To receive Part A for free, individuals generally have had to pay into Medicare for ten years (40 quarters). However, if individuals do not have enough work history during which time they paid Social Security taxes, they may be required to pay a monthly premium for Part A coverage.

Although Part A covers nursing care, it is meant to provide coverage for those recovering from acute illness or injury and not long-term chronic care in a nursing home facility.

*ii. Part B—Medical Insurance*

Part B is medical insurance and helps to pay for doctors' services and medical services and supplies that are not covered by Part A hospital insurance. This includes diagnostic studies, imaging scans, blood work, outpatient care, doctors' services, durable medical equipment used at home, some home care, and ambulance transportation. Part B is optional and individuals must proactively choose to enroll. There is a monthly premium that is based on income and an annual deductible. The premium for 2025 is $185 (or higher depending on income levels). The annual deductible was $257 in 2025. After individuals meet their deductible, they are responsible for a 20 percent cost-share amount for any medical expenses for the rest of the year. Part B does not have an out-of-pocket maximum, which can leave individuals with very high out-of-pocket costs, especially when receiving expensive cancer care.

Parts A and B together are often referred to as "Original Medicare." Individuals who have Original Medicare are entitled to receive services from any health care provider or facility that accepts Medicare nationwide. In other words, there is a national network of providers.

*iii. Part C—Medicare Advantage*

Part C is an alternative way to receive the benefits under Parts A and B.[52] Part C plans are also referred to as Medicare Advantage plans. Medicare Advantage was created in 1997, to "allow beneficiaries to have access to a wide array of private health plan choices in addition to traditional fee-for-service Medicare."[53] In 2024, 32.8 million Americans opted to enroll in a Medicare Advantage plan, equating to one-half of all Medicare participants.[54] Part C plans are provided through private health insurers. Similar to individual insurance, there are different types of Medicare Advantage plans, including HMOs and PPOs.

---

52. *Id.* § 1395w-21(a).

53. H.R. Conf. Rep. No. 105-217, at 585 (1997).

54. Meredith Freed et al., *Medicare Advantage in 2024: Enrollment Update and Key Trends*, KFF (Aug. 8, 2024), https://www.kff.org/medicare/issue-brief/medicare-advantage-in-2024-enrollment-update-and-key-trends/.

Not all types of plans are available in all areas or to all Medicare beneficiaries. The private insurance companies selling Medicare Advantage plans must be approved and must provide all hospital and medical benefits covered by Medicare Part A and Part B. Each plan is able to establish the amounts they charge for premiums, deductibles, services, and out-of-pocket maximums. The out-of-pocket maximum for 2025 is $9,350. The specific Medicare Advantage plan decides how much individuals pay for the covered services they receive. Part C beneficiaries will pay at least the premium for Part B, and may pay more to cover additional services being offered in the plan. In 2025, the estimated average monthly Part C plan premium was $17, but premiums ranged from $0 to more than $200.[55] Some Medicare Advantage plans provide extra benefits outside of those traditionally provided by Medicare (e.g., vision, hearing, and dental coverage). However, many Medicare Advantage plans have a network of providers and do not provide coverage for services received out of that network. In plans that do provide some coverage for out-of-network services, individuals will likely have to pay more to see those providers. Part C plans may or may not include prescription coverage through Part D.

*iv. Part D—Prescription Drug Coverage*

Part D is prescription drug coverage that will pay for medications prescribed by a doctor that are purchased from retail, mail-order, home infusion, specialty, and long-term care pharmacies. Part D was added to Medicare in 2006 by the Medicare Prescription Drug, Improvement, and Modernization Act of 2003.[56] Unlike Medicare Parts A and B, Part D coverage is provided by private companies that have contracted with the Centers for Medicare and Medicaid Services (CMS). Individuals can enroll in Part D as part of a Medicare Advantage plan or can purchase stand-alone drug coverage if they have Original Medicare.

How much individuals pay for Medicare Part D and out-of-pocket prescription drug costs depends on a number of factors, like which Part D plan they choose, how many prescriptions they take and how often, whether the pharmacy is in the plan's network, and whether the prescription drugs are on the Part D plan's formulary. The Medicare website has a tool to help individuals find Part D plans available to them: https://www.medicare.gov/plan-compare.

In 2025, Part D premiums generally ranged from $3–$128 per month (depending on the plans available in the area and on the specific plan chosen).[57]

55. *What Are the Costs of Medicare Advantage?*, Nat'l Council on Aging (Jan. 8, 2025), https://www.ncoa.org/article/what-are-the-costs-of-medicare-advantage-part-c/.

56. Pub. L. No. 108-173, 117 Stat. 2066.

57. Juliette Cubanski & Anthony Damico, *Medicare Part D in 2025: A First Look at Prescription Drug Plan Availability, Premiums, and Cost Sharing*, KFF (Nov. 22, 2024), https://www.kff.org/medicare/issue-brief/medicare-part-d-in-2025-a-first-look-at-prescription-drug-plan-availability-premiums-and-cost-sharing/.

In 2023, a standard Part D plan was structured with a maximum deductible of $505. After paying the deductible, an individual would pay 25 percent of their drug costs. When the total out-of-pocket drug costs reached $7,400, then the patient would enter catastrophic coverage. Then, patients would pay the greater of 5 percent of the drug costs, or $10.35 for brand-name drugs ($4.15 for generics) for the remainder of the year. There was no out-of-pocket maximum for Part D prescription drug costs.

Patient Medicare drug costs in 2023 were as follows:

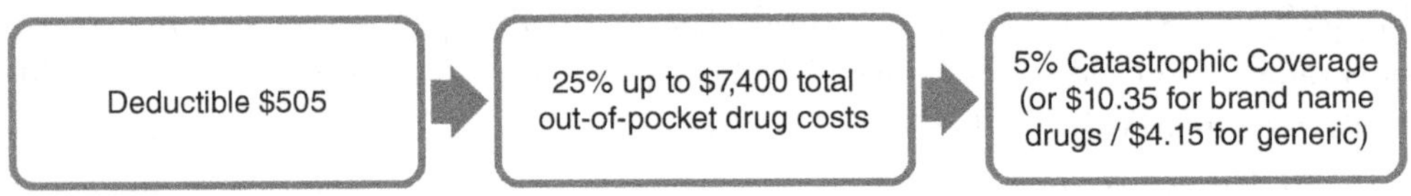


As a result of the passage of the Inflation Reduction Act of 2022 (IRA), in 2024, the structure of the standard Part D drug benefit changed.[58] In 2024, the maximum deductible for a Part D plan was $545. After paying the deductible, patients pay 25 percent of their drug costs, until their total out-of-pocket drug costs reach $8,000. Based on this language, it would appear patient costs would be calculated as follows:

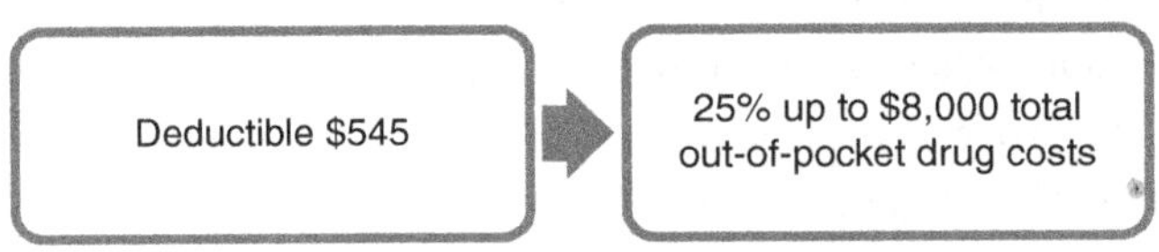


However, the devil is in the details. The total out-of-pocket drug costs include what patients have actually spent out of pocket, plus the value of the 70 percent manufacturer price discount on brand-name drugs in the former coverage gap (FCP). This means that individuals who took only brand-name drugs in 2024 would reach the $8,000 catastrophic coverage threshold by spending a total of $3,333 out of pocket. And, they would then have no additional costs for their Part D prescriptions for the rest of the year.

The brand-name discounts and the math involved creates significant confusion. The following chart illustrates what individual patients will pay when taking an oral chemotherapy brand-name drug covered under Part D that costs $12,000.

58. Note to Medicare Advantage Organizations, Prescription Drug Plan Sponsors, and Other Interested Parties, From CMS, Announcement of Calendar Year (CY) 2024 Medicare Advantage (MA) Capitation Rates and Part C and Part D Payment Policies (May 31, 2023), https://www.cms.gov/files/document/2024-announcement-pdf.pdf.

| | |
|---|---|
| **Deductible**<br>**\$0–\$545** | **\$545** |
| **Initial Coverage Period (ICP)**<br>\$545–\$5,030 | 25% of cost of covered drugs = \$1,121.25<br><br>How you get there:<br>\$545 up to \$5,030 in total drug costs (what a patient and their plan pays together) = \$4,485<br>\$4,485 × 25% = \$1,121.25 |
| **Former Coverage Gap (FCP)**<br>\$5,030–\$8,000 | 25% of cost of covered drugs = \$1,666.75<br><br>How you get there:<br>\$8,000 catastrophic threshold − \$545 deductible already paid − \$1,121.25 ICP amount already paid = \$6,333.75 left to pay (95% of total drug costs)<br><br>However, the total amount a patient gets credit for spending during the FCP = 95% of total drug costs. This includes the 25% actually paid by patient and a 70% drug manufacturer's discount on brand-name drugs. The 5% paid by the plan, is not included.<br>100% of the costs during this period is \$6,667.11.<br>\$6,667.11 × 25% = \$1,666.75 |
| **Catastrophic Coverage** | \$0 |
| **Total amount a patient actually pays out of pocket if they only take brand-name drugs** | \$3,333<br><br>How you get there:<br>\$545 deductible + \$1,121.25 ICP + \$1666.75 FCP = \$3,333 |

Starting in 2025, the structure for patient out-of-pocket drug costs will be simplified considerably. Patients will pay a deductible of \$590 and then will pay 25 percent of their drug costs until they have spent a total of \$2,000 out of pocket. They will then have no additional costs for their Part D prescriptions for the rest of the year.

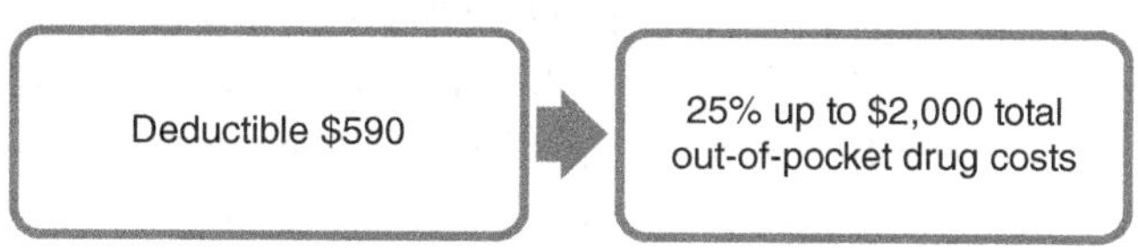


It is important to note that under the IRA, the \$2,000 cap on drug costs will be indexed to rise each year after 2025, at the rate of growth in per capita Part D costs.

Also starting in 2025, individuals will have the option of spreading out their out-of-pocket prescription drug costs over the year, rather than face high out-of-pocket costs in any given month. For example, if a patient takes an expensive brand-name drug in January, instead of paying the full $2,000 out-of-pocket cost in January, the patient can make payments throughout the year.

Understanding the parts of Medicare and what they cost is imperative for individuals to ensure adequate health care coverage and to minimize expenses. That also includes understanding options to help with out-of-pocket costs associated with Medicare, such as Medigap supplemental plans.

***b. Medigap Supplemental Plans***

Part B of Medicare has an 80/20 cost-share, and no out-of-pocket maximum, which can result in a significant financial burden for individuals with Medicare who are diagnosed with chronic or expensive medical conditions like cancer. One study found that Medicare beneficiaries without supplemental insurance paid out-of-pocket costs between 23.7 percent and 63.1 percent of their household income for their cancer care.[59] In order to help individuals pay for the 20 percent cost-share amount and other Medicare-related out-of-pocket costs, Medicare created an option to purchase additional coverage through a Medicare supplemental insurance policy, also called a Medigap plan. These supplemental insurance plans are purchased through a private insurer and they pick up out-of-pocket costs related to care received under Medicare Part A and Part B benefits. Although Medigap plans have an additional monthly premium, the premium amount may be significantly less than paying the 20 percent cost-share out of pocket.

There are different Medigap plans, named by letters A–N, which are offered by private health insurance companies. Medicare provides a chart comparing benefits within Medigap plans A–N. For example, Medigap plan A does not cover the cost-share for skilled nursing facility care, while Medigap plan F does. Medigap plans K and L have an out-of-pocket maximum, while the other 12 plans do not. Medigap plans F and C are no longer available to individuals who are newly eligible for Medicare. Medigap policies are regulated and standardized by federal and state law, which means that while any insurance company can sell a Medigap policy, the policies are standardized. It is important to note that three states—Massachusetts, Minnesota, and Wisconsin—offer Medigap plans not available in other states.

Medigap policies are only available to individuals who purchase Original Medicare (Parts A and B). Individuals who opt for a Medicare Advantage plan (Part C) are ineligible to purchase a Medigap policy. Individuals who do not enroll in a Medigap plan when they are first eligible for Medicare may face barriers to accessing a Medigap plan. Within the initial enrollment period, companies selling Medigap plans cannot deny selling policies to individuals with preexisting conditions, or charge them more than other 65-year-olds. However, outside of that initial enrollment period, companies selling Medigap policies are allowed to use medical underwriting to decide if they are

59. Amol K. Narang & Lauren Hersch Nicholas, *Out-of-Pocket Spending and Financial Burden among Medicare Beneficiaries with Cancer*, 3 JAMA Oncology 757, 757 (2017).

going to sell an individual a policy and what they charge. Individuals with preexisting conditions who try to purchase a Medigap plan outside of the initial enrollment period may have a six-month preexisting condition exclusion period. During those six months, the Medigap plan will not pay for any out-of-pocket expenses related to the preexisting condition. After six months, the Medigap plan will begin paying its portion. Medicare's website allows individuals to enter their zip code and determine whether or not they already have a Medigap plan.[60] The site then shows individuals the various Medigap plans available to them. Medigap plans may only be available in certain states depending on how an individual qualifies for Medicare. To see how states handle access to Medigap plans, visit https://triagecancer.org/state-laws.

***c. Enrolling in Medicare***

Choosing the right Medicare plan can be daunting for individuals. In an attempt to simplify the process, the following figure illustrates the two paths an individual can take when signing up for Medicare benefits.

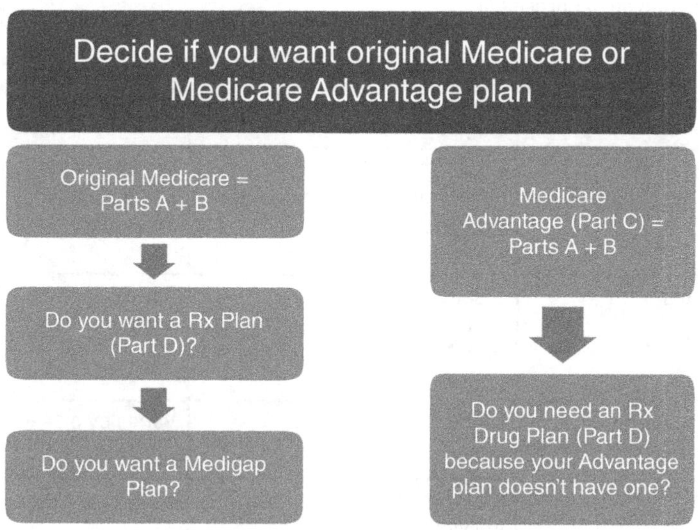


There is no one right answer for everyone as to which path to take. There are pros and cons of each option and individuals should weigh their options carefully (see tables in this subsection).

Some questions an individual may ask if considering a Medicare Advantage plan include:

60. Medicare.gov, *Find a Medigap Policy That Works for You*, https://www.medicare.gov/medigap-supplemental-insurance-plans/ (last visited Jan. 29, 2025).

- Do I want to see specific health care providers? Would having a limited network of providers be concerning?
- Am I able to coordinate and keep track of different premiums and deductibles?
- Do I need dental and vision services?

| **Pros of Medicare Advantage Plans** | **Cons of Medicare Advantage Plans** |
|---|---|
| Out-of-pocket maximum is at most $9,350 a year (in 2025) | Could have a small network of providers = out-of-network providers not part of out-of-pocket max, if covered at all |
| Many plans cost exactly the same amount as a Part B plan | Plans are difficult to compare since no two plans are alike |
| Usually includes drug coverage (without separate premium/deductible) | Usually only localized coverage (i.e., no nationwide coverage) |
| Can include "extras" like dental, vision | Primarily HMO plans that require referrals from primary care physicians to see specialists |
| Can switch to another Advantage plan or Original Medicare during open enrollment | May not be able to get Medigap later |

| | **Original Medicare** | **Medicare Advantage** |
|---|---|---|
| Network of Providers | No<br>Individuals can see any provider in the United States that accepts Medicare | Yes; varies by plan<br>Some plans offer no out-of-network coverage |
| Monthly Premium | Standardized<br>Part A: typically, free<br>Part B: $185–$628.90 (depending on income) | Part B premium + $128 more for additional services |
| Annual Deductible | $257 | Varies by plan |
| Co-Payments | $9,350 in 2025 | Varies by plan |
| Cost-Share Amount | Medicare 80%<br>Individual 20% | Varies by plan |
| Out-of-Pocket Maximum | No | Varies by plan<br>Maximum $9,350 in 2025 |
| Includes Vision, Dental, and Hearing Benefits | No | Varies by plan |
| Includes Prescription Drug Coverage | No<br>Individuals must elect Part D for prescription drug coverage | Varies by plan<br>Prescription drug coverage varies by plan; if individuals chose a Medicare Advantage plan without prescription drug coverage, they may also choose a Part D plan |
| Eligible to Purchase a Medigap Plan | Yes | No |

In addition to choosing the right path, there are specific times when an individual becomes eligible to enroll in Medicare for the first time. The initial enrollment periods for Medicare include:

- Becoming newly eligible for Medicare upon turning 65. Individuals have a seven-month period to pick plans. The seven-month period starts three months before the month individuals turn 65, includes the month they turn 65, and ends three months after the month they turn 65.
- Becoming newly eligible for Medicare because the individual has a disability and has been receiving SSDI for 24 months
- Already having Medicare because of a disability, and turning 65
- Having Medicare Part A coverage, and obtaining Medicare Part B for the first time by enrolling during the Part B general enrollment period (GEP) (January 1–March 31)

Enrollment in Part A is automatic for most individuals who have paid into the Social Security retirement system and have turned 65. However, individuals who are not already receiving Social Security retirement benefits must take proactive steps to enroll in Parts B, C, or D. Individuals who opt not to enroll in Medicare during their initial enrollment period will most likely have to pay a lifetime penalty. However, if they enroll in coverage later, individuals may be eligible for a SEP that allows them to delay enrolling in Part A, B, C, or D, and avoid a penalty. SEPs for Parts A and B are available to individuals who work for an employer with 20 or more employees and who have health insurance through their job, union, or a spouse's job when they turn 65. Individuals in that circumstance can get a SEP to sign up for Parts A and/or B:

- Any time they are still covered by the employer, union, or spouse's group health plan
- During the eight months following the month the employer, union, or spouse's group health plan coverage ends, or when the employment ends (whichever is first)

After individuals in this situation sign up for Part B, they then also have a six-month SEP to enroll in a Medigap plan. Individuals may be eligible for a SEP to purchase a Part C plan (i.e., Medicare Advantage plan) after the employer or union group health plan coverage ends, or when the employment ends, whichever is first. Additionally, if an individual enrolled in a Medicare Advantage plan when they initially became eligible for Medicare, the individual is entitled to a Medicare Advantage "trial period" special enrollment. Individuals have up to 12 months to change their minds and switch to an Original Medicare plan (i.e., Parts A and B). They will also be eligible to purchase a guaranteed issue Medigap supplemental policy.[61] Individuals

---

61. Medicare.gov, *Joining a Plan*, https://www.medicare.gov/basics/get-started-with-medicare/get-more-coverage/joining-a-plan (last visited Jan. 29, 2025).

may be eligible for a SEP to purchase a Part D plan after the employer or union group health plan coverage ends, or when the employment ends, whichever is first. Additionally, individuals may be able to choose a different Part C or D plan if circumstances in their lives change—for example, they move out of the service area for the current plan; they enter or leave a long-term care facility; the original plan no longer serves their area; or they get Extra Help program assistance for their Medicare prescription drug costs. For details about each of these SEPs, visit https://www.medicare.gov/basics/get-started-with-medicare/get-more-coverage/joining-a-plan/special-enrollment-periods.

If individuals do not enroll in Medicare Part B during their initial enrollment period, or their SEP, they may be able to enroll during the GEP, which is January 1 through March 31, every year, but they may have to pay a penalty. The Part B late enrollment penalty can be as high as 10 percent for each full 12-month period that the individual was eligible to have Part B, but did not sign up. For example, Jed became eligible for Part B on January 1, 2022. However, he waited to enroll until February 15, 2024. Since Jed waited 25 months to enroll in Part B, he will have to pay a 20 percent penalty, added to his Medicare Part B monthly premium, for as long as he has Medicare.

Because Part B is an extra cost, some individuals choose not to elect Part B coverage. However, refusing Part B coverage is a decision that has important ramifications, so individuals should consider it carefully. One of the primary reasons that individuals refuse Part B coverage is because they have other health insurance coverage. But they need to understand the rules about how their coverage works with Medicare. For example:

- Individuals are still working and are covered through their employer, or their spouse is still working and their employer offers coverage. Individuals should ask their employer or union benefits administrator if they require eligible individuals to sign up for Part B. If the employer does not require eligible individuals to sign up for Part B right away, individuals can usually sign up for Part B later during a SEP without a late enrollment penalty.
- Individuals are retired but have health insurance coverage through a former employer, COBRA, or the Veterans Health Administration. For individuals who are retired and have retiree health insurance from a former employer or union, COBRA, or U.S. Department of Veterans Affairs (VA) coverage, Medicare generally will become their primary health insurance. Medicare will pay its part of the costs for any health care services an individual receives, and then any amount not covered by Medicare can be submitted to the non-Medicare plan. If individuals do not keep Part B, the non-Medicare coverage may not pay for medical costs during any period in which the individual was eligible for Medicare Part B, but did not sign up for it.

- Once eligible for Medicare, individuals who have coverage through the Health Insurance Marketplace as an individual are no longer eligible for financial assistance for a Marketplace plan once their Part A coverage begins.
- Individuals with TRICARE coverage (insurance for active-duty military, military retirees, and their families). Eligible individuals must have Part B to keep TRICARE coverage. However, if they are an active-duty service member or the spouse or dependent child of an active-duty service member, they may not have to get Part B right away.
- Individuals with Civilian Health and Medical Program of the VA (CHAMPVA) coverage. Eligible individuals must have Part B to keep their CHAMPVA coverage.
- Individuals with coverage through a private insurance plan. If individuals accept Medicare Part B, Medicare will pay its part of the costs for any health care services received, and then any amount not covered by Medicare can be submitted to the private plan, which becomes the secondary payer.

The late enrollment penalty for Part D is added to individuals' Part D premiums each month. If subject to a penalty, individuals will have to pay it each month for as long as they have Medicare drug coverage. The Part D late enrollment penalty is calculated as 1 percent of the national base beneficiary premium for each full month the individual did not have Part D or other creditable coverage.

For example, Ainsley did not have Part D or creditable prescription drug coverage for 14 months after her initial enrollment period. Her Part D penalty will be calculated in the following way:

$$\$36.78 \text{ (2025 base beneficiary premium)} \times 1\% = .368$$
$$.368 \times 14 \text{ months} = \$5.152$$
$$\$5.152 \text{ rounded to the nearest } \$.10 = \$5.20$$

Ainsley would have $5.20 added to her monthly Part D premium for as long as she has Medicare Part D (which will probably be the remainder of her life). So, each year she will pay close to an additional $62 in Part D penalties. Over 20 years, that would be more than $1,200 in avoidable penalties.

Every year, individuals who are enrolled in Medicare will receive an "evidence of coverage" (EOC) document from their plan. The EOC provides information about covered benefits and costs. Individuals can typically expect their EOC in the fall, prior to open enrollment. Open enrollment starts October 15 and ends December 7 each year. During this time frame, individuals who already have Medicare can sign up for a new plan or make changes to their existing plans. Coverage for these plans begins January 1. While individuals are not required to make changes, the open enrollment period is a valuable opportunity to review their coverage, review the cost of plans, and change plans if they choose.

For more information about signing up for Medicare, visit Medicare.gov, or call (800) MEDICARE.

*d. Medicare Specialty Coverage*

There are some lesser-known services that Medicare covers that may be particularly relevant to individuals coping with cancer, specifically home health care and hospice.

Medicare covers home health care services for eligible individuals. Home health care can be less expensive, more convenient, and provide better quality of life for many individuals. For more information about who is eligible, what is covered, and how to find and choose a home health care agency, see CMS's "Medicare & Home Health Care" at https://www.medicare.gov/publications/10969-medicare-and-home-health-care.pdf.

Another service that Medicare provides coverage for is hospice care. Hospice is specifically for individuals who have been diagnosed with a terminal medical condition. The focus of hospice care is on ensuring that an individual is comfortable, rather than on curing an illness. In hospice, a specially trained team of professionals and caregivers provide care for the "whole person," including physical, emotional, social, and spiritual needs. There are hospice facilities, but hospice care is often provided in the individual's home. Hospice care can even include specialized care, such as reading to a patient, playing music, and companionship. Hospice care providers can also provide respite for caregivers.

Medicare recognizes the importance of hospice and covers it fully under Part A services as long as the services are provided by a Medicare-approved hospice provider. If, while in hospice, an individual requires outpatient care that is not associated with the terminal illness (e.g., they fall and break an arm), those services would be covered by Part B or Part C Medicare benefits.

Once an individual has determined that they no longer wish to pursue curative treatment for a medical condition, that decision should be discussed with the health care team. The health care team should be able to provide assistance coordinating hospice care. Individuals should also remember that at any time they have the right to stop hospice care, and to seek curative treatment. For more information on hospice care, visit https://www.nhpco.org.

For more information about Medicare's coverage of hospice benefits and how to find and choose a hospice provider, see CMS's "Medicare Hospice Benefits" at https://www.medicare.gov/Pubs/pdf/02154-Medicare-Hospice-Benefits.PDF.

*e. Services Medicare Does Not Cover*

There are still some health care services that Medicare does not cover. For example, Medicare will not provide coverage for the following services:

- Long-term care (also called custodial care)
- Most dental care
- Eye examinations related to prescribing glasses

- Dentures
- Cosmetic surgery
- Acupuncture
- Hearing aids and exams for fitting them
- Routine foot care

To find out if a test, service, or exam is covered by Original Medicare, visit https://www.medicare.gov/coverage/your-medicare-coverage.html. Individuals who have a Part D or Medicare Advantage plan should contact the plan itself to learn more.

*f. Help Paying for Medicare*

Individuals with lower incomes and limited assets may be eligible for financial assistance to pay for their Medicare coverage. There are four main programs to help individuals pay for Medicare costs:

- **Medicaid** (discussed in detail later). Individuals who also have Medicaid will receive help paying for Medicare costs such as premiums, deductibles, co-payments, and cost-share. Eligibility requirements for Medicaid vary by state. Individuals who qualify for both Medicare and Medicaid are referred to as "dual-eligibles."
- **Medicare savings programs (MSPs)**. Provides individuals financial assistance to help pay their Medicare premiums. In some cases, individuals may also receive help to pay for their deductibles, co-payments, and cost-share amounts. There are four types of MSPs:
  - Qualified Medicare Beneficiary (QMB) Program helps eligible individuals pay for Part A and Part B premiums, as well as deductibles, coinsurance, and co-payments. To be eligible in 2025, individuals cannot have monthly incomes over $1,325 and more than $9,660 in resources, and married couples could not have monthly incomes over $1,783 and more than $14,470 in resources. Health care providers are not permitted to bill individuals who are designated as a QMB for deductibles, co-payments, and cost-share amounts when the individual receives services Medicare covers. However, pharmacists may charge QMBs a very limited amount for prescription drugs covered by Medicare Part D.[62]
  - Specified Low-Income Medicare Beneficiary (SLMB) Program helps eligible individuals pay for Part B premiums. To be eligible, individuals cannot have monthly incomes over $1,585 and more than $9,660 in resources, and married couples cannot have monthly incomes over $2,135 and more than $14,470 in resources.[63]

---

62. *Medicare Savings Programs*, MEDICARE.GOV, https://www.medicare.gov/basics/costs/help/medicare-savings-programs (last visited Nov. 4, 2024).
63. *Id.*

- o Qualifying Individual (QI) Program helps pay the Part B premiums for certain individuals who are not eligible for Medicaid. Individuals must apply each year for the QI Program, and benefits are awarded on a first come basis. Priority is given to prior recipients. To be eligible for the QI Program, individuals cannot have monthly incomes over $1,781 and more than $9,660 in resources, and married couples cannot have monthly incomes over $2,400 and more than $14,470 in resources.[64]
- o Qualified Disabled and Working Individuals (QDWI) Program helps eligible individuals pay their Part A premiums. To be eligible, individuals must be under 65 and working with a disability; have lost their premium-free Part A when they went back to work; and have limited income and resources. Individuals cannot have monthly incomes over $5,302 and more than $4,000 in resources, and married couples cannot have monthly incomes over $7,135 and more than $6,000 in resources.[65]

- **Program of All-Inclusive Care for the Elderly (PACE).**[66] A joint Medicare and Medicaid program that helps individuals pay for some medical and long-term care. Individuals older than 55 who would qualify for nursing home level care but choose, and are able, to live in their communities may be eligible for PACE.[67] PACE is not available in all states. To locate PACE programs, visit https://www.npaonline.org/find-a-pace-program.
- **Prescription drug assistance programs.** Even with Part D coverage, prescription drugs can be expensive. Depending on individuals' income and resource levels, they may qualify for a low-income subsidy (also called the Extra Help program) to help pay for their prescription drugs.

Individuals who qualify for an MSP may qualify for Extra Help. Extra Help is a program that helps pay Medicare Part D premiums, deductibles, co-payments, and cost-share amounts. Individuals who are dual-eligible or those that have Medicare and receive Supplemental Security Income may automatically qualify for Extra Help. Generally, to be eligible, individuals cannot have an annual income higher than $23,712 or $31,968 for a married couple living together. The value of their resources cannot be more than $17,600 for an individual or $35,130 for a married couple living together.[68] Resources are things like real estate (excluding a primary residence), bank accounts, bonds, retirement accounts, and cash.[69] Individuals with higher incomes

---

64. *Id.*
65. *Id.*
66. 42 C.F.R. § 460.98(b)(2).
67. *PACE,* MEDICARE.GOV, https://www.medicare.gov/health-drug-plans/health-plans/your-coverage-options/other-medicare-health-plans/PACE (last visited Nov. 4, 2024).
68. *Help with Drug Costs,* MEDICARE.GOV, https://www.medicare.gov/basics/costs/help/drug-costs (last visited Nov. 4, 2024).
69. *Id.*

may still be eligible for some assistance if they support other family members who live with them; have income from work; or live in Alaska or Hawaii.[70]

To apply for the Medicare low-income subsidy, individuals should fill out an "Application for Extra Help with Medicare Prescription Drug Plan Costs"[71] online at https://www.ssa.gov/medicare/part-d-extra-help, by calling (800) 771-1213, or in person at their local Social Security office.

State Pharmaceutical Assistance Programs (SPAPs) also provide assistance for paying Part D premiums or drug costs. Programs are not available in every state. To locate SPAPs, visit https://www.medicare.gov/plan-compare/#/pharmaceutical-assistance-program/states/. For information on how to reduce prescription drug costs, see Chapter 6, Finances.

***g. Assistance with Medicare***

Individuals who qualify for Medicare, but need assistance, should contact the State Health Insurance Assistance Program (SHIP). SHIP was created under section 4360 of the Omnibus Budget Reconciliation Act (OBRA) of 1990.[72] Specifically, SHIP counselors are trained to provide one-on-one assistance and to do the following:

- Answer questions about Medicare, Medigap, long-term care insurance, Medicare Advantage, and other health insurance plans
- Answer questions about Part D plans
- Organize and assist in filing Medicare and Medigap claims
- Appeal claim denials
- Answer questions about and help complete applications for Extra Help

There are SHIP grantees in all states, Puerto Rico, Guam, the District of Columbia, and the U.S. Virgin Islands, which include thousands of local SHIP programs and counselors. The majority of SHIP programs are housed under State Departments on Aging or State Departments of Insurance.[73] SHIP programs are not affiliated with any insurance company and do not sell any insurance. The contact information for each state's SHIP program can be found at https://triagecancer.org/stateresources.

## 2. Medicaid

Medicaid is a federal health insurance program that provides health care coverage for individuals with low incomes.[74] The Medicaid program started in 1965, and was created by the same law that created the Medicare program.[75] Currently, Medicaid is the

70. *Id.*
71. Social Security Form SSA-1020.
72. Pub. L. No. 101-508, § 4360, 104 Stat. 1388.
73. Carol O'Shaughnessy, National Health Policy Forum, The Basics: The State Health Insurance Assistance Program (SHIP) (2010), https://www.nhpf.org/library/the-basics/Basics_SHIP_03-29-10.pdf.
74. 42 U.S.C. § 1396 *et seq.*
75. Pub. L. No. 89-97, 79 Stat. 286 (1965).

largest source of funding for medical and health services for low-income individuals in the United States. Medicaid funding is provided by both federal and state governments. Federal law set broad national guidelines for Medicaid eligibility, but states have discretion in setting their own eligibility standards, and scope and duration of services under the program.[76] Thus, a person who is eligible for Medicaid in one state may not be eligible in another state, and the services provided by one state may differ from services provided in a neighboring state. States are also responsible for administering their Medicaid programs.

While details vary by state, Medicaid generally covers inpatient hospital services, outpatient hospital services, laboratory and x-ray services, skilled nursing home services, physicians' services, physical therapy, hospice care, and rehabilitative services.

States have the discretion, within federal guidelines, to establish a network of providers and provider payment rates.[77] There are two types of payment schemes: FFS and managed care. Under FFS arrangements, states pay providers directly for services. Typically, the rate states agree to pay is based on the average costs of the service; what consumers pay for the same service in the private market; and/or a percentage of what Medicare pays for equivalent services. With managed care arrangements, state Medicaid agencies contract with managed care organizations (MCOs) to provide health care services for Medicaid-eligible individuals. In return, states pay the MCO a set amount per member, per month.[78]

States can make enrollment in an MCO voluntary, or obtain a waiver from CMS to require certain individuals to enroll in an MCO. If a state provides a choice of at least two plans, they can mandate that individuals enroll in an MCO.[79] For more details about state-specific plans, individuals should contact their state Medicaid agency, https://triagecancer.org/stateresources.

As discussed later in the chapter, the ACA allowed states to expand eligibility for Medicaid. To avoid confusion, *traditional Medicaid* refers to the program in existence before January 1, 2014, and *Medicaid expansion* refers to expansion of the program after January 1, 2014. Even in states that have expanded Medicaid under the ACA, the traditional Medicaid option still exists.

### *a. Traditional Medicaid*

To be eligible for traditional Medicaid, one must have limited assets, a low income, and fall into at least one of the following categories:

76. 42 U.S.C. § 1396a.

77. *Section 1115 Demonstrations*, Medicaid.gov, https://www.medicaid.gov/medicaid/section-1115-demonstrations/index.html (last visited Nov. 4, 2024).

78. 42 C.F.R. pt. 438 (2002).

79. *Medicaid 101: Provider Payment and Delivery Systems*, MACPAC, https://www.macpac.gov/medicaid-101/provider-payment-and-delivery-systems/ (last visited Nov. 4, 2024).

- Have a disability[80]
- Be blind
- Have a minor child or children
- Be a child younger than 19 years old
- Be a pregnant woman (coverage will last until six months after the child is born)
- Have been diagnosed with breast or cervical cancer through the National Breast and Cervical Cancer Early Detection Program (NBCCEDP)

These categories can be thought of as different doors into Medicaid, as illustrated in the following figure.

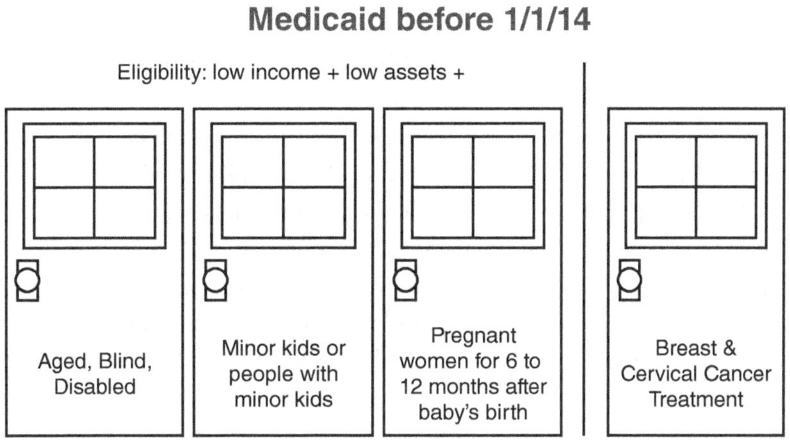


If an individual has too high of an income or too many assets but is otherwise eligible for Medicaid, the individual may be able to participate in a spend-down program. These vary state by state and individuals should contact their state Medicaid office for more information. Generally, spend-down programs allow people to pay for a portion of their health care costs, up to a certain amount that is determined based on their income and asset levels. After individuals can show that they have paid the predetermined amount toward health care costs, Medicaid will pick up the remainder of the costs. Several types of expenses are eligible for the spend-down program, such as doctor services, hospital services, nursing home services, prescription medicines and medical supplies, health insurance premiums, transportation to and from medical care, and co-payments or deductibles. Individuals can typically submit bills each

80. You may be deemed disabled by the U.S. Social Security Administration (SSA) if you cannot do work that you did before; the SSA decides that you cannot adjust to other work because of your medical condition(s); and your disability has lasted or is expected to last for at least one year or to result in death. *See Disability*, SSA, https://www.ssa.gov/benefits/disability/ (last visited Nov. 4, 2024).

month to prove that they have met their spend-down amount. However, sometimes large bills can be submitted all at once to receive a card showing that the amount has been met for several future months. For details about Medicaid in a particular state, contact the state's Medicaid agency: https://triagecancer.org/stateresources.

**Spend-Down Example**

Ann's spend-down amount is $200. Ann has a doctor bill for $100 and a hospital bill for $900 on the same day. She will owe only the $100 doctor bill and $100 of the hospital bill. The hospital will bill Medicaid for the remaining $800.

*b. Dual-Eligible Individuals*

Some individuals are eligible for both Medicare and Medicaid; these individuals are referred to as "dual-eligible" beneficiaries. Typically, these individuals have low incomes and receive Medicare Parts A and B. Because they are eligible for both programs, their health care is primarily covered by Medicare, but Medicaid helps pay for Medicare-related co-payments, deductibles, and cost-share amounts. Medicaid may also provide some benefits that Medicare does not cover, such as vision and dental care. It is also worth noting that as of January 2006, outpatient prescription drugs are covered under Medicare Part D for individuals who are dual-eligible.[81] It is estimated that 12.5 million Americans are dual-eligible.[82] Details vary by state, so individuals should contact their state's Medicaid agency for more information.

*c. Medicaid Additional Services*

A number of programs provide additional assistance for individuals receiving Medicaid.

*i. Health Insurance Premium Payment Program*

The Health Insurance Premium Payment (HIPP) Program is available to individuals who would be eligible for Medicaid, but have private insurance through their employers or COBRA. OBRA authorized states to implement a HIPP Program.[83] As of August 2024, the following states have HIPP Programs: Alabama, Alaska, Arkansas, California, Colorado, Florida, Georgia, Hawaii, Illinois, Iowa, Kansas, Kentucky, Louisiana, Maine, Massachusetts, Minnesota, Missouri, Montana, Nebraska, Nevada, New Hampshire, North Carolina, Oregon, Pennsylvania, Rhode Island, South Carolina, South Dakota, Texas, Utah, Vermont, Virginia, Washington, West

81. Medicare Prescription Drug, Improvement, and Modernization Act of 2003, Pub. L. No. 108-173, 117 Stat. 2066.

82. Maria T. Peña et al., *A Profile of Medicare-Medicaid Enrollees (Dual Eligibles)*, KFF (Jan. 31, 2023), https://www.kff.org/medicare/issue-brief/a-profile-of-medicare-medicaid-enrollees-dual-eligibles.

83. Pub. L. No. 101-508, 104 Stat. 1388.

Virginia, Wisconsin, and Wyoming.[84] For the contact information and more information about each state's HIPP Program, visit https://triagecancer.org/stateresources.

In addition to helping individuals with lower incomes pay for the cost of health insurance, it allows individuals to keep their employer-sponsored or COBRA coverage, which may cover services or providers not covered by Medicaid.

*ii. Compensation for Caregiving*

Medicaid also offers some compensation for individuals who are providing caregiving services to individuals with Medicaid as a way to help them remain in their homes when they are unable to fully care for themselves. Under this program, individuals receive nonmedical personal care. This is an alternative to out-of-home care institutions like nursing homes. The services can include domestic tasks (meal preparation, cleaning, laundry, shopping, and errands), personal care, accompaniment to medical appointments, and supervision for individuals with cognitive impairment. For more details about these in-home caregiving services, see Chapter 7.

*iii. Transportation*

If individuals with Medicaid obtain medical services from medical providers that are a distance from their homes, many states provide nonemergency medical transportation (NEMT) or contract their local agencies and vendors to provide transportation. States are required to provide NEMT to individuals with Medicaid to assure access to medical care and services. In most states, there must be preapproval before one can arrange for NEMT. For more information about NEMT, see Triage Cancer's "Quick Guide to Medicaid Transportation Coverage" at https://triagecancer.org/QuickGuide-MedicaidTransportation-PDF.

### *d. Breast and Cervical Cancer Treatment Program and NBCCEDP*

In 1990, Congress passed the Breast and Cervical Cancer Mortality Prevention Act.[85] This law created the NBCCEDP. The purpose of the NBCCEDP was to allow the Centers for Disease Control and Prevention (CDC) to provide women who have low incomes, or are uninsured or underinsured, access to breast and cervical cancer screenings and early detection services.[86] "Low income" for the purposes of this program is defined as incomes at or below 250 percent of the FPL. In addition to having a low income, women must also be between the ages of 21 and 64 for cervical cancer screening and 40 and 64 for breast cancer screening. Services available under the NBCCEDP include clinical breast examinations, mammograms, pap tests, pelvic

84. DOL, Premium Assistance under Medicaid and the Children's Health Insurance Program (CHIP) (2024), https://www.dol.gov/sites/default/files/ebsa/laws-and-regulations/laws/chipra/model-notice.pdf.

85. Pub. L. No. 101-354, 104 Stat. 409 (1990).

86. *National Breast and Cervical Cancer Early Detection Program—About the National Breast and Cervical Cancer Early Detection Program*, CDC, https://www.cdc.gov/breast-cervical-cancer-screening/about/ (last updated Sept. 19, 2024).

examinations, and testing for human papillomavirus (HPV).[87] In 1993, Congress amended the act to expand these services to women who are members of American Indian and Alaska Native tribes and tribal organizations.[88] The NBCCEDP operates in all 50 states, the District of Columbia, six U.S. territories, and 12 American Indian/Alaska Native organizations.

Although the NBCCEDP has made great strides in helping to screen and diagnose women with breast and cervical cancer, many women who were diagnosed with cancer through their participation in the program had limited treatment options. In 2000, Congress passed the Breast and Cervical Cancer Prevention and Treatment Act.[89] This law allowed states to provide Medicaid coverage to women diagnosed with breast or cervical cancer or precancerous conditions through the NBCCEDP. Every state and the District of Columbia exercised the option to expand Medicaid coverage to these women. In 2002, the Native American Breast and Cervical Cancer Treatment Technical Amendment Act was signed into law.[90] This law clarifies that women who are members of American Indian and Alaska Native tribes and tribal organizations are eligible for similar services provided by the Indian Health Service (IHS) or a tribal organization.[91]

***e. Medicaid after 2010***

The major flaw in traditional Medicaid is that it does not provide health care coverage to childless adults with low incomes because poverty alone does not necessarily qualify someone for Medicaid. Furthermore, the resource test for traditional Medicaid was often a barrier to access. Individuals were forced to deplete any savings before becoming eligible for health care services under Medicaid.

The ACA expanded access to Medicaid as of January 1, 2014, as part of its goal to increase the numbers of Americans covered by health insurance. The federal government was fully responsible for funding the expansion for three years, and beginning in 2017, the federal government would pay at least 90 percent of the expansion costs.[92] The ACA intended every state to expand their Medicaid programs or risk losing federal funding for their existing programs. However, the 2012 U.S. Supreme Court decision in *National Federation of Independent Business v. Sebelius* changed the way this expansion would unfold.[93]

In *National Federation*, the Court determined that it was constitutional for Congress to ask states to expand their Medicaid programs. However, if a state chooses

87. *Id.*
88. Pub. L. No. 103-183, 107 Stat. 2226 (1993).
89. Pub. L. No. 106-354, 114 Stat. 1381 (2000).
90. Pub. L. No. 107-121, 115 Stat. 2384 (2002).
91. *Id.*
92. *Id.*
93. 132 S. Ct. 2566 (2012).

not to comply with the expansion, Congress cannot withhold all federal funding for that state's Medicaid program. The Court noted:

> Nothing in our opinion precludes Congress from offering funds under the Affordable Care Act to expand the availability of health care, and requiring that States accepting such funds comply with the conditions on their use. What Congress is not free to do is to penalize States that choose not to participate in that new program by taking away their existing Medicaid funding.[94]

In other words, even if states do not expand their Medicaid programs, they will continue to receive any funding they have gotten in the past to run their programs, but they will not receive any additional funding from the federal government.

The result of the Supreme Court's decision was to make the Medicaid expansion voluntary for states, creating a nationwide patchwork of options for low-income adults. While some states moved forward with the expansion and some chose to opt out completely, other states pursued other models of expansion. As of 2024, some states are still debating whether they will expand the program.

The following illustration demonstrates what the Medicaid program looks like now, in states that have chosen to expand their programs under the ACA.

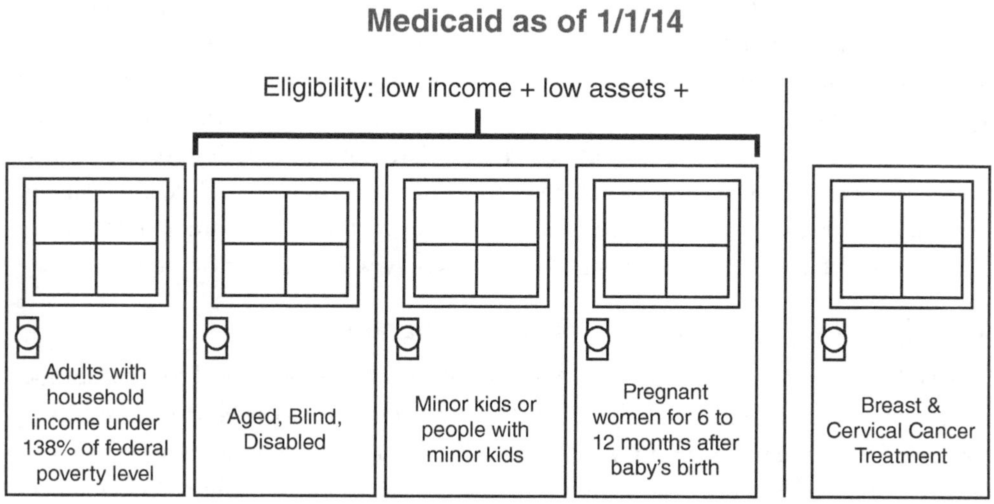


However, there is some additional variation within states. For example, Minnesota and New York have used the ACA Basic Health Program[95] option to cover adults with incomes between 138 percent and 200 percent of the FPL, rather than requiring

94. *Id.*
95. Pub. L. No. 111-148, § 1331, 124 Stat. 119 (2010).

these individuals to purchase coverage in the state Marketplaces. Due to this state variation, it is especially important for people who are coping with cancer to understand what is happening in their state. If their state has not moved forward with Medicaid expansion, there may continue to be a gap in coverage for childless adults with low incomes. For individuals who are unsure of their eligibility, HHS suggests:

- Individuals check with their states directly
- Individuals still apply even if their state is not expanding Medicaid, because they may qualify under existing state rules
- Individuals continue to check back because states are still making coverage choices and could accept the expansion in the future[96]
- Individuals who believe they are eligible for these programs should contact their state Medicaid agencies

## 3. CHIP

CHIP provides health insurance coverage for children in low-income households. The CHIP program was created by the Balanced Budget Act of 1997.[97] Like Medicaid, CHIP is a state-federal partnership. The program is administered by states based on federal requirements. The federal government provides matching funds to states to pay for the program.

The eligibility rules and details vary by state, but each state provides comprehensive coverage, which includes routine checkups, immunizations, doctor visits, prescription drugs, dental and vision care, inpatient and outpatient hospital care, laboratory and x-ray services, and emergency services. The costs for CHIP also vary by state. Some states charge a monthly premium. Additionally, individuals will have to pay a copayment for some services; however, routine "well child" doctor and dental visits are free. Individuals can apply for CHIP at any point during the year. For more information about the CHIP program in each state, visit https://www.insurekidsnow.gov.

## 4. Federal Employees Health Benefits Program

The Federal Employees Health Benefits (FEHB) Program provides health insurance benefits to most employees of the federal government,[98] retirees, and their surviving spouses.[99] The FEHB Program was created by the Federal Employees Health Benefits Act of 1959[100] and is administered by the U.S. Office of Personnel Management. Eligible individuals can enroll in comprehensive coverage through an FFS plan, an HMO, or even an HDHP. The annual time period when individuals can enroll or

---

96. *Medicaid Expansion & What It Means for You*, HEALTHCARE.GOV, https://www.healthcare.gov/medicaid-chip/medicaid-expansion-and-you/ (last visited Nov. 4, 2024).
97. Pub. L. No. 105-33, 111 Stat. 251.
98. 5 C.F.R. pt. 890 (1978).
99. *Id.* pt. 891.
100. Pub. L. No. 86-382, 73 Stat. 708.

make changes within the FEHB Program is referred to as "Open Season," and generally runs from November 13 through December 11. Coverage begins January 1 of the following year. For more information about the FEHB Program, visit https://www.opm.gov/healthcare-insurance/healthcare.

## 5. Military-Related Health Insurance

Active-duty service members and veterans who have been diagnosed with cancer have access to government-sponsored health care programs that provide coverage to certain family members and dependents and operate on a network of military treatment facilities. TRICARE provides medical and dental coverage to active-duty military members, and the VA provides health care for veterans. TRICARE and VA health care options are helpful to individuals diagnosed with cancer because they make treatment more affordable. However, both programs contain some limitations that may be problematic for people seeking cancer treatment.

### *a. TRICARE*

TRICARE is a health care program sponsored by the U.S. Department of Defense. TRICARE provides medical and dental coverage to active-duty military personnel and their dependents, eligible members of the reserve component and their dependents, and uniformed services dependents and retirees and their survivors.

Overall, TRICARE is an important resource for active-duty service members who are either personally coping with cancer or have someone in their family coping with cancer. For more information about TRICARE, visit https://tricare.mil/.

### *b. Veterans' Health Care*

The VA administers the Veterans Health Administration, which is the largest integrated health care system in the country and currently provides care to millions of veterans at more than 1,000 facilities each year.[101]

Individuals who served in the active military, naval, or air service and were separated under any condition other than dishonorable may qualify for veterans' health care benefits.[102] Current and former members of the Reserves or National Guard who were called to serve in active duty and completed the full period that they were ordered to serve may also qualify for VA health benefits.[103] Generally, veterans who enlisted after September 7, 1980, or entered active duty after October 16, 1981, must have served 24 consecutive months or completed the full period that they were called to serve in order to be eligible. This minimum duty requirement may not apply to veterans who enlisted earlier than September 7, 1980, or to those who were discharged

101. *Veterans Health Administration*, VA, https://www.va.gov/health/ (last updated Oct. 7, 2024).

102. *See Eligibility for VA Health Care*, VA, http://www.va.gov/healthbenefits/apply/veterans.asp (last updated May 15, 2024).

103. *Id.*

due to a disability sustained in the line of duty.[104] There are also some new ways to qualify for VA coverage, which can be found here: https://www.va.gov/health-care/eligibility.

VA health care is free for many veterans who have a service-connected disability or meet other requirements. Veterans are required to complete a financial assessment or means test at the time of enrollment to determine if they qualify for free health care services.[105] Veterans who refuse to complete a means test or those whose income exceeds VA income limits may be required to pay co-payments for health care services.[106] If a veteran has private health insurance, the VA will bill that insurance policy for any care the veteran receives.[107] Generally, the veteran will not be responsible for any costs the private health insurance policy does not cover. For more information about how costs and co-payments work within VA health care, visit https://www.va.gov/healthbenefits/cost/index.asp.

Veterans can apply for VA health care benefits in person, by telephone, or by mail. One of the easiest ways to apply is online at https://www.va.gov/health-care/how-to-apply/. Once the VA receives the application, it will determine whether the applicant is eligible for enrollment. If the VA approves the application, it will send the new enrollee a Veterans Health Benefits Handbook and provide details on the specific benefits that the enrollee is entitled to receive. Enrollees will also receive information on their enrollment priority group assignment and co-payment status.[108] If the applicant is unable to be enrolled or disagrees with the enrollment decision, then the applicant may appeal the decision. The handbook will contain instructions on the appeal process or, if the applicant cannot be enrolled, the VA will notify the applicant with a letter that contains information on how to appeal the decision.[109]

## 6. IHS

IHS, an agency within HHS, provides health services to American Indians and Alaska Natives. IHS provides a variety of health care services, including inpatient, ambulatory, emergency, dental, public health nursing, and preventive health care. IHS provides a variety of cancer screenings and diagnostic services. Health care services vary by IHS facility, but services are provided free to eligible individuals regardless of their ability to pay.[110] IHS is not an insurance plan; rather, it provides health care services to individuals directly or through contracts with Indian tribes or tribal orga-

---

104. *Id.*

105. *Current VA Health Care Copay Rates*, VA, http://www.va.gov/healthbenefits/cost/copays.asp (last updated May 29, 2024).

106. *Id.*

107. *Id.*

108. *How to Apply for VA Health Care*, VA, http://www.va.gov/healthbenefits/apply/application_process.asp (last updated July 11, 2024).

109. *Id.*

110. Congressional Research Service, The Indian Health Service (IHS): An Overview (2016).

nizations.[111] As of 2022, IHS coordinates health care for approximately 2.8 million American Indians and Alaska Natives who belong to 574 federally recognized tribes in 37 states.[112]

The legal basis for providing federal funds for health services to recognized Indian tribes is the Snyder Act of 1921.[113] However, subsequent legislation has refined how this program operates. The Indian Self-Determination and Education Assistance Act[114] allows the "Secretary of Health, Education, and Welfare to enter into contracts with Indian tribes," and the Indian Health Care Improvement Act (IHCIA) called for "improving the services and facilities of federal Indian health programs and encouraging maximum participation of Indians in such programs."[115] Finally, the ACA included provisions to amend and permanently reauthorized the IHCIA.[116] For more information about IHS, visit https://www.ihs.gov.

## IV. Health Care Consumer Rights and Protections

Arguably, every American is a consumer of health care at some point in their lives. There are various laws and benefits that exist to protect health care consumers. This section describes some of the consumer protections that are relevant to individuals with a cancer diagnosis.

### A. ACA's Consumer Benefit Reforms

In addition to providing certain individuals with new health insurance options, the ACA made significant reforms as to how health insurance companies can do business and provided health care consumers with additional protections.

**ACA Key Insurance Reforms**

- No annual or lifetime limits
- No rescissions
- Coverage for preventive services
- Medical loss ratio

111. Under the authority of the Indian Self-Determination and Education Assistance Act, Pub. L. No. 93-638, 88 Stat. 2203 (1975).

112. *IHS Profile*, IHS, https://www.ihs.gov/newsroom/factsheets/ihsprofile (last visited Nov. 4, 2024).

113. Pub. L. No. 67-85, 42 Stat. 208.

114. Pub. L. No. 93-638, 88 Stat. 2203 (1975).

115. Pub. L. No. 94-437, 90 Stat. 1400 (1976).

116. Pub. L. No. 111-148, 124 Stat. 782 (2010).

## 1. Lifetime and Annual Limits

Many insurance plans had limits on the amount of benefits someone could use during each year or in a lifetime. These are called annual limits or lifetime limits. These benefit limits were very easy to reach, especially when someone was being treated for a serious medical condition, such as cancer. After a limit was reached, it left that person virtually uninsured, because the insurance company would no longer pay for medical expenses and individuals could not purchase a new policy because of their preexisting conditions.

As of September 23, 2010, insurance companies can no longer impose lifetime limits on payments for EHBs. As of January 1, 2014, annual limits on EHBs were also eliminated. The exact definition for EHBs differs from state to state, but generally includes items and services in the following categories: ambulatory patient services; emergency services; hospitalization; maternity and newborn care; mental health and substance use disorder services, including behavioral health treatment; prescription drugs; rehabilitative and habilitative services and devices; laboratory services; preventive and wellness services and chronic disease management; and pediatric services, including oral and vision care.

Each state was required to choose a benchmark plan. All individual and small group health insurance plans in the state must at least provide coverage for the benefits that are contained in the benchmark plan. To find the benchmark plans for each state, visit https://www.cms.gov/marketplace/resources/data/essential-health-benefits.

## 2. Rescissions

In the past, insurance companies often cancelled an individual's policy if the individual got sick. The ACA prohibits insurers from canceling an individual's plan unless that individual failed to pay their monthly premiums, committed fraud, or made an intentional misrepresentation of a material fact (i.e., lied about something very important) about their medical history on the initial application for coverage. Furthermore, if an insurance company rescinds a policy, it must provide a minimum of 30 days' notice to the enrollee and include in that notice information on the enrollee's right to appeal the rescission decision.

## 3. Preexisting Condition Protections and Premium Rating

Prior to the ACA, health insurance companies could charge higher premiums or even outright deny selling coverage to someone with a preexisting medical condition. As of January 1, 2014, no one can be denied health insurance coverage because of a preexisting condition. Also, as of 2014, insurance companies will be limited in what they can consider in deciding how much to charge someone for their monthly premiums. Specifically, insurance companies are only able to look at the type of plan they are purchasing (i.e., individual or family plan), age, tobacco use, and rating area (zip code) to determine how much someone will be charged for insurance coverage. Some states have gone further and eliminated the ability of insurance companies to charge individuals who use tobacco more for their premiums.

With respect to age, insurers are allowed to vary rates based on age within a 3:1 ratio for adults.[117] This means that, at most, a 64-year-old can only be charged three times more than a similarly situated 21-year-old for the same plan. For more information, visit https://www.cms.gov/marketplace/private-health-insurance/market-rating-reforms.

## 4. Free Preventive Services

Most insurance companies must cover specific preventive services without charging co-payments or making individuals first meet their deductibles. These free preventive services include items such as screenings for blood pressure, cholesterol, diabetes, and cancer, and immunizations such as flu shots. The goal was to make screenings and other preventive services more accessible to people with insurance. For more information about which preventive services are covered under this rule, see https://www.healthcare.gov/coverage/preventive-care-benefits. Grandfathered plans are not required to provide free preventive services.

## 5. Medical Loss Ratio

The ACA also requires that health insurance companies spend a minimum percentage of what they collect in premiums on actual health care, rather than administrative costs, marketing, and salaries. Insurance companies in the individual and small-group markets must spend at least 80 percent of the collected premiums (large-group insurers must spend at least 85 percent of the collected premiums) on health care and quality improvement activities. This is referred to as the medical loss ratio. If insurance companies do not meet these requirements, they must provide rebates to their customers by August 1 of each year. To learn more about the medical loss ratio, see https://www.healthcare.gov/health-care-law-protections/rate-review.

## 6. SBC

All group health plans and health insurance companies offering group or individual health insurance are now required to provide members with a standardized SBC. These SBCs should describe the benefits and coverage under the plan and must be presented in a standardized format. As of September 23, 2012, SBCs must be made available to a member upon application for coverage, by the first day of coverage (if information has changed), upon renewal or reissuance, and upon request.

Different entities are responsible for providing the SBCs:

- Individual health insurance plans: insurance company is responsible

117. 45 C.F.R. § 147.102(a)(1)(iii) (2013).

- Insured group plans: insurance company and the group health plan including the plan administrator (as defined by ERISA) are responsible
- Self-insured group plans: group health plan or designated administrator of the plan (as defined under ERISA) are responsible[118]

For more information about SBCs, visit https://www.cms.gov/marketplace/health-plans-issuers/summary-benefits-coverage.

The following table shows which types of plans must comply with various ACA provisions. This chart is not exhaustive, but rather focuses on the provisions that are most relevant to consumers.

**Summary of ACA Provisions and Applicable Plan Types**

| Provision | Individual Policies | Group Policies (Funded/ Insured) | Group Policies (Self-Funded/ Self-Insured) | Grandfathered Policies | Retiree Only Policies |
|---|---|---|---|---|---|
| Staying on parents plan until age 26 | X | X | X | X | |
| Covering preventative services for free | X | X | X | | |
| Caps on annual & lifetime limits | X | X | X | X | |
| Prohibition on preexisting condition discrimination | X | X | X | X | X |
| Limits on premium ratings | X | X | X | X | X |
| Prohibition on rescissions | X | X | X | X | |
| Standardized SBC | X | X | X | X | |
| Minimum EHB | X | X | | | |

## B. Insurance Coverage While Participating in Clinical Trials

Participating in a clinical trial might be an excellent treatment option for individuals diagnosed with cancer. However, in the past, some insurance companies denied

118. 26 C.F.R. §§ 54.9815–2715, *id.* §§ 2590.715–2715, and 45 C.F.R. § 147.200, published Feb. 14, 2012, at 77 Fed. Reg. 8,668.

claims for individuals who participated in clinical trials. Coverage for clinical trials will depend on an individual's type of insurance.

### 1. Private Insurance

As of January 1, 2014, the ACA required that non-grandfathered health plans (i.e., those that were created after March 23, 2010) cannot deny a qualified individual participation in an approved clinical trial, or deny or limit the coverage of "routine costs" in connection with participation in the trial. An "approved clinical trial" is one that tests ways to prevent, detect, or treat cancer and are funded or approved by the federal government and have submitted a U.S. Food and Drug Administration Investigational New Drug (IND) application or are exempt from IND requirements. "Routine costs" are those that would normally be involved in standard care, such as doctor visits, blood tests, imaging scans, and so on.

State laws may go even further in protecting consumers' rights to participate in clinical trials. Thirty-seven states and the District of Columbia have laws regarding clinical trial coverage.[119]

### 2. Medicaid

As of January 1, 2022, the federal government requires states to cover individuals who participate in clinical trials through state Medicaid plans. This includes coverage for out-of-state clinical trials.[120]

### 3. Medicare

Like private insurance, Medicare covers the routine costs of items and services in covered research studies. Examples of these items and services include room and board at a hospital, the treatment of side effects and complications that may occur as a result of the study, and operations to implant an item that is being tested. For more information about Medicare coverage for clinical trials, visit https://www.medicare.gov/coverage/clinical-research-studies.

### 4. TRICARE and VA

TRICARE will reimburse the medical costs related to taking part in National Cancer Institute (NCI)-sponsored trials for cancer prevention and treatment. The VA allows eligible veterans to participate in NCI-sponsored clinical trials at VA medical centers.

For specific information about state laws, visit https://triagecancer.org/state-laws. For more information about clinical trials, visit https://www.clinicaltrials.gov.

---

119. *See State Laws*, Triage Cancer, https://triagecancer.org/state-laws (last visited Nov. 4, 2024).

120. Letter from Daniel Tsai, Deputy Administrator and Director, CMS, to State Medicaid Director, Updated: Mandatory Medicaid Coverage of Routine Patient Costs Furnished in Connection with Participation in Qualifying Clinical Trials (Apr. 13, 2022), https://www.medicaid.gov/federal-policy-guidance/downloads/smd21005.pdf.

## C. Cancer Screening Mandates

Insurance coverage for cancer screenings varies by federal and state law and by the type of insurance coverage (e.g., private insurance, Medicare, or Medicaid). The ACA does not change existing state law protections; however, it does require that any new health insurance plans offer free preventive care, including some cancer screenings. However, this ACA provision does not apply to grandfathered plans. *Free* means that the insurance plan not only will cover the cancer screening, but it also cannot apply any costs to the deductible or charge a co-payment or cost-share amount. Some of the cancer-related preventive services include the following:

- Breast cancer mammography screenings every one to two years for women over 40 years old
- Cervical cancer screenings for sexually active women
- Colorectal cancer screenings for adults over 45 years old
- Genetic counseling and BRCA testing
- Immunizations for HPV
- Tobacco use screenings and cessation interventions

A complete list of preventive services to which this new provision applies can be found at https://www.healthcare.gov/coverage/preventive-care-benefits.

## D. Oral Chemotherapy Parity Laws

Oral cancer medications are typically covered under a health plan's pharmacy benefit. This means that patients are often required to pay higher out-of-pocket co-payments to fill these prescriptions. There are often no intravenous (IV) substitutes for oral chemotherapy drugs, which can leave patients with a significant financial burden. There have been various federal bills proposed to address this issue, but none have become law, to date. More than 43 states, plus the District of Columbia and Puerto Rico, have enacted oral chemotherapy parity access laws.[121] Each state's law varies, but generally insurance companies are required to treat and cover oral chemotherapy similarly to the way they would cover IV chemotherapy, which may reduce the out-of-pocket expenses incurred by patients.

## E. Women's Health and Cancer Rights Act

The Women's Health and Cancer Rights Act (WHCRA) is a federal law that may be especially important to women who are diagnosed with breast cancer. This law requires that if an insurance company covers a mastectomy or a partial mastectomy (i.e., a lumpectomy), it must also cover breast prostheses or the costs of reconstruction. Those costs can include reconstruction of the breast on which the mastectomy

121. See *State Laws*, *supra* note 119, for an updated list and links to each state's laws.

was performed, reconstruction of the other breast to achieve a symmetrical (balanced) appearance, and/or implants. Insurance companies must also pay for the treatment of any physical complications of a mastectomy.

If a patient has a mastectomy while covered by one plan but then moves to another health insurance plan before having reconstructive surgery, the new plan must also pay for the reconstructive surgery if it would have covered the original mastectomy.[122]

Although the WHCRA applies to most private health insurance plans, it may apply differently to certain church plans, and does not apply to Medicare or Medicaid. For more information on the WHCRA, visit https://www.dol.gov/agencies/ebsa/laws-and-regulations/laws/whcra.

## F. Privacy of and Access to Medical Records

The confidentiality of health care information is regulated by federal, state, and local laws, agency regulations, and case law. HIPAA of 1996[123] provides several different types of consumer protections. Under what is commonly known as the Privacy Rule, covered entities must keep medical records private and provide copies to individuals when requested. Entities that have to comply with the HIPAA Privacy Rule include:

- **Health care providers.** Every health care provider, regardless of size of practice, who electronically transmits health information in connection with certain transactions, including claims, benefit eligibility inquiries, referral authorization requests, and other transactions under the HIPAA Transactions Rule
- **Health plans.** Entities that provide or pay the cost of medical care (e.g., health, dental, vision, and prescription drug insurers; Medicare; Medicaid; Medigap insurers; long-term care insurers (excluding nursing home fixed-indemnity policies); employer-sponsored group health plans, government- and church-sponsored health plans, and multi-employer health plans)
- **Business associates.** A person or organization (other than a member of a covered entity's workforce) using or disclosing individually identifiable health information to perform functions, activities, or services including claims processing, data analysis, utilization review, and billing
- **Health care clearinghouses** (i.e., entities that facilitate and process the flow of information between health care providers and payers)[124]

Entities that are not covered under HIPAA typically include employers (unless they are acting as the health care provider or plan) or other types of insurers, such as those that provide life and disability insurance.

---

122. Employee Benefits Security Administration, DOL, FAQs about Women's Health and Cancer Rights, https://www.dol.gov/sites/default/files/ebsa/about-ebsa/our-activities/resource-center/faqs/whcra.pdf (last visited Nov. 4, 2024).

123. Pub. L. No. 104-191, 110 Stat. 1936.

124. 45 C.F.R. § 160.103 (2000).

Individuals have the right to obtain a copy of their medical records from any health care provider or health plan at any time, for any reason. A patient has the right to request a full or partial copy of their medical record. A full record is helpful for a patient's own records or if the patient has a new provider. A partial record is helpful to access specific information, such as allergies, immunization history, test results, and medications. Providers must also make clinical notes available, including consultation notes, discharge summary notes, history and physicals, imaging narratives, laboratory and pathology report narratives, procedure notes, and progress notes. A patient can decide what format the medical records are provided in. Options include email, paper, fax, mail, USB drive, digital/smartphone health apps with application programming interfaces (APIs), or an online portal.

A health care provider may not withhold access to medical records because a patient may have an outstanding medical bill. If a patient thinks that there is information in the medical or billing record that is incorrect, they can ask their health care provider or health plan to make a change to the record. The health care provider or health plan must respond to the request and make the change or addition to the record. If they refuse, the patient has the right to submit a statement of disagreement that the provider or plan must add to the patient's record.

The federal 21st Century Cures Act (Cures Act), passed in 2016, made it easier for patients to get copies of their health records. Hospitals and doctors cannot "block" patients from accessing their health records (known as "information blocking"). Patients have the right to see their electronic medical records, "without delay" and without charge.

Providers may charge reasonable, cost-based fees for copying and mailing hard copies of medical records. Patients may *not* be charged a fee for searching and retrieving records, nor if someone else searches for a patient's records. Providers may also charge reasonable, cost-based fees for supplying copies of electronic health information. Per page fees are not allowed if records are stored electronically; however, fees related to labor, supplies, postage, and preparation of explanations or summaries are. Some states also allow for fees, and amounts vary by state.

Under HIPAA's Privacy Rule, providers must provide a patient with a copy of their medical records within 30 days of the request, or 60 days if records are kept off-site. If the provider cannot either respond or provide the records within this time frame, they can use one 30-day extension. The Cures Act does not specify a time frame in which health care providers must provide patients with access to their electronic health records, but it does state that the records should be provided "without delay."

Health records can be withheld if required by law, or if they fall within one of eight exceptions to the Cures Act's "information blocking" rule. For example, health records may be withheld if doing so would prevent harm to the patient or someone else.

If a patient is denied access to records or a patient believes that their information was shared improperly, the patient can file a complaint about a possible HIPAA violation (denial of access to records or improper sharing of health information) by contacting the HHS Office for Civil Rights online at https://www.hhs.gov/hipaa/filing-a-complaint/index.html or by phone at (800) 368-1019. Patients can also file a complaint about a possible Cures Act violation (information blocking) by contacting the Office of the National Coordinator for Health Information Technology online at https://www.healthit.gov/.

## V. Choosing a Health Insurance Plan

### A. Tips for Picking a Plan

Three key factors are important to compare when considering health insurance options: (1) costs; (2) the health care providers and facilities covered by the plan; and (3) whether or not recommended prescriptions drugs are included on the list of covered drugs (formulary).

#### 1. Math Matters

When comparing prices for different plans, many individuals only look at the monthly premium. However, for individuals with an expensive medical condition such as cancer, it is imperative to not only focus on the monthly premium of a plan, but to also pay attention to the out-of-pocket maximums.

The out-of-pocket maximum is defined as the most amount of money an individual will pay on their own, each year, for medical expenses. In order to assess the total annual cost of an insurance plan, individuals should use this formula:

[monthly premium × 12 (months)] + out-of-pocket maximum

This formula can be used when comparing plans sold in the state Marketplace, plans offered by an employer, between Marketplace plans and employer plans, and between different Medicare Advantage or Part D plans. In some cases, choosing a plan with a higher monthly premium and a lower out-of-pocket maximum can save individuals thousands of dollars each year. For example:

Madeline is currently in treatment for cancer and is being offered three different health insurance plans from her employer. Assuming she will reach her out-of-pocket maximum during the year, which option is the most affordable?

A. HMO: $25 premium; $2,500 deductible; 70/30 cost-share amount; $8,000 out-of-pocket maximum

$25 × 12 month = $300 + $8,000 = $8,300

B. PPO: $100 premium; $1,500 deductible; 80/20 cost-share amount; $6,000 out-of-pocket maximum

$100 × 12 month = $1,200 + $6,000 = $7,200

C. PPO: $200 premium; $0 deductible; 90/10 cost-share amount; $4,000 out-of-pocket maximum

$200 × 12 month = $2,400 + $4,000 = $6,400

Just based on the math, option C is the least expensive, even though it has a higher monthly premium. However, there are additional things to take into consideration. Individuals should also look at the deductible; some plans have a higher monthly premium and a lower deductible. The advantage of these plans is that while they are more expensive, they start covering a higher percentage of the cost-share immediately. This helps to spread the costs out over the year, rather than requiring a large lump-sum payment up front. Tools like Triage Cancer's Health Insurance Comparison Worksheet can be helpful for individuals when comparing choices: https://triagecancer.org/Worksheet-HealthInsurance.

### 2. Provider Networks

Individuals must also consider the network of providers when choosing a health insurance plan. Some plans will not cover visits to out-of-network providers at all, and others only cover those services in a limited way. Additionally, most plans only apply out-of-pocket payments to in-network providers to the annual out-of-pocket maximum. Therefore, if individuals pick plans with limited provider networks, which do not include their health care providers, they will end up with higher out-of-pocket costs. Providers can include individual doctors, medical groups, hospitals and other health care facilities, pharmacies, and labs.

### 3. Formularies

Similarly, it is beneficial for individuals to review the prescription drug formularies for each plan they are considering. Individuals should communicate with their health care teams about any existing or anticipated prescription drug needs. Picking a plan that covers their prescription drug needs can greatly reduce out-of-pocket costs.

## B. Changes to Health Insurance

Obtaining health insurance is not a one-time chore. Individuals will likely have several different policies throughout their lives, and the source of those policies may also change as their life circumstances change. Individuals may have to make decisions about their health insurance coverage if they find themselves in a situation where they are losing their existing coverage.

### 1. Employer-Sponsored Health Insurance

When individuals receive their health insurance coverage through an employer, it can compound the overwhelming nature of having to make decisions about taking time off, switching jobs, or ending their employment. Fortunately, there are several laws that enable individuals with cancer to maintain health insurance when losing employer-sponsored coverage.

### *a. COBRA*

COBRA[125] was enacted in 1986.[126] It is a federal law that allows qualified beneficiaries the right to continue their health coverage after the occurrence of a qualifying event. To be eligible for COBRA, an individual must work for a private employer with 20 or more employees[127] or work for the state or federal government.[128] A qualified beneficiary generally is an individual covered by a group health plan on the day before a qualifying event (i.e., an employee or an employee's spouse or child).[129] A qualifying event is an event that causes a qualified beneficiary to lose coverage, such as voluntary or involuntary termination of employment (excluding termination for gross misconduct) or reduction in the number of hours the employee works (see the following table).[130] For example, Beagle Studios only provides health insurance benefits to full-time employees. Sue has decided that due to her treatment and recovery she can only work part-time, thus losing her health insurance benefits. That would be a qualifying event under COBRA even though she is still employed by Beagle Studios.

**COBRA Coverage[131]**

| COBRA Qualifying Event | Maximum COBRA Coverage* |
|---|---|
| Employment ends or hours reduced | 18 months |
| Loss of dependent child status | 36 months |
| Employee enrolls in Medicare | 36 months |
| Divorce or legal separation | 36 months |
| Death of employee | 36 months |

*COBRA coverage may be extended in limited circumstances.

COBRA coverage must be substantially similar, if not the exact same coverage, to what the employee received while working. However, it is typically going to cost a lot more. Often with employer-sponsored coverage, the employer pays a portion of the plan's monthly premium and the employee pays a portion. When individuals elect

125. Pub. L. No. 99-272, 100 Stat. 82 (1986).

126. COBRA is placed in three different laws: ERISA, the Internal Revenue Code, and the Public Health Service Act. The IRS and the DOL are responsible for issuing regulations.

127. 29 U.S.C. pt. 6.

128. 42 U.S.C. § 300bb-1.

129. Employee Benefits Security Administration, DOL, FAQs on COBRA Continuation Health Coverage for Workers, https://www.dol.gov/sites/dolgov/files/ebsa/about-ebsa/our-activities/resource-center/faqs/cobra-continuation-coverage.pdf (last visited Nov. 4, 2024).

130. *Id.* Note that certain events only apply to certain beneficiaries. For example, if a dependent child loses dependent status, that would be considered a qualifying event for the dependent and would not be a qualifying event for the employee.

131. 26 C.F.R. § 54.4980B-4 (1999).

COBRA coverage, they will be responsible for up to 102 percent of the applicable premium (i.e., the full cost of the plan plus a 2 percent administration fee).[132]

For example, Phoebe's premium is $400 per month, and her employer contributed $200 and she contributed $200 per month. Phoebe chose to move to part-time and, therefore, no longer qualifies for benefits at her job. Phoebe is entitled to elect COBRA coverage for 18 months. She is now responsible for paying the entire $400 monthly premium and perhaps an additional $8 per month (2 percent of $400) for administrative fees.

Even with the high premium costs, there may be some benefits to electing COBRA coverage rather than trying to find coverage in the Marketplace or open individual market. For example, if individuals are in the middle of treatment, they would not have to worry about finding insurance that had the same coverage for their doctors, hospitals, and prescription drugs. Additionally, if someone has already met the out-of-pocket maximum or deductible for the year, it may make more sense financially to elect COBRA for the remainder of the plan year rather than finding a new plan and having to pay another deductible or out-of-pocket maximum.

There are two times when individuals can extend their COBRA coverage:

- Individuals who experience a second qualifying event during their first 18 months of COBRA coverage may be entitled to an 18-month extension for a maximum total of 36 months of coverage.[133]
- Individuals who are deemed to be disabled by the Social Security Administration within the first 60 days of COBRA coverage may be entitled to an 11-month extension, for a total of 29 months of COBRA coverage. However, during the 11-month extension, the premiums may increase to 150 percent of the cost of coverage.[134]

There are a few instances when COBRA coverage may end early:[135]

- The employee does not pay the premiums
- The employee becomes eligible for Medicare (however, dependents can maintain their COBRA coverage)
- The employee commits fraud
- The employer stops offering a health plan to all employees
- The employer goes out of business

If an individual is eligible for COBRA, some specific notice requirements and deadlines must be met, as outlined in the following table.[136]

---

132. Employee Benefits Security Administration, DOL, FAQs on COBRA Continuation Health Coverage for Workers, https://www.dol.gov/sites/dolgov/files/ebsa/about-ebsa/our-activities/resource-center/faqs/cobra-continuation-health-coverage-consumer.pdf (last visited Nov. 4, 2024) (see Q15).

133. 26 C.F.R. § 54.4980B-7 (1999).

134. *Id.*

135. 29 U.S.C. § 1162.

136. *Id.* § 1166.

**COBRA Deadlines**

| Notice | Deadline |
|---|---|
| For divorce, legal separation, or loss of dependent status, employee must notify the employer. | 60 days after the qualifying event |
| For divorce, legal separation, or loss of dependent status, the employer must notify the health plan. | 14 days after receiving a notice from an employee |
| For employment ending or an employee reducing the number of working hours, an employee enrolling in Medicare, or the death of an employee, the employer must notify the health plan. | 30 days after the qualifying event |
| The health plan must notify the employee and any covered dependents of the right to elect COBRA. | 14 days after receiving a notice from the employer |
| The employee and dependents must notify the health plan of electing COBRA. | 60 days after receiving a notice from the plan administrator; the employee has 45 days to pay the first premium after notification |

It is important to remember that COBRA is not an actual health plan; it is the right to keep the same health insurance individuals had while they were employed. Keeping the same policy can be extremely beneficial to someone who is in the middle of cancer treatment because they would not have to find another health insurance policy that covers the same doctors and has the same prescription drug benefits.

*b. State COBRA*

Several states have passed state COBRA laws, some of which are more protective than the federal law. The details vary by state, but generally the state laws cover smaller employers with two to 19 employees, which is beneficial to employees who work for smaller employers.[137]

*c. SEPs (ACA and Medicare)*

If individuals experience a life-changing event that results in the loss of creditable coverage, they may be eligible for SEPs both through the State Health Insurance Marketplaces and through Medicare, if eligible. Insurance purchased in the Marketplaces would be a completely new policy, unlike with COBRA coverage, and individuals may also be eligible for financial assistance.

Since 2014, individuals losing their employer-sponsored insurance have more options to maintain health insurance coverage. However, individuals in this situation must think strategically before making any decisions. Typically, once individuals pick a path, they cannot change their minds until the next open enrollment period. For example, if someone decides to elect COBRA coverage after losing employer-sponsored insurance, they cannot decide midyear to stop paying the premiums and purchase a Marketplace plan instead. Voluntarily ending COBRA coverage will not trigger a SEP in the Marketplace.

---

137. *Health Insurance State Laws: Options*, Triage Cancer, https://triagecancer.org/state-laws/health-insurance-options (last visited Nov. 4, 2024).

There is a misconception that the ACA made COBRA irrelevant. COBRA is still a very important option for some individuals losing their employer-sponsored health insurance. For example, the coverage available under the employer's plan may be superior to the coverage available in the Marketplace. Or, perhaps the individual has already reached the out-of-pocket maximum for the year. In that case, it may make more financial sense for individuals to pay the high COBRA premiums and know that is all they will have to pay for their health care for the rest of the year. As discussed earlier, when making the decision between electing COBRA coverage or purchasing a new plan in the Marketplace, it is critical to "do the math" as well as compare the coverage.

## 2. Young Adults

Under the ACA, eligible young adults now have the option of staying on their parents' health insurance plans until they are 26 years old.[138] These young adults do not have to be dependents under IRS standards; they can live on their own, be married, and even have their own children.[139] This rule gives young adults additional options and helps to bridge the gap that may occur between leaving school and finding a job that offers health insurance benefits. It is important to note, however, that "retiree-only" plans are not subject to this requirement. So, if a parent has a retiree-only plan, the young adults may not be able to get coverage.

If a young adult is 26 and, therefore, aging out of a parent's plan, there may be several options:

- If they have an income less than 138 percent of the FPL and live in a state that has expanded its Medicaid program, they may be able to receive Medicaid.
- If they are employed, they may be eligible for an employer-sponsored plan.
- If they are married, they may be able to join a spouse's employer-sponsored plan.
- If they have an income more than 138 percent of the FPL or they live in a state that has not expanded its Medicaid program, they may be eligible for a SEP to buy coverage through the State Health Insurance Marketplaces.
- If they have a disability and have been receiving SSDI payments for 24 months, they may be eligible for Medicare.

## 3. Medicaid If Income Increases

If an individual is losing access to Medicaid because their income has increased past the Medicaid eligibility threshold, and the person is under 65, there may be several options:

- If they are under the age of 26, they may be able to join a parents' health insurance plan.

138. 45 C.F.R. § 147.120.
139. *Id.*

- If they are married, they may be able to join a spouse's employer-sponsored plan.
- If they begin working, they may be eligible for an employer-sponsored plan.
- They will be eligible for a SEP to buy coverage through the State Health Insurance Marketplaces.
- If they are over 65 and are also enrolled in Medicare, they will maintain their Medicare coverage and they may be eligible for MSPs or Extra Help.

### 4. Medicare If No Longer Deemed Disabled

Individuals who are under 65 and have had access to Medicare due to having a disability will lose their eligibility if the disability is no longer present. Individuals in this circumstance may have several options:

- If they are under the age of 26, they may be able to join a parents' health insurance plan.
- If they are married, they may be able to join a spouse's employer-sponsored plan.
- If they have an income less than 138 percent of the FPL and live in a state that has expanded its Medicaid program, they may be able to receive Medicaid.
- If they begin working, they may be eligible for an employer-sponsored plan.
- If they have an income more than 138 percent of the FPL or they live in a state that has not expanded its Medicaid program, they may be eligible for a SEP to buy coverage through the State Health Insurance Marketplaces.

As discussed previously, when making the decision between various health insurance options, individuals should make sure to "do the math" as well as compare the coverage.

## VI. Using Health Insurance Effectively

In order to avoid unexpected medical bills, it is important for individuals to understand how their health plan works.

### A. Pre-authorization

Health insurance companies may require patients to obtain their written approval before they receive certain medical care, including specific treatments, medical devices, and prescriptions. This approval is called pre-authorization, but might also be called pre-auth, prior authorization, prior auth, prior approval, precertification, treatment authorization request, or advanced approval. Insurance companies are not required to pay for medical care that requires pre-authorization, if a patient receives these services without the pre-authorization. Patients may then have to pay the full cost of the medical care. Medical care that might require pre-authorization includes:

- Medical treatments that have lower-cost, but equally effective, alternatives available
- Medical treatments and medications that should only be used for certain health conditions
- Lab tests, imaging scans, and biomarker tests
- Medical treatments and medications that are often misused or abused
- Medications that may be unsafe when combined with other medications
- Drugs often used for cosmetic purposes
- Medical care that is provided out of network

Most insurance companies do not provide a list with the medical care that requires a pre-authorization, so individuals have to ask. The insurance company may also change its pre-authorization requirements at any time.

Sometimes, a patient's health care team will request a pre-authorization for them. But if they do not, and a patient gets the medical care without the pre-authorization, then their insurance company may refuse to pay for the care. Ultimately, it is the patient's responsibility to get the pre-authorization. This means that it is always helpful for patients to ask their health care team if they will be getting any necessary pre-authorizations on their behalf. If they are not, then the patient needs to get the pre-authorization from their insurance company.

There are some key steps to getting a pre-authorization. First, a patient needs to contact their health insurance company to find out if the care they need requires pre-authorization. If it does, then the patient should ask the health insurance company about the process to get a pre-authorization. Then, a patient should contact their health care team to find out if they will request the pre-authorization on the patient's behalf. If a patient has to file a pre-authorization on their own, the patient can still ask for help from their health care team to medically justify the care. Many insurance companies have specific deadlines. It is important for patients to request the pre-authorization as early as possible, so that waiting for a pre-authorization does not delay medical care. Patients should keep a copy of their request in case it is lost. If pre-authorization is approved, patients should keep that paperwork in a safe place, in case their insurance company later claims that they did not approve the pre-authorization. If the health insurance company denies a pre-authorization, meaning that they are saying they will not cover the care prescribed by the health care team, patients do not have to take no for an answer. They can appeal that decision. See Section VI.C for a discussion of appeals.

## B. Step Therapy

Step therapy refers to when an insurance company requires patients to try a generic or lower-cost drug before getting access to a brand-name or more expensive drug. If the lower-cost drug does not work or causes an adverse reaction, the patient would be allowed to "step up" to another medicine. If an insurance company uses step therapy, patients can file an exception request to try to get access to the drug prescribed by their health care team. If an insurance company has denied coverage for a prescription, a patient can *appeal. See the following section for a discussion of appeals.*

## C. Appealing Claim Denials

At some point during cancer treatment, individuals may find that they are faced with a denial of coverage for their treatment from an insurance company. Therefore, they may be forced to become a self-advocate and appeal the insurance company's decision. The types of appeals available to individuals and the appeals process will differ based on how individuals access health insurance coverage.

Many individuals assume that their insurance company has accurately assessed their coverage, accept the denial of coverage, and then try to find a way to pay for the medical care themselves. However, if an insurance company denies coverage, patients have the right to appeal the decision. Triage Cancer has created an appeals tracking form to help consumers through this process, available for free download at https://triagecancer.org/AppealTrackingForm.

The following flowcharts demonstrate a generic life cycle of an appeal. The first flowchart applies if individuals are submitting a claim after they have received a benefit. The second flowchart is the process if individuals requested a preauthorization from their insurance company to cover a service before they received the care.

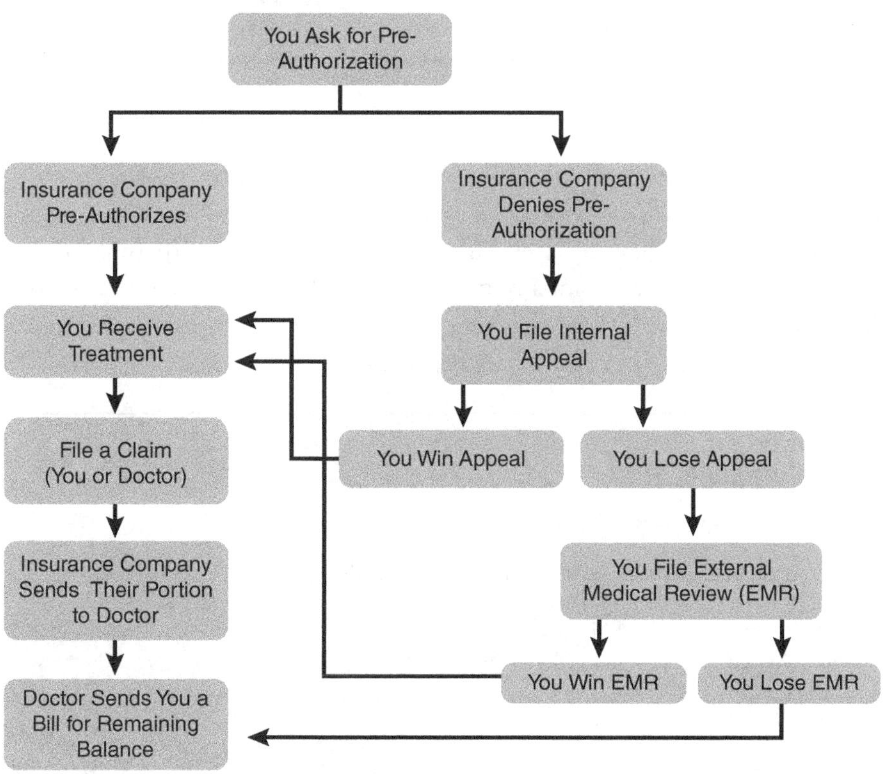

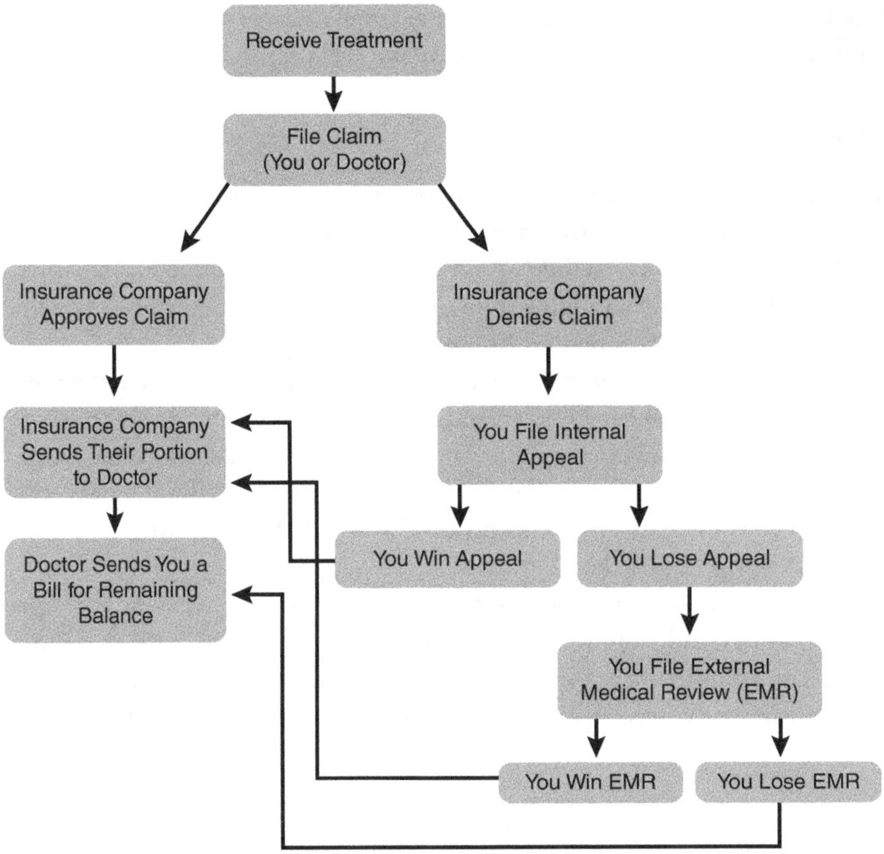


## 1. Private Health Insurance

Generally, there are two types of appeals in private health insurance: internal and external. In many states, individuals are required to exhaust their plan's internal appeals process before they can seek an external appeal, unless there is an extraordinary or urgent case. Each company may have a different internal appeals process, and the policyholder must follow that process exactly. If individuals are unsure about their company's process, they should contact the company and ask for it in writing.

### Internal Appeals Tips

- Be patient and persistent.
- Use an appeals tracking sheet to write everything down.
- Get decisions in writing.
- Pay attention to deadlines.
- Send items via certified mail.
- Get a copy of your files from the insurance company.

All health insurance companies are required to notify individuals in writing if they deny claims for coverage:

- Within 15 days, if individuals are seeking prior authorization for a treatment
- Within 30 days, for medical services already received
- Within 72 hours, for urgent care that has not yet been received

Individuals who disagree with a health plan's decision have the right to file one of two types of internal appeals:

- **Expedited appeal.** An expedited, or urgent, appeal can be filed if individuals have not yet received treatment or if they are in the middle of treatment and their health care providers believe their condition could involve imminent or serious threat to their health. The health plan is required to respond to the appeal within 72 hours of receiving a qualifying appeal.
- **Standard appeal.** For all situations that are not urgent, a standard appeal can be filed. The health plan is required to provide an answer, in writing, within 30 calendar days of receiving an appeal.

When preparing an appeal, individuals should include all the information requested by the insurance company. For instance, the member's name and identification number, the name of the provider who will or has provided the care, the dates of service, the claim reference number for the specific decision being appealed, and the precise reason for disagreement with the initial decision should all be included. Any other relevant documents, records, or other materials can also be included.

Internal appeals must be filed within 180 days (six months) of receiving notice that the claim was denied. If an internal appeal is unsuccessful, individuals may have the right to file an external appeal. Individuals who have an urgent health situation may be able to request an external appeal concurrently with the internal appeal.

## 2. Appeals for Plans Governed by ERISA

If an individual has an employer-sponsored health insurance plan, ERISA is often the governing law. ERISA requires that health plans let policyholders see their plan documents, forbids plans from setting a fee to file an internal appeal, and only allows for a maximum of two levels of internal appeals.

Section 503 of ERISA requires that plans provide notice of adverse benefit determinations and an opportunity for participants to appeal the adverse decision. An adverse benefit determination includes a denial, reduction, or termination of a benefit or failure to pay for a benefit. Appeals must be requested in writing.

In 2000, the DOL issued regulations requiring that initial urgent care claims and urgent appeals be decided within 72 hours of receiving the claim. In addition, pre-service initial claims needed to be decided within 15 days, and appeals of pre-service claims needed to be decided within 30 days—whereas post-service initial claims had to be decided within 30 days, and post-service appeals needed to be decided within 60 days. The 2000 regulations also extended the time frame a member had to appeal from 60 days to 180 days. Furthermore, the 2000 regulations required that the plan administrator decide a disability claim within 45 days (although the plan administrator could request up to two 30-day extensions). The ACA changed the time frame for deciding urgent claims to 24 hours for non-grandfathered plans (grandfathered plans still have 72 hours).

ERISA also requires that the claims and appeal procedures be outlined in the summary plan description. It is important to note that participants are generally required to exhaust internal appeal remedies before filing an ERISA claim for denial of benefits; otherwise, ERISA claims may be dismissed.

It is important to note that nonfederal government self-funded plans are not governed by ERISA. These plans are regulated by HHS.

## 3. ACA Requirement for External Appeals

Once individuals have exhausted the insurance company's internal appeals process and the decision is still not favorable to them, they may be able to file an external appeal called an external medical review (EMR), or independent medical review.

This was already law in some states, and the ACA made it federal law. This means that an external, independent specialist will review the appeal and the decision is binding on the insurance company. Individuals can only request an external review if their internal appeal was denied or was not satisfactorily resolved within the 30 days, or 72 hours in cases of an expedited appeal.

Unlike internal reviews, where the insurance company is the decision maker, external reviews employ a completely independent medical review organization. The decision of this independent body is typically binding on both parties. Generally, individuals must seek an EMR within four months from the date they receive written notification that they have exhausted the internal appeals process. Individuals should be able to seek an EMR when the denial for coverage of services was because of the following:

- The service is not medically necessary.
- The service is considered experimental or investigational.
- The condition is preexisting.
- There is a recession (cancellation) of coverage for a reason other than nonpayment of premiums.

All states are required to participate in an EMR process that meets the consumer protection standards of the ACA. Some states have an external review process that is more protective than the federal law. To find out about the external review process in each state, visit https://triagecancer.org/stateresources.

If a state does not have an external review process that meets the minimum consumer protection standards, HHS will oversee that state's external review process for health insurance companies.

Individuals will likely not qualify for an EMR if:

- They have coverage through Medicare, Medicaid, the FEHB Program, TRICARE, or other military coverage.
- They are part of a self-insured employer or union plan (unless the employer or union plan has opted for the state process).
- They have a group plan issued in another state.
- The coverage is only for a specified disease (such as cancer); a specified accident or accident; and/or credit, dental, disability income, hospital indemnity, long-term care, vision, or other limited supplemental benefits.

For more information about the external appeals process, visit https://www.cms.gov/marketplace/about/affordable-care-act/external-appeals.

## 4. Medicare Appeals

Individuals with Medicare also have the right to appeal coverage and payment decisions. There are five levels of appeals for Medicare Part A and Part B denials:[140]

- **Redetermination by a Medicare administrative contractor (MAC).** Individuals must file a written request for a redetermination within 120 days from the date of receipt of the initial claim determination. It is assumed the notice was received five days after the date of the notice unless there is evidence to the contrary. The MAC must issue a decision within 60 days.
- **Reconsideration by a qualified independent contractor (QIC).** Individuals must file a written request for a reconsideration within 180 days from the date of receipt of the redetermination notice. The QIC must issue a decision within 60 days.
- **Hearing by an administrative law judge (ALJ) in the Office of Medicare Hearings and Appeals.** Individuals must file an appeal within 60 days from the date of receipt of the reconsideration notice. Only cases involving at least $150 in dispute are eligible for ALJ hearings.[141] The ALJ must issue a decision within 90 days.
- **Review by the Medicare Appeals Council.** Individuals may request a review of the ALJ decision in writing within 60 days. There are no requirements regarding the amount of money in controversy. The written request must specify the issues and findings that are being contested. The Medicare Appeals Council must issue a decision within 90 days.
- **Judicial review in federal district court.** An individual may file for judicial review within 60 days of the Medicare Appeals Council decision. Cases must

140. 42 C.F.R. pt. 405, subpt. I (2005).
141. For cases filed on or after January 1, 2016.

satisfy the amount in controversy (AIC) thresholds for that year. For 2025, the AIC threshold for review in federal district court was $1,900.[142]

There is a similar process to appealing a decision of a Medicare Part D prescription drug coverage provider or of a Medicare Advantage (Part C) plan. For more information about Part D appeals, visit https://www.medicare.gov/providers-services/claims-appeals-complaints/appeals/drug-plans. For more information about Part C appeals, visit https://www.medicare.gov/providers-services/claims-appeals-complaints/appeals/medicare-health-plans.

There may also be an opportunity for individuals to file for an expedited appeal in both hospital and nonhospital settings. For more information, visit https://www.medicare.gov/providers-services/claims-appeals-complaints/appeals/fast-appeals.

Individuals with coverage through PACE have different appeal rights.[143] These individuals should contact the PACE organization for written information about appeal rights.

For more information about Medicare appeals, see https://www.medicare.gov/providers-services/claims-appeals-complaints/appeals. Individuals who need help filing an appeal should contact their SHIP: https://www.shiphelp.org/.

## 5. Medicaid Appeals

Federal law entitles individuals with Medicaid to receive notice of state Medicaid agency decisions, and provides the ability to appeal those decisions.[144] That applies to decisions around eligibility for the Medicaid program and for claim denials. Rules around the appeals process are federally mandated, and states must comply.[145] A notice of action must be sent to individuals ten days before a proposed termination, suspension, or reduction of their Medicaid eligibility or covered services.[146] Individuals then have a state-specified amount of time, not to exceed 90 days, to appeal the claim denial in writing.[147] Furthermore, individuals who are covered by Medicaid are generally able to request that their services continue during the appeal.[148]

Generally, there are two levels of appeals within the Medicaid program: an evidentiary hearing and an administrative fair hearing. Some states have eliminated the evidentiary hearing and only allow individuals an administrative fair hearing. These hearings are the only opportunity individuals have to provide evidence to support

142. 42 C.F.R. § 405.1006(c) (2025).
143. *Id.* § 460.122.
144. *Id.* pt. 431, subpt. E.
145. Social Security Act § 1902(a)(3); CMS, State Medicaid Manual § 2900, https://www.cms.gov/Regulations-and-Guidance/guidance/Manuals/Paper-Based-Manuals-Items/CMS021927.html.
146. 42 C.F.R. § 431.210.
147. *Id.* § 431.221(d).
148. *Id.* § 431.230.

their assertion that the state agency decided incorrectly.[149] However, individuals who do not win their appeal may have the ability to seek judicial review in state court. The state Medicaid agency must make a final decision on the appeal within 90 days of the individual's appeal request. Expedited appeals may be available if delaying a decision would "jeopardize the individual's life, health or ability to attain, maintain, or regain maximum function."[150]

As rules and procedures vary by state, individuals should contact their state Medicaid agency for details on how to appeal an adverse decision. Contact information for each agency can be found at https://triagecancer.org/stateresources.

### 6. Veterans' Appeals

Individuals who receive VA health care have the right to appeal adverse decisions.[151] The VA has changed the appeals process to the decision review process. If a veteran disagrees with a VA benefit or claim decision, they have three options to pursue a decision review: a supplemental claim,[152] a higher-level review,[153] or an appeal with the Board of Veterans' Appeals.[154] If a veteran is not satisfied with the outcome of the first option, they can try another option. If a veteran disagrees with a VA medical decision, the veteran can request a clinical appeal.[155]

For more information about appealing a health insurance claim within the VA, visit https://www.va.gov/decision-reviews/insurance-claims/.

## VII. Care for the Uninsured

Since the passage of the ACA, the number of people without health insurance in the United States was an estimated 27.1 million people in 2024.[156] In 2022, 64 percent of uninsured nonelderly adults said that they were uninsured because the cost of coverage was too high.[157] Populations that remain uninsured include noncitizens (both

---

149. MaryBeth Musumeci, Kaiser Commission on Medicaid and the Uninsured, A Guide to the Medicaid Appeals Process (2012).

150. 42 C.F.R. § 431.224.

151. *VA Decision Reviews and Appeals*, VA, https://www.va.gov/decision-reviews (last updated May 15, 2024).

152. *Supplemental Claims*, VA, https://www.va.gov/decision-reviews/supplemental-claim (last updated Nov. 4, 2024).

153. *Higher-Level Reviews*, VA, https://www.va.gov/decision-reviews/higher-level-review (last updated May 15, 2024).

154. *Board Appeals*, VA, https://www.va.gov/decision-reviews/board-appeal (last updated July 23, 2024).

155. *Clinical Appeals of Medical Treatment Decisions*, VA, https://www.va.gov/decision-reviews/clinical-appeals (last updated Mar. 29, 2024).

156. Assistant Secretary for Planning and Evaluation, HHS, National Uninsured Rate at 8.2 Percent in the First Quarter of 2024 (Aug. 2024), https://aspe.hhs.gov/sites/default/files/documents/ee0475e44e27daef00155e95a24fd023/nhis-q1-2024-datapoint.pdf.

157. Jennifer Tolbert et al., *Key Facts about the Uninsured Population*, KFF (Dec. 18, 2023), https://www.kff.org/uninsured/issue-brief/key-facts-about-the-uninsured-population/.

lawfully present and undocumented immigrants). Undocumented immigrants and legal immigrants residing in the United States for fewer than five years are ineligible for federally funded health coverage (e.g., Medicaid and CHIP) except in emergency situations.[158] Some states provide Medicaid to individuals who are undocumented, using state funds, and as of 2024, Colorado and Washington allow individuals who are undocumented to buy plans through the State Health Insurance Marketplaces.[159]

Individuals who do not qualify for, or cannot afford, health insurance have very limited options to access health care. They have three main options for accessing health care: federally funded health centers, community clinics, and emergency departments.

## A. Free or Low-Cost Options for Health Care

Some hospitals and clinics provide health care to individuals, even if they do not have health insurance.

- **Charity care.** Nonprofit hospitals are required to offer free or discounted care to patients with certain income. This is called charity care, patient financial assistance, or an ability to pay program. Charity care includes emergency care or hospitalization. Nonprofit hospitals are required to post their financial assistance policy online and in the hospital. Some for-profit hospitals also offer financial help. See Triage Cancer's Quick Guide to Charity Care Programs at https://triagecancer.org/quick-guides/charity-care-programs. Dollar For, https://dollarfor.org/triagecancer, is a nonprofit organization that can check to see if an individual is eligible for charity care at a hospital, and help them apply. They can even help after an individual receives a medical bill that they cannot pay.
- **Federally qualified health centers (FQHCs).** These centers must provide care on a sliding fee scale based on ability to pay. They cannot deny care because someone does not have insurance. FQHCs offer a range of services, including primary care. To find a FQHC, visit https://findahealthcenter.hrsa.gov/.
- **Rural health clinics (RHCs).** These clinics provide health care in rural areas. Many use a sliding fee scale based on an individual's ability to pay. To find an RHC, see CMS's "CASPER Report 0006DL Name and Address Listing for Rural Health Clinic Based on Current Survey" at http://www.cms.gov/Outreach-and-Education/Medicare-Learning-Network-MLN/MLNProducts/Downloads/rhclistbyprovidername.pdf.

158. *Coverage for Lawfully Present Immigrants*, HealthCare.gov, https://www.healthcare.gov/immigrants/lawfully-present-immigrants/ (last visited Nov. 4, 2024).

159. Claire Heyison & Shelby Gonzales, Center on Budget and Policy Priorities, States Are Providing Affordable Health Coverage to People Barred from Certain Health Programs Due to Immigration Status (2024), https://www.cbpp.org/sites/default/files/12-15-23health.pdf.

- **Community clinics.** Generally, community clinics may be an option for individuals without insurance to access health care. The availability of these clinics varies widely by location. Often, these clinics are nonprofit organizations and are funded by religious groups, grants, and donations. They typically provide primary care, immunizations, and limited other health care. These clinics are rarely equipped to provide comprehensive cancer treatment. The National Association of Free and Charitable Clinics has a search tool for individuals to find a clinic in their area, available at https://nafcclinics.org.
- **Hill-Burton facilities.** The Hospital Survey and Construction Act of 1946,[160] more commonly referred to as the Hill-Burton Act, is a federal law that gave hospitals grants and loans to modernize in exchange for the hospital providing free care to a certain number of uninsured individuals per year. Although the program no longer provides additional funds to hospitals, approximately 127 facilities are still obligated to provide free or reduced-cost care.[161] To find a Hill-Burton facility, visit https://www.hrsa.gov/get-health-care/affordable/hill-burton/facilities.

## B. Accessing Care in an Emergency

Congress enacted the Emergency Medical Treatment and Active Labor Act of 1986 (EMTALA)[162] in response to growing concern that emergency rooms across the country were refusing to treat indigent and uninsured patients.[163] EMTALA requires all hospitals with emergency departments "provide for an appropriate medical screening examination within the capability of the hospital's emergency department . . . to determine whether or not an emergency medical condition . . . exists."[164] In other words, emergency departments must screen individuals who come to the emergency department for treatment and to stabilize or transfer those suffering from emergency medical conditions.[165] EMTALA applies to all hospitals that offer emergency room services and that are Medicare-participating hospitals; however, it covers all patients who seek medical services from that hospital, not just the Medicare patients.[166] The definition of "emergency" can be subjective and EMTALA screening requirements do not necessarily guarantee that an accurate diagnosis is made.[167]

---

160. 42 U.S.C. § 291.

161. *Hill-Burton Free and Reduced-Cost Health Care*, Health Res. & Servs. Admin., https://www.hrsa.gov/get-health-care/affordable/hill-burton/index.html (last reviewed Sept. 2023).

162. 42 U.S.C. § 1395dd.

163. Lynn Healey Scaduto, *The Emergency Medical Treatment and Active Labor Act Gone Astray: A Proposal to Reclaim EMTALA for Its Intended Beneficiaries*, 46 UCLA L. Rev. 943, 943 (1999).

164. 42 U.S.C. § 1395dd(a).

165. *Id.* § 1395dd.

166. Lauren A. Dame, *The Emergency Medical Treatment and Active Labor Act: The Anomalous Right to Health Care*, 8 Health Matrix 3, 10 (1998).

167. Baber v. Hosp. Corp. of Am., 977 F.2d 872 (4th Cir. 1992).

Additionally, many times the care an individual with cancer may need is not going to be considered emergent (e.g., chemotherapy or radiation therapy). So, while EMTALA is an important protection, it does not solve all needs for access to health care, especially for those with a cancer diagnosis.

## VIII. Conclusion

The U.S. health care system is incredibly complex. Individuals are often required to learn a new lexicon to navigate the complexities of health insurance options. This complexity is compounded by the political nature of how health care is delivered in the United States. Changes occur at the state and federal levels on a regular basis. All of this creates uncertainty with respect to the future of the American health care landscape. The long-term impact of this uncertainty on the Marketplace, on access to quality, affordable health insurance, and on individuals coping with cancer is also unclear. This chapter is as accurate as can be at the date of publication. For up-to-date information, visit https://triagecancer.org/cancer-health-insurance-finances-cost.

## IX. Resources

For information about health insurance and how to pick a plan:

Triage Cancer, Cancer & Health Insurance: https://triagecancer.org/cancer-health-insurance-finances-cost

Triage Cancer Presents: Health Insurance Basics: https://triagecancer.org/video-HealthInsuranceBasics

For state insurance agencies:

Triage Cancer, Resources by Location: https://triagecancer.org/stateresources

For information about individual health insurance options:

Health Insurance Marketplace: https://www.healthcare.gov

Marketplace Application Checklist: https://Marketplace.cms.gov/outreach-and-education/Marketplace-application-checklist.pdf

Health Insurance Marketplace, Find Local Help: https://www.healthcare.gov/find-local-help/

CMS—Medicaid: https://www.medicaid.gov or (800) 633-4227

For information about Medicare:

CMS—Medicare: https://www.medicare.gov or (800) 633-4227

SHIP: https://www.shiphelp.org/

For information on programs providing health care to people who are geographically isolated, or economically or medically vulnerable:

HHS—Health Resources and Services Administration: https://www.hrsa.gov

For information about COBRA and WHCRA:

DOL—Employee Benefits Security Administration: https://www.dol.gov/agencies/ebsa or (866) 444-3272

For information about cancer screening programs:

CDC—Division of Cancer Prevention and Control: https://www.cdc.gov/cancer

## X. Exercises and Discussion Topics

### A. Case Studies

1. Samantha is 44 years old and has been working as an accountant for the past ten years at a small firm, with 25 employees. When diagnosed with cancer, she had surgery and chemotherapy treatment. She is still experiencing some fatigue, "chemo brain," and some neuropathy in her feet. Due to these ongoing side effects, Samantha thinks that she may need to stop working. She is particularly concerned about what she is going to do for health insurance if she does take time off work since she has a preexisting condition. She is also worried about how she will afford to pay for her policy without a steady income.
   a. If Samantha chooses to leave her job to focus on treatment and recovery she will lose her employer-sponsored health insurance coverage. Because the employer has more than 20 employees, Samantha is entitled to elect COBRA to keep the same coverage she has. The benefits of doing so could include keeping the same providers, drug formulary, and everything she has paid towards her deductible and out-of-pocket maximum so far. Samantha would also be eligible for a SEP to purchase a new plan through the State Health Insurance Marketplace. Depending on her household size and income she may also be eligible for financial assistance to purchase a plan in the Marketplace; however, she will have to start over to meet her deductible and out-of-pocket maximum. If she has a spouse with employer-sponsored health insurance she may be able to join that plan. Before she decides which option is best, she should check each plan's cost, provider network, and drug formulary to ensure it meets her needs. Once she makes a choice, she will not be able to change that choice until the next open enrollment period. Finally, if she is no longer working and has no income, she may also be eligible for Medicaid depending on if her state has expanded the Medicaid program.
2. Mark graduated from college in June, is 21 years old, and lives in Texas. He has not been able to find a job since graduation, so he has no income except what he earns doing odd jobs around his neighborhood. He is considering going to graduate school. He had health insurance coverage through his college, but

that ended in June. He has not been able to find a health insurance plan that will cover him, because he is a childhood cancer survivor. Although Mark is aware that he could stay on his parents' health insurance plan until he is 26, he has a strained relationship with his parents. They will not allow him to use their insurance and they have given him until the end of the year to move out. They have claimed him as a dependent on their taxes up until now. Mark is not sure if they will claim him as a dependent for this tax year and if this will affect his ability to get health insurance coverage. He has also heard about some kind of new Marketplace to get insurance and is wondering if there are health insurance plans available to him there.

3. Emily is 34 and lives in Washington state. She works full-time for a large employer with about 250 employees and she makes $40,000 a year. Her employer offers health insurance coverage, but each year it costs her about 10 percent of her income, so it is very expensive for her. Also, she is concerned because her co-worker told her that their policy has a lifetime limit of $1 million and Emily is very close to reaching that amount, because of her ongoing cancer treatment. She is wondering what her other health insurance options might be and if she qualifies for any financial help to get insurance coverage. Emily also wants to participate in a clinical trial that her doctor recommended, which starts next week, but her insurer is saying that they will not cover anything related to her care if she participates in the clinical trial.
4. Ann is 44 years old and lives in New York with her "stay-at-home" husband and two children. When she was 37, she was diagnosed with cancer. She participated in a local cancer community event and was interviewed by the local newspaper about her survivor experience. She is now in the midst of changing jobs and she Googled herself to see what was out there and to prepare for her job interviews. The local newspaper is now online and the article comes up when she searches for her name. She is now looking for health insurance options because her COBRA coverage from her previous employer is ending at the end of January. She is worried about a potential health insurer finding out about her cancer history because of this article and either denying her coverage or charging her more because of her past diagnosis. Last year, she made $55,000. Ann is also wondering how she determines what her family's options are through the State Health Insurance Marketplace because she does not know what their household income will be this year.
5. Tom is 60 years old and lives in Florida. He was diagnosed with cancer and went through treatment two years ago. He has a job with a small accounting firm, but it does not offer him health insurance coverage. He lost his previous job when he took time off for treatment and he was not able to afford COBRA. He has been uninsured since then and knows that he has a few years before he can be eligible for Medicare.

6. Antonio is 53 years old and lives in California. He works for a large wine producer with more than 200 employees. He was diagnosed with cancer last week and he has been trying to figure out his treatment options and if he will need to take time off work. He is concerned that if he loses his job, he will lose access to his health insurance coverage and will not be able to get medical care.

## B. Discussion Topics

1. With the rising cost of health insurance, many insurance companies are narrowing their networks (i.e., the number of providers that are available to each consumer). As a consumer of health insurance, would you rather pay less and have fewer providers available to you or would you rather pay more and have more available providers available? What do you think?
2. Is health insurance really "insurance"? Compare it to other types of insurance, for example car insurance or homeowners insurance. The latter types of insurance cover "unexpected" events. Are health care needs really "unexpected?" Or should health insurance be treated more like a tax—similar to how school funding operates? Should we pay doctors like we pay teachers?

   Following that, should "expected" and "unexpected" events be treated differently? For example, should a routine office visit for preventive screening be covered differently than treatment for breast cancer? Certain preventive coverage is covered at 100 percent, whereas treatment for cancer will include some sort of cost-sharing, either through a deductible or cost-share amount until the out-of-pocket maximum is met.
3. Consider this situation: You recently were diagnosed with Stage 1 laryngeal cancer. You are insured by Aetna. You go online and look at Aetna's provider list and they have two doctors, Dr. Tim and Dr. Sam, who both specialize in treatment of laryngeal cancer. Your aunt had the same surgery and she went to Dr. Ed who is at the same hospital as Dr. Tim and Dr. Sam, but Dr. Ed is not on your provider list. You did some digging and found that while all doctors had positive outcomes and quality ratings, Dr. Ed's ratings were off the charts—100 percent success rate. What do you do? If you go to Dr. Ed, do you expect to pay more or should your insurance pay for all/some of it?
4. Do we need health insurance companies? Consider single-payer proposals. What is the benefit of having multiple payers? Is there one?
5. Company X comes to you and asks if you think they should self-fund their employee benefit plan or if they should buy a fully insured plan. Remember, insurance premiums are higher for fully insured plans and self-funded plans assume all the risk of paying for claims. Company X is just starting out so they do not have much money in their reserves. Company X has 1,000 employees. What do you tell them? Make sure to take into account the issue of

reinsurance/stop-loss insurance: many plans buy stop-loss insurance to protect themselves against large claims. Stop-loss insurance is not health insurance, and is not subject to the ACA or ERISA.

6. Sarah works at the supermarket as a full-time cashier. She is covered under the supermarket's employee welfare benefit health plan. Sarah's husband, Al, is covered under his own employer's health plan. Sarah's daughter, Kiley, is covered under the supermarket's plan. Sarah is then fired from the supermarket. Who does the supermarket need to offer COBRA to?
7. Sally has three chemotherapy treatments per month and her employer just informed her that her services are no longer needed. Employment discrimination issues aside, when does her employer have to offer her coverage? How long does Sally have to elect the coverage? How long does Sally have to pay the initial premium? Should Sally elect COBRA coverage? What if Sally was on Family and Medical Leave Act (FMLA) leave and she decides she does not want to return?
8. Consider the ACA's Marketplace and the future of COBRA. Is COBRA needed at all? What are some circumstances when COBRA could potentially be more beneficial than purchasing new insurance through the Marketplace?

# CHAPTER TWO

# Employment

## *Case Study: Evan*

*Evan has been diagnosed with cancer. He is a full-time truck driver for a large, national shipping company with more than 100 employees. Evan is married, with two kids. His wife only works part-time, so he knows that he needs to work to pay his family's bills. His family has health insurance coverage through his employer. Evan does not remember the details of whether he has any employee benefits because he has not taken any time off work in three years. He has not discussed his treatment plan with his health care team. He is concerned about telling anyone at work about his diagnosis, for fear that they might treat him differently, or, worse yet, his boss might let him go. Evan's co-worker, Mark, was fired a few weeks after he asked for time off to take care of his dad, who had Alzheimer's.*

## I. Introduction

Nearly 50 percent of cancer survivors are diagnosed at "working age."[1] Yet, this is a conservative estimate, as there are many more people who are now working long past the "standard" retirement age of 65. With an estimated two million people having been diagnosed with cancer in 2024, there is a significant number of people who need credible information about their legal rights and options in order to make educated decisions and to navigate cancer-related employment issues.

---

1. Angela B. Mariotto et al., *Projections of the Cost of Cancer Care in the United States: 2010–2020*, 103 J. Nat'l Cancer Inst. 117 (2011).

A cancer diagnosis may have a significant impact on employment and income for people with cancer and their caregivers. The probability of employment drops 10 percent for an individual diagnosed with cancer. Within two years of diagnosis, earnings of cancer patients decreased almost 40 percent and remained low, while total family income dropped 20 percent and took up to five years after diagnosis to rebound, suggesting that caregivers' income levels are also affected.[2]

When a child is diagnosed with cancer, one parent typically has to stop working, which also has an impact on household finances. Twenty-five percent of families lost more than 40 percent of their total household income, and 33 percent experienced housing, energy, or food insecurity.[3] Thirty-seven percent of adults were forced to cut their hours or had to take a leave of absence from work, while 15 percent of parents either had to quit or were laid off from their jobs.[4] Young adults diagnosed with cancer may feel a disproportionate financial impact, as they are less likely to have career longevity or health insurance coverage, but are more likely to have lower paying jobs and higher student loan debt.[5]

The inability to work and the subsequent loss in income can contribute to the financial burden of a cancer diagnosis, exacerbating the financial burden of costs associated with cancer care. In 2013, researchers coined the term "financial toxicity" to refer to the financial side effects induced by the cost of cancer treatment.[6] One-third of working-age cancer survivors go into debt.[7] Being unable to work and other factors that contribute to financial toxicity are also linked with health outcomes, including quality of life,[8] therapy compliance,[9] and symptom burden.[10] According to a Centers for Disease Control and Prevention study, those who were unemployed had worse physical and mental health than those who were employed, regardless

---

2. Anna Zajacova et al., *Employment and Income Losses among Cancer Survivors: Estimates from a National Longitudinal Survey of American Families*, 121 Cancer 4425 (2015).

3. Kira Bona et al., *Impact of Socioeconomic Status on Timing of Relapse and Overall Survival for Children Treated on Dana-Farber Cancer Institute ALL Consortium Protocols (2000–2010)*, 63 Pediatric Blood Cancer 1012 (2016).

4. *Id.*

5. Samantha Watson & Michelle S. Landwehr, *Financial Toxicity and the Young Adult Cancer Survivor*, 21 AMJC SP482 (2015), https://www.ajmc.com/view/financial-toxicity-and-the-young-adult-cancer-survivor.

6. S. Yousuf Zafar & Amy P. Abernethy, *Financial Toxicity, Part I: A New Name for a Growing Problem*, 27 Oncology (Williston Park) 80 (2013), https://www.ncbi.nlm.nih.gov/pmc/articles/PMC4523887.

7. *Health Affairs January Issue: High-Cost Populations, Medicaid Spending, and More*, Health Affs. (Jan. 5, 2016), http://www.healthaffairs.org/do/10.1377/hblog20160105.052511/full/.

8. S. Yousuf Zafar et al., *Population-Based Assessment of Cancer Survivors' Financial Burden and Quality of Life: A Prospective Cohort Study*, 11 J. Oncology Prac. 145 (2015).

9. Alfred I. Neugut et al., *Association between Prescription Co-Payment Amount and Compliance with Adjuvant Hormonal Therapy in Women with Early-Stage Breast Cancer*, 29 J. Clinical Oncology 2534 (2011).

10. Christopher S. Lathan et al., *Association of Financial Strain with Symptom Burden and Quality of Life for Patients with Lung or Colorectal Cancer*, 34 J. Clinical Oncology 1732 (2016).

of whether or not they had health insurance.[11] Bankrupt cancer patients are nearly 80 percent more likely to die than patients who do not file for bankruptcy.[12] A 1.95 times higher odds of having a depressed mood was found in cancer survivors with financial burdens due to cancer.[13]

While many patients continue to work through their treatment to maintain their income and access to health insurance coverage, this is not the only reason they choose to work. Sixty-five percent of cancer survivors surveyed reported that working can be an effective coping strategy, helping them to have a routine, providing a distraction from their health, and allowing them to feel productive.[14] For many of these reasons, a study found that 44 percent of people diagnosed with metastatic cancer continue to work.[15] However, not everyone diagnosed with cancer can work through treatment or even return to work after treatment has been completed. The most significant factor associated with no longer working was a higher burden of side effects.[16] In addition to short-term, long-term, or late-term side effects from treatment, patients' ability to work might be significantly impacted by their type of cancer, stage of cancer, type of treatment, prognosis, comorbidities, environment, geographic location, and commute. For instance, a 2017 study found that working patients were more likely to experience substantial employment disruptions if they received more aggressive treatment.[17]

A patient who is newly diagnosed with cancer has a number of employment options that might vary based on these factors, including working through treatment; reducing work hours to part-time; changing jobs; taking time off work, either for a short or longer period of time; filing for short-term or long-term disability benefits to replace wages while taking time off work; resigning; or even retiring from employment based on age and seniority at work. A recent survey of patients on the financial hardship of cancer found that among those working full-time when diagnosed,

11. Steven Reinberg, *Even with Insurance, Unemployed Have Worse Health Outcomes*, HealthDay News (Jan. 24, 2012), https://www.healthday.com/health-news/public-health/even-with-insurance-unemployed-have-worse-health-outcomes-661028.html.

12. Scott Ramsey et al., *Washington State Cancer Patients Found to Be at Greater Risk for Bankruptcy Than People without a Cancer Diagnosis*, 32 Health Affs. 1143 (2013).

13. Hrishikesh P. Kale & Norman V. Carroll, *Self-Reported Financial Burden of Cancer Care and Its Effect on Physical and Mental Health-Related Quality of Life among US Cancer Survivors*, 122 Cancer 283 (2016).

14. Press Release, Cancer and Careers, More Than Half of Cancer Patients and Survivors Are Concerned about Changes to Their Healthcare Access (June 14, 2017), https://www.prnewswire.com/news-releases/more-than-half-of-cancer-patients-and-survivors-are-concerned-about-changes-to-their-healthcare-access-300473461.html.

15. Amye J. Tevaarwerk et al., *Working after a Metastatic Cancer Diagnosis: Factors Affecting Employment in the Metastatic Setting from ECOG-ACRIN's Symptom Outcomes and Practice Patterns Study*, 122 Cancer 438 (2015).

16. *Id.*

17. Reshma Jagsi et al., *Treatment Decisions and Employment of Breast Cancer Patients: Results of a Population-Based Survey*, 123 Cancer 4791 (2017).

66 percent reported resigning, reducing their hours, or taking a leave of absence.[18] Caregivers are also often faced with employment decisions. Nearly half of survivors surveyed said a household member reduced their work hours to provide caregiving services.[19]

Making decisions about these options is challenging for all individuals diagnosed with cancer, but they may be particularly burdensome for individuals employed in low-wage hourly jobs. These individuals are more likely to experience job insecurity, live paycheck to paycheck, and have limited access to workplace protections, paid leave, employer-sponsored health insurance benefits, flexible work hours, and flexible work arrangements, such as telecommuting.[20] Only 39 percent of the lowest 10 percent of wage earners who worked for private employers in 2023 had access to paid sick leave.[21]

Employment issues can come into play at different times across the continuum of cancer care and there is also an employment continuum after a cancer diagnosis, as described in the following table.

| **Employment Continuum after a Cancer Diagnosis** | | | | | |
|---|---|---|---|---|---|
| Newly Diagnosed | Working through Treatment | Taking Time off Work | Returning to Work (same job) | Returning to Work (different job) | Retiring or Resigning from Work |

## A. Where to Find Employment Rights and Benefits

There are three key places to look for information about an employee's employment rights and benefits.

### 1. Employment Laws

Laws that could provide relevant rights and benefits to individuals diagnosed with cancer include federal fair employment laws, state fair employment laws, federal leave laws, state and local leave laws, and other federal, state, and local wage and hour laws. Fair employment laws provide employees with protections against discrimination in the workplace. This chapter will focus on federal and state fair employment laws that protect against disability discrimination in the workplace. Federal, state, and local leave laws allow employees to take time off work and offer job protection.

---

18. Press Release, Cancer*Care,* New Cancer*Care*® Survey Illuminates the Financial Hardship of Cancer (June 23, 2017), https://www.cancercare.org/press/releases/147-2017_06_23.

19. *Id.*

20. Jennifer E. Swanberg et al., *Managing Cancer and Employment: Decisions and Strategies Used by Breast Cancer Survivors Employed in Low-Wage Jobs*, 35 J. Psychosoc. Oncology 180 (2017).

21. *Table 6. Selected Paid Leave Benefits: Access*, U.S. Bureau Lab. Stat., https://www.bls.gov/news.release/ebs2.t06.htm (last modified Sept. 19, 2024).

Federal, state, and local wage and hour laws provide employee protections in the areas of wages, overtime, rest periods, time off from work, and more.

## 2. Employment Contracts

Employment contracts can provide for additional protections and benefits than those provided under the law. These include union contracts, collective bargaining agreements, and general employment contracts. In some cases, employees working under a contract may waive their rights to other protections and benefits. For example, employees who are members of a union (e.g., teachers) sometimes have their own retirement system into which they pay. Because they do not pay Social Security retirement taxes, they are unable to qualify for Social Security Disability Insurance benefits. However, they may have access to other disability insurance benefits under their union contract. Therefore, employees diagnosed with cancer must look not only to federal, state, and local laws, but also check to see how their employment contracts might have an impact.

## 3. Employer Policies

Laws only establish a minimum level of protection for employees in the workplace; however, many employers choose to create policies that are more protective than the legal requirement. For example, an employer can choose to offer health, dental, vision, life, and disability insurance options to employees. Employers may only offer access to coverage, or they may pick up some or all of the costs of those policies. Employers may also offer sick days,[22] vacation days, or other forms of paid time off beyond local and state requirements. Employers may allow for employees to donate their leave hours to co-workers in need. Employers may also establish policies allowing for the use of flex time, job-sharing, or even telecommuting. Financial counseling and employee assistance programs may be additional benefits that employers provide, which may be useful for employees diagnosed with cancer.

Employees who are looking for information about their employers' policies should review their employee handbook, manual, or policies and procedures document. If such a document is not available, employees can talk with a human resources (HR) representative. If their company is too small to have an HR department, then often the person on staff who handles employee benefits or an office manager can answer questions about company policies. Many employers also describe an internal process for employees who need to ask for a reasonable accommodation or medical leave, so that employees do not have to reinvent the wheel when trying to navigate how to access these benefits.

---

22. Note: Some states and cities have laws that require certain or all employers to provide a minimum amount of sick time to their employees (e.g., Connecticut and California). *See* Section III.

## B. Employment Concepts

There are a number of other employment concepts that are relevant to the discussion of how federal and local laws apply to certain categories of individuals.

Generally, "at-will" employment means that an employer can terminate an employee for any reason, except an illegal one, or for no reason, without incurring legal liability. This also means that employees are free to resign at any time for any reason without any legal consequences.[23] There are some exceptions to the at-will presumption, including when an employer fires an employee for a discriminatory reason, in violation of a federal or state discrimination law that covers a protected class. Protected classes can include race, ethnicity, age, gender, religion, sexual orientation, and disability. Unions may also have negotiated rights to employment that supersede the presumption of at-will employment.

Other classes of employees may have different protections under the law. Generally, part-time employees and full-time employees are treated similarly under fair employment laws such as the Americans with Disabilities Act (ADA) and leave laws such as the Family and Medical Leave Act (FMLA). Also, generally, under the ADA, temporary employees have two "employers": the temp agency and the employer with whom they are placed.[24] On the other hand, independent contractors often waive many of the rights of "employees" in their contract and may not be able to access the same legal protections and benefits. Generally, to determine whether someone is an independent contractor, multiple factors are considered to help determine whether the independent contractor has sufficient autonomy and control over their duties to constitute an independent contractor under the law.[25] And, finally, undocumented immigrants are generally protected under most federal and state wage and hour laws, discrimination laws, and health and safety laws. However, undocumented employees may face challenges such as retaliation from an employer if they try to enforce their rights.[26]

---

23. *At-Will Employment—Overview*, NAT'L CONF. STATE LEGISLATURES, https://www.ncsl.org/labor-and-employment/at-will-employment-overview (last updated Apr. 15, 2008).

24. *Enforcement Guidance: Application of the ADA to Contingent Workers Placed by Temporary Agencies and Other Staffing Firms*, U.S. EQUAL EMP. OPPORTUNITY COMM'N, https://www.eeoc.gov/laws/guidance/enforcement-guidance-application-ada-contingent-workers-placed-temporary-agencies-and (last visited Nov. 8, 2024).

25. *Independent Contractor (Self-Employed) or Employee?*, INTERNAL REVENUE SERV., https://www.irs.gov/Businesses/Small-Businesses-&-Self-Employed/Independent-Contractor-Self-Employed-or-Employee (last updated Oct. 2, 2024).

26. *Employment Rights of Undocumented Workers*, LEGAL AID WORK, https://legalaidatwork.org/factsheet/employment-rights-of-undocumented-workers (last updated Oct. 2024).

# II. Federal Fair Employment Laws

## A. ADA of 1990 and ADA Amendments Act of 2008

The ADA[27] is a federal law passed in 1990, which prohibits discrimination against individuals with disabilities, as follows:

- Title I: Employment
  - Protects eligible employees with disabilities from discrimination in all employment practices
  - Provides access to reasonable accommodations
- Title II: Public Entities (and Public Transportation)
  - Covers access to all programs/services offered by the entity
  - Applies to all state and local public housing, housing assistance, and housing referrals
- Title III: Public Accommodations and Commercial Facilities
  - Includes most places of lodging, recreation, transportation, education, and dining, along with stores, care providers, and places of public displays
- Title IV: Telecommunications
- Title V: Miscellaneous

Most people are more familiar with titles II and III of the ADA, as this is the section of the ADA that requires public places to have wheelchair accessible parking spots, restrooms, crosswalks, and buildings. However, there are many protections in the ADA that are relevant to individuals diagnosed with cancer. This chapter will focus on the ADA's title I protections related to employment.

The passage of the ADA was an attempt by Congress to address the discrimination faced by people with disabilities in various facets of life and to fill a gap in civil rights laws, as described in the language of the statute:

> 42 U.S.C. § 12101. Findings of the ADA
> **(a) Findings**
> *The Congress finds that—*
> *(1) physical or mental disabilities in no way diminish a person's right to fully participate in all aspects of society, yet many people with physical or mental disabilities have been precluded from doing so because of discrimination; others who have a record of a disability or are regarded as having a disability also have been subjected to discrimination;*
> *(2) historically, society has tended to isolate and segregate individuals with disabilities, and, despite some improvements, such forms of discrimination*

27. 42 U.S.C. § 12101 *et seq.*

*against individuals with disabilities continue to be a serious and pervasive social problem;*
*(3) discrimination against individuals with disabilities persists in such critical areas as employment, housing, public accommodations, education, transportation, communication, recreation, institutionalization, health services, voting, and access to public services;*
*(4) unlike individuals who have experienced discrimination on the basis of race, color, sex, national origin, religion, or age, individuals who have experienced discrimination on the basis of disability have often had no legal recourse to redress such discrimination;*
*(5) individuals with disabilities continually encounter various forms of discrimination, including outright intentional exclusion, the discriminatory effects of architectural, transportation, and communication barriers, overprotective rules and policies, failure to make modifications to existing facilities and practices, exclusionary qualification standards and criteria, segregation, and relegation to lesser services, programs, activities, benefits, jobs, or other opportunities;*
*(6) census data, national polls, and other studies have documented that people with disabilities, as a group, occupy an inferior status in our society, and are severely disadvantaged socially, vocationally, economically, and educationally;*
*(7) the Nation's proper goals regarding individuals with disabilities are to assure equality of opportunity, full participation, independent living, and economic self-sufficiency for such individuals; and*
*(8) the continuing existence of unfair and unnecessary discrimination and prejudice denies people with disabilities the opportunity to compete on an equal basis and to pursue those opportunities for which our free society is justifiably famous, and costs the United States billions of dollars in unnecessary expenses resulting from dependency and nonproductivity.*[28]

Between 1990 and 2007, a number of disability discrimination cases with ADA-related claims were heard by the U.S. Supreme Court. Many of those cases focused on whether or not employees qualified as having a disability under the ADA, and were therefore entitled to protection. In 1999, a trilogy of cases was heard by the Supreme Court, the result of which was a significant narrowing of the applicability of the ADA to people with disabilities: *Sutton v. United Air Lines, Inc.*, *Murphy v. United Parcel Service*, and *Albertsons v. Kirkingburg*.[29] The Court held in these cases that in order to determine whether or not a disability substantially limited a major life activity, the

---

28. *Id.* § 12101.

29. Sutton v. United Air Lines, Inc., 527 U.S. 471 (1999); Murphy v. United Parcel Serv., 527 U.S. 516 (1999); Albertsons v. Kirkingburg, 527 U.S. 555 (1999). See the details of these cases discussed in this section.

ameliorative effects of mitigating measures must be taken into account. The practical result of this ruling was that anyone who took any medication or used any device to improve their medical condition might make themselves ineligible for protection under the ADA. In addition, the Court held that an employee seeking protection under the "regarded as" prong of the ADA must demonstrate that the employer mistakenly believes that the employee has a substantially limiting impairment that the employee does not have. This requirement would mean that employees would have to demonstrate that the employer thought their impairment was "substantially limiting," a near impossible burden of proof, making this protection within the ADA unusable.

Then, in 2002, the Supreme Court's ruling in *Toyota Motor Manufacturing, Kentucky, Inc. v. Williams*[30] further limited the protections afforded in the ADA, holding that the terms "substantially limits" and "major life activities" need to be "strictly interpreted to create a demanding standard for qualifying as disabled."[31] The Court further defined "substantially limits" as preventing or severely restricting a person from performing a major life activity, and that "major" means activities that are of central importance to most people's daily lives.

To address the practical effects of these rulings, in 2008, Congress passed the ADA Amendments Act (ADAAA) in order to more clearly iterate which individuals are intended to be protected by the ADA, as follows:

> **Pub. L. No. 110–325. Findings and purpose of the ADA Amendments Act**
> *(b) Purposes.—The purposes of this Act are—*
> *(1) to carry out the ADA's objectives of providing "a clear and comprehensive national mandate for the elimination of discrimination" and "clear, strong, consistent, enforceable standards addressing discrimination" by reinstating a broad scope of protection to be available under the ADA;*
> *(2) to reject the requirement enunciated by the Supreme Court in Sutton v. United Air Lines, Inc., 527 U.S. 471 (1999) and its companion cases that whether an impairment substantially limits a major life activity is to be determined with reference to the ameliorative effects of mitigating measures;*
> *(3) to reject the Supreme Court's reasoning in Sutton v. United Air Lines, Inc., 527 U.S. 471 (1999) with regard to coverage under the third prong of the definition of disability and to reinstate the reasoning of the Supreme Court in School Board of Nassau County v. Arline, 480 U.S. 273 (1987) which set forth a broad view of the third prong of the definition of handicap under the Rehabilitation Act of 1973;*
> *(4) to reject the standards enunciated by the Supreme Court in Toyota Motor Manufacturing, Kentucky, Inc. v. Williams, 534 U.S. 184 (2002), that the*

30. 534 U.S. 184 (2002).
31. *Id.* at 197.

*terms "substantially" and "major" in the definition of disability under the ADA "need to be interpreted strictly to create a demanding standard for qualifying as disabled," and that to be substantially limited in performing a major life activity under the ADA "an individual must have an impairment that prevents or severely restricts the individual from doing activities that are of central importance to most people's daily lives";*

*(5) to convey congressional intent that the standard created by the Supreme Court in the case of Toyota Motor Manufacturing, Kentucky, Inc. v. Williams, 534 U.S. 184 (2002) for "substantially limits", and applied by lower courts in numerous decisions, has created an inappropriately high level of limitation necessary to obtain coverage under the ADA, to convey that it is the intent of Congress that the primary object of attention in cases brought under the ADA should be whether entities covered under the ADA have complied with their obligations, and to convey that the question of whether an individual's impairment is a disability under the ADA should not demand extensive analysis; and*

*(6) to express Congress' expectation that the Equal Employment Opportunity Commission will revise that portion of its current regulations that defines the term "substantially limits" as "significantly restricted" to be consistent with this Act, including the amendments made by this Act.*[32]

## 1. Definitions

The ADA applies to eligible job applicants and employees of a private employer with 15[33] or more employees, or a state or local government of any size. Employers also include employment agencies, labor organizations, or joint labor-management committees. The ADA does not apply to these employers:

- The United States, a corporation wholly owned by the government of the United States, Indian tribes, or a bona fide private membership club (other than a labor organization) that is exempt from taxation under 26 U.S.C. § 501(c)[34]

Federal employees are covered by the Rehabilitation Act of 1973, which was actually the precursor to the ADA and is discussed in more detail later.

Eligible employees are those who are qualified, who have a disability, and who are able to perform the essential functions of the job with or without a reasonable accommodation.[35] The ADA gives consideration to the employer's judgment as to

32. ADAAA, Pub. L. No. 110-325, § 2, 122 Stat. 3553.

33. When first enacted, the ADA applied to employers with 25 or more employees. On July 26, 1994, it changed to 15. *See Titles I and V of the Americans with Disabilities Act of 1990 (ADA)*, U.S. Equal Emp. Opportunity Comm'n, https://www.eeoc.gov/laws/statutes/ada.cfm (last visited Nov. 4, 2024).

34. 42 U.S.C. § 12111(5)(B).

35. *Id.* § 12111(8).

what functions of a job are essential, and if an employer has prepared a written job description before advertising or interviewing applicants for the job.[36] In addition, according to the U.S. Equal Employment Opportunity Commission (EEOC), the following factors should be considered to determine if a job function is essential:

- The reason the position exists is to perform that function
- How many other employees are available to perform the function or among whom the performance of the function can be distributed
- The degree of expertise or skill required to perform the function[37]

Under the ADA, disability is defined as a physical or mental impairment that substantially limits one or more major life activities.[38] The ADA provides protections for an individual who currently has a disability; for example, if an individual is currently going through cancer treatment and is suffering from extreme fatigue and nausea that makes getting through a regular workday very difficult.

An employee or job applicant with a record or history of a physical or mental impairment also qualifies for protection under the ADA[39]—such as a cancer survivor with no current limitations on a major life activity, who is protected under the ADA when a potential employer refuses to hire the applicant because of their history of having cancer. Even if an employee's cancer is in remission, the employee may be protected from discriminatory employment practices based on the ADAAA, which includes within the definition of "disability," "[a]n impairment that is episodic or in remission is a disability if it would substantially limit a major life activity when active."[40]

In addition, an employee or job applicant who is regarded by an employer as having an impairment also qualifies for protection under the ADA.[41] For instance, an employee is going through treatment but not experiencing any major side effects except hair loss, and the employer treats the employee differently because the employer perceives the employee as having a disability.

In the context of a cancer diagnosis, often it is not the cancer diagnosis itself that impacts an individual's ability to do their job, but rather the side effects of the treatment (e.g., nausea, cognitive difficulties, fatigue, neuropathy, and/or depression) are what have a substantial impact on a major life activity.

Major life activities include, but are not limited to, "caring for oneself, performing manual tasks, seeing, hearing, eating, sleeping, walking, standing, lifting, bending, speaking, breathing, learning, reading, concentrating, thinking, communicating,

---

36. *Id.*

37. *The ADA: Your Responsibilities as an Employer*, EEOC, https://www.eeoc.gov/facts/ada17.html (last visited Nov. 8, 2024).

38. 42 U.S.C. § 12102(1).

39. *Id.*

40. *Id.* § 12102(4)(D).

41. *Id.*

and working."[42] Major life activities also include the operation of a major bodily function, including "functions of the immune system, normal cell growth, digestive, bowel, bladder, neurological, brain, respiratory, circulatory, endocrine, and reproductive functions."[43]

Although disability determinations are made on a case-by-case basis, the inclusion of the operation of major bodily functions as a major life activity that could be substantially impacted to qualify someone as having a disability under the ADA has created a situation where even individualized assessment of some impairments will virtually always result in the determination of disability.[44] For example, a cancer diagnosis substantially limits normal cell growth, by definition, and would therefore suggest that an individual with a diagnosis of cancer would always qualify as having a disability.[45] This scenario also applies to other types of medical conditions.[46]

An impairment is a disability if it substantially limits the ability of an individual to perform a major life activity as compared to most people in the general population. An impairment need not prevent, or significantly or severely restrict, the individual from performing a major life activity in order to be considered substantially limiting.[47]

For less obvious disabilities, in order to determine whether an individual is substantially limited in a major life activity, it may be useful to consider:

1. The difficulty, effort, or time required to perform a major life activity
2. Any pain experienced when performing a major life activity
3. The length of time a major life activity can be performed and/or the way an impairment affects the operation of a major bodily function[48]

The determination of whether a disability substantially limits a major life activity must be made without considering the ameliorative effects of mitigating measures,

42. *Id.* § 12102(2)(A).

43. *Id.* § 12102(2)(B).

44. Job Accommodation Network, Accommodation and Compliance Series: The ADA Amendments Act of 2008 (2009), https://www.ars.usda.gov/ARSUserFiles/ODEO/ADA%20Amendments%20Act%202008.pdf.

45. But see *Fierro v. Knight Transportation, Inc.*, 2012 WL 4321304 (W.D. Tex. Sept. 18, 2012), where the court ruled that merely alleging that the employee had adenoid cystic carcinoma, a form of cancer, without alleging any facts describing a substantial limitation in a major life activity, was insufficient to state a claim.

46. Deafness substantially limits hearing; blindness substantially limits seeing; an intellectual disability substantially limits brain function; diabetes substantially limits endocrine function; epilepsy substantially limits neurological function; HIV infection substantially limits immune function; multiple sclerosis substantially limits neurological function; and major depressive disorder, bipolar disorder, post-traumatic stress disorder, obsessive compulsive disorder, and schizophrenia substantially limit brain function. *See* 29 C.F.R. § 1630.2(j)(3)(iii) (2011).

47. *Id.* § 1630.2(j)(1)(ii).

48. Press Release, Cancer*Care*, *supra* note 18.

such as medicine, mobility devices, assistive technology, and auxiliary aids (e.g., hearing aid compatible telephones).[49]

For an employee who is being regarded as having a disability, it is sufficient to show that the employee has been subjected to discrimination because of an actual or perceived physical or mental impairment whether or not the impairment limits or is perceived to limit a major life activity.[50] However, this does not apply to impairments that are transitory and minor. A transitory impairment is an impairment with an actual or expected duration of six months or less.[51]

Finally, the ADA provides protection against discrimination to employees who have a relationship or association with a person who has a disability.[52] This can be useful to caregivers of individuals who have been diagnosed with cancer, who might face discrimination in the workplace because of their status as a caregiver.[53] The ADA does not require a familial relationship for the individual to be protected by the association provision.

## 2. Fair Employment Protections

The ADA applies to all employment practices and all phases of the employment process, including hiring, firing, application, leave, reinstatement, promotion, testing and training, compensation, and benefits.[54] This means that both job applicants and employees are protected. Discriminatory acts by an employer include:

> *(1) limiting, segregating, or classifying a job applicant or employee in a way that adversely affects the opportunities or status of such applicant or employee because of the disability of such applicant or employee;*
> *(2) participating in a contractual or other arrangement or relationship that has the effect of subjecting a qualified applicant or employee with a disability to the discrimination prohibited by this title;*
> *(3) utilizing standards, criteria, or methods of administration—*
> > *(A) that have the effect of discrimination on the basis of disability; or*
> > *(B) that perpetuate the discrimination of others who are subject to common administrative control;*
>
> *(4) excluding or otherwise denying equal jobs or benefits to a qualified individual because of the known disability of an individual with whom the qualified individual is known to have a relationship or association;*

---

49. 42 U.S.C. § 12102(4)(E).
50. *Id.* § 12102(3)(A).
51. *Id.* § 12102(3)(B).
52. *Id.* § 12112(b)(4).
53. *Questions & Answers: Association Provision of the ADA*, EEOC, https://www.eeoc.gov/laws/guidance/questions-answers-association-provision-ada (last visited Jan. 29, 2025).
54. 42 U.S.C. § 12112(a).

*(5)(A) not making reasonable accommodations to the known physical or mental limitations of an otherwise qualified individual with a disability who is an applicant or employee, unless such covered entity can demonstrate that the accommodation would impose an undue hardship on the operation of the business of such covered entity; or*

*(B) denying employment opportunities to a job applicant or employee who is an otherwise qualified individual with a disability, if such denial is based on the need of such covered entity to make reasonable accommodation to the physical or mental impairments of the employee or applicant;*

*(6) using qualification standards, employment tests or other selection criteria that screen out or tend to screen out an individual with a disability or a class of individuals with disabilities unless the standard, test or other selection criteria, as used by the covered entity, is shown to be job-related for the position in question and is consistent with business necessity; and*

*(7) failing to select and administer tests concerning employment in the most effective manner to ensure that, when such test is administered to a job applicant or employee who has a disability that impairs sensory, manual, or speaking skills, such test results accurately reflect the skills, aptitude, or whatever other factor of such applicant or employee that such test purports to measure, rather than reflecting the impaired sensory, manual, or speaking skills of such employee or applicant (except where such skills are the factors that the test purports to measure).*[55]

In all of these circumstances, the ADA protects against discrimination in the workplace.

## 3. Reasonable Accommodations

In addition to providing protection against discriminatory employment practices, the ADA also entitles employees who currently have a disability or who have a record of having a disability to reasonable accommodations in the workplace.[56] A reasonable accommodation is "any change in the work environment or in the way things are customarily done that enables an individual with a disability to enjoy equal employment opportunities."[57] Reasonable accommodations are a primary method for employees to get assistance in continuing to perform their job responsibilities during treatment, returning to work after treatment, and taking time off work. Reasonable

---

55. *Id.* § 12112(b).

56. *Id.* § 12112(b)(5)(A).

57. *Enforcement Guidance: Reasonable Accommodation and Undue Hardship under the Americans with Disabilities Act*, EEOC (citing 29 C.F.R. § 1630(o)), https://www.eeoc.gov/laws/guidance/enforcement-guidance-reasonable-accommodation-and-undue-hardship-under-ada (last visited Nov. 8, 2024).

accommodations can often help to mitigate side effects from treatment that employees may find are challenging or interfering with their work performance.[58]

There are a plethora of short-term and long-term side effects that an individual diagnosed with cancer might experience, including visual side effects such as surgical scars or hair loss, and hidden side effects, such as fatigue, pain, and cognitive challenges. There are also late-term side effects, which can appear months or even years after a cancer diagnosis.[59] For example, young adults who had chemotherapy as a child may experience poorer thinking flexibility and short-term memory.[60] All of these side effects might impact an individual's ability to effectively perform job responsibilities.

Some of the most common and significant side effects that may impact a patient's ability to work are the cognitive side effects collectively referred to as "chemo brain." These cognitive challenges may include difficulties with short-term memory, an inability to concentrate or trouble focusing, challenges with executive function, trouble with learning new things, and difficulties when working with numbers. Scientific research on the causes, prevention, and treatment of chemo brain are limited. However, some recent studies have shown that people can experience cognitive challenges, not only when receiving chemotherapy treatment, but also when receiving radiation or endocrine therapy. Some of the predictors of whether or not someone will experience chemo brain include age, genetics, and cognitive reserve before treatment begins (e.g., IQ, education, occupation, hobbies, etc.). There are other factors that can affect cognitive function, regardless of cancer treatment, including lack of sleep, hydration, nutrition, and exercise; and whether an individual is experiencing stress, depression, anxiety, pain, or other comorbidities.

Some side effects can be addressed through medication or other practical changes, but when there needs to be a change at work that can be provided by an employer, that is when reasonable accommodations can be utilized.

Some practical examples of reasonable accommodations include:

- Changing a work schedule (e.g., telecommuting, reducing hours to part-time, working a flexible schedule, using additional rest breaks, reducing overtime shifts,[61] or taking time off work)

---

58. Irena Stepanikova et al., *Exploring Long-Term Cancer Survivors' Experiences in the Career and Financial Domains: Interviews with Hematopoietic Stem Cell Transplantation Recipients*, 34 J. Psychosoc. Oncology 2 (2015).

59. Michelle C. Janelsins et al., *Cognitive Complaints in Survivors of Breast Cancer after Chemotherapy Compared with Age-Matched Controls: An Analysis from a Nationwide, Multicenter, Prospective Longitudinal Study*, 35 J. Clinical Oncology 506 (2017).

60. Iris Elens et al., *Neurocognitive Sequelae in Adult Childhood Leukemia Survivors Related to Levels of Phosphorylated Tau*, 109 JNCI djw321 (2017).

61. Note: There have been cases to suggest that in some circumstances an essential function of a particular position is working overtime hours (*see* Tardie v. Rehab. Hosp. of R.I., 168 F.3d 538 (1st Cir. 1999); Manigan v. Sw. Ohio Reg'l Transit Auth., 385 F. App'x 472 (6th Cir. 2010)).

- Using technology (e.g., a tape recorder, smartphone, tablet, or speak/type software)
- Changing a physical work environment (e.g., moving your work location closer to the elevator or restroom, moving your workspace to a location with less distractions, or adding hand controls to your work vehicle)
- Changing a workplace policy (e.g., the ability to wear a head covering due to hair loss)
- Shifting nonessential job responsibilities
- Changing a job position and/or duties (e.g., moving to a vacant position)

See the table in this subsection for additional reasonable accommodation suggestions based on different types of side effects from cancer treatment.[62]

The legal definition of a "reasonable accommodation" is very broad, as it states "any change" is possible. However, accommodations do need to be reasonable based on an individual's job responsibilities. For example, school bus drivers are not going to be able to telecommute to their job. While it may not be realistic or reasonable for certain types of jobs, telecommuting is offered by 59 percent of U.S. employers, and can be cost-effective for both the employer and the employee.[63] The employee saves money on commuting costs and the employer saves money on real estate, electricity, and other utilities. As of 2023, 35 percent of employees in the United States, with teleworkable jobs, now work from home full-time and 41 percent are working a hybrid schedule.[64] This suggests that telecommuting may be a very realistic option for individuals working through cancer treatment or returning to work, as a way to avoid commuting, to take breaks as needed, and to have a more flexible work schedule, while still working full-time and fulfilling their job responsibilities.

In addition, a reasonable accommodation does not have to be related to an essential job function.[65] For additional information on possible reasonable accommodations that may be available, the Job Accommodation Network (JAN), a program of the U.S. Department of Labor (DOL), was specifically established to help employers and employees navigate reasonable accommodations. JAN has a Searchable Online Accommodation Resource system that allows people to explore various accommodation options for people with different types of medical conditions in particular workplace settings.[66]

---

62. *Cancer*, Job Accommodation Network, https://askjan.org/disabilities/Cancer.cfm (last visited Nov. 8, 2024).

63. Dana Wilkie, *How to Create an Effective Telecommuting Program*, Soc'y for Hum. Res. Mgmt. (June 1, 2015), https://www.shrm.org/hr-today/news/hr-magazine/Pages/0615-how-to-create-an-effective-telecommuting-program.aspx.

64. Kim Parker, *About a Third of U.S. Workers Who Can Work from Home Now Do So All the Time*, Pew Rsch. Ctr. (Mar. 23, 2023), https://www.pewresearch.org/short-reads/2023/03/30/about-a-third-of-us-workers-who-can-work-from-home-do-so-all-the-time.

65. Feist v. Louisiana, 730 F.3d 450, 452–54 (5th Cir. 2013).

66. *See* JAN, https://askjan.org (last visited Nov. 8, 2024).

| Fatigue or Weakness | Temperature Sensitivity |
|---|---|
| • Reduce or eliminate physical exertion and workplace stress<br>• Schedule periodic rest breaks away from the workstation<br>• Allow a flexible work schedule and flexible use of leave time<br>• Allow work from home<br>• Implement ergonomic workstation design<br>• Provide a scooter or other mobility aid if walking cannot be reduced<br>• Provide parking close to the worksite<br>• Install automatic door openers<br>• Make sure materials and equipment are within reach<br>• Move workstation close to other work areas, office equipment, and break rooms<br>• Reduce noise with sound-absorbent baffles/partitions, environmental sound machines, and headsets<br>• Provide alternate workspace to reduce visual and auditory distractions | • Modify worksite temperature<br>• Modify dress code<br>• Use fan/air-conditioner or heater at the workstation<br>• Allow flexible scheduling and flexible use of leave time<br>• Allow work from home during extremely hot or cold weather<br>• Maintain the ventilation system<br>• Redirect air-conditioning and heating vents<br>• Provide an office with separate temperature controls |
| **Skin Irritations** | **Ongoing Medical Treatment** |
| • Avoid infectious agents and chemicals<br>• Avoid invasive procedures (activities that could exacerbate skin condition)<br>• Provide alternative and protective clothing | • Provide flexible schedule and leave time<br>• Allow a self-paced workload with flexible hours<br>• Allow employee to work from home<br>• Provide part-time work schedules |
| **Respiratory Difficulties** | |
| • Provide adjustable ventilation<br>• Keep work environment free from dust, smoke, odor, and fumes<br>• Implement a "fragrance-free" workplace policy and a "smoke-free" building policy<br>• Avoid temperature extremes<br>• Use fan/air-conditioner/heater at workstation<br>• Redirect air-conditioning and heating vents | |

While employees who currently have or previously had a disability are able to access reasonable accommodations, employees who are regarded as having a disability and employees who have a relationship or association with a person with a disability are not.[67] However, those employees may still want to consider if there are accommodations that may assist them in performing their job functions and ask their employers for those accommodations. Employers may be willing to provide

67. *Questions & Answers: Association Provision of the ADA*, *supra* note 53; Den Hartog v. Wasatch Acad., 129 F.3d 1076, 1084 (10th Cir. 1997).

accommodations even though they are not required to by law, especially if it would facilitate the retention and performance of a valued employee.

***a. Requesting an Accommodation***

An employee may ask a supervisor, another superior, or an HR representative for a reasonable accommodation.[68] "The ADA" or the specific words "reasonable accommodation" do not need to be used. In addition, the request does not need to be in writing, but it is a good practice for employees to document in writing any agreed-upon reasonable accommodations. Even a short thank-you email summarizing a conversation with an employer can be a simple way to document what was discussed with respect to reasonable accommodations. There are no specific forms for an employee to complete to request a reasonable accommodation under the ADA. For employers that want to have a written request, JAN has developed a sample request form.[69] Some employers simply ask for a note from a doctor. (See Section VI, Disclosure.)

A reasonable accommodation can be requested during the job application process, or at any point during employment.[70] There is not a specific time frame required in which to request an accommodation. However, it may be in the best interest of employees to ask for a reasonable accommodation as soon as employees realize that a challenge with performing their job functions has arisen. If an employee waits or fails to ask for a reasonable accommodation and the work performance of the employee begins to suffer, employers are within their rights to make nondiscriminatory workplace decisions based on poor work performance.[71]

The "interactive process" is the name of the informal conversation(s) during which employees and employers identify, discuss, negotiate, choose, implement, and monitor an effective reasonable accommodation for an employee. An employer has an obligation to respond to a request for a reasonable accommodation in a timely manner, as well as to maintain the confidentiality of the employee throughout the accommodation process.[72] The following figure describes this process.[73]

---

68. *Enforcement Guidance: Reasonable Accommodation and Undue Hardship under the Americans with Disabilities Act*, *supra* note 57.

69. JAN, Accommodation and Compliance Series: Sample Reasonable Accommodation Form for Employers, https://askjan.org/Forms/upload/raform.doc (last visited Nov. 8, 2024).

70. 29 C.F.R. § 1630.9(a) (2011).

71. *Enforcement Guidance: Reasonable Accommodation and Undue Hardship under the Americans with Disabilities Act*, *supra* note 57.

72. *Id.*

73. *Interactive Process*, JAN, https://askjan.org/topics/interactive.cfm (last visited Nov. 8, 2024).

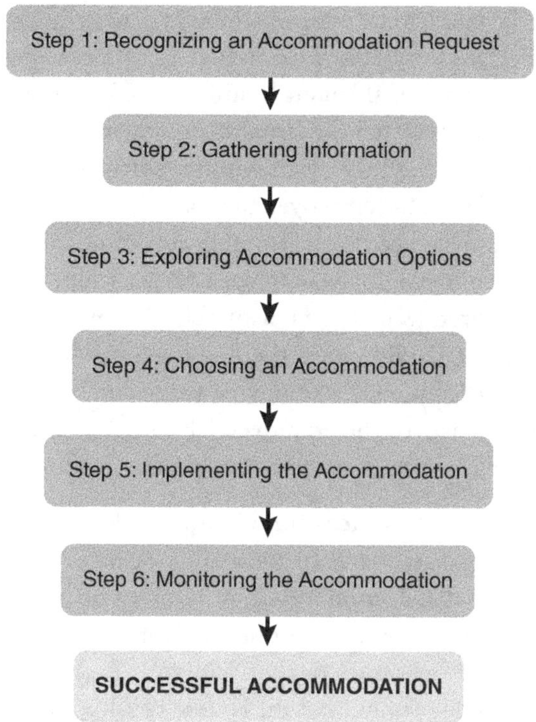


Before employees engage in the interactive process, it can be helpful for employees to consider more than one accommodation that might work to address their workplace challenges, and to be as creative as possible in their possible accommodation options. For some employees, there may be more than one accommodation needed to allow the employees to effectively perform the essential functions of their jobs.

When there is more than one reasonable accommodation available, the employer may choose an accommodation that costs less or is easier to provide, as long as the chosen accommodation is effective. If more than one accommodation is effective, "the preference of the individual with a disability should be given primary consideration. However, the employer providing the accommodation has the ultimate discretion to choose between effective accommodations."[74]

On a practical level, the interactive process does not end, as there is an obligation on both the employer and employees to assess the effectiveness of the chosen accommodation on an ongoing basis.[75] There are many reasons why the need for an accommodation may change over time, particularly for an employee working through cancer treatment. "In some cases, an accommodation stops being effective for various reasons such as: the employee's limitations change, workplace equipment changes, the job changes, the workplace itself changes, or the accommodation becomes an

74. 29 C.F.R. § 1630.9 (2011).

75. *Interactive Process*, *supra* note 73.

undue hardship for the employer."[76] For example, in the context of a cancer diagnosis, an employee's need for a flexible work schedule as a reasonable accommodation to allow the employee to work through treatment may change when the employee completes treatment and now has neuropathy in their fingertips, necessitating an accommodation of the use of speak/type computer software.

According to the EEOC, an employer may ask an employee with a known disability whether the employee needs a reasonable accommodation when the employer reasonably believes that the employee may need an accommodation.[77]

An employer is required to provide reasonable accommodations for an employee with a disability, unless it would cause the employer an "undue hardship."[78] To be considered an undue hardship on the employer, the accommodation must require significant difficulty or expense for the employer.[79] Factors to be considered when determining if an accommodation poses an undue hardship include:

- The nature and cost of the accommodation needed
- The overall financial resources of the facility or facilities involved in the provision of the reasonable accommodation; number of persons employed at such facility; effect on expenses and resources; or impact otherwise of such accommodation upon the operation of the facility
- The overall financial resources of the covered entity; overall size of the business of a covered entity with respect to the number of its employees; number, type, and location of its facilities
- The type of operation or operations of the covered entity, including the composition, structure, and functions of the workforce of such entity; the geographic separateness, administrative, or fiscal relationship of the facility or facilities in question to the covered entity[80]

Many employers fear their employees asking for accommodations because there is a preconceived notion that it will be too expensive or inconvenient for an employer to provide the accommodation. According to a JAN study,[81] 59 percent of job accommodations cost the employer nothing, while 36 percent have a one-time cost, typically under $500. In addition, the study found that 83 percent of employers who called JAN for information or help were doing so to retain or promote a current employee. Additional employer benefits to accommodating employees include being able to retain a valued employee (90 percent); increase the employee's productivity (72 percent); increase the employee's attendance (56 percent); and avoid the costs of training a new employee (61 percent).[82]

---

76. *Id.*
77. *Id.*
78. 42 U.S.C. § 12112(b)(5)(A).
79. *Id.*; *id.* § 12111(10).
80. *Id.* § 12111(10)(B).
81. *Costs and Benefits of Accommodation*, JAN, https://askjan.org/topics/costs.cfm?csSearch=6286901_1 (last updated Apr. 5, 2024).
82. *Id.*

For additional information about the ADA or reasonable accommodations, see https://www.eeoc.gov/laws/guidance/cancer-workplace-and-ada and https://www.eeoc.gov/laws/guidance/enforcement-guidance-reasonable-accommodation-and-undue-hardship-under-ada.

## B. Rehabilitation Act of 1973

The Rehabilitation Act is very similar to the ADA, but it prohibits discrimination against employees with disabilities by three types of federal employers:[83]

- **Section 501.** Prohibits *federal agency employers* from discriminating against qualified individuals with disabilities and requires them to take affirmative action to employ and advance employment of qualified individuals with disabilities. *Each federal agency enforces section 501 for its own job applicants and/or employees. For additional information on specific section 501 policies, contact the relevant agency's Equal Employment Opportunity (EEO) office.*
- **Section 503.** Prohibits disability discrimination in the workplace and requires affirmative action in the hiring, placement, and advancement of people with disabilities by *federal contractors or subcontractors* who have federal contracts or subcontracts in excess of $10,000. *The Office of Federal Contract Compliance Programs of the DOL's Employment Standards Administration enforces section 503.*
- **Section 504.** Prohibits disability discrimination by *federal programs or activities* that receive federal financial assistance from, or are conducted by, a federal agency. *The federal agency providing the financial assistance or conducting the program/activity enforces section 504. For additional information on specific section 504 policies, contact the relevant agency's EEO office.*[84]

The Rehabilitation Act defines a disability as a physical or mental impairment that results in a substantial impediment to employment, or any condition that constitutes a disability under the ADA.[85]

## C. Filing a Complaint

If an individual believes that their fair employment rights have been violated, the individual has the right to file a complaint against an employer.

### 1. Against Private-Sector Employers and State and Local Governments

In order to file a complaint against an employer for violations of the ADA, a "charge of discrimination" should be filed through the EEOC. Complaints should be filed

83. 29 U.S.C. § 701 *et seq*. (Rehabilitation Act of 1973).

84. *Employment Laws: Disability & Discrimination*, DOL Off. Disability Emp. Pol'y, https://www.dol.gov/agencies/odep/publications/fact-sheets/employment-laws-disability-and-discrimination (last visited Nov. 8, 2024).

85. 29 U.S.C. § 705.

within 180 calendar days from the day the discrimination took place. There are a few exceptions to this deadline:

- Individuals who live where a state or local agency also has a relevant fair employment law (300 days)
- Individuals who feel they were discriminated against during the job application process (45 days)
- Individuals who are employees of the federal government (45 days) (see following section)

It is generally in an individual's best interest to file the complaint as soon as possible. An individual can start the process of filing a complaint in person, over the phone, or by mail. While the EEOC does not accept online complaints, they do have an online assessment tool that may be useful for someone who is unsure if they should file a complaint. This tool can be found at https://publicportal.eeoc.gov/Portal. The site will first ask general questions about an individual's complaint to determine whether or not the EEOC can provide assistance. Next, an individual will need to fill out a questionnaire regarding specifics about their employment situation. After an individual fills out the questionnaire, they should bring the questionnaire to the nearest EEOC office to begin filing a charge.[86]

Once the charge is filed, the EEOC will notify the employer and provide the employer with the charge investigator's contact information. After a claim is filed with the EEOC, they may suggest completing mediation before they launch an official investigation.[87] Both the employee and the employer must agree to mediation, which is when an independent third party attempts to resolve the issues. Participating in the EEOC's mediation program is free, voluntary, and confidential. There may be several benefits to mediation, including avoiding a potentially costly lawsuit and perhaps even retaining employment.[88] If an employee is unable to resolve the issues through mediation, the EEOC will investigate the charge of discrimination to determine if there is reasonable cause to believe that the employee was discriminated against. The employer may need to supply a statement of its position and copies of policies, files, and other evidence, and the employer may also need to allow on-site investigations and employee interviews.

Once the EEOC has completed its investigation, it will determine whether or not there is "reasonable cause" to believe that discrimination occurred. If there is not enough evidence to support a finding of reasonable cause, the EEOC will distribute a dismissal and notice of rights stating that the employee or job applicant has the right to file a lawsuit against the employer in federal court within 90 days

86. To find the closest EEOC office, visit *EEOC Field Offices*, https://www.eeoc.gov/field-office (last visited Nov. 8, 2024).

87. *Mediation*, EEOC, https://www.eeoc.gov/mediation-0 (last visited Nov. 8, 2024).

88. *Id.*

of receipt of notice. Conversely, if the EEOC finds reasonable cause, it will issue a letter of determination and try to reconcile the charge. When the charge cannot be resolved through conciliation, the EEOC will either file a lawsuit on behalf of the employee or job applicant or it will issue a notice of right to sue to the employee or job applicant, stating that the employee or job applicant is entitled to file a lawsuit against the employer within 90 days of receipt of the notice. If the process is taking a long time, the employee or job applicant may also request a notice of right to sue from the EEOC if 180 days have passed since originally filing the charge with the EEOC.[89] Individuals who choose to pursue a lawsuit against their employer in federal court should consider hiring a lawyer who specializes in employment discrimination matters.

For more information about filing a complaint on the basis of disability discrimination, visit https://www.eeoc.gov/how-file-charge-employment-discrimination.

## 2. Against Federal Agencies

An employee, or job applicant, of the federal government who feels that their ADA rights were violated has 45 days from the date the discrimination occurred to contact an EEO counselor at the agency where the employee works or applied for a job. The EEO representative will try to resolve the dispute through counseling or alternative dispute resolution (ADR). Usually, counseling concludes within 30 days and ADR concludes within 90 days.

If counseling and ADR are unsuccessful, the charging party may file a complaint with the agency and the agency must investigate the complaint unless it is dismissed. Once the agency concludes its investigation, the employee or job applicant may request an immediate final decision from the agency or a hearing from an EEOC judge. Where a hearing is requested, the administrative judge decides the outcome of the case and issues a notice of that decision to both parties. If the agency does not issue a final order within 40 days of receiving the judge's decision, the judge's decision becomes the agency's final action. Both parties are also entitled to appeal the judge's final decision. The employee or job applicant has 30 days and the federal agency has 40 days to file an appeal.[90]

For more information about the process of filing a complaint as a federal employee, visit https://www.eeoc.gov/federal-sector/overview-federal-sector-eeo-complaint-process.

---

89. For more information on this procedure, see *What You Can Expect after a Charge Is Filed*, EEOC, https://www.eeoc.gov/employers/what-you-can-expect-after-charge-filed (last visited Nov. 8, 2024).

90. For more information, see *Background Information for EEOC Final Rule on Title II of the Genetic Information Nondiscrimination Act of 2008*, EEOC, https://www.eeoc.gov/laws/regulations/gina-background.cfm (last visited Nov. 8, 2024).

## III. State Fair Employment Laws

While the ADA is a federal law, some states may have their own laws that are similar to the ADA. These laws cannot contradict the ADA,[91] but may provide the same, or greater, recourse at the state level, thereby supplementing an employee's rights under the ADA. Only the laws of the state in which an employee works will apply to the employee.[92] If an employee's rights under both federal and state laws have been violated, an employee could have legal claims under both and is not necessarily precluded from bringing both claims.

Some state laws have a broader definition of "disability" than the ADA. For example, under the California Fair Employment and Housing Act, the definition of a "medical condition" specifically includes a health impairment related to a diagnosis of cancer.[93]

Most state laws cover smaller employers than the ADA covers (see following table). If a state is not listed in the table, then it covers 15 or more employees, the same as the ADA.

| **Minimum Number of Employees an Employer Must Have to Be Covered under the State Fair Employment Law** | | | | | | | | |
|---|---|---|---|---|---|---|---|---|
| **1** | **2** | **3** | **4** | **5** | **6** | **8** | **9** | **12** |
| AK<br>CO<br>CT<br>DC<br>HI<br>IL<br>ME<br>MI<br>MN<br>MT<br>NJ<br>NY<br>ND<br>SD<br>VT<br>VA<br>WI | WY | | IA<br>KS<br>NM<br>OH<br>PA<br>RI | CA<br>ID | IN<br>MA<br>MO<br>NH<br>OR | KY<br>TN<br>WA | AR (but 15 for RAs) | WV |

* Note: The EEOC enforces state antidiscrimination law in Arkansas, which only applies to employers with nine or more employees. The state antidiscrimination law only covers discrimination, and does not provide for reasonable accommodations. Therefore, in order to access reasonable accommodations in Arkansas, employees must look to the ADA, which covers private employers with 15 or more employees.

---

91. U.S. CONST. art. VI, cl. 2 (Supremacy Clause).

92. Where an employee legally works may not always be clear and it is a good idea to seek guidance. For example, it may be confusing when an employee physically works in a different state than where the employer is located, or when an employee performs work in multiple states and the employer also has a presence in multiple states. If an employee works under an employment agreement, that contract may also assign and determine which state laws will apply.

93. CAL. GOV'T CODE § 12926.

## IV. Taking Time off Work

Employees may need to take time off work if they are diagnosed with cancer or are caring for a family member who has been diagnosed with cancer. Often, it is the specific policies of an employer that provide the greatest ability to take time off work, as there are limited options for medical leave under federal law, and state and local laws vary greatly. For example, under federal law, employers are not required to provide paid sick leave. Given the burden this places on employees, there have been significant legislative efforts at the state and local levels to provide this benefit. As of January 2025, 20 states and the District of Columbia, as well as numerous cities, have passed laws requiring employers to offer paid sick leave to their employees.[94]

In response, some employers have lobbied their state legislatures to ban these local paid sick leave laws.[95] And, nearly 80 percent of working cancer survivors without health insurance also lack paid sick leave.[96] Private-sector employees who do have sick leave only receive an average of seven days per year, not enough for cancer care.[97] This patchwork legislative approach to providing paid sick leave emphasizes the need for a federal approach, similar to the federal law that provides employees with family and medical leave.

### A. FMLA

The FMLA is a federal law passed in 1993,[98] which provides eligible employees with the right to take up to 12 weeks of leave per year for the following:

- A serious health condition that makes the employee unable to perform the essential functions of their job
- The care of an employee's spouse, child, or parent who has a serious health condition
- The birth of a child and to care for the newborn child within one year of birth
- The placement with the employee of a child for adoption or foster care and to care for the newly placed child within one year of placement
- Any qualifying exigency arising out of the fact that the employee's spouse, son, daughter, or parent is a covered military member on "covered active duty"

---

94. *Employment State Laws: Paid Leave*, Triage Cancer, https://triagecancer.org/state-laws/taking-time-off#paid (last visited Nov. 8, 2024).

95. H. Elizabeth Peters et al., Urban Institute, State Preemption of Local Paid Sick Days Ordinances: Lessons from a Pandemic (2020), https://www.urban.org/sites/default/files/publication/103150/state-preemption-of-local-paid-sick-days-ordinances_0.pdf.

96. Zhiyuan Zheng et al., *Paid Sick Leave among Working Cancer Survivors and Its Associations with Use of Preventive Services in the United States, 20* JNCCN 1244 (2022).

97. *National Compensation Survey: Employee Benefits in the United States, March 2023,* U.S. Bureau Lab. Stat., https://www.bls.gov/ebs/publications/employee-benefits-in-the-united-states-march-2023.htm (last modified Sept. 21, 2023).

98. 29 U.S.C. § 2601 *et seq*. (FMLA of 1993).

The FMLA also provides for 26 weeks of leave during a single 12-month period to care for a covered service member with a serious injury or illness if the eligible employee is the service member's spouse, son, daughter, parent, or next of kin (military caregiver leave).[99]

This section will focus on an employee's need to take leave due to their own serious medical condition or to take care of a child, parent, or spouse with a serious medical condition.

While the FMLA's 12 weeks of medical leave is the minimum amount of leave that covered employers must provide under the FMLA, employers may offer more generous leave policies. Therefore, employees should review their employers' leave policies.

According to a 2018 DOL study, only 56 percent of workers are protected by the FMLA, and 56 percent of employees believe the FMLA covers more reasons for leave than it does, such as caring for a sibling.[100] In addition, millions of employees eligible for the FMLA do not take it because they are worried about losing their job or cannot afford to take unpaid leave.[101]

In passing the FMLA, Congress attempted to address the increasing needs of families to balance work and family life, as expressed in the language of the statute:

> 29 U.S.C. § 2601. Purpose of the FMLA
> ***(b) Purposes***
> *It is the purpose of this Act—*
> *(1) to balance the demands of the workplace with the needs of families, to promote the stability and economic security of families, and to promote national interests in preserving family integrity;*
> *(2) to entitle employees to take reasonable leave for medical reasons, for the birth or adoption of a child, and for the care of a child, spouse, or parent who has a serious health condition;*
> *(3) to accomplish the purposes described in paragraphs (1) and (2) in a manner that accommodates the legitimate interests of employers;*
> *(4) to accomplish the purposes described in paragraphs (1) and (2) in a manner that, consistent with the Equal Protection Clause of the Fourteenth Amendment, minimizes the potential for employment discrimination on the basis of sex by ensuring generally that leave is available for eligible medical reasons*

---

99. *Family and Medical Leave Act*, DOL Wage & Hour Div., https://www.dol.gov/agencies/whd/fmla (last visited Nov. 8, 2024).

100. Scott Brown et al., DOL, Employee and Worksite Perspectives of the FMLA: Who Is Eligible? (2020), https://www.dol.gov/sites/dolgov/files/OASP/evaluation/pdf/WHD_FMLA2018PB1WhoIsEligible_StudyBrief_Aug2020.pdf.

101. National Partnership for Women and Families, Key Facts: The Family and Medical Leave Act (2023), https://nationalpartnership.org/wp-content/uploads/2023/02/key-facts-the-family-and-medical-leave-act.pdf.

*(including maternity-related disability) and for compelling family reasons, on a gender-neutral basis; and*
*(5) to promote the goal of equal employment opportunity for women and men, pursuant to such clause.*[102]

## 1. FMLA-Covered Medical Conditions

The FMLA defines a serious health condition as an illness, injury, impairment, or physical or mental condition that involves inpatient care or continuing treatment by a health care provider.[103] In order to demonstrate that an employee is undergoing "continuing treatment," an employee or the employee's family member must experience:

- A period of incapacity of more than three consecutive, full calendar days plus treatment by a health care provider twice, or once with a continuing regimen of treatment
- Any period of incapacity related to pregnancy or for prenatal care
- Any period of incapacity or treatment for a chronic serious health condition
- A period of incapacity for permanent or long-term conditions for which treatment may not be effective
- Any period of incapacity to receive and/or recover from multiple treatments or surgery[104]

The regulations specify that if an employee asserts a serious health condition under the requirement of a "period of incapacity of more than three consecutive, full calendar days and any subsequent treatment or period of incapacity relating to the same condition," the employee's first treatment visit (or only visit if coupled with a regimen of continuing treatment) must take place within seven days of the first day of incapacity. The FMLA also allows an employee to take leave for chronic serious health conditions. A chronic serious health condition is one that:

- Requires periodic visits for treatment by a health care provider or nurse (e.g., two or more times a year)
- Continues across an extended period of time
- May cause episodic rather than continuing periods of incapacity[105]

The diagnosis and treatment of cancer typically qualifies as a serious health condition under the FMLA.

---

102. 29 U.S.C. § 2601.
103. *Id.* § 2611(11).
104. *Frequently Asked Questions and Answers about the Revisions to the Family and Medical Leave Act*, DOL Wage & Hour Div., https://www.dol.gov/agencies/whd/fmla/final-rule/faq (last visited Nov. 8, 2024).
105. *Id.*

## 2. FMLA-Covered Family Members

Under the FMLA, an employee is permitted to take time off to provide physical or psychological care for a family member, as well as assistance with basic daily needs, including transportation.[106] The FMLA allows employees to take time off to care for the following:

- **Child.** A child includes a biological, adopted, stepchild or foster child, legal ward, or other child for whom the employee is acting in loco parentis.
- **Parent.** A parent includes a biological, adoptive, stepchild or foster father or mother, or any other individual who stood in loco parentis to the employee.[107]
- **Spouse.** A spouse means a husband or wife as defined or recognized under state law for purposes of marriage in the state where the employee resides, including common-law marriage in states where it is recognized.

## 3. FMLA-Covered Employers

To be eligible to take FMLA leave, an employee must work for a covered employer, which includes the following:

- A public employer of any size (e.g., federal, state, and local governments)
- A public and private elementary or secondary school of any size
- A private employer with 50 or more employees who work within a 75-mile radius of an employee's worksite[108]

In order for an employer to be covered by the FMLA, the employer must have 50 or more employees during 20 or more calendar workweeks in either the current or the preceding calendar year.[109] The 20 workweeks do not have to be consecutive.[110] Any employee whose name appears on the employer's payroll will be considered employed each working day of the calendar week and must be counted even if no compensation was received for the week.[111] Any part-time employees and employees who are on paid or unpaid leave, FMLA leave, a leave of absence, or disciplinary suspension, are counted as long as the employer reasonably expects the employee to return to active employment.[112]

If an employee works in a branch of a larger company (e.g., chain restaurant, retail store, or bank branch), the employee may count any employee that works for the company within 75 miles of the employee's worksite to meet the 50-employee

106. 29 C.F.R. § 825.124(a)–(c) (2015).
107. Note: This does not include parents-in-law or grandparents (*id.* § 825.122(b)).
108. *Id.* § 825.104(a).
109. *Id.* § 825.105(e).
110. *Id.*
111. *Id.* § 825.105(b).
112. *Id.* § 825.105(c).

requirement.[113] The 75-mile radius is determined not by using an "as the crow flies" method, but by "using surface transportation over public streets, roads, highways, and waterways, by the shortest route from the facility where the employee requesting leave is employed."[114] It is important to be aware of franchise businesses, as they are often owned by different employers, so those employees cannot be added together. However, one employer/owner may own more than one branch or location of a franchise and those employees may be added together. For employees who telecommute, their worksite is the site from which work is assigned or the site to which they report.[115]

## 4. FMLA-Covered Employees

In addition to working for a large enough employer, in order to be eligible for FMLA leave, an employee must have worked for the employer long enough. The FMLA requires that an employee work for an employer for at least 12 months and at least 1,250 hours in the 12 months immediately prior to taking leave, which is slightly more than part-time in most employment situations.[116] For example, an employee may meet the 1,250-hour requirement by working:

- Twenty-four hours per week for 52 weeks in a row
- Forty hours per week for 31 weeks in a year
- More than 104 hours each month for 12 months in a row[117]

In order to meet the 1,250-hour requirement, an employee can only include hours actually worked for the employer. Any hours of paid leave, unpaid leave, or FMLA leave may not be included.[118]

If an employer does not maintain adequate records of the employee's hours, then the employer has the burden of demonstrating that the employee has not met the 1,250-hour requirement under the FMLA.[119]

The 12 months worked for an employer to meet the FMLA requirement do not need to be consecutive, only cumulative.[120] The FMLA allows employees to look

113. 29 U.S.C. § 2611(2)(B)(ii).
114. 29 C.F.R. § 825.111(b).
115. *Id.* § 825.111(a)(2).
116. 29 U.S.C. § 2611(2)(A).
117. This list is exemplary and not exhaustive. Some calculations of the number of hours worked for potentially eligible employees may be simple, but some are more complex. The FMLA gives some additional instructions for some job positions, such as for individuals who are members of flight crews. *Id.* § 2611(2 (D).
118. *FMLA Frequently Asked Questions,* DOL Wage & Hour Div., https://www.dol.gov/agencies/whd/fmla/faq#4 (last visited Nov. 8, 2024).
119. 29 C.F.R. § 825.110(c)(3).
120. 29 U.S.C. § 2612(b)(1).

back seven years[121] into their work history to determine whether they meet this requirement.[122]

"If an employee is maintained on the payroll for any part of a week, including any periods of paid or unpaid leave (sick, vacation) during which other benefits or compensation are provided by the employer (e.g., workers' compensation, group health plan benefits, etc.), the week counts as a week of employment" towards the 12-month requirement.[123] The following figure describes this process.[124]

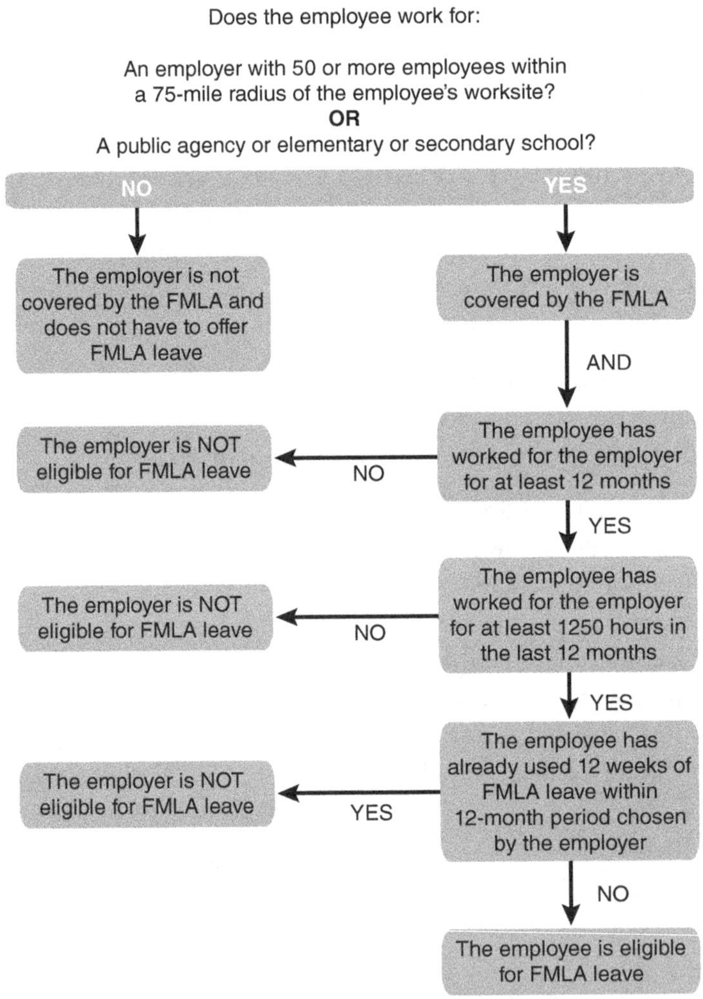


121. Some states have similar laws that do not place a time period of how far to look back into an employee's work history to meet this requirement.

122. 29 C.F.R. § 825.110(b)(1). Also, if a break in service for an employee lasts longer than seven years, but is the result of the employee's service in the National Guard or Reserve Military, or there is a written agreement that states the employer intends to rehire the employee after a break in service, then the previous employment can be used to meet the 12-month requirement (*id.* § 825.110(b)(2)).

123. *Id.* § 825.110(b)(3).

124. DOL, Need Time? The Employee's Guide to the Family and Medical Leave Act (2015), https://www.dol.gov/whd/fmla/employeeguide.pdf.

## 5. Amount of Medical Leave

Under the FMLA, eligible employees who work for a covered employer are entitled to take up to 12 weeks of unpaid leave per 12-month period to deal with their own serious medical condition or to care for a child, parent, or spouse.[125] Leave may be taken all at once or in shorter periods of time (intermittent leave) if it is medically necessary.[126] For example, an employee may take 12 weeks off at once for surgery and recovery; or take two weeks off a month for chemotherapy and recovery; or take every Monday off for radiation appointments. It is important to note that any time spent performing "light duty" work does not count against an employee's FMLA leave entitlement, and if an employee is voluntarily performing a light-duty assignment, the employee is not on FMLA leave.[127]

Employees are eligible for 12 weeks of leave in a 12-month period and there are four different ways in which an employer can calculate the 12-month period:

- A calendar year
- The 12-month period based on the date when an employee first begins FMLA leave, not from the date the leave is requested[128]
- The 12-month period measured backward from the date an employee uses the FMLA leave
- Any other fixed 12-month period (e.g., fiscal year or anniversary of employee hiring date)[129]

An employer must choose one of these ways as a policy. If the employer does not specify one of these four options, then the option that is most favorable to the employee is automatically applied.

Part-time employees who are otherwise eligible to take FMLA leave receive prorated amounts of FMLA leave based on their normal workweek.[130] For example, an employee who regularly works 24 hours a week and takes six hours of FMLA leave would be considered to have used one-fourth of a workweek of leave.

## 6. FMLA Job and Benefit Protections

FMLA leave is job-protected, meaning that when an employee returns from leave, generally the employee must be reinstated into the same or an equivalent position as the one the employee had prior to taking time off.[131]

---

125. 29 U.S.C. § 2612(a)(1)(C), (D).
126. *Id.* § 2612(b)(1).
127. Wage and Hour Division, DOL, Fact Sheet: Final Rule to Amend the Definition of Spouse in the Family and Medical Leave Act Regulations (2015), https://www.dol.gov/whd/fmla/finalrule/factsheet.pdf.
128. Ragsdale v. Wolverine World Wide, Inc., 535 U.S. 81 (2002).
129. 29 C.F.R. § 825.200(b).
130. *Id.* § 825.205(b)(1).
131. *Id.* § 825.214.

An employee's health insurance benefits are also protected while the employee is out on FMLA leave. If an employer pays for a portion or all of an employee's health insurance coverage, the employer must continue to do so while the employee is on leave (i.e., the employer cannot force the employee to elect Consolidated Omnibus Budget Reconciliation Act (COBRA) during the employee's FMLA leave).[132] However, that rule applies only to health insurance, not disability or life insurance or any other employer-sponsored benefit. After an employee returns from leave, all benefits that the employee received prior to FMLA leave must be reinstated. If an employee voluntarily does not return to work after an FMLA leave, an employer can recover the cost of benefits paid while the employee was on FMLA leave.[133]

While the FMLA provides 12 weeks of leave time per year, that leave is unpaid. Many employees are unable to afford taking 12 weeks of unpaid leave from work. In order to address this, the FMLA allows an employee to request a substitution of paid leave for unpaid leave under the FMLA. In addition, an employer may require an employee to first use any accrued vacation or paid leave.[134]

Employees who want to take time off work under the FMLA must provide notice to their employers that they need to take leave. If the leave is foreseeable, then the employee must provide notice of at least 30 days,[135] or if the leave is unforeseeable, an employee must provide notice as soon as it is practicable.[136] An employer may sometimes classify leave retroactively as FMLA leave, if the employee learns of a qualifying leave after the fact.

## 7. How the FMLA and ADA Interact

If an employee has used their 12 weeks of FMLA leave and is still unable to return to work, the ADA may provide the employee with additional leave time as a reasonable accommodation.[137] For example, if an employee takes 12 weeks of FMLA leave and is unable to return to work, the employee may ask the employer for some additional time off as a reasonable accommodation under the ADA. Generally, the employer must grant this additional leave if it is for a definite period of time (e.g., two additional weeks) and it is not an undue hardship on the employer.[138] If a health care provider can only provide an approximate or projected date of return for an employee

132. *Id.* § 825.209.

133. *Id.* § 825.213.

134. 29 U.S.C. § 2612(d)(2).

135. *Id.* § 2612(e).

136. The FMLA also requires that the employee make reasonable efforts to schedule medical treatment at such times that will not unduly burden the employer. *Id.*

137. 29 C.F.R. § 825.702.

138. See *Valdez v. McGill*, No. 11-2051, D.C. No. 1:08-CV-00453-JCH-RLP (D.N.M. Feb. 13, 2012), wherein a cancer survivor, Doyle Brown, exercised his right to use FMLA leave. However, he continued to need additional time off after exhausting his legally required leave time. Brown made continuing requests and eventually it became unclear and indefinite when he would return to work. The employer terminated Brown's employment, and was not held to have violated the FMLA or ADA.

or a range of return dates, the request for additional leave is not necessarily for an indefinite period of time. An employer is not required to provide leave when an alternative accommodation would be equally effective.

### 8. Information to Gather before Taking Leave

It is important for employees to understand how much leave they are entitled to and which policy or law they are taking leave under. In addition, if an employee is taking leave and the employee pays a portion of their health insurance premiums by having them withdrawn from the employee's paycheck, the employee should ask their employer how to make those payments while out on leave. It is also important for employees to ask about any other benefits they pay for through paycheck deductions (e.g., vision, dental, life, disability insurance) and to confirm how to make those payments while on leave, so that the policies do not lapse. It is also useful for employees to understand their employer's policies about contact while on leave. For example, are there rules about using work email or a work phone, or are other employees allowed to contact an employee on leave?

### 9. Filing a Complaint under the FMLA

An employer is not permitted to interfere with or deny an employee FMLA rights. Employers are also not permitted to retaliate or discriminate against employees because they took FMLA leave.[139]

The DOL's Wage and Hour Division is the federal agency that enforces the FMLA.[140] If employees feel that their rights under the FMLA have been violated, employees may file a complaint with the DOL;[141] however, unlike with the ADA, it is not necessary to do so before bringing a private lawsuit in federal court. An employee should file a claim within a reasonable time of when the employee discovers that their FMLA rights have been violated, or at the latest no more than two years after the alleged violation of the FMLA occurred, or three years in the case of a willful violation of the FMLA.[142]

## V. State and Local Leave Laws

While the FMLA is a federal law, some states may have laws that are similar to the FMLA. These laws cannot contradict the FMLA,[143] but may provide similar or the same recourse at the state level, thereby augmenting an employee's rights, or they may provide additional rights, thereby expanding an employee's rights beyond what

139. 29 C.F.R. § 825.220(a).

140. *Id.* § 825.401.

141. Local offices can be found at *Wage and Hour Division*, DOL, https://www.dol.gov/agencies/whd (last visited Nov. 8, 2024).

142. 29 C.F.R. § 825.401(b).

143. U.S. Const. art. VI, cl. 2 (Supremacy Clause).

is provided under the FMLA. Only the laws of the state in which an employee works will apply to the employee.[144] In most circumstances, leave under the FMLA and the employee's state's laws may be taken simultaneously, so that the first 12 weeks of leave count against both an employee's leave under FMLA and state laws.

For example, the California Family Rights Act (CFRA) is similar to the FMLA, but applies to private employers with five or more employees, rather than the 50 employees required under the FMLA.[145] The CFRA also has a broader definition of whom an employee can care for, using a "designated person" standard, which includes anyone related by blood or who is like family to the employee.

Another example is the Oregon Family Leave Act, which generally requires that an employee must have only been employed with the employer for 180 days and worked an average of 25 hours per week during the 180 days prior to taking leave.[146] This is less than the 12-month requirement to take leave under the FMLA.

There are also state, county, and city leave laws that may be useful to individuals diagnosed with cancer and their caregivers. For example, some cities have paid sick leave laws. For more information about state and local laws, visit https://triagecancer.org/state-laws/taking-time-off.

## VI. Disclosure

An individual's choice to disclose a cancer diagnosis in the workplace is a personal decision, and should only be made after thoughtful consideration of many factors. Some individuals feel very confident that sharing their diagnosis in the workplace and in other arenas is right for them. Others have concerns about sharing their diagnosis for a variety of reasons. There is no one-size-fits-all answer to disclosure. This section will discuss factors to help individuals make disclosure decisions and identify potential areas of inadvertent disclosure. For individuals diagnosed with cancer, these are some questions to consider when making disclosure decisions:

- Will my diagnosis affect my ability to do the job?
- What is my proposed treatment schedule?
- What are the likely side effects of my treatment and when are they likely to occur?
- How will my cancer be "visible" in the workplace, if at all?
- Will I need any accommodations at work?
- Will I need any medical leave time?

---

144. Where you legally work may not always be clear. Some situations where it may be confusing is when you physically work in a different state than where your employer is located, or when you perform work in multiple states and your employer also has a presence in multiple states. If you have an employment agreement, that contract may also assign and determine what state laws will apply for you.

145. Cal. Gov't Code § 12945.2.

146. Or. Rev. Stat. § 659A.156.

- What are my financial worries?
- What are my insurance worries?
- What laws might protect me?
- What are my employer's policies?
- How will disclosure affect my relationship with my employer and with my co-workers?
- How will disclosure affect my comfort level at work?
- What is the reputation of this employer toward employees in a similar situation?
- Do I plan on staying with my current employer for a long time?
- Do I want to explain my diagnosis to a future employer?

## A. Disclosure and the ADA

If an employee requests a reasonable accommodation under the ADA or state fair employment law, and the disability or the need for a reasonable accommodation is not obvious, the employer may ask for medical documentation to certify that the employee has a qualifying disability.[147] Although an employee must say that the request for a change in work environment or policy is a result of a medical condition, the employee does not need to disclose the exact nature of that condition (e.g., an employee does not necessarily have to tell the employer that the employee has been diagnosed with cancer) if the employee can provide sufficient information that describes the nature and the duration of the impairment, the activity the impairment limits, and why the employee needs a reasonable accommodation.[148] Employees who are concerned about disclosing their diagnosis to their employer should have a conversation with their health care team when asking them to complete an employer's medical certification paperwork. It is important to communicate a desire for privacy and nondisclosure, so that when health care professionals are describing an employee's medical condition they focus on the side effects of treatment, rather than the diagnosis of cancer.

The issue of disclosure also arises when employers make other medical inquiries or ask prospective or current employees to take medical exams. There are limitations on an employer's ability to make medical inquiries or require medical exams, depending on the stage of employment:

- **Pre-offer.** During the application process, before a job offer is made, an employer may not ask about an applicant's health, or require that the applicant undergo a medical exam.[149] This includes questions intended to elicit information about

147. JAN, Employers' Practical Guide to Reasonable Accommodation under the Americans with Disabilities Act (ADA), https://askjan.org/publications/employers/employers-guide.cfm (last visited Nov. 8, 2024).

148. *Enforcement Guidance on Disability-Related Inquiries and Medical Examinations of Employees under the ADA*, EEOC, https://www.eeoc.gov/policy/docs/guidance-inquiries.html (last visited Nov. 8, 2024).

149. 42 U.S.C. § 12112(d)(2)(A).

an applicant's disability, such as how much sick leave the applicant used in the past or if the applicant has ever taken FMLA leave. Employers are allowed to ask only if the applicant is able to perform the essential functions of the job and how they will be performed.

> Fatima is 35 years old. When she was 24, she was diagnosed with cancer. She participated in a local run/walk to raise money for cancer research and was interviewed by the local newspaper about her survivor experience. She is now looking for a new job. When she Googled herself to see what a potential employer might see, she found that the local newspaper is now online and includes her name and that she is a cancer survivor. She is worried about a potential employer finding out about her cancer history because of this article. *What options does Fatima have?*

- **Post-offer.** After an applicant is offered a job, an employer does have the right to make the offer conditional based on the results of a medical exam, but only if other applicants in the same job category are required to take the same exam. If the applicant is not hired because of the results of that exam, the employer must be able to demonstrate both of the following:
    - Not hiring the applicant was consistent with business necessity (e.g., the applicant would pose a direct threat or a significant risk of substantial harm to the health or safety of the applicant or others)
    - That threat cannot be eliminated or reduced significantly through reasonable accommodation(s)[150]

All of an employee's medical information, including any requests for reasonable accommodations, must be kept confidential and in a medical file separate from the employee's personnel file.[151] Only the following people may have access to such information:

- Supervisors and managers may be informed regarding necessary restrictions on the work or duties of the employee and necessary accommodations.
- First aid and safety personnel may be informed, when appropriate, if the disability might require emergency treatment.
- Government officials investigating compliance with the ADA shall be provided relevant information on request.[152]

---

150. *Enforcement Guidance on Disability-Related Inquiries and Medical Examinations of Employees under the ADA*, *supra* note 148.

151. Many states have labor laws entitling an employee to review and/or receive copies of their personnel file. For example, California has codified these rights in California Labor Code sections 226 and 1198.5.

152. 42 U.S.C. § 12112(d)(3)(B).

## B. Disclosure and the FMLA

If an employee requests time off under the FMLA, the employer has the right to ask for a medical certification from a health care provider to demonstrate that the employee has a serious medical condition under the FMLA.[153] Health care providers who are permitted to complete the FMLA certification include:[154]

- Doctors of medicine or osteopathy
- Podiatrists, dentists, clinical psychologists, optometrists, and chiropractors
- Nurse practitioners, nurse-midwives, and clinical social workers and physician assistants
- Christian Scientist practitioners
- Any health care provider recognized by the employer or the employer's benefits manager

If the employer requires medical certification, the employer must allow the employee at least 15 calendar days to secure the certification unless that is not practicable.[155] The employee is responsible for paying for any costs associated with getting the medical certification and for making sure the certification is provided to the employer. If the certification is not complete or sufficient, the employer must inform the employee in writing and state what additional information is necessary to make the certification complete and sufficient. The employee must provide the additional information to the employer within seven calendar days, in most circumstances.[156]

The DOL offers model medical certification forms for employees to complete;[157] however, many employers use their own forms. Employers are not entitled to request additional information beyond that requested on the model form. A medical certification may include contact information and practice area for the health care provider; the date the serious health condition began and how long it will last; a description of medical facts about the condition; and information showing that the employee cannot perform the essential functions of the job.[158] For employees who need leave to care for a family member, a certification should include a statement of the care needed.[159]

It is important for employees to communicate with their health care team if they wish to keep their exact diagnosis confidential from their employers because medical certification forms may request information that will disclose a diagnosis. For example, an employer's customized medical certification form may include a space for the

---

153. 29 U.S.C. § 2613, but note: an employer may not request a certification for leave to bond with a newborn child or a child placed for adoption or foster care.
154. 29 C.F.R. § 825.125 (2015).
155. *Id.* § 825.305(b).
156. *Id.* § 825.305(c).
157. *Id.* § 825.306(b).
158. *Id.* § 825.306.
159. *Id.* § 825.306(a).

employee's doctor to write in the employee's diagnosis or it may just have a space for the health care provider's medical specialty.

There may be limited instances when an employer may contact an employee's health care provider. Under the FMLA, an employer may contact an employee's health care provider only to "authenticate" and "clarify" the information provided on a medical certification form.[160] Authentication means that the employer can verify that the health care provider actually signed the paperwork and that it was not forged. Clarification means that the employer can ask questions of the health care provider because it cannot read the handwriting or there is something else confusing about the medical certification form. Employers cannot ask for additional information from an employee's health care provider. Employers are not permitted to ask for copies of an employee's medical records or to put medical information in an employee's regular personnel file. Under no circumstances may an employee's direct supervisor contact an employee's health care provider.[161] Additionally, if the employer has reason to doubt the validity of the certification, it may require the employee to obtain a second opinion at the employer's expense.[162]

The employer can choose the health care provider to provide the second opinion, but generally may not select a health care provider who it employs on a regular or routine basis.[163] If the second opinion differs from the original certification, the employer may require the employee to obtain a third certification from a health care provider selected by both the employee and employer.[164] The opinion of the third health care provider is final and must be used by the employer. The employer is responsible for paying for the second and third opinions, including any reasonable travel expenses for the employee or family member.[165] While waiting for the second (or third) opinion, the employee is provisionally entitled to FMLA leave.[166]

There are circumstances where an employer would want to recertify that an employee is still in need of taking medical leave. Under the FMLA, an employer may request the employee to provide a recertification no more often than every 30 days.[167] If a certification indicates that the minimum duration of the serious health condition is more than 30 days, the employer must generally wait until that minimum duration expires before requesting recertification.[168]

Employers may also ask all similarly situated employees who take leave for similar health conditions to provide a return to work, or "fitness-for-duty," certification

160. *Id.* § 825.307.
161. *Id.* § 825.307(a).
162. 29 U.S.C. § 2613(c).
163. 29 C.F.R. § 825.307(b).
164. *Id.* § 825.307(c).
165. *Id.* § 825.307(e).
166. *Id.* § 825.307(b)(2).
167. *Id.* § 825.308(a).
168. *Id.* § 825.308(b).

from the employee's health care provider showing that the employee is able to resume work.[169] An employer may contact an employee's health care provider to clarify or authenticate a fitness-for-duty certification, but cannot delay the employee's return to work while making that contact.[170] An employer may not require second or third opinions for a fitness-for-duty certification.[171] The employee is responsible for any costs to obtain the fitness-for-duty certification.[172]

## C. Other Disclosure Issues

In addition to the medical privacy protections offered by the ADA and FMLA, and their requirements around medical certification, there are other disclosure issues that may arise for individuals diagnosed with cancer in the context of their impact on employability.

Many individuals diagnosed with cancer have an online footprint that includes activity on social media platforms, blogs, and websites. Using social media platforms and online tools can be very helpful as a source of information and support. However, it is important to remember that disclosing a cancer diagnosis online makes the information public and many employers search social media platforms and the internet in order to research job applicants and employees. An estimated 60 percent of employers use social media sites to screen job candidates, while 41 percent use social networking sites to research current employees.[173] Therefore, if you are concerned about disclosure, there are some online and social media options that provide greater levels of privacy and allow you to only invite certain people to the conversation, such as MyLifeLine.org and CaringBridge. Online fundraisers (otherwise known as "crowdfunding") have become very popular over the past few years as a way to help raise funds for individuals coping with cancer. However, it is important to remember that these fundraisers are typically searchable by name in online search engines like Google.

Other places ripe for inadvertent disclosure in the context of employment include background checks during the hiring process. Some states still allow employers to include a credit check as part of a background check.[174] If an individual's credit score has suffered as a result of medical debt, then that is something to be aware of and prepared to answer questions about.

169. *Id.* § 825.312.

170. *Id.* § 825.312(b).

171. *Id.*

172. *Id.* § 825.312(c).

173. *60% of Employers Are Peeking into Candidates' Social Media Profiles*, CAREERBUILDER, https://www.careerbuilder.com/advice/blog/60-of-employers-are-peeking-into-candidates-social-media-profiles (last visited Nov. 8, 2024).

174. *State Laws*, TRIAGE CANCER, https://triagecancer.org/state-laws (last visited Nov. 8, 2024).

Specific to the work context, remember that most employers legally "own" their employees' work voicemail, email, and computer equipment. For individuals concerned about disclosure in the workplace, they should consider using personal voicemail or email for communication with health care providers. Furthermore, with the explosion in the use of social media, some employers have started to ask for access to employees' personal social media passwords. Many states have begun to address this legislatively; see https://triagecancer.org/state-laws for more information.

## VII. Other Employment Topics

There are other employment issues that may arise for an individual diagnosed with cancer and their caregivers.

For instance, if an employee's cancer was caused in whole or in part by their work conditions, they may also have rights and claims for compensation and relief under workers' compensation laws. Injuries that occur in the course and scope of employment entitle employees to certain wage replacement and medical treatment compensation through an employer's workers' compensation coverage. Many employers have workers' compensation insurance, and in some states are required to have such coverage.[175]

This section will highlight a few of the other topics that are important for employees to consider.

### A. Individuals Who Are Self-Employed

For an individual who is self-employed, a cancer diagnosis can pose a number of challenges. Self-employed individuals may be faced with stepping away from their work because of their diagnosis and treatment, but may not have the support systems in place that employees of larger companies might have. For example, if an individual who is self-employed has not been paying into the Social Security retirement system within the past five years, and that individual can no longer work because of a medical condition, that individual will not be able to access Social Security Disability Insurance benefits. The Social Security Administration has more information about self-employment and paying Social Security taxes in its document "If You Are Self-Employed" at https://www.ssa.gov/pubs/EN-05-10022.pdf. A similar issue arises for self-employed individuals who live in states that have state-sponsored short-term disability insurance programs. If they were not paying into those systems, then they would be unable to draw on those benefits. See Chapter 3, Disability Insurance, for more information.

---

175. For example, California requires employers to have either workers' compensation insurance or be self-insured as authorized. CAL. LAB. CODE § 3700 (2002).

Being self-employed can also pose other work-related challenges when it comes to making decisions about working through treatment or taking time off work. For instance, a self-employed individual may have limited options in accessing reasonable accommodations that involve shifting workload. Without another staff member to share the work, a self-employed individual may need to hire additional staff; however, this would impact a self-employed individual's income. Furthermore, the ability to take time off work may be hindered by ongoing client projects with pressing deadlines. A self-employed individual may also have more significant concerns about disclosing a cancer diagnosis to existing or potential clients and business partners, for fear of losing business opportunities.

Alternatively, after coping with a cancer diagnosis, some individuals are compelled to change careers and start working for themselves. Self-employment may provide some flexibility around balancing work and a cancer diagnosis that working for a larger company might not. However, there may be a different set of challenges when working for themselves (e.g., income stability, the cost of health insurance, and access to disability benefits). The U.S. government provides information on starting a business and self-employment: https://www.usa.gov/start-business.

## B. Unemployment Benefits

Generally, when an individual is let go from a job, the individual is eligible for unemployment benefits. The amount that an individual will receive depends on where an individual lives and their past earnings. If an employee chooses to leave a job, they are generally not eligible for unemployment benefits. However, if an employee leaves a job because it is not safe for the employee to remain working, the employee may still be eligible for unemployment benefits. It may be helpful for an employee to talk to their health care team about documenting their medical condition and why it was not safe for the employee to remain at work. Generally, an individual cannot be eligible for both Social Security Disability Insurance benefits and unemployment benefits. Every state's program has different rules and processes, but most states require individuals to certify that they are able to work and are actively looking for work, while the Social Security Administration requires individuals to be unable to work because of a medical condition. If an individual is denied unemployment benefits, they can file an appeal. For more information about unemployment benefits, visit https://triagecancer.org/stateresources.

## C. Considerations When Returning to Work

When returning to work, an employee may be returning to a previous employer after extended time off, or may be starting a new job. The rights and benefits of employees depend on their situation and their employer. As a starting point, it is helpful for employees to consult their employer's policies, as many employers provide benefits beyond what the law requires.

For employees returning to work after a period of time off, there are different right-to-work rights under the FMLA and ADA.

If an employee took leave under the FMLA, then the law requires that the employee be reinstated to the same or an "equivalent" position as the one the employee had before taking **time off.**[176] An equivalent position is one with equivalent pay, benefits, responsibilities, and other conditions of employment.[177] There are some exceptions when an employer will not be required to reinstate an employee:[178]

1. If the employee notifies the employer that they do not plan to return to work
2. If the employee's job position was eliminated while they were on leave (e.g., a reduction in force)
3. If the employee would have been terminated for a legitimate reason (e.g., misconduct)
4. If the employee was a highly paid key employee and the leave would cause substantial economic injury to the business[179]
5. If the employee is unable to return to work after exhausting their allotted FMLA leave (but be aware of an employer's ongoing duty to accommodate an eligible employee under the ADA)

For employees who take leave under the ADA as a reasonable accommodation, the law requires reinstatement to the same job, unless reinstatement to the same job is an undue hardship for the employer. If so, the employer may have to reinstate an employee to any available vacant position the employee is qualified to perform.

For employees who need support for preparing to go back to work, vocational rehabilitation may be useful. Vocational rehabilitation programs are run by state Departments of Rehabilitation (DORs) and provide different services, including peer support, skills development, systems advocacy, referrals, assistive technology services, transition services, housing assistance, and personal assistance services. To find a state's DOR, visit https://triagecancer.org/stateresources.

Once an employee has returned to work, they can consider using reasonable accommodations or medical leave to balance any long- or late-term side effects that may impact the ability to work.

For information about returning to work and transitioning off disability insurance, see Chapter 3, Disability Insurance.

---

176. 29 C.F.R. § 825.215.
177. *Id.*
178. *Id.* § 825.216.
179. *Id.* § 825.216(b).

## D. Considerations When Leaving Work

Individuals diagnosed with cancer or caregivers may find that they need to take time off, for a short period of time, for a longer period of time, or stop working entirely. Employees may also find themselves experiencing a loss of employment unrelated to cancer, such as when an employer goes out of business. These are some key issues for employees to consider when leaving a job:

- Confirm how and when a last paycheck will be received, if applicable.
- Check to see if owed payment for any unused vacation time. Employers may have policies about what they will pay out, and the rules vary from state to state.
- If an employee is eligible for COBRA or state COBRA, the employee should make sure to have the necessary paperwork and know where to send completed paperwork and payments in the future.
- Are there employee benefits that can be converted into an individual policy (e.g., vision, dental, supplemental, disability, or life insurance policy)? Note that if an employer paid the premiums for these policies before, an employee will likely have to pay the premiums moving forward.
- An employee should understand the options with respect to any retirement accounts (e.g., can the employee roll over funds into an individual retirement account?). If unsure of the best course of action, meeting with a financial planner may be useful (https://findanafc.org/search).
- If considering applying for unemployment benefits, will the employer contest the application?
- If an employee is planning on moving, make sure that the past employer has the new address to send tax documents in the future.
- Be prepared to return any equipment that belongs to the employer. For example, if an employee has a company cell phone, they should make sure to save any personal contacts. If an employee has a company computer, the employee should make sure to clean off any personal information.
- If an employee is interested, they can ask their employer to set up an automatic response for the employee's email account that provides forwarding contact information.

Generally, an employer should have someone available to help answer these questions for employees who are preparing to leave their job. Some employers have an internal HR department or staff person; some hire an external company to handle their HR needs. Some smaller employers do not have any HR staff. If an employee is not sure whom to ask, the employee can start with the person who handles timesheets or other employment paperwork. There are usually deadlines to make these decisions, so it is important for employees to not delay getting the information they need to make them.

## E. Considerations for Caregivers

In addition to the many psychosocial aspects of caregiving, there are also legal issues that can impact caregivers, particularly in the area of employment.

The ADA and state fair employment laws protect caregivers against discrimination in the workplace.[180] This means that employers cannot make employment-related decisions based on an employee's caregiver status, such as decisions around hiring, firing, benefits, promotions, bonuses, and more.

For a caregiver who needs to take time off work to fulfill caregiving responsibilities, the FMLA can be a useful tool. The challenge with the FMLA is that while it provides up to 12 weeks per year of job-protected leave, it is unpaid leave. For a caregiver who does not have access to paid time off, taking unpaid leave may not be a realistic option. And, there are limited options available to caregivers to replace those lost wages.

One option is state-sponsored paid family leave. As of 2024, 12 states and the District of Columbia provide paid family leave benefits for caregivers: California, Colorado, Connecticut, Delaware, Maryland, Massachusetts, New Jersey, New York, Oregon, Rhode Island, Washington, and Washington, D.C.

### 1. State Paid Family Leave Programs

**California.** The Paid Family Leave (PFL) program began in 2004 and covers all private-sector employers as well as some public-sector employers. An employee must have paid into the State Disability Insurance (SDI) program during the previous 18 months. An employee must have earned at least $300 in gross wages during the base period from which SDI deductions were taken. The program does not have a waiting period, but the employer may require that an employee use up to two weeks of vacation time or other paid time off before getting PFL benefits. The program does not provide job protection, but an employee may be covered by other laws that provide such protection. An employee can receive between 60 and 70 percent of pay, depending on their income, for up to eight weeks in a 12-month period. For details, visit https://edd.ca.gov/en/disability/paid-family-leave.

**Colorado.** The Paid Family and Medical Leave Insurance program began January 1, 2024. It covers employers with one or more employees during each of 20 or more calendar workweeks during the year. It excludes federal employers, and local government employers may opt out. However, self-employed persons and local government employees may choose to pay into the program. To qualify, an employee must have earned at least $2,500 in wages during the base year or year prior. The program requires continuation of health insurance benefits, as well as reinstatement to the previous or equivalent position if employed at least 180 days before taking leave. An employee can receive up to 90 percent of the state average weekly wage and

180. *Questions & Answers: Association Provision of the ADA*, *supra* note 53.

50 percent of the portion of their wage that exceeds the state average weekly wage. Benefits last up to 12 weeks, or up to 16 weeks if the disability is pregnancy-related. For details, visit https://famli.colorado.gov.

**Connecticut.** The Paid Family and Medical Leave program began January 1, 2022, and covers all employers. To qualify, employees must work in the state, have earned at least $2,325 during the highest earning quarter within the base period, and be either presently employed or have been employed in the previous 12 weeks by an employer. This program does not offer job protection. An employee can receive 95 percent of their weekly wage on a sliding scale. Benefits last up to 12 weeks, or 14 weeks if the disability is pregnancy-related. For details, visit https://portal.ct.gov/dol.

**Delaware.** The Healthy Delaware Families Act will begin January 1, 2026. Individuals who work for an employer with ten or more employees will have access to parental leave during the first year after a child's birth, adoption, or foster care placement. Individuals who work for an employer with 25+ employees will have access to leave to care for a family member with a serious health condition or their own serious health condition. Employees must work for their employer for one year and at least 1,250 hours in the past 12 months to be eligible. Individuals may receive up to 80 percent of their average weekly wage, and continuation of health benefits, and reinstatement to their previous position, or an equivalent one, after leave. Qualified individuals will receive up to 12 weeks of leave. For details, visit https://www.jacksonlewis.com/sites/default/files/docs/HealthyDelawareFamiliesActEngrossment.pdf.

**Maryland.** The Time to Care Act provides access to paid family and medical leave beginning July 1, 2026. Leave can be taken to care for a family member, or an employee's own serious medical condition. Individuals will be eligible if they have worked 680 hours in the past 12 months. Self-employed individuals can opt in. Individuals can receive up to 12 weeks of paid leave. For details, visit https://paidleave.maryland.gov.

**Massachusetts.** The Massachusetts Paid Family and Medical Leave program began January 1, 2021, and covers all employers. Employers may use the state plan or a state-approved private plan. Self-employed individuals may choose coverage under certain conditions. If an employee has earned at least $6,000 during the past four calendar quarters, and at least 30 times more than how much the employee is eligible to get each week in benefits, the employee qualifies for benefits. Employers covered by this program must provide continuation of health insurance benefits, and reinstatement to an employee's previous or equivalent position. An employee can receive 80 percent of their income, up to 50 percent of the state average weekly wage, and then 50 percent of the employee's wage that exceeds the state average weekly wage. Benefits last up to 12 weeks for family leave, 20 weeks for medical leave, and 26 weeks for military caregiver leave. For details, visit https://www.mass.gov/orgs/department-of-family-and-medical-leave.

**New Hampshire.** The Granite State PFL Plan began January 1, 2023, and covers state employers. However, private employers may opt in. Even if they do not, if the employer has more than 50 employees, employees may still opt in. If employers do opt in, they receive a tax credit of 50 percent of the premium paid, and employees receive job protection. An employee can receive 60 percent of their wages for up to six weeks of leave in a 12-month period. The program has a seven-month waiting period, a one-week elimination period, and a 60-day annual open enrollment period. For details, visit https://www.paidfamilymedicalleave.nh.gov.

**New Jersey.** The New Jersey Family Leave Insurance program began in 2009, and covers all employers. Employers can use the state plan or a state-approved private plan. To have qualified in 2024, an employee must have either (1) worked 20 calendar weeks in New Jersey in the base year, earning $283 or more each week; or (2 earned $14,200 or more in the past year prior to the start of family leave. There is no waiting period. An employee may choose to (but an employer cannot require them to) use vacation/paid time off at 100 percent of pay instead of receiving benefits through this program. This program provides job protection. An employee can receive from 85 percent of their average weekly wage up to the maximum amount. Benefits last up to 12 weeks (56 days) or until the benefits equal one-third of the employee's total wages during the year, whichever is less. For details, visit https://www.nj.gov/labor/myleavebenefits/worker/fli/index.shtml.

**New York.** The New York PFL program began in 2018, and covers most employers. To qualify, an employee must be scheduled for at least 20 hours per week for 26 consecutive weeks, or if scheduled for fewer than 20 average hours per week, must show 175 days worked. This program has no waiting period. It does provide job protection. An employee can receive 67 percent of their average weekly wage or New York state average weekly wage, whichever is less. Benefits last for 12 weeks in a 12-month period. For details, visit https://paidfamilyleave.ny.gov/paid-family-leave-family-care.

**Oregon.** The Oregon Paid Family and Medical Leave (PFML) program began September 3, 2023, and covers any employer with one or more employees working in the state (excluding federal government employers). Tribal governments and self-employed workers may opt in. To qualify, an employee must have contributed to the PFML Insurance Fund during the base year (four of the past five quarters worked) and have earned at least $1,000 in wages during the base year or the prior year. This program requires the continuation of the employee's health insurance benefits and reinstatement to the previous or equivalent position, if employed at least 90 days before taking leave. The employee can choose to supplement this program with earned paid time off. An employee can receive up to 100 percent of their average weekly wage on a sliding scale, and benefits last up to 12 weeks in a 12-month period, or 14 weeks if the disability is pregnancy-related. For details, visit https://paidleave.oregon.gov/.

**Rhode Island.** The Temporary Caregiver Insurance (TCI) program began in 2014, and covers all private employees and some public employees. To qualify, the employee (1) must have been paid wages in Rhode Island and have paid into the TCI fund; and (2) must have been paid at least $16,800 in the base period or earned at least $2,800 in one quarter with total taxable wages at least 1.5 times the highest quarter of earnings and base period taxable wages equal to at least $5,600. This program requires maintenance of health benefits while on leave and provides job protection. Leave must last for seven or more consecutive days to be eligible for benefits. An employee can receive 4.62 percent of wages paid in the highest base period quarter, and benefits last up to six weeks. For details, visit https://dlt.ri.gov/individuals/temporary-disability-caregiver-insurance.

**Washington.** The Paid Family and Medical Leave program began in 2020, and covers all employers. Self-employed workers may opt in. To qualify for the state plan, an employee must have been employed for at least 820 hours in the qualifying period. To qualify for the voluntary plan, an employee must have worked 340 hours in the past 12 months. There is a one-week waiting period, except for leave to bond with a new child and qualifying exigency leaves. The state plan provides job protection and health insurance protection for employees who have worked at least 12 months, worked 1,250 hours in the 12 months immediately preceding leave, and work for an employer who has 50+ employees. An employee can receive up to 90 percent of their average weekly wage up to the state average weekly wage, and then 50 percent of the employee's average weekly wage exceeding that. Benefits last for up to 12 weeks for medical or family leave and up to 16 weeks of combined family and medical leave if an employee has more than one qualifying event in the same claim year. For details, visit https://paidleave.wa.gov.

**Washington,** D.C. The Universal PFL program began in 2020, and covers all private employers, unless they are exempt from D.C. taxes by federal law or treaty. A self-employed individual may opt in. To qualify, an employee must work more than 50 percent of the time in D.C. in the 52 calendar weeks immediately preceding leave or regularly spend a substantial amount of time working in D.C. without spending more than 50 percent of their work time in another jurisdiction. There is a one-week waiting period for this program. This program does not provide job protection. An employee can receive up to 90 percent of their average weekly wage up to 150 percent of D.C.'s minimum wage, and then 50 percent of their average weekly wage that exceeds 150 percent of D.C.'s minimum wage. Benefits last up to six weeks for family caregiver leave, up to six weeks for medical leave, and up to eight weeks for parental leave. For details, visit https://does.dc.gov/page/dc-paid-family-leave.

## 2. In-Home Support Services

There is another benefit that may be available to individuals who need to take time off work for their caregiving responsibilities, but who are concerned about potential lost wages. Some state Medicaid programs have benefits to help Medicaid-eligible individuals remain in their homes. Eligibility requirements vary from state to state, but in most circumstances, an individual must be over the age of 65 or have a disability to qualify. Programs are named differently in each state; for example, in California, "In-Home Supportive Services," and in Michigan, the "Choice Waiver." Caregiving services that may be covered under these programs include housecleaning, meal preparation, laundry, grocery shopping, personal care services (e.g., bowel and bladder care, bathing, and grooming), and accompaniment to medical appointments. If an individual qualifies for a program, it may be possible for a family member to provide the caregiving services and get paid by the program. However, only 23 states allow spouses to be compensated as caregivers: Alabama, Arizona, California, Colorado, Delaware, Florida, Hawaii, Indiana, Kentucky, Louisiana, Maryland, Minnesota, Montana, New Hampshire, New Jersey, New Mexico, North Carolina, North Dakota, Oklahoma, Oregon, Utah, Vermont, and Wisconsin.[181] State programs can be found at https://triagecancer.org/stateresources.

### 3. Respite Care

Caregivers may sometimes need help with or need a break from their caregiving responsibilities. Caregivers should consider asking other family members, friends, neighbors, or other members of their support community to help. Professional respite services can also be provided through in-home care agencies, adult day services, facilities that allow short-term stays, and individuals that are hired directly. There may also be local support programs for caregivers, which can be found here: https://eldercare.acl.gov/Public/Resources/Topic/Caregiver.aspx.

## F. Medical Marijuana

Although medical marijuana has been legalized for medical purposes in 39 states, the District of Columbia, and Guam, as of February 2024, it is still illegal to use, possess, or sell marijuana under federal law. This creates a conflict in the law and confusion for individuals diagnosed with cancer who are trying to make medical decisions about using marijuana to alleviate side effects from treatment. State laws vary widely in what they allow for and some specify medical conditions, limiting use to those who have been diagnosed with epilepsy or seizure disorders.[182]

This area of the law is changing rapidly and one issue that poses a potential challenge for patients is how employers treat medical marijuana usage. Generally, employers are required to accommodate an eligible employee, unless it poses an undue hardship on the employer or a direct threat to the employee or others. There are also some professions (e.g., public safety, military, pilots, bus drivers, etc.) that have additional regulations or requirements (e.g., Occupational Safety and Health

---

181. *Spouses Can Be Paid Caregivers for Their Husbands or Wives*, Paying for Senior Care, https://www.payingforseniorcare.com/paying-spousal-caregivers (last visited Nov. 8, 2024).

182. *Other Cancer-Related State Laws*, Triage Cancer, https://triagecancer.org/state-laws/cancer-related (last visited Nov. 8, 2024).

Administration, U.S. Department of Transportation, Federal Aviation Administration, etc.) that are relevant to the discussion of whether or not employers should or must accommodate employees who use medical marijuana.

In *Garcia v. Tractor Supply Co.*,[183] a New Mexico federal court ruled that employers do not need to accommodate drug use that is illegal under federal law. However, there are some state exceptions that may impact the ruling in this case. For example, Connecticut and Delaware state laws mandate employers accommodate medical marijuana cardholders. Some states (e.g., Arizona, Connecticut, Delaware, Rhode Island) prohibit employers from discriminating against employees for their use of medical marijuana.

Further complicating the issue, marijuana has also been legalized for recreational use in 24 states.[184] However, employers are not required to accommodate recreational use of marijuana. In Colorado, for example, employers are not required to accommodate recreational use, whereas Washington state law does not specifically address workplace accommodation of medical marijuana usage.

Given the recent tide in state laws, some employers are creating accommodations for their employees who use medical marijuana even though they are not required to accommodate. Employees diagnosed with cancer should ensure that they are not violating employer policies by using medical or recreational marijuana, or risk termination.

### G. Genetic Discrimination

Some employees who have been diagnosed with cancer or who have a genetic predisposition to developing cancer may be concerned about employment discrimination. For a discussion on genetic employment discrimination, see Chapter 4, Biomarkers and Genetics.

## VIII. Case Law

Often, even after a law is passed, there are still questions about how the law will be applied in real life situations. As a result, individuals must rely on court interpretations of the law to gain a better understanding of their rights. Court interpretations of the ADA and FMLA offer a deeper understanding of protections against discrimination and the use of medical leave.

183. No. 15-cv-00735 (D.N.M. Jan. 7, 2016).

184. Kate Bryan, *Cannabis Overview*, NCSL (June 20, 2024), https://www.ncsl.org/civil-and-criminal-justice/cannabis-overview.

## A. Post-ADAAA Cases Addressing Whether Cancer Is a Disability

### 1. *Norton v. Assisted Living Concepts, Inc.*

In *Norton,*[185] Michael J. Norton brought suit against his employer, Assisted Living Concepts, Inc. (ALC), alleging that ALC violated the ADA.[186] Norton claimed that ALC fired him because he suffered from *renal cancer*.[187] ALC moved for summary judgment and argued that the plaintiff's cancer did not qualify as a disability under the ADA because it was in remission at the time that the plaintiff was fired.[188] Therefore, the issue in this case was whether Norton's renal cancer constituted a disability under the ADA.

The court noted that in order to show a prima facie case of discrimination under the ADA, the plaintiff must establish "(1) he suffers from a disability; (2) he is qualified for the job despite the disability; (3) he was subjected to an adverse employment action due to the disability; and (4) he was treated less favorably than non-disabled employees."[189] The act defines a person with a disability as one who (1) has an actual "physical or mental impairment that substantially limits one or more major life activities of such individual" (the actual disability prong); (2) "a record of such an impairment"; or (3) "being regarded as having such an impairment."[190]

The definition of "major life activities" under the ADA's first prong encompasses "major bodily functions," including normal cell growth.[191] Furthermore, the ADA emphasized that as long as a disability substantially limits one major life activity, such as normal cell growth, it need not limit other life activities.[192] Finally, the ADA makes clear that "an impairment that is episodic or in remission, is a disability if it would substantially limit a major life activity when active."[193]

Applying the definition of "disability" to the facts of the case, the court held that Norton's renal cancer qualified as a disability for purposes of the ADA.[194] The court also held that renal cancer, when active, substantially limits the major life activity of normal cell growth.[195] Therefore, the court concluded that (1) the fact that Norton's renal cancer was in remission when he returned to work was irrelevant, and (2) Norton's renal cancer qualified as a disability even if the only major life activity it substantially limited is normal cell growth.[196]

---

185. Norton v. Assisted Living Concepts, Inc., 786 F. Supp. 2d 1173 (E.D. Tex. 2011).
186. *Id.*
187. *Id.*
188. *Id.*
189. *Id.* at 1184 (citing McInnis v. Alamo Cmty. Coll. Dist., 207 F.3d 276, 279–80 (5th Cir. 2000)).
190. *Id.* (citing 42 U.S.C. § 12102(1)).
191. 42 U.S.C. § 12102(2)(b).
192. *Id.*
193. *Id.* § 12102(4)(D).
194. *Norton*, 786 F. Supp. 2d at 1185.
195. *Id.* (citing 42 U.S.C. § 12102(4)(A), (B); *id.* § 12102(2)(B)).
196. *Id.*

*Note:* Norton *is significant case law because it gives individuals with cancer legal recourse against workplace discrimination even if the cancer is in remission when the discrimination occurs. Additionally,* Norton *saves individuals with cancer from the burden of proving that cancer substantially limits a major life activity. Cancer, by its very nature, limits normal cell growth in all cases and* Norton *says that limitation is enough for cancer to qualify as a disability for ADA purposes. Despite the outcome in this case, an individual analysis is used to determine if someone with cancer has a disability under the ADA.*

## 2. *Haley v. Community Mercy Health Partners*

In *Haley*,[197] the plaintiff, a registered nurse, alleged she was terminated after 32 years of employment because she took leave to care for a parent and then leave for her own breast cancer treatment. The court rejected the argument that the plaintiff could not be an individual with a disability under the ADA definition because she denied in her deposition that she is disabled, holding that an employee does not need to affirmatively self-identify as "disabled" in order to meet the legal definition of having a disability under the ADA.[198]

## 3. *Angell v. Fairmount Fire Protection District*

In *Angell*,[199] undisputed facts that the plaintiff had been diagnosed with *cancer*, and had undergone surgeries and treatment for his cancer, were adequate to defeat summary judgment on the question of whether the plaintiff was substantially limited in a major life activity. In reaching this conclusion, the court cited the ADAAA's "episodic or in remission rule" and the addition of the major bodily function of "normal cell growth," and quoted the new statutory provisions, legislative history, and various provisions of the EEOC's regulations, including 29 C.F.R. § 1630.2(j)(3)(iii) ("it should easily be concluded that . . . cancer substantially limits [the major life activity of] normal cell growth") and the appendix to 29 C.F.R. § 1630.4 ("We hope this will be an important signal to both lawyers and courts to spend less time and energy on the minutia of an individual's impairment, and more time and energy on the merits of the case—including whether discrimination occurred because of the disability. . . .") (internal quotation omitted).

## 4. *Hoffman v. Carefirst of Fort Wayne, Inc.*

In *Hoffman*,[200] the plaintiff, a medical equipment service technician, was diagnosed with stage III renal carcinoma in November 2007, took short-term disability leave for surgery and recovery, returned to work January 2, 2008, without restrictions, and did

197. Haley v. Cmty. Mercy Health Partners, Case No. 3:11-cv-232, 2013 WL 322493 (S.D. Ohio Jan. 28, 2013).
198. *Id.*
199. Angell v. Fairmount Fire Prot. Dist., 907 F. Supp. 2d 1242 (D. Colo. 2012).
200. Hoffman v. Carefirst of Fort Wayne, Inc., 737 F. Supp. 2d 976 (N.D. Ind. 2010).

not take any significant time off after returning to work. One year later, in response to a new requirement that all service technicians work overtime (between 65 and 70 hours per week) and do a night shift once a week, the plaintiff sought a reasonable accommodation, providing a doctor's note stating that "[p]atient may not work more than 8 hours/day, 5 days/week. Dx: Stage III renal cancer."[201] In the plaintiff's subsequent action challenging the denial of accommodation and resulting termination, the employer argued that the plaintiff did not have a substantially limiting impairment because at the time in question his cancer was in remission and he had been working for a year without restrictions. Rejecting this argument, the court held:

> [It] is bound by the clear language of the ADAAA . . . [which] clearly provides that "an impairment that is episodic or in remission is a disability if it would substantially limit a major life activity when active[.]" . . . In other words, under the ADAAA, because Hoffman had cancer in remission (and that cancer would have substantially limited a major life activity when it was active), Hoffman does not need to show that he was substantially limited in a major life activity at the actual time of the alleged adverse employment action.[202]

## B. Reasonable Accommodations Cases

The following cases provide further guidance on accessing and providing reasonable accommodations under the ADA.

1. *Kravits v. Shinseki*, No. 10-861, 2012 WL 604169 (W.D. Pa. Feb. 24, 2012) (oral request for accommodation is legally sufficient despite contrary employer policy)
2. *Cox v. Wal-Mart Stores, Inc.*, 441 F. App'x 547 (9th Cir. 2011) (employer's failure to tell employee that request is submitted on wrong form, or to provide time to return paperwork, can render the employer responsible for the breakdown in the interactive process)
3. *Valle-Arce v. Puerto Rico Ports Authority*, 651 F.3d 190 (1st Cir. 2011) (employer's denial of request on ground that information provided was not specific enough, without advising employee and asking for the additional details needed, can render the employer responsible for the breakdown in the interactive process)
4. *Colwell v. Rite Aid Corp.*, 602 F.3d 495 (3d Cir. 2010) (if the employer flatly turns down requested accommodation and fails to offer an available alternative that did not pose an undue hardship, the employer is responsible for the breakdown in the interactive process)

201. *Id.* at 982.
202. *Id.* at 985.

5. *Zombeck v. Friendship Ridge*, No. 08-1626, 2011 WL 666200 (W.D. Pa. Feb. 14, 2011) (employer at its peril simply ignores accommodation request because it believes employee does not have a disability)
6. *Green v. BakeMark USA LLC*, No. 16-3141, 2017 WL 1147168 (6th Cir. Mar. 27, 2017) (an employer is not required to provide a part-time schedule as an accommodation if full-time attendance is an essential function of the employee's job and duties could not be performed within restricted hours)

## C. FMLA Cases

The following cases provide additional guidance on accessing leave under the FMLA.

1. *Ragsdale v. Wolverine*, 535 U.S. 81 (2002) (an employer is not required to provide an additional 12 weeks of leave if they did not inform their employee that the leave the employee had already taken was FMLA leave)
2. *Smith v. Diffee Ford-Lincoln-Mercury, Inc.*, 298 F.3d 955 (10th Cir. 2002) (once an employee proves that they were entitled to FMLA leave and were terminated while on that leave, the burden of proof shifts to the employer to show that the employee would have been terminated for reasons unrelated to the FMLA leave (e.g., misconduct))
3. *Brown v. Eastern Maine Medical Center*, 514 F. Supp. 2d 104 (D. Me. 2007) (an employee is not protected by intermittent leave under the FMLA, when an employee is chronically late for work—usually only by a few minutes)
4. *Ballard v. Chicago Park District*, No. 13-1445 (7th Cir. Jan. 28, 2014) (an employee can use FMLA leave to serve as a caregiver, even if the person for whom the employee is caring is traveling)
5. *Whitaker v. Milwaukee County*, 772 F.3d 802 (7th Cir. 2014) (attendance may be an essential function of a job)

## D. Intersection of ADA and FMLA Cases

The following cases provide further guidance on how the ADA and FMLA may intersect.

1. *EEOC v. BMO Harris Bank*, No. 12-C-7793 (N.D. Ill. May 2, 2013) (employer paid $400,000 to settle a lawsuit filed by the EEOC, charging that the employer violated the ADA by terminating 14 employees whose medical leaves had run out, rather than offering accommodations that would have allowed them to return to work)[203]

---

203. Press Release, EEOC, BMO Harris Bank to Pay $400,000 to Resolve EEOC Disability Lawsuit (May 9, 2013), https://www.eeoc.gov/newsroom/bmo-harris-bank-pay-400000-resolve-eeoc-disability-lawsuit.

2. *EEOC v. United Road Towing, Inc.*, No. 10-CV-6259 (N.D. Ill. June 20, 2012) (employer paid $380,000 to settle a lawsuit filed by the EEOC, charging that the company maintained an inflexible leave policy that required termination at the end of medical leaves in violation of the ADA)[204]
3. *Severson v. Heartland Woodcraft, Inc.*, No. 15-3754 (7th Cir. Sept. 20, 2017) (despite previous rulings and EEOC guidance[205] to the contrary, an extended leave of absence for an employee is not a reasonable accommodation under the ADA) (*Note: The* Heartland *case has caused a jurisdictional split in court decisions, and will ultimately need to be decided by the U.S. Supreme Court.*)

## IX. Conclusion

With an increasing number of cancer survivors in the United States, nearly 50 percent of cancer survivors being of working age, and the fact that cancer survivors are more likely to be unemployed,[206] there is an increasing need to address cancer-related employment issues. Approximately 70–80 percent of working-age cancer survivors return to their jobs after a cancer diagnosis.[207] Furthermore, 20 percent of cancer survivors report work limitations affected by cancer-related problems five years after diagnosis.[208] Many cancer survivors want and are able to return to work after diagnosis and treatment.[209] Patients often correlate returning to work with regaining normalcy.[210] Employment is also associated with a higher quality of life.[211] However, in 2022, the EEOC received 760 cancer discrimination claims, suggesting that cancer survivors are still experiencing cancer-related legal issues that pose barriers to thriving in the workplace.[212] Therefore, cancer community advocates, health care professionals, and lawyers must continue to provide education and navigation around cancer-related employment issues.

---

204. Press Release, EEOC, United Road Towing to Pay $380,000 to Resolve EEOC Disability Discrimination Suit (June 25, 2012), https://www.eeoc.gov/newsroom/united-road-towing-pay-380000-resolve-eeoc-disability-discrimination-suit.

205. EEOC, Employer-Provided Leave and the Americans with Disabilities Act (2016), https://www.eeoc.gov/laws/guidance/employer-provided-leave-and-americans-disabilities-act.

206. Angela G.E.M. de Boer et al., *Cancer Survivors and Unemployment: A Meta-analysis and Meta-regression*, 301 JAMA 753 (2009).

207. Reshma Jagsi et al., *Impact of Adjuvant Chemotherapy on Long-Term Employment of Survivors of Early-Stage Breast Cancer*, 120 Cancer 1854 (2014).

208. Michael Feuerstein, Work and Cancer Survivors (2009).

209. Barbara Hoffman, *Cancer Survivors at Work: A Generation of Progress*, 55 CA: Cancer J. for Clinicians 271 (2005).

210. F. Kennedy et al., *Returning to Work Following Cancer: A Qualitative Exploratory Study into the Experience of Returning to Work Following Cancer*, 16 Eur. J. Cancer Care 17 (2007).

211. Evelien R. Spelten et al., *Factors Reported to Influence the Return to Work of Cancer Survivors: A Literature Review*, 11 Psychooncology 124 (2002).

212. *Enforcement and Litigation Statistics*, EEOC, https://www.eeoc.gov/data/enforcement-and-litigation-statistics-0 (last visited Nov. 8, 2024).

# X. Resources

For more information about employment and cancer:

Triage Cancer:
http://triagecancer.org/employment

For information about the ADA:

EEOC: https://www.eeoc.gov or (800) 669-4000

For information about the Rehabilitation Act of 1973:

U.S. Department of Justice—Civil Rights Division: https://www.justice.gov/crt or (800) 514-0301

For information about job accommodations:

JAN: https://askjan.org

For information about the FMLA:

DOL—Wage and Hour Division: https://www.dol.gov/agencies/whd/fmla or (866) 487-9243

For information about state fair employment agencies, fair employment laws, and leave laws:

Triage Cancer: https://triagecancer.org/stateresources; https://triagecancer.org/state-laws

# XI. Exercises and Discussion Topics

## A. Case Studies

1. Evan has been diagnosed with cancer. He is a full-time truck driver for a large, national shipping company with more than 100 employees. Evan is married, with two kids. His wife only works part-time, so he knows that he needs to work to pay his family's bills. His family has health insurance coverage through his employer. He does not remember the details of whether he has any employee benefits because he has not taken any time off work in three years. He has not discussed his treatment plan with his health care team. He is concerned about telling anyone at work about his diagnosis, for fear that they might treat him differently, or, worse yet, his boss might let him go. Evan's co-worker, Mark, was fired a few weeks after he asked for time off to take care of his dad, who had Alzheimer's. *What are Evan's options?*

   Evan could contact his HR representative to determine what employee benefits he is entitled to (e.g., paid sick days or disability insurance). Evan may also be eligible for 12 weeks of FMLA leave if his company has at least 50 employees. He has worked there at least three years and because he has not taken any time off work in three years, he has probably worked 1,250 hours in the past 12 months. If Evan will not be able to return to work after 12 weeks of FMLA leave, then he may be able to ask for additional time off as a reasonable accommodation under the ADA. If Evan chooses to leave his job to focus on treatment and recovery, and he loses access to his health insurance coverage, he may elect COBRA coverage or he could investigate his family's health insurance options in his State Health Insurance Marketplace (https://www.healthcare.gov).

2. Carlos is 24 years old and is a childhood cancer survivor. He is very excited about graduating from college in a few weeks. Carlos has some trouble with mild depression, fatigue, anxiety, and memory problems, so he took a lighter load each semester, setting back his graduation date. He is ready to start looking for a job and is concerned about how to enter the job market with a history of cancer and his ongoing health issues. He is wondering if he has to disclose his medical history and if people will still hire him if he does. He is also wondering about his health insurance options. *What are Carlos's options?*
3. After Mariko was diagnosed with cancer of the tonsils and larynx, she decided to work through her treatment. Mariko works as a cashier at a large supermarket chain. She has not told anyone at work about her medical condition. She took two weeks of vacation time for her surgery and recovery. She is now in the third week of her chemotherapy and is having trouble with fatigue and is limited in how long she can stand at a time. She also has to constantly drink water because of the effect of treatment on her salivary glands. As a result of the large volume of water she consumes, she has to urinate frequently. The supermarket does not allow employees to have beverages at the checkout stand and she is only allowed breaks every four hours. *What options does Mariko have?*
4. Marcus is 51 and has been diagnosed with cancer. Marcus has been an executive at a bank for four years and often works 60+ hours a week. He often comes home for dinner with his family and then works late at night from his home office. The bank branch where he works has 16 employees, but there are two other branches in town, one with 19 employees and one with 24. Marcus has not talked to his health care team about his treatment options yet, but thinks he will need to take time off work for treatment. However, he is worried about losing his job, his family's health insurance coverage, and his life insurance coverage that he gets through his employer. He has four weeks of vacation time accrued because he rarely gets an opportunity to use it, and 24 hours of sick time that he can use. He thinks his employer offers some type of disability insurance. He is also thinking about asking if he can work from home, depending on his treatment. *What are his options? What should his next steps be?*
5. Liam's mother has cancer. He works at a large company and would like to take time off work, but his employer said this is a "bad time." When Liam asked

about the FMLA, the employer gave him a large stack of paperwork to fill out. Included in the stack of papers was a document that asked Liam to provide the contact information for his mother's doctor and a release form to allow the employer to get a copy of his mother's medical record. Liam is not only a private person and has not shared at work what his family is going through, but his mother has a hereditary cancer. Liam has taken a genetic test to learn about his predisposition for a cancer diagnosis, and is waiting for the test results. Liam is concerned about sharing his mother's diagnosis with his employer. *What are Liam's options?*

## B. Class Exercises

1. **Reasonable accommodations.** Count off in the room or assign groups of two or three to work together. Identify a numbered list of jobs, corresponding to a numbered list of common side effects of cancer treatment. Assign each group a job and a side effect and ask group members to think about the requirements of that particular job, determine what might be challenging about doing the job while experiencing the specific side effect, and then identify possible reasonable accommodations that might assist that employee in doing their job. For example:

| | |
|---|---|
| Nurse—neuropathy | School teacher—weakened immune system |
| Firefighter—fatigue | Construction worker—limited range of motion |
| Executive assistant—chemo brain | Airline pilot—need to change ostomy bags |

2. **Mock interview.** Draft questions for a job interview that contain a mixture of permissible and impermissible questions. After you have completed your questionnaire, pair up with another classmate and interview them. When you finish the interview, ask your classmate which questions they think are impermissible and why. Then, practice the interview again and try to develop model responses to prohibited questions, with the understanding that just because they are impermissible does not mean that a job applicant will not face those questions in an interview. When the class is finished with mock interviews, each team should share their sample impermissible questions and model responses with the class. Some examples of questions include:

   Are there any accommodations that you might need to meet the requirements of this job?

   Do you have any medical conditions that I should know about?

   What did you do during this gap on your resume?

   It is really important that you are available to come to work. Is there any reason why you think you will not be able to meet the attendance requirements of the job?

I noticed on your LinkedIn profile that you are a volunteer for a lot of groups related to cancer. Are you a cancer survivor?

3. **Review job applications.** Collect or have students collect job applications from their community. Review the applications for questions that might pose a challenge for someone with a cancer diagnosis, and in particular someone who does not want to disclose that diagnosis while applying for a job.
4. **Review FMLA forms.** Look at the model DOL FMLA forms for employees who want to take time off for their own medical condition or as a caregiver. What questions on the model form may pose a challenge for someone who does not want to disclose a diagnosis while applying for a job?

## C. Discussion Topics

1. The FMLA only applies to private employers with 50 or more employees. In addition, the FMLA only allows eligible employees to take off work up to 12 weeks per year, to care for a spouse, a parent, or a child. What are some ways in which this could be limiting for someone diagnosed with cancer or their caregiver? How might access to the FMLA be expanded? What are the public policy pros and cons of expanding access to the FMLA's protections? Should there be some version of federal paid leave in the United States?
2. What are some of the practical challenges for individuals with cancer to enforce their employment rights? What does it take to prove discrimination? Are there ways to lessen the burden of proof on employees?
3. The ADA protects eligible employees with a disability from discrimination in the workplace. The ADA defines disability as a physical or mental impairment that substantially limits a major life activity. The ADA also defines major life activities as activities such as breathing, eating, thinking, and the operation of major bodily functions. If the ADA includes cell growth as a major bodily function, is there an argument to be made that all people diagnosed with cancer qualify as having a disability under the ADA, by definition? Does this change the intent of the ADA? Are there other types of medical conditions where this would apply? Do disability determinations still need to occur on a case-by-case basis? Why or why not?
4. The FMLA limits the information to which employers are entitled with respect to an employee's medical condition, while still giving an employer enough information to determine if an employee is eligible for medical leave. The DOL has model forms that employers can use for the employees to complete. Some employers choose to use their own forms, some of which ask for more information than the model forms. What challenges might this pose for someone with a cancer diagnosis? Should all employers be required to use the model forms? Why or why not?

# CHAPTER THREE

# Disability Insurance

## *Case Study: Mary*

*Mary is a 62-year-old nurse who was diagnosed with cancer early last year. When she had her surgery, she took six weeks off under the Family and Medical Leave Act (FMLA) and was paid a portion of her salary through an employer-sponsored short-term disability policy. A co-worker recommended that she retire early, but Mary really loves her job. As a result of her treatment, she is suffering from depression and "chemo brain" (short-term memory loss, inability to focus, etc.) as well as a tremor in her left hand. These side effects of treatment make her feel like she cannot continue to do her nursing job. The hospital pays for her health insurance coverage and has a rule that they will pay 100 percent of her premiums while receiving employer-sponsored disability benefits, but does not cover health insurance for retirees. She has some other benefits through her job at the hospital and as a union member, but she has not looked at that binder of paperwork in several years. She has some savings but is concerned about how she is going to pay her bills after her savings are exhausted. She is also concerned that if she applies for disability benefits she would never be able to go back to work. What are Mary's options?*

## I. Introduction

As of January 2021, 61 million Americans, or one in four, live with disabilities.[1] Twenty-five percent of today's 20-year-olds will experience a disability before they

1. *Disability and Health Data System (DHDS)*, Ctrs. for Disease Control & Prevention, http://dhds.cdc.gov (last visited Nov. 16, 2024).

retire.[2] Approximately 7.5 million people receive Supplemental Security Income (SSI)[3] and 9.3 million people receive Social Security Disability Insurance (SSDI) benefits.[4]

Experiencing a serious medical diagnosis like cancer can have a devastating impact on an individual's entire life, especially if the cancer diagnosis and subsequent treatment prevent the individual from working. One survey found that 90 percent of individuals felt that their "ability to earn an income" was "valuable" or "very valuable" in helping them achieve long-term financial security.[5] The study also revealed a belief that an individual's ability to earn an income was even more valuable to them than retirement savings, medical insurance, personal possessions, other forms of savings, or the individual's home.[6]

If an individual is unable to work for a short or long period of time as a result of a cancer diagnosis and subsequent treatment, they will likely need to find alternative sources of income. One option may be to use disability insurance benefits. Disability insurance is insurance coverage that provides individuals with some income (generally 45 percent to 90 percent of an individual's monthly salary) while they are unable to work as a result of a serious medical condition. In one review of private long-term disability (LTD) claims, cancer ranked as the second leading cause of new disability claims, accounting for 15 percent of all claims.[7]

While Social Security disability benefits can be useful, there are some barriers to getting access to these benefits. It can be challenging to obtain benefits. The average processing time for an initial application decision in 2023 was 225 days.[8] Two-thirds of individuals who apply are denied and must go through an appeals process that can sometimes take years. The first level of appeal is a reconsideration. The average time the Social Security Administration (SSA) took to make a decision on a reconsideration was 182 days in 2022.[9] The next level of appeal is a hearing before an administrative law judge (ALJ). The SSA anticipated that the average wait time for a hearing

2. Social Security Administration, Fact Sheet: Social Security, https://www.ssa.gov/news/press/factsheets/basicfact-alt.pdf (last visited Nov. 16, 2024).

3. Center on Budget and Policy Priorities, Policy Basics: Supplemental Security Income (2024), https://www.cbpp.org/sites/default/files/atoms/files/PolicyBasics_SocSec-IntroToSSI.pdf.

4. Social Security Administration, Annual Statistical Report on the Social Security Disability Insurance Program, 2021 (2022), https://www.ssa.gov/policy/docs/statcomps/di_asr/2021/di_asr21.pdf.

5. Council for Disability Income Awareness, CDA 2010 Consumer Disability Awareness Survey—The Disability Divide (2010), http://www.disabilitycanhappen.org/research/pdfs/ConsumerResearchReport_Consumer.pdf.

6. *Id.*

7. Integrated Benefits Institute, IBI Health and Productivity Benchmarking 2019: Long-Term Disability Program (2020), https://files.ibiweb.org/uploads/general/Sample-Reports.zip (all employers, condition-specific results).

8. *Social Security (SSA) Monthly Data for Combined Title II Disability and Title XVI Blind and Disabled Average Processing Time*, SSA, https://www.ssa.gov/open/data/Combined-Disability-Processing-Time.html (last updated Oct. 3, 2024).

9. *Social Security (SSA) Annual Data for Disability Reconsideration Average Processing Time*, https://www.ssa.gov/open/data/disability_reconsideration_average_processing_time.html (last updated Mar. 8, 2024).

would be 390 days at the end of fiscal year (FY) 2023.[10] After the hearing, individuals could wait an estimated 78 to 120 days to find out the judge's decision. When considered in total, the average applicant is waiting 917 days, or two years and six months, before receiving an award of benefits.

Cancer is one of the top six categories of conditions that qualify someone for disability insurance benefits, according to the SSA. Therefore, it reasons that tens of thousands of individuals coping with cancer are stuck in the SSDI backlog. Fortunately, there are some steps individuals can take during the initial application processes to increase the likelihood of approval.

It is also common for caregivers of people coping with cancer to need to take time off work to fulfill their caregiving duties. The Americans with Disabilities Act (ADA) and the Family and Medical Leave Act (FMLA) provide some protections in the workplace for caregivers (see Chapter 2, Employment). However, disability insurance is only applicable if an individual cannot work due to their own disability. To address this gap, some states have acted legislatively to create state paid leave programs for caregivers (see Chapter 2).

Within disability insurance policies there are short-term policies and long-term policies. The details will vary widely depending on the policy itself. Generally, a short-term policy will provide benefits if the disability an individual is experiencing lasts fewer than 12 months, whereas a long-term policy will provide benefits if the disability is expected to last 12 months or longer. There are several ways an individual can acquire a disability insurance policy. Individuals may have access to private plans (i.e., individual, employer-sponsored, or other group plans), state disability insurance (SDI) programs, and federal disability insurance benefits. Note that this discussion does not include workers' compensation benefits for work-related injuries.

## II. Private Disability Insurance

### A. Individual Disability Insurance

Private disability policies are often purchased directly from an insurance company. Unfortunately, there are very few regulations around the sale of these policies, so companies are allowed to take into consideration preexisting conditions, like cancer, and health history when determining whether to sell an individual a policy and what to charge for that policy. This process, where the insurance company reviews an individual's medical records and health history, is called medical underwriting. Generally, policies will define a preexisting condition based on two time periods: a "look back period" and a "preexisting condition waiting period." A look-back provision defines which conditions will be considered "preexisting" and, therefore, not covered.

---

10. FY 2023 Operating Plan: Social Security Administration General Statement (2023), https://www.ssa.gov/budget/assets/materials/2023/2023OP.pdf.

Look-back periods typically range from three to 12 months. A preexisting condition waiting period is the amount of time an individual must be covered by a policy before that policy will provide disability benefits related to that preexisting condition. Waiting periods are often from one to two years, but each insurance company has its own rules.

### Questions to Ask about a Private Disability Policy

**Definition of "disability."** How does the plan define a "disability?" Is it the inability to fully perform "your job," or "any job?"

**Benefit amount.** Is it a fixed amount? Is it a percentage of your income (e.g., 70 percent of your salary)? Is there a maximum?

**Benefit reductions.** Are benefits reduced for any reason (e.g., if an individual is getting SSDI or workers' compensation benefits)?

**Length of benefit.** How long will benefits last (e.g., is it for a set length of time, or until reaching a set age)?

**Are benefits taxable?** (Note: It depends on whether it is an individual plan or an employer plan and if the premiums were paid with pre- or post-tax dollars.)

**Elimination period.** Is there a waiting period before benefit payments start (e.g., 180 days)?

**Exclusion period.** Are there any exclusions relating to preexisting conditions?

**Residual disability.** Does the plan pay a smaller benefit if an individual is working fewer hours in their regular job or a different job, because of their medical condition?

**Payments.** If an individual gets coverage through an employer, do payments end if the individual is let go while on disability?

**Conversion.** If an individual gets coverage through an employer, can an individual convert the policy to an individual policy?

**Policy information.** Is there a booklet describing the policy? For group policies, is the policy governed by the Employee Retirement Income Security Act of 1974 (ERISA)?

Disability insurance companies may also require that an individual take a medical examination before issuing a policy. However, once a policy is issued, it cannot be canceled as long the individual pays the premiums and does not misrepresent any information about medical conditions.

The lack of protection for individuals with preexisting conditions can make it difficult, and sometimes impossible, for individuals with cancer to purchase a private, individual disability insurance policy. Every insurance company has different approaches as to how they handle covering individuals with preexisting conditions. Individuals should research and compare individual, private disability insurance policies. Individuals can start by contacting their state insurance agency to find out which companies sell policies in their state. Moreover, there is little standardization among private disability policies. Each policy could have a different definition of "disability," different term lengths, and different prices. For instance, some policies may only cover disabilities that prevent an individual from doing any job, rather than just their own job. Therefore, it is critical for an individual purchasing a private policy to understand the details of that particular policy (see "Questions to Ask about a Private Disability Policy" text box).

Some insurance companies will offer add-on provisions, for an additional fee, that may make the policy more valuable. For example, an inflation protection provision might be purchased for an additional fee. This protection ensures that any benefits an individual receives over time will be adjusted for cost-of-living increases.

## B. Employer-Sponsored and Group Disability Insurance

Although not a requirement, some employers offer short-term disability or LTD insurance as a benefit of employment. These employers buy a policy from a private insurance company for their employees. These group plans are "guaranteed issue," but may contain exclusions for preexisting conditions. Therefore, an employee cannot be denied overall coverage, but if the disability that keeps the employee from working was preexisting, the policy may impose an exclusion period for the preexisting condition, or exclude all coverage related to that preexisting condition. Each employer has a different structure for offering disability insurance. Some employers will pay the total cost of the premiums for their employees, and some will only pay a portion of the premiums and require that the employees pay the remaining amount. Some employers do not contribute at all to the cost of disability insurance; they simply offer employees the opportunity to join the group plan. In those cases, employees will be responsible for the entire premium. Employers may also offer both an LTD policy and a short-term disability policy, while some employers only offer either a short-term disability policy or LTD policy. In states that have state short-term disability programs, it is more common for an employer to only offer an LTD policy.

Many of these employer-sponsored plans are governed by ERISA.[11] Knowing if a particular plan is governed by ERISA is critical for individuals to understand their rights. For example, under ERISA, plans are required to make a claim decision within 45 days, unless the plan can show there is a reason beyond its control for the delay.

---

11. 29 U.S.C. § 1001 *et seq*. Note: Some plans sponsored by certain religious organizations, professional associations, and government agencies are exempt from ERISA.

In that case, the plan has a maximum of 30 additional days to make a decision. If the claim is denied, the plan administrator must provide notice, in writing, with a detailed explanation of why the claim was denied and how an individual can appeal that decision. The notice may also include a specific request to provide the plan with additional information.

If an individual does not have access to an employer-sponsored disability insurance plan, they can explore if any of the professional organizations, alumni groups, or clubs the individual belongs to offer group coverage.

## C. Filing a Claim

When individuals need to stop working because of their medical condition, they can file a claim to access their disability insurance benefits. Each policy has a different process to file a claim, so it is in the individual's best interest to contact their insurance company or employer's human resources representative for more information on how to submit claims. Typically, the first step is to complete a claim form by providing information about the date the individual last worked, a description of the medical condition, and contact information. Once that is completed, individuals will have to request their employer and health care provider complete the relevant portions of the form. Generally, the employer will be asked questions about the individual's job description and salary, and the health care provider will be asked about the individual's medical condition and ability to work. Upon receiving this form, the insurance company will typically request medical records to corroborate the information contained on the claim form.

Keep in mind that the need for disability insurance may not necessarily end when active cancer treatment ends. Individuals may continue to experience long-term or late-term side effects or have other medical conditions that keep them from being able to work. Furthermore, individuals who have a private or employer-sponsored disability insurance policy may be entitled to retroactive benefits if they did not file a claim while they were out of work, but now are back at work.

## D. Appealing a Claim Denial

If a disability claim is denied, individuals have the right to appeal that decision. Some of the information that could be submitted with an appeal includes medical records; letters of support from members of their health care team, family members, friends, and former co-workers; information about their job duties, salary, and work experience; and if they have been awarded federal disability benefits. Individuals should strongly consider working with their health care team to gather relevant information for an appeal. Furthermore, if an appeal reaches the courts, an individual may want to consider hiring an attorney to assist with the case. The appeals process is specific to the individual's type of disability insurance coverage.

### 1. Individual Disability Insurance Plans

If an individual bought a private policy directly from an insurance company, they will have to follow the insurance company's rules for appeal. If individuals follow all of the steps outlined by the insurance company and their claim is still denied, they may have the ability to sue in court. There are two main causes of action to dispute a denial of benefits: breach of contract and bad faith. The rules regarding what constitutes "bad faith" vary among states, but a legitimate dispute over coverage or benefits will mostly likely not rise to the level of a bad-faith claim. Individuals choosing to file suit in court may consider hiring an attorney. For information about finding legal assistance, see Chapter 7, Conclusion.

### 2. Employer-Sponsored Disability Insurance Plans Governed by ERISA

It is important for individuals to understand if their policy is governed by ERISA. ERISA is a federal law that limits an individual's remedy to the benefits that should have been paid under the plan, plus, potentially, attorney fees. For example, if the plan failed to cover a $200 test, then the remedy will only be $200. ERISA specifically precludes other state-law remedies, such as claims for bad-faith failure to pay an insurance claim, or fraud, and punitive damages. The plan documents for an employer-sponsored disability insurance plan should indicate if the plan is governed by ERISA.

If the plan is governed by ERISA, an individual must submit an administrative appeal to the insurance company within 180 days of the date on the written denial notice. In most cases, if individuals do not submit an appeal to the insurance company first, within those 180 days, they will lose the right to sue in court. If a claim is still denied after an administrative appeal, usually the denial notice will state that administrative remedies have been exhausted and that the individual has a right to sue in court under ERISA.

## E. Tax Implications

As disability insurance replaces lost income, there may be some tax implications. Taxability of disability insurance benefits depends on what type of benefits are received, if the individual paid the premiums with pre-tax or post-tax dollars, and if a portion of the premiums were paid for by an employer.[12]

- For individual policies, premiums are paid for with post-tax dollars; therefore, the income received from a policy will not be taxed.
- For employer-sponsored or other group policies, taxes will depend on who pays the premium:

12. *Provisions Affecting Taxation of Benefits*, SSA, https://www.ssa.gov/oact/solvency/provisions/taxbenefit.html (last visited Nov. 16, 2024).

- o If an individual pays the premium with post-tax dollars, the benefits will not be taxed.
- o If the employer pays the total premium, and does not include the amount paid as part of the individual's gross income, the benefits will be taxed.
- o If the individual pays a portion of the premium and the employer pays a portion, the tax liability will be split proportionally.

If individuals have concerns about whether or not benefits will be taxed, they should consult a tax professional or accountant.

## III. State Short-Term Disability Insurance Programs

There are a few states and territories that have short-term disability insurance programs: California, Hawaii, New Jersey, New York, Puerto Rico, and Rhode Island. The maximum amount of time that you can receive short-term disability benefits is between six and 12 months, depending on the state. You may be able to receive both federal SSDI benefits and state disability benefits, but rules also vary by state.

### A. California

California State Disability Insurance (SDI) is a program that most California employees contribute to through payroll deductions. All employers not specifically exempt from coverage must provide disability insurance for their employees either through the SDI program or through their own self-insured or commercial plan. The weekly benefit amount is about 60 to 70 percent (depending on income) of wages earned five to 18 months before the claim start date up to the maximum weekly benefit amount. The maximum weekly benefit in 2024 was $1,620, for a total of 52 weeks. There is a seven-day non-payable waiting period. Employees must have earned at least $300 in wages subject to SDI contributions during a 12-month base period. A health care provider must certify the disability. For information, visit https://edd.ca.gov/.

### B. Hawaii

Hawaii Temporary Disability Insurance (TDI) requires most employers to provide disability benefits to employees. Employers must obtain private coverage, self-insure, or provide coverage through a sick leave plan under a collective bargaining agreement. The type of plan the employer carries will determine the benefits the employee can receive. The benefit received will be 58 percent of the employee's average weekly wages rounded to the next higher dollar, not to exceed the maximum weekly benefit. In 2024, the maximum weekly benefit was $798, for a maximum of 26 weeks. An employee must have worked at least 14 weeks in Hawaii, during which the employee was paid for 20 hours or more, and earned at least $400 in the 52 weeks before the first day of disability. The 14 weeks can be with different employers and do not need to be consecutive. The employee must be currently employed. For information, visit https://labor.hawaii.gov/.

## C. New Jersey

The New Jersey Temporary Disability Insurance program covers all employers subject to the state unemployment insurance law. Employers have the option of participating in TDI or buying a private plan that provides benefits equal to or more than the state plan. As of 2024, claimants are paid 85 percent of their average weekly wage, up to the maximum weekly benefit of $1,055, for a maximum of 26 weeks. Individuals are not initially paid for the first seven days of their claim. If they are still unable to work on the 22nd day of their claim, they will receive back pay benefits for the first week they were out of work. For information, visit https://www.nj.gov/labor/myleavebenefits/worker/tdi/.

## D. New York

The New York Disability Benefits Law requires most employers to provide short-term disability benefits for employees. Employers may participate in the state's insurance fund, purchase private insurance, or provide self-insured plans. Premiums are paid entirely by the employer or jointly paid by the employer and the employee. Specific eligibility criteria defining which kinds of employees are covered and not covered are available on the state Workers' Compensation Board website at https://www.wcb.ny.gov/. Disability benefits will pay 50 percent of an individual's average wages up to a maximum weekly benefit of $170, for a maximum of 26 weeks. Calculations are based on the eight weeks prior to application. However, employers can add money to the amount the state program pays. There is a seven-day unpaid waiting period. Benefits paid by the employer or insurance carrier are subject to taxes. For information, visit https://www.wcb.ny.gov/.

## E. Puerto Rico

Puerto Rico's law, Seguro por Incapacidad No Ocupacional Temporal (SINOT), or Temporary Non-Occupational Disability Insurance, requires most employers to provide disability coverage for employees. Employers may participate in the Puerto Rico insurance fund, purchase private insurance, or provide self-insured plans. Both employers and employees must contribute to SINOT. The employee must have received at least $150 of insured employment in the base year. The 2024 maximum weekly benefit was $113 for a maximum of 26 weeks. For information, call (787) 754-5353 or visit https://trabajo.pr.gov/.

### F. Rhode Island

Rhode Island's Temporary Disability Insurance program was the first of its kind in the United States. Employers can elect to contribute to the state temporary disability fund, which is otherwise funded through employee payroll deductions. The 2024 maximum weekly benefit was $1,043, for a maximum of 30 weeks. The weekly benefit rate will be equal to 4.62 percent of the wages paid to the employee in the highest quarter of the base period. The base period is the first four of the past five completed calendar quarters before the starting date of a new claim. TDI benefits are not subject to federal or state income taxes. For information, visit https://dlt.ri.gov/individuals/temporary-disability-caregiver-insurance.

## IV. Federal LTD Insurance Programs

Most Americans do not have a plan for maintaining some income in the event that they experience a cancer diagnosis, or other serious illness that prevents them from working. In fact, seven out of ten employees who work for private employers lack private LTD insurance. Therefore, a majority of Americans rely on the federal disability programs, but few understand their complexities. The two federal LTD programs most typically utilized by someone coping with cancer are SSDI and SSI. Although these programs are different, both are administered by the SSA and are based on an inability to work as a result of an LTD. For both SSDI and SSI, an individual must meet the Social Security Act's definition of a "disability," which is an "inability to engage in any substantial gainful activity by reason of any . . . physical or mental impairment which can be expected to result in death or which has lasted or can be expected to last for a continuous period of not less than 12 months."[13]

Practically speaking, this means that the SSA would consider individuals to have a disability if:

- They cannot do the work that they did previously because of a medical condition.
- They cannot adjust to other work because of their medical condition.
- Their medical condition has lasted, or is expected to last, for at least one year, or result in death.

### A. Five-Step Disability Determination Process

The SSA uses a five-step sequential evaluation[14] to determine if an individual has a disability and is therefore eligible for SSA disability benefits (see "Disability Determination Process" text box). In order to answer these questions, the SSA performs an in-depth analysis of an individual's unique situation. This analysis is completed

13. 42 U.S.C. § 423(d)(1)(A); 20 C.F.R. § 404.1505(a).
14. 20 C.F.R. § 404.1520.

by local SSA field offices and state agencies called Disability Determination Services (DDS).[15]

An application for SSDI benefits can be completed online at https://www.ssa.gov/disability. For SSI, begin the process online at https://www.ssa.gov/ssi. Alternatively, individuals can call (800) 772-1213 to make an appointment to file either type of disability claim at a local Social Security office or to set up an appointment for an SSA agent to complete the claim by telephone. The disability claims interview typically lasts about one hour.

**Disability Determination Process**

1. Are you working, earning more than $1,620* (substantial gainful activity (SGA)) a month?

   If yes, review ends and you will not be deemed disabled for SSA disability benefits.

   If no, go to step 2.

2. Is your medical condition "severe"?

   If yes, go to step 3.

   If no, review ends and you will not be deemed disabled for SSA disability benefits.

3. Is your medical condition on the "List of Impairments"?

   If yes, presumptively deemed disabled for SSA disability benefits.

   If no, then agency looks at severity of condition. If severe enough go to step 4.

4. Can you do the work you did before?

   If yes, review ends and you will not be deemed disabled for SSA disability benefits.

   If no, go to step 5.

5. Can you do any other type of work?

   If yes, review ends and you will not be deemed disabled for SSA disability benefits.

   If no, you will be deemed disabled for SSDI.

* For non-blind individuals in 2025.

15. *Disability Determination Process*, SSA, https://www.ssa.gov/disability/determination.htm (last visited Nov. 16, 2024).

## 1. SGA

One of the most common questions that individuals with cancer have is, "Do I have to stop working before applying for Social Security disability benefits?" And the answer is, "It depends." The SSA determines, each year, a dollar amount threshold called "substantial gainful activity." In 2025, SGA for a non-blind individual was $1,620 a month.[16] Therefore, if an individual earns less than $1,620 a month, the individual is not engaging in SGA, or not "working" according to the SSA.

The Social Security Act's definition of a "disability" may be misleading, because it is possible that an individual could still be working, earning a limited income under the SGA amount, and still be able to answer no to the first question and possibly qualify for SSDI benefits.

## 2. Severe Medical Condition

An individual's disability will be considered severe (see step 2 in the "Disability Determination Process" text box) if it "significantly limits [an individual's] physical or mental ability to do basic work activities."[17] According to the SSA, basic work activities include:

- Physical activities (e.g., standing, walking, sitting, lifting)
- Speaking, hearing, seeing
- Responding appropriately to typical work situations and supervision
- Using reasonable judgment[18]

## 3. Condition Included in the SSA List of Impairments

If the individual's medical condition is deemed to be severe, the SSA will determine if the condition is specifically listed in the SSA's listing of disabling impairments (see step 3 in the "Disability Determination Process" text box). The official title of the list is "Disability Evaluation under Social Security"; however, it is commonly referred to as the "Blue Book."[19] In addition to listing the impairments that are most often considered severe enough to prevent an individual from working, the Blue Book also provides information about the medical evidence needed to support a claim. Cancer-related medical conditions are included in section 13. If an individual's condition meets or equals a condition in the Blue Book, there will be an irrebuttable presumption that the individual has a disability and should be granted SSA disability benefits.

---

16. *Substantial Gainful Activity*, SSA, https://www.ssa.gov/oact/cola/sga.html (last visited Nov. 16, 2024).

17. *Understanding Supplemental Security Income If You Are Disabled or Blind—2024 Edition*, SSA, https://www.ssa.gov/ssi/text-disable-ussi.htm (last visited Nov. 16, 2024).

18. *Id.*

19. *Disability Evaluation under Social Security, Listing of Impairments—Adult Listings (Part A)*, SSA, https://www.ssa.gov/disability/professionals/bluebook/AdultListings.htm (last visited Nov. 16, 2024).

To facilitate prompt disability determinations, individuals should ask their health care team to consult the Blue Book to determine the most relevant medical information to include in their application for Social Security disability benefits.

## 4. Residual Functional Capacity

If the individual's condition is not included in the Blue Book, the SSA will consider an individual's "residual functional capacity (RFC) and the vocational factors of age, education, and work experience, as appropriate," to make the determination (see steps 4 and 5 in the "Disability Determination Process" text box). The RFC is a determination of what work an individual can do, on a full-time basis, in spite of the disability.[20] The RFC form[21] is completed by a specialist at DDS[22] based on the information included in the original application. However, individuals are permitted to have their own health care providers complete these forms as well, which may improve their chances of being awarded benefits.

If the individual has a physical disability, the SSA will indicate the level of work that can be maintained (i.e., sedentary, light, medium, or heavy).[23] This determination will be based on factors such as one's ability to lift, stand, carry, sit, and walk.[24] If the individual's disability is mental or emotional, a mental residual functional capacity (MRFC) will be conducted.[25] This assessment will include one's ability to do the following:

- Understand and carry out instructions
- Maintain concentration for extended periods of time
- Perform tasks on a reasonable schedule
- Perform without special supervision
- Interact appropriately with others[26]

It can be challenging to successfully assert a claim of limited MRFC without the input of a psychiatrist or licensed psychologist. After cancer treatment, individuals may experience side effects that impact their cognitive function. These cognitive challenges may include difficulties with short-term memory, an inability to concentrate or trouble focusing, challenges with executive function, trouble with learning new things, and difficulties when working with numbers. Collectively, these challenges are typically referred to as "chemo brain." However, it is a misnomer because these

20. SSR 96-8p (July 2, 1996), https://www.ssa.gov/OP_Home/rulings/di/01/SSR96-08-di-01.html.
21. The form can be downloaded at https://www.ssa.gov/forms/ssa-3373-bk.pdf.
22. DDS is a state agency that is federally funded and helps the SSA make decisions about individuals' eligibility for disability benefits.
23. SSR 83-14 (Nov. 28, 1978), https://www.ssa.gov/OP_Home/rulings/di/02/SSR83-14-di-02.html.
24. The SSA's "Function Report" form can be found online at https://www.ssa.gov/forms/ssa-3373-bk.pdf.
25. SSR 85-16, https://www.ssa.gov/OP_Home/rulings/di/01/SSR85-16-di-01.html.
26. *Id.*

cognitive deficits can result from many types of cancer treatment, including radiation and endocrine therapy. Even if individuals believe that they are suffering from chemo brain as a result of their cancer treatment, they should enlist the help of a health care professional to provide support for the mental disability claim.

Once the RFC/MRFC is completed, an examiner from DDS will look to see what type of work an individual has done over the past 15 years and compare that with the RFC determination.[27] For example, if a review of one's work history indicates that the majority of an individual's work in the past 15 years was sedentary and the RFC deems that an individual can perform sedentary work, the disability claim will likely be denied, unless there are also mental limitations.

If the DDS examiner finds that an individual cannot do their prior job, they will then use the SSA's medical-vocational rules grid to determine whether the individual can do another job. Many times, an individual will not be able to satisfy the requirement that they are unable to do any type of work (see step 5 in the "Disability Determination Process" text box). It is at this stage that the burden shifts to the SSA to demonstrate that there are alternative jobs that the individual could perform.[28] The examiner will take into consideration an individual's RFC, age, education, and skills when deciding if the individual can perform another job.

Any job that the SSA suggests an individual could adjust to "must exist in significant numbers in the national economy (either in the region where the individual lives or in the national economy)."[29] This analysis is typically conducted during a hearing in front of an ALJ during an appeals process. The burden to prove that there are jobs that exist in significant numbers is on the SSA.[30] The SSA often uses vocational experts to testify, given a set of restrictions (e.g., job must be sedentary), how many jobs exist regionally or nationally. The law does not provide a numerical value to help determine what "significant numbers" means. However, the courts have provided some guidance. For example, the Ninth Circuit Court of Appeals clarified that when only 135 jobs that an individual could perform existed regionally and 1,680 jobs existed nationally, there were not a significant number of jobs. Therefore, the individual was deemed eligible for SSA benefits.[31]

---

27. SSA, Program Operations Manual System (POMS) DI 24510.006 Assessing Residual Functional Capacity (RFC) in Initial Claims (SSR 96-8p) (2024), https://secure.ssa.gov/poms.nsf/lnx/0424510006.

28. Allen v. Califano, 613 F.2d 139, 145 (6th Cir. 1980).

29. 20 C.F.R. § 404.1560(c)(1).

30. Tackett v. Apfel, 180 F.3d 1094, 1099 (9th Cir. 1999).

31. Beltran v. Astrue, 676 F.3d 1203 (9th Cir. 2012).

### 5. Practical Tips for the Application Process

Applying for Social Security disability benefits can be time-consuming and daunting. However, there are a few practical steps individuals can take to improve their chances of being approved for benefits, as follows:

- **Submit sufficient information about health care providers.** Individuals should list all health care professionals, hospitals, clinics, and other facilities where they received treatment, even if tangentially related to their cancer diagnosis. For example, an individual may see a psychiatrist to cope with the anxiety experienced during cancer treatment. That individual should include the psychiatrist's name and contact information in the application for disability benefits, even though the psychiatrist did not treat the individual for cancer. The SSA will contact the health care providers listed in the application to gather medical information, including medical records.
- **Communicate with health care team.** Individuals should let members of their health care team know that they are applying for disability insurance, and share any physical, mental, and emotional challenges they are facing and how those challenges are impacting their ability to work. Individuals can work with their health care team to ensure that information is documented in their medical records, before any records are submitted to the SSA.
- **Avoid mistakes and omissions in the application itself.** Individuals should ensure that everything is spelled correctly (e.g., diagnoses, medications, names of health care providers and facilities). Additionally, individuals should answer all of the questions posed in the application, with as much detail as possible. If a field is not applicable to an individual, it is best to include a notation like "N/A" so DDS does not assume it was left blank by mistake.
- **Do not work and earn more than the SGA amount at the time of application.** If an individual does continue to work and makes more than the SGA threshold, the application will be denied.

## B. SSDI

In addition to meeting the SSA's definition of "disability," an individual must be fully insured to collect SSDI payments, meaning that an individual has worked and paid into the Social Security retirement system through Social Security taxes. To be fully insured and, therefore, eligible for this program, an individual must have enough "credits" within the recent past.

In 2025, individuals earned one credit for each $1,810 of wages or self-employment income. When an individual has earned $7,240, the individual has earned the maximum four credits per year.

**SSA Credits Needed by Age (non-blind individuals)**

< 24 years old: 6 credits in 3 years before disability

24–31 years old: credit for working half the time between 21 and disability

31+ years old: 40 credits (20 earned in the 10 years before disability)

Generally, individuals 31 and older will need 40 credits, 20 of which were earned in the ten years immediately before their disability began. Practically, this means an individual with cancer must have worked and paid into the Social Security retirement system five of the past ten years to qualify for SSDI. Even if an individual has not worked recently enough for SSDI, they would still qualify for Social Security retirement benefits when eligible.

If an individual becomes disabled before 24 years of age, the individual may qualify for SSDI if the individual has earned six credits in the three-year period ending when the disability began. If individuals become disabled between the ages of 24 and 31, they may be eligible for SSDI benefits if they have credit for working half the time between age 21 and the time their disability began. For example, if they became disabled at 27, they would need credit for three years of work (12 credits) in the past six years (between 21 and 27 years old).[32]

## 1. Accessing Your Social Security Statement

If an individual currently has, or had, a job where the individual earned money and paid into the Social Security retirement system, they likely received a Social Security statement in the mail, at some point. These statements used to be sent by mail each year, but now are available online. By setting up a **mySSA** account, individuals can see their Social Security statement, to learn the estimated amount they will get paid if they retire at full retirement age, if they retire early, or if they qualify for SSDI benefits because they are unable to work.

An individual's monthly disability payment is calculated using a formula that takes into account how much the individual has paid in Social Security taxes over their work history. The average amount received by a worker with a disability is $17,868 annually (approximately $1,489 per month).[33] Getting this information can help individuals make strategic financial decisions about which path to take. They can also find out if they will qualify for premium-free Medicare Part A.

---

32. *Disability*, SSA, https://www.ssa.gov/disability (last visited Nov. 16, 2024).

33. *Monthly Statistical Snapshot, October 2024*, SSA, https://www.ssa.gov/policy/docs/quickfacts/stat_snapshot/ (last released Nov. 2024).

It is also useful for individuals to check, each year, that their income is correct on their statement, as retirement and disability benefit amounts are based on an individual's income over their work history. Creating a mySSA account is free, secure, and accessible on any device.

## 2. Medicare Eligibility

Many individuals receive health insurance through their employers. This can be an issue for an individual who has to stop working due to a cancer diagnosis. Fortunately, each federal LTD program is paired with a federal health insurance program. Medicare is a federal health insurance program for individuals over 65 or those with a disability. Individuals under the age of 65 become eligible for Medicare once they receive SSDI for 24 months. For more information about Medicare, see Chapter 1, Health Insurance.

## 3. Important Dates in the SSDI Application Process

When thinking about when an individual applying for SSDI benefits will actually start receiving payments, there are a few different dates to keep in mind:

- **Disability onset date (DOD).** Once an individual's claim is approved, they will receive a letter with a date of "disability onset." This is the date that the SSA believes the individual's disability began. It is important to recognize that for an individual with cancer, the DOD is not usually the diagnosis date, but the date that treatment begins, because it is usually needing to receive treatment or side effects from treatment that keep an individual from working.
- **Application date.** This is the date on which an individual files an application with the SSA.
- **Waiting period.** SSDI requires a five-month waiting period before an individual is entitled to receive SSDI benefits. The waiting period begins the first month after the month of the DOD.
- **Date of entitlement.** This is the first month after the five-month waiting period when an individual is entitled to receive benefits.
- **Approval date.** This is the date the SSA actually approves an individual's application.
- **Medicare eligibility date.** This date is 24 full months from the date of entitlement.

It is crucial for individuals to understand these dates in order to accurately assess when they will begin receiving benefits, and how much they will get paid, because the SSA does provide for SSDI back payments and retroactive payments.

## 4. Back Payments versus Retroactive Payments

The application and approval process for Social Security disability benefits can take months. To compensate for the time that an individual should have received benefits, the SSA allows for back payments. Back payments cover the time between the date of application and the date when the SSA approves the individual's application. If an individual is not also receiving retroactive payments, then the five-month waiting period is subtracted out, to calculate the total number of months eligible for back payments. Back payments are also available to SSI applicants.

The SSA also understands that individuals may not apply for SSDI benefits until long after their disability began. Therefore, the SSA also provides retroactive payments. Retroactive payments cover up to 12 months from the date of application back to the DOD. Only SSDI applicants are eligible for retroactive benefits; SSI applicants are not.

The process of determining these dates and eligibility for benefits is often confusing in real life and is best explained through examples.

## *Case Study #1: Jackson*

*Jackson began treatment for cancer on February 28, 2021 (which the SSA determined was his DOD). He applied for disability benefits on June 1, 2022. His waiting period ran from March 2021 through July 2021. Therefore, his entitlement date is August 1, 2022. The SSA approved Jackson's application on September 1, 2022. Jackson would be eligible for back pay for the months of June 2022 through August 2022. He would also be entitled to retroactive payments for August 1, 2021, to May 31, 2022. He would also become eligible to receive Medicare benefits on August 1, 2023.*

The following figure illustrates Jackson's SSDI timing:

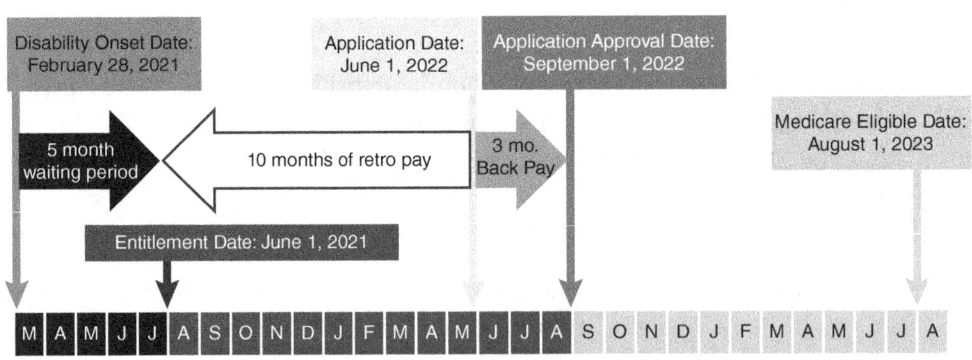

## *Case Study #2: Isabelle*

*Isabelle applied for disability benefits on June 1, 2022, due to her cancer diagnosis. The SSA deemed her DOD was October 31, 2020. Isabelle's waiting period was from November 1, 2020, to March 31, 2021. Her date of entitlement was June 1, 2021. However, her application was not approved until December 31, 2022.*

*Isabelle is entitled to retroactive payments for the time between her entitlement date backwards to when the waiting period ended. However, since retroactive payments are capped at 12 months, she will only receive payment for the months of June 1, 2021–May 31, 2022. Therefore, for April and May 2021, she will not receive any benefits. Isabelle will also receive back pay for the six months from June 1, 2022, when the application was submitted, to December 31, 2022, when the application was actually approved. She would also become eligible to receive Medicare benefits on June 1, 2023—24 full months after her date of entitlement.*

The following figure illustrates Isabelle's SSDI timing:

## 5. SSDI and Retirement Benefits

It can be beneficial for an individual to understand how SSDI and SSA retirement benefits work together. For most SSDI beneficiaries born after 1960, their full retirement age is 67 years old.[34] If an individual is considering filing for Social Security disability benefits, but is also close to Social Security early retirement age or full retirement age,

34. *Retirement Age Calculator*, SSA, https://www.ssa.gov/planners/retire/ageincrease.html (last visited Nov. 16, 2024).

they should consider checking their Social Security statement, to compare the amount of monthly payments if the individual were to receive SSDI, retire early, or wait until reaching full retirement age. This information can be found on one's mySSA account online, as discussed earlier.

Once an individual who is receiving SSDI reaches full retirement age, their benefits will switch from SSDI to Social Security retirement benefits. This switch is effectively in name only and there should be no disruption in an individual's monthly payments. The amount of the monthly payment does not decrease when it switches from disability to retirement benefits.

The SSA also imposes a "disability freeze" during the months or years an individual has a disability. In other words, the period of time an individual is unable to work due to a disability is not counted in the calculation for their total retirement benefits and the individual is able to maintain the "insured" status for future disability benefits.[35]

Once an individual who has been receiving SSDI benefits reaches full retirement age, then the rules change. An individual who was on SSDI but has reached full retirement age can work and earn any amount and not have their monthly Social Security retirement benefits reduced.

An individual may decide to file for early retirement (starting at age 62) while awaiting their disability claim to be approved. The individual would receive a reduced retirement benefit (currently 25 percent less than the full retirement benefit amount) right away. If the individual is approved for SSDI, they will begin to receive the higher dollar amount. The individual could also receive prorated retroactive payments for any time that they were determined to be disabled and were receiving reduced benefits.

If an individual is found to have a disability that began after taking early retirement, the individual would not get the benefit of a "disability freeze." In addition, they would receive the higher SSDI payments only until the time of reaching full retirement age, then the payments would return to the reduced early retirement amount for the remainder of the individual's life. If an individual selects early retirement and then never applies, or is never approved, for SSDI, they will receive a reduced monthly retirement benefit amount for the rest of the individual's life.

## 6. Bridging the Five-Month Waiting Period

The five-month waiting period for SSDI benefits to begin can pose a practical challenge, as most people are not able to go multiple months without any income. There are some limited options on how to bridge that gap.

If an individual does not have income, and does not have significant resources or assets, they may also qualify for SSI. Individuals could apply for SSI and SSDI at the

35. 42 U.S.C. §§ 423(a), 426(b)(f); 20 C.F.R. § 404.320.

same time. Once approved, they would start receiving SSI sooner because SSI does not have a waiting period. When that individual starts receiving SSDI benefits, typically the amount of the SSDI benefit makes the individual ineligible for SSI.

However, some individuals earned a lower amount while working and paying into the Social Security retirement system. Therefore, their SSDI payments may be low enough to receive SSI and SSDI at the same time moving forward.

If someone does not qualify for SSI, but lives in one of the five states or Puerto Rico that have SDI programs, the money from those programs may also help bridge an income gap during the SSDI five-month waiting period. Alternatively, if an individual has access to a private short-term disability or LTD policy, those can help bridge that gap until they begin receiving SSDI payments.

### 7. SSDI and Private LTD Plans

Many private LTD plans require individuals to also apply for SSDI. Typically, the private policy will begin paying benefits without a waiting period and before the SSA makes a determination about SSDI eligibility. It is possible to receive benefits from both SSDI and a private LTD policy. However, the amount received from the private policy will be prorated. For example, assume an individual is eligible for 80 percent of their monthly income from the private policy and SSDI pays 60 percent. The individual will get 60 percent from SSDI and 20 percent from the private policy.

If an individual does qualify for SSDI, then they may be eligible for back payments or retroactive payments. If a private LTD policy has been paying benefits to the individual for the same months that SSDI paid back pay or retroactive payments, then the LTD policy will likely require repayment of any SSDI back payments or retroactive payments received.

For example, Todd has an LTD policy through his employer that pays him 70 percent of his monthly income. He is awarded SSDI benefits that amount to 50 percent of his monthly income as well as $2,000 in retroactive payments. Moving forward, SSDI will pay 50 percent of Todd's monthly income and the private policy will pay him 20 percent of his monthly income. Todd will have to send the private disability company the $2,000 he received in retroactive payments because he was already paid for those months from the private company.

## *Case Study #3: Paul*

*Paul started cancer treatment on January 1, 2021, and as a result he could not work and began using his LTD policy through his employer, which pays 80 percent of his income. In May, the LTD policy sent him a letter saying he had to apply for SSDI. He applied for SSDI on June 1, 2021, and kept receiving LTD benefits until he received his first SSDI check. Paul's first SSDI check arrived January 2022, which included back payment benefits from June–December 2021. His SSDI benefit amount equals*

*60 percent of his income when working. From January 2022 moving forward, Paul will receive 60 percent of his salary from SSDI and the additional 20 percent from his LTD policy. When Paul receives his back pay SSDI benefits from June–December 2021, he has to give them back to the LTD company. Note: He does not have to pay back the additional 20 percent that LTD is paying him per month on top of his SSDI.*

The following figure illustrates Paul's scenario:

**Case Study: Paul**

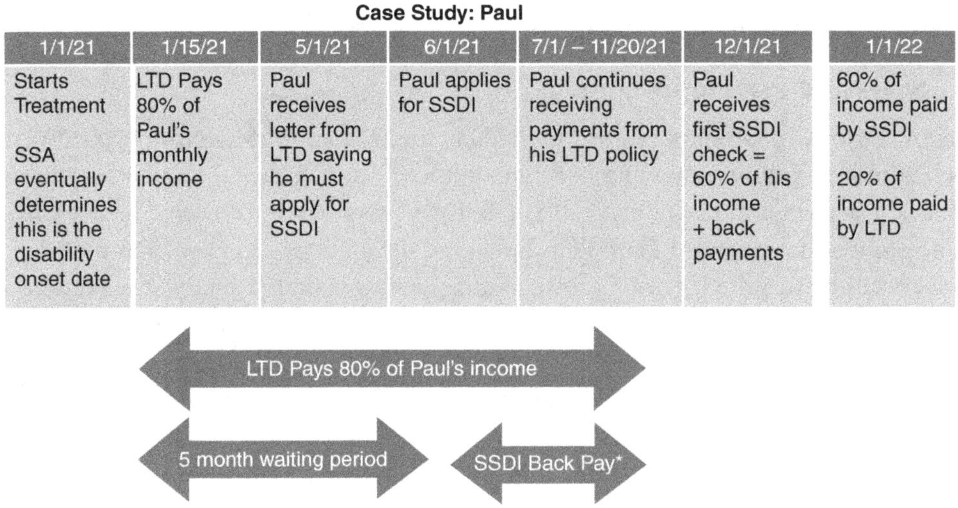


*SSDI back payments must be paid back to LTD

If an individual is denied SSDI benefits, a private LTD company may offer to help the individual with the appeals process, including hiring an attorney for the individual.

## C. SSI

Unlike SSDI, SSI provides individuals with disability benefits based on financial need, rather than previous work history. Eligibility is determined based on having a low income, few resources, and falling into at least one of three categories: 65 or older, blind, or disabled.[36]

The following items will be needed to complete an application:

- Social Security card
- Birth certificate or other proof of age

36. 42 U.S.C. § 1381a.

- Proof of U.S. citizenship or eligible noncitizen status
- Information about the home where the applicant lives (e.g., mortgage or lease)
- Payroll slips, bankbooks, insurance policies, burial fund records, and other information about the applicant's income and assets
- Checkbook or other documents with bank, credit union, or savings and loan account number(s)
- Names and contact information for the applicant's doctors, hospitals, and clinics

## 1. Income and Resource Limits

To determine SSI eligibility, the SSA will use the five-step analysis discussed earlier to determine if an individual has a disability. The SSA will also look at the total amount of an individual's income, including wages, Social Security disability and retirement benefits, pensions, and interest accrued on savings and other accounts.[37] The amount of income an individual can earn each month and still receive SSI is set by law and is called the federal benefit rate (FBR). The FBR increases annually if there is a cost-of-living adjustment. In 2025, the FBR was $967 a month for an individual and $1,450 a month for a couple (even if only one spouse is applying for SSI). The income and resource determinations are complicated. For more information, visit https://www.ssa.gov.

### *a. What Counts as Income*

The SSA will consider income that an individual receives, in cash or in-kind, that can be used to meet their needs for food and shelter. Typically, the types of income individuals receive include:

- **Earned income.** Wages from employment, income received in exchange for services, and so on[38]
- **Unearned income.** Social Security disability and retirement benefits, pensions, unemployment, interest on accounts, dividends from investments, donations or loans from friends and family, and so on[39]
- **In-kind support and maintenance.** Shelter that someone other than the individual pays for (e.g., parents pay for an individual's rent or utilities)[40]

---

37. *Id.* § 1382a.

38. SSA, POMS SI 00820.000 Earned Income (2024), https://secure.ssa.gov/apps10/poms.nsf/lnx/0500820000.

39. SSA, POMS SI 00830.000 Unearned Income (2024), https://secure.ssa.gov/apps10/poms.nsf/lnx/0500830000.

40. SSA, POMS SI 00835.001 Introduction to Living Arrangements and In-Kind Support and Maintenance (2023), https://secure.ssa.gov/apps10/poms.nsf/lnx/0500835001; Omitting Food From In-Kind Support and Maintenance Calculations, 89 Fed. Reg. 21,199 (Mar. 27, 2024), https://www.federalregister.gov/documents/2024/03/27/2024-06464/omitting-food-from-in-kind-support-and-maintenance-calculations.

*b. What Does Not Count as Income*

The SSA will not consider the following items when determining an individual's income:

- The first $20 per month of most income received
- The first $65 per month earned from working and half the amount greater than $65
- Supplemental Nutrition Assistance Program (SNAP) benefits
- Food or shelter assistance received from nonprofit organizations (e.g., food banks)
- Most home energy assistance
- Some income tax refunds, scholarships, and loans
- Direct payments by someone other than the individual for expenses other than food or shelter (e.g., medical bills, car insurance)

For more information about what is and is not counted as an individual's income for the purposes of SSI eligibility, visit https://www.ssa.gov/ssi/text-income-ussi.htm.

*c. What Is a Resource*[41]

In addition to income, the SSA requires that an individual has limited resources to be eligible for SSI. An individual must have less than $2,000 worth of resources and a couple may have no more than $3,000 worth of resources. Resources include cash, personal property, and real property that an individual, or the individual's spouse

- owns;
- has the legal right to sell or convert to cash; and
- is not legally restricted from using for their support and maintenance.[42]

Resources could include stocks, bonds, bank accounts, vehicles, jewelry, tools, vacation homes, timeshares, and life insurance policies.

*d. What Is Not Included as a Resource*

However, not every asset an individual owns will be seen as a resource by the SSA. For example, the SSA generally exempts the following, when calculating an individual's resource level:

- A primary residence and the land it is on
- Household goods and personal property (e.g., furniture)
- One vehicle
- Life insurance policies worth less than $1,500
- Burial plots for the individual and/or the immediate family

---

41. SSA, POMS SI 01110.100 Distinction between Assets and Resources (2024), https://secure.ssa.gov/apps10/poms.nsf/lnx/0501110100.

42. *Id.*

- Up to $1,500 in burial funds for an individual and up to $1,500 in burial funds for the spouse
- Retroactive SSA benefits up to nine months after receipt[43]
- Grants, scholarships, fellowships, or gifts set aside to pay educational expenses up to nine months after receipt
- Up to $100,000 in an Achieving a Better Life Experience (ABLE) account established through a state ABLE program
- Assets held in a special needs trust (see Chapter 5, Estate Planning and Medical Decision-Making)

For more information about what is and is not counted as a resource for the purposes of SSI eligibility, visit https://www.ssa.gov/ssi/text-resources-ussi.htm. The SSA may presumptively determine that individuals with certain conditions, like cancer, have a disability.[44] In those cases, the individual may receive SSI payments while their application is pending, for up to six months. If the SSA denies an individual's application for SSI, the individual typically does not have to pay those advanced payments back.

## 2. State SSI Supplemental Payments

In 44 states, individuals who are collecting SSI benefits may also be eligible for an additional payment from the state, generally referred to as the state supplemental payment (SSP). The following states do not offer SSPs: Arizona, Arkansas, Mississippi, North Dakota, Northern Mariana Islands, Tennessee, and West Virginia.

## 3. SSI and Children

Children who have a disability may also qualify for SSI.[45]

To qualify for SSI benefits, a child must:

- Be under 18 years old (or under age 22 if a student regularly attending school)
- Be unmarried, nor head of a household
- Have a disability within the SSA's definition of "disability" for children, meaning that the child
  - o has a physical or mental condition(s) that very seriously limits activities; and
  - o the condition(s) has, or is expected to, last for one year or to result in death

43. SSA, POMS SI 01130.600 Retroactive Supplemental Security Income (SSI) and Retirement, Survivors, and Disability (RSDI) Payments (2024), https://secure.ssa.gov/apps10/poms.nsf/lnx/0501130600.

44. *Understanding Supplemental Security Income Expedited Payments—2024 Edition*, SSA, https://www.ssa.gov/ssi/text-expedite-ussi.htm (last visited Nov. 16, 2024).

45. *Understanding Supplemental Security Income SSI for Children—2024 Edition*, SSA, https://www.ssa.gov/ssi/text-child-ussi.htm (last visited Nov. 16, 2024).

Children can receive SSI benefits until they turn 18 years old. Once a child turns 18, the SSA will review the individual's condition and will use the adult disability rules to decide whether they are still eligible for SSI benefits.

The SSA considers the income and resources of family members living in a child's household, including stepparents and adoptive parents, when deciding if a child is eligible. Also, if the child is working, they cannot earn more than $1,620 per month (in 2025). For information about SSI and children, visit https://www.ssa.gov/ssi/text-child-ussi.htm.

### 4. SSI and Medicaid

In most states, SSI recipients are automatically eligible for Medicaid as soon as they become eligible for SSI. These states do not provide automatic eligibility: Connecticut, Hawaii, Illinois, Minnesota, Missouri, New Hampshire, North Dakota, and Virginia. Individuals living in these states must meet additional state requirements and can contact their state Medicaid program for more information.

## D. Expediting Disability Determinations

It generally takes between three and six months for an individual to receive a decision on the initial application for Social Security disability benefits. However, the SSA has some ways that certain disability determinations are expedited. Keep in mind that even if an individual has their application expedited, there will still be a five-month waiting period before SSDI benefits are received.

### 1. Compassionate Allowances

The Compassionate Allowances List (CAL) is a list of certain medical conditions that would make an individual presumptively eligible for disability benefits. Having a diagnosis on this list is not a guarantee of being awarded benefits; however, the SSA tends to require only a minimal amount of medical evidence from applicants who have a medical condition listed. There are more than 60 cancer diagnoses on the CAL. For the full list, visit https://www.ssa.gov/compassionateallowances/conditions.htm.

### 2. Terminal Illness

The terminal illness (TERI) case flag is a way for the SSA to expedite a disability determination in cases where an individual has a terminal illness. The SSA defines "terminal illness" as "a medical condition that is untreatable and expected to result in death."[46] This is an SSA internal determination, and not enforceable by the individual. The following cancer diagnoses are considered eligible for the TERI flag:

---

46. SSA, POMS DI 23020.045 TERMINAL ILLNESS (TERI) CASES (2023), https://secure.ssa.gov/poms.nsf/lnx/0423020045.

Any malignant neoplasm (cancer) that is:

- Metastatic (has spread)
- Defined as stage IV
- Persistent or recurrent following initial therapy
- Inoperable or unresectable

An allegation or diagnosis of:

- Cancer of the esophagus
- Cancer of the liver
- Cancer of the pancreas
- Cancer of the gallbladder
- Mesothelioma
- Small cell or oat cell lung cancer
- Cancer of the brain
- Acute myelogenous leukemia (AML) or acute lymphocytic leukemia (ALL)[47]

## 3. Quick Disability Determination

Finally, the SSA utilizes a computer program that analyzes applications for factors that indicate a high likelihood the individual would be found to have a disability. If an application is flagged, it is sent to a special Quick Disability Determinations (QDD) group for review and decision. In these cases, the QDD examiner can approve a case without having to request that a medical consultant look at the file (unlike the regular Social Security disability determination process). These QDD cases are typically only for individuals who file their application soon after their alleged DOD. If the alleged DOD was more than a few months prior to the application date, the case will likely go through the normal disability determination process.

The following table compares the SSDI and SSI programs.

| Comparing Programs: SSDI versus SSI | | |
|---|---|---|
| | **SSDI** | **SSI** |
| Must have paid Social Security retirement taxes to qualify for program? | Yes | No |
| Must have a low income and asset level? | No | Yes |
| Waiting period before benefits begin? | Yes, five months | No |
| Retroactive benefits? | Yes, up to 12 months | No |
| Back payments? | Yes | Yes |

47. *Id.*

| Comparing Programs: SSDI versus SSI | | |
|---|---|---|
| | **SSDI** | **SSI** |
| Minimum duration of disability required? | 12 months | 12 months |
| Disability freeze available? | Yes | No |
| Compassionate Allowances program applicable? | Yes | Yes |
| Benefits maintained during trial work period? | Yes | Yes |

## E. Appealing an SSA Decision

The rate of SSDI and SSI approvals vary state by state, with the national average of approximately 33 percent. This can be discouraging to many applicants. Fortunately, individuals have the right to appeal the SSA's denial decision.

There are four levels of appeals for initial SSA determinations:

1. **Request for reconsideration.**[48] This is an initial request for the SSA to review an individual's application again. The first appeal must be in writing and sent within 60 days of receiving the denial letter. The SSA assumes that individuals have received the letter five days after the date on the letter, unless individuals can prove otherwise.[49]
2. **Hearing with an Administrative Law Judge (ALJ).**[50] The hearing will be conducted by an ALJ, and can be held online or in person, at a location that is usually within 75 miles of an individual's home. If possible, it is in the individual's best interests to attend the hearing, because the judge might ask the individual questions about their job or medical condition. Individuals may also bring a representative, like an attorney, and medical professionals to testify to their medical condition and inability to work.
3. **Review by the Appeals Council.** The Appeals Council may deny a request if it believes the ALJ hearing decision was correct.
4. **Review by a federal court.** If individuals disagree with the Appeals Council's decision, or if the Appeals Council decides not to review their case, individuals may file a lawsuit in federal district court.

48. The form "Request for Reconsideration" can be found online at https://www.ssa.gov/forms/ssa-561.pdf (last visited Nov. 16, 2024).

49. *Understanding Supplemental Security Income Appeals Process—2024 Edition: Appeals Process*, SSA, https://www.ssa.gov/ssi/text-appeals-ussi.htm (last visited Nov. 16, 2024).

50. The form "Request for Hearing by Administrative Law Judge" can be found online at https://www.ssa.gov/forms/ha-501.pdf (last visited Nov. 16, 2024).

Each level of appeal will delve into great detail about the individual's medical condition and the severity of the disability.[51] Individuals coping with cancer should enlist their health care team's assistance in their initial application for, and appeal of a denial of, SSA benefits.

If an individual decides to appeal an SSDI or an SSI determination, the individual may consider hiring an attorney. Social Security disability attorneys work on a contingency fee, meaning they will take a case even if the individual does not have the money up front to pay for the attorney's services. If the attorney wins an appeal, they will take a percentage of past-due benefits (retroactive and back payments) an individual receives. Any fee charged by a representative must be approved in writing by the SSA. The SSA will not approve a fee that exceeds 25 percent of the past-due benefits an individual is awarded, up to a maximum of $9,200.[52] However, individuals should keep in mind that this representation may not be totally free. Attorneys are entitled to charge clients for other expenses that are not related to the fee for representation, such as reimbursement for the cost of obtaining medical records, postage, or travel expenses. Individuals should make sure they understand what an attorney is planning on charging for these types of items, prior to signing a contract with the attorney.

**Attorney Fee Calculation Example**

Sally appeals the SSA's denial of her cancer-related disability claim. Sally wins and is awarded $20,000 in back pay and retroactive benefits.

Sally's attorney will be paid $5,000 (25 percent of $20,000) and Sally will receive $15,000.

The other caveat is when an individual has a particularly complicated case that requires multiple hearings or an appeal to the Appeals Council or federal court. In those circumstances, a disability lawyer is permitted to file a fee petition with the SSA to request to be paid more than the $9,200 limit.[53] The SSA will review the fee petition and will approve it only if it is reasonable. At that point, the individual has the right to decide to end the appeal. To find a reputable Social Security appeals attorney, see the resources in Section VI.

51. *See* 20 C.F.R. § 416.912(b).

52. *Fee Agreements*, SSA, https://www.ssa.gov/representation/fee_agreements.htm (last visited Nov. 16, 2024).

53. *Id.*

## F. Continuing Disability Reviews

Once individuals become eligible for SSDI or SSI, they should expect that the SSA will conduct a review of their medical condition periodically, to ensure they are still experiencing a qualifying disability. This process is referred to as a continuing disability review (CDR). The frequency of CDRs will depend on their disability and if they are expected to improve. If the SSA feels improvement is "expected," it will generally conduct a review six to 18 months after the date it determined an individual became disabled. If the SSA believes that improvement is "possible, but can't be predicted," it will conduct a review approximately every three years. If the SSA believes that improvement is "not expected," it will conduct a review every seven years.[54]

During a CDR, individuals will be mailed a notice of review and likely asked to complete an SSA-454-BK, Continuing Disability Review Report.[55] This form asks questions about an individual's medical information for the past year, including medical conditions, treatment received, and medications. Additionally, the report inquires as to engagement in any education, training, employment, and daily activities. With an individual's permission, the SSA may contact health care providers for additional information or corroboration.

If, upon review, the SSA concludes that the individual no longer has the disability, the individual will be sent a termination notice. In order to justify a termination of SSI benefits, the SSA has the burden to prove that the individual has experienced "medical improvement."[56] Individuals have 60 days after receiving the letter to file an appeal for termination of benefits. The SSA assumes that the letter was received five days after the date on it, unless an individual can prove otherwise. If the appeal is filed within ten days, the individual can request that their benefits continue while the appeal is processed. However, if an individual's appeal is unsuccessful, the individual may be asked to pay back the benefits received during the appeal period.[57]

## G. Taxes and Social Security Disability Benefits

Some individuals will be required to pay taxes on Social Security disability benefits they receive. Typically, this is only an issue if the individual receives some other substantial income.

Individuals receiving SSDI will likely have to pay federal taxes on their disability benefits if they:

---

54. *Understanding Supplemental Security Income Continuing Disability Reviews—2024 Edition: Continuing Disability Reviews*, SSA, https://www.ssa.gov/ssi/text-cdrs-ussi.htm (last visited Nov. 16, 2024).

55. SSA, POMS DI 13005.040 Completion of the Form SSA-454-BK (Continuing Disability Review Report) in Adult and Title XVI Child Continuing Disability Review (CDR) Cases (2023), https://secure.ssa.gov/poms.nsf/lnx/0413005040.

56. 20 C.F.R. § 404.1594.

57. *Id.* § 404.1597A.

- File a federal tax return as an "individual," and have an annual income more than $25,000
- File a joint federal tax return, and collectively have an annual income of more than $32,000
- Are married and file a separate return[58]

It may be in an individual's best interest to consult with a tax professional. For more information about Social Security benefits and taxes, visit https://triagecancer.org/quick-guides/taxes-disability-retirement.

Generally, individuals who receive SSI do not meet the income threshold to be required to pay federal taxes on their benefits.[59] However, it may still be in an individual's best interest to file a tax return, even if they do not owe taxes. (See Chapter 6, Finances.)

## H. Social Security Overpayments

Occasionally, the SSA makes mistakes and overpays beneficiaries. The amount of the overpayment is the difference in the amount one received and the amount of benefits one should have actually received. Overpayments can occur for a number of reasons including that the beneficiary's income is more than estimated; the beneficiary no longer has a disability but continued to receive benefits; the beneficiary's living situation changes; or the benefits are incorrectly calculated due to incorrect or incomplete information.[60]

The SSA will send a written notice explaining the overpayment and asking for a refund within 30 days. The notice must include the reason for overpayment, the time period where there was an overpayment of benefits, and the amount of overpayment for each time period. The overpayment notice must also include information about the beneficiary's rights and how to take next steps. If an individual receives an overpayment notice, they can take one of three steps.

1. Challenge that the individual received an overpayment or the amount of the overpayment by filing a request for reconsideration. Generally, the burden of proof is on the SSA to provide a logical explanation of why the overpayment happened and how it was calculated. The request must be filed in writing, within 60 days, using Form SSA-561.[61] The form can be submitted online using

58. SSA, WHAT YOU NEED TO KNOW WHEN YOU GET SOCIAL SECURITY DISABILITY BENEFITS (2024), https://www.ssa.gov/pubs/EN-05-10153.pdf.

59. *Publication 17 (2023), Your Federal Income Tax*, INTERNAL REVENUE SERV., https://www.irs.gov/publications/p17/ch01.html#en_US_2016_publink1000170388 (last updated Sept. 10, 2024).

60. *Repay Overpaid Social Security Benefits*, SSA, https://www.ssa.gov/manage-benefits/repay-overpaid-benefits (last visited Nov. 16, 2024).

61. The form can be found here: https://www.ssa.gov/forms/ssa-561-u2.pdf (last visited Nov. 16, 2024).

the SSA's iAppeals system, by calling (800) 772-1213, by certified mail with a return receipt, or in person at a local SSA office.

2. Ask the SSA to waive its right to collect the overpayment. In order to get a waiver to avoid repayment, the individual must be without fault in causing the overpayment and recovery would either defeat the purpose of the Social Security Act, or "be against equity and good conscience." The individual has the burden of proof to show that they qualifies for the waiver by a preponderance of evidence.
3. Try to negotiate a lower repayment amount using Form SSA-634 to request a change in the repayment rate. For SSDI beneficiaries, there is no limit to how much to recoup. For SSI benefits, the SSA limits the recoup amount to just 10 percent of monthly benefits. The decision made after the negotiation cannot be appealed.

The SSA has acknowledged the challenge of overpayments and is seeking ways to improve this system.

## I. Social Security Disability Benefits and Unemployment

Due to the often lengthy determination process for Social Security disability benefits, some individuals may attempt to collect unemployment benefits while they are waiting for the SSA to make a determination. Generally, individuals cannot be eligible for both Social Security disability benefits and unemployment benefits. The rationale is that every state's unemployment program requires individuals to certify that they are able to work and actively looking for work. However, the SSA program requires an individual to be unable to work because of a medical condition. This is certainly true for SDI programs and unemployment. However, although the two programs seem to be in conflict, there are limited circumstances when collecting both unemployment benefits and Social Security disability benefits is possible. For example:

- If you are seeking some work, but the type of work is limited due to your disability and will pay you less than $1,620 per month (in 2025) you may be able to collect unemployment and SSDI.
- If you are collecting unemployment, and then become disabled, you may be able to continue collecting unemployment while you apply for SSDI.
- If you receive SSDI, start working through the Ticket to Work Program for at least six months, and are then laid off, you may be entitled to collect unemployment benefits while receiving SSDI.

In *Cleveland v. Policy Management Systems Corp.*,[62] Carolyn Cleveland suffered from a stroke, which damaged her concentration, memory, and language skills.

62. 526 U.S. 795 (1999).

Cleveland applied for SSDI stating she was completely disabled. A few months later, and prior to the SSA making a determination on her SSDI claim, Cleveland returned to her job and was subsequently fired. Prior to receiving notice from the SSA about her SSDI approval, Cleveland brought suit against her former employer alleging they violated the ADA. The lower court granted summary judgment, claiming that "the application for or the receipt of social security disability benefits creates a *rebuttable* presumption that the claimant or recipient of such benefits is judicially estopped from asserting that he is a 'qualified individual with a disability.'"[63] On appeal, the U.S. Supreme Court held that (1) claims for SSDI benefits and for ADA damages do not inherently conflict, and (2) an individual is entitled to an opportunity to explain any discrepancy between their statement in pursuing SSDI benefits that they were totally disabled and the individual's ADA claim that they could perform essential functions of the job. A similar analysis can be applied to the simultaneous applications for unemployment and SSDI. In other words, just because an individual is able to work, it does not mean that the individual will be able to earn an amount above the SGA threshold.

Furthermore, the SSA's official stance is that receiving unemployment benefits does not automatically preclude an individual from receiving Social Security disability benefits. However, ALJs may consider an individual's application for or receipt of unemployment benefits as an indication that the individual is able to work and, therefore, ineligible for disability benefits.

Therefore, while the law does not preclude an individual from applying for both unemployment and SSDI benefits, it could be problematic during an SSDI appeals hearing. If an individual believes they fall in the limited exceptions, the individual should consider contacting a disability attorney.

## J. How Employment Laws and Disability Insurance Interact

Often, the way that federal laws, state laws, and employer policies work together are like puzzle pieces fitting together—except that each puzzle looks a little different, depending on which laws apply to an individual, the state the individual lives in, and what benefits an individual's employer offers.

When an individual is deciding whether to take time off work for cancer treatment or recovery, the individual may have multiple options available. Some individuals ask, "Can I use my sick time, then my vacation time, then my FMLA, and then I also have a short-term disability policy at work. Can I string them all out to cover all the time that I need to be away from work because of my cancer treatment?" And the answer is, "It depends."

63. Cleveland v. Pol'y Mgmt. Sys. Corp., 120 F.3d 513, 518 (5th Cir. 1997) (emphasis added).

## 1. The FMLA Can Work with Paid Leave Options and Disability Insurance

- **FMLA.** The FMLA is a federal law that provides eligible employees with up to 12 weeks of unpaid, but job-protected, leave per year. (See Chapter 2, Employment.)
- **Paid time off (PTO).** Employers may offer paid vacation days, sick days, or just a general bank of PTO hours for employees to use for vacation or sick leave. (See Chapter 2.)
- **Disability insurance.** If an employee needs to take time off because of a medical condition, or is unable to work at all, an employee may be able to replace lost wages using disability insurance.

Step 1: Find out if any of these options are available to you.
Step 2: Figure how they can work together.

## *Case Study: Nancy*

*Nancy has three weeks of vacation and three weeks of sick time, her employer is covered by the FMLA, and her employer offers a short-term disability insurance policy that lasts up to 12 months. Nancy thinks that she will need to be out of work for 12 weeks. What are Nancy's options?*

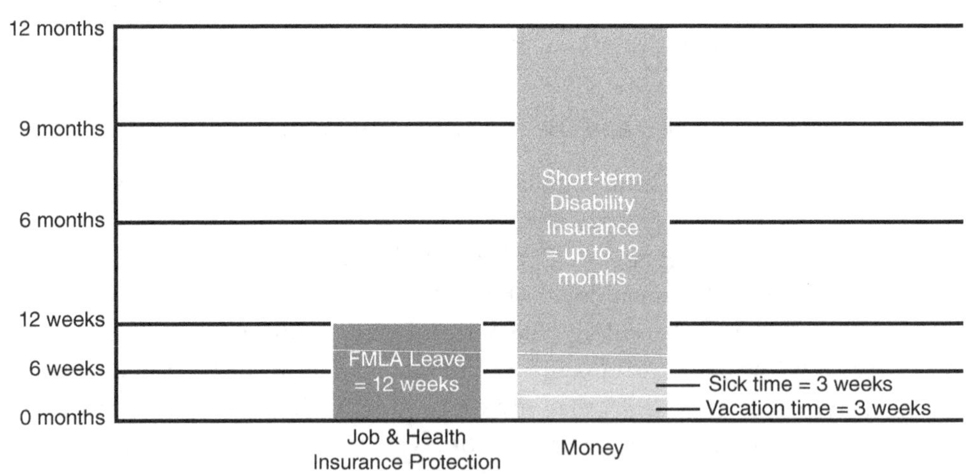


As shown in the previous figure, Nancy can use all of her benefits together, concurrently, to get access to job and health insurance protections as well as paid leave. In fact, her employer can require her to substitute the unpaid leave under the FMLA with any paid leave that she has (e.g., her sick time hours). But, if her employer does not require her to do that, and she still wants to, her employer must allow the following:

1. Take her 12 weeks off work under the FMLA, which provides her with job protection and maintains her health insurance
2. For the first three weeks that she is off, she is paid by her vacation days
3. For the next three weeks that she is off, she is paid by her sick time
4. And, for the final six weeks, she is paid a portion of her salary by her short-term disability policy

Using these benefits together allows Nancy to maintain her income, while also protecting her job and access to health insurance coverage.

If Nancy prefers to string out her sick time and vacation time, use her FMLA, and then use her short-term disability benefits, she may be able to do that, but only if her employer allows her to. However, Nancy should know that just taking sick time or vacation time, or receiving short-term disability benefits, does not protect her job. In this situation, it is the FMLA that is providing the job protection.

## 2. The FMLA Can Work with Paid Leave, Disability Insurance, and the ADA (or State Fair Employment Law)

## *Case Study: Mark*

*Mark has three weeks of vacation and three weeks of sick time, his employer is covered by the FMLA, and his employer offers a short-term disability insurance policy that lasts up to 12 months. Mark thinks that he will need to be out of work for 15 weeks. What are Mark's options?*

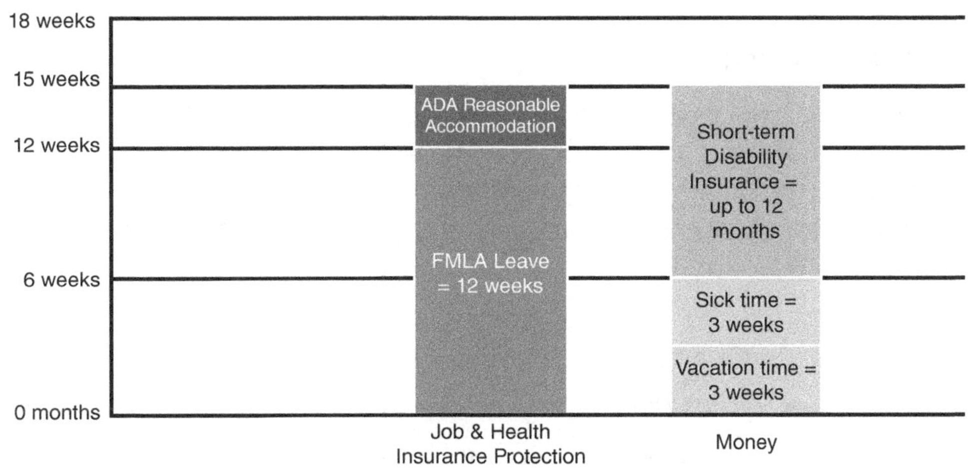

As shown in the previous figure, Mark can use all of his benefits together, concurrently. If he wants to, his employer must allow the following:

- Take his 12 weeks off work under the FMLA, which provides him with job protection and maintains his health insurance
- Take the remaining three weeks off work as a reasonable accommodation under the ADA, which also provides him with job protection
- For the first three weeks that he is off, he is paid by his vacation days
- For the next three weeks that he is off, he is paid by his sick time
- And, for the final nine weeks, he is paid a portion of his salary by his short-term disability policy

Using these benefits together allows Mark to maintain his income, while also protecting his job and access to health insurance coverage.

## K. Reporting Changes

Individuals collecting both SSDI and SSI are responsible for reporting changes in their circumstances to the SSA. Changes should be reported as soon as possible and no later than ten days after the end of the month in which the change occurred. Failing to report changes in a timely manner could result in underpayment, overpayment for which the individual would have to pay monies back to the SSA plus a penalty, or, at worst, the SSA could withhold payments for up to 12 months.[64]

The types of changes that should be reported to the SSA include any changes in work status, household size, address, immigration status, income, marital status, or health status.[65] For a complete list of changes that must be reported by individuals receiving SSI, and how to report those changes, visit https://www.ssa.gov/ssi/text-report-ussi.htm. For individuals receiving SSDI, see the SSA's "What You Need to Know When You Get Social Security Disability Benefits" at https://www.ssa.gov/pubs/EN-05-10153.pdf.

## L. Returning to Work

Many individuals who receive disability benefits through SSDI and SSI after a cancer diagnosis eventually want to return to work. However, there is often a fear about trying to return to work, but being unable to work at the same capacity they could prior to a cancer diagnosis, and how that might affect their disability and health insurance benefits.

---

64. *Understanding Supplemental Security Income Reporting Responsibilities—2024 Edition: Reporting Responsibilities*, SSA, https://www.ssa.gov/ssi/text-report-ussi.htm (last visited Nov. 16, 2024).

65. SSA Form SSA-16-INST, https://www.ssa.gov/forms/ssa-16-inst.pdf (last visited Nov. 16, 2024).

Fortunately, the SSA has programs in place to assist individuals who want to return to work. Collectively, these programs are referred to as "work incentives." The programs available can vary depending on if an individual is receiving SSI or SSDI.[66] For example, the trial work period allows an individual to attempt to return to work while keeping access to cash benefits and Medicare. Other work incentives include help with education, training, and rehabilitation to start in a new line of work.

For more information about returning to work and disability insurance benefits, visit https://triagecancer.org/cancer-finances-disability-insurance.

## M. Social Security Benefits for Family Members

Family members may be eligible for different types of benefits from the SSA such as SSDI benefits; retirement benefits; survivor benefits; and death benefits.

### 1. SSDI Benefits

If an individual receives SSDI benefits, the individual's family members may be able to receive benefits based on the individual's work history, including:

- A spouse
  - o age 62+, unless the spouse collects a higher Social Security benefit based on their earnings, or
  - o at any age if they are caring for the individual's child under age 16, or who was disabled before age 22 and is entitled to benefits
- A divorced spouse
  - o who was married to the individual for at least ten years and is now unmarried,
  - o is at least 62 years old, or
  - o is not eligible for an equal or higher benefit on their own Social Security record, or on someone else's Social Security record
- Children (including biological children, adopted children, or stepchildren)
- Adult children with a disability (if the disability began before age 22)

Based on a formula, each family member could receive a monthly benefit up to 50 percent of the individual's disability benefit amount. But that amount is capped for the family. Typically, the total amount the individual and their family can receive is around 150 to 180 percent of the individual's disability benefit. Note: A divorced spouse's benefits are not included in the family maximum.[67]

---

66. *Ticket to Work*, SSA, https://www.ssa.gov/work/ (last visited Nov. 16, 2024).
67. *Family Benefits*, SSA, https://www.ssa.gov/family (last visited Nov. 16, 2024).

## 2. Retirement Benefits

If an individual receives Social Security retirement benefits, the family members may be able to receive benefits, based on the record of the individual who retires. Payments to family members will not decrease the amount of the retiree's retirement benefit.

**Spouse.** A spouse or former spouse may get up to 50 percent of the retiree's full benefit when an individual starts receiving Social Security retirement benefits. To get benefits, the spouse or former spouse must be either

- age 62 or older; or
- younger than 62, if taking care of a child who is younger than age 16 or has a qualifying disability; and is also eligible for benefits on the retiree's record.[68]

This can be helpful for a spouse who has never worked or had a job that did not pay into the Social Security retirement system. Also, if the spouse earned less than the retiree, and, therefore, their benefits are lower than the retiree's then the spouse could get an additional payment so that the benefits are equal.

For example, Jane qualifies for a retirement benefit of $1,250 and her spouse's benefit is $1,400. At her full retirement age, she will get her own $1,250 retirement benefit. The SSA will also add $150 to match her spouse's benefit, for a total of $1,400. Her spouse will also receive the full $1,400. If either of them takes their retirement benefit before their full retirement age, both amounts are reduced.

**Children.** A dependent child may get up to 50 percent of a retiree's full benefit when an individual starts receiving Social Security retirement benefits. To get benefits, the child must be unmarried and

- younger than age 18;
- 18–19 years old and a full-time student (no higher than grade 12); or
- have a disability, even if older than 18, and the disability began before age 22.[69]

A stepchild is eligible for benefits only if the stepparent financially supported the stepchild before the stepparent becomes eligible for benefits or dies. Social Security may also pay benefits to grandchildren, when the grandparent retires, becomes disabled, or dies, if certain rules are met. Generally, the biological parents of the child must be deceased or have a disability, or the grandparent legally adopts the grandchild.

For more information about Social Security retirement benefits, visit https://www.ssa.gov/retirement.

---

68. *Id.*
69. *Id.*

## N. Survivor Benefits

Social Security survivors benefits are payments made to family members of deceased workers who were receiving or were eligible for Social Security benefits. Most of the time, survivor benefits are based on the amount the worker was receiving (or was entitled to receive) from Social Security at the time of death.[70] Family members eligible for survivor benefits are:

Widows and widowers:

1. If they are 60 or older
2. If they are 50 or older and have a disability
3. If they are under 50 and they take care of the individual's child who is under 16 or has a disability

Divorced widows and widowers:

1. If they are 60 or older and the marriage lasted at least ten years
2. If they are 50, have a disability, and the marriage lasted at least ten years
3. If they are under 50 and they take care of the individual's child who is under 16 or has a disability

Unmarried children:

1. If they are under 18 (or up to age 19 if they are attending elementary or secondary school full time)
2. If they are over 18 and they have a disability that began before they were 22
3. Under certain circumstances, benefits can also be paid to stepchildren, grandchildren, stepgrandchildren, or adopted children

Dependent parents:

1. If they are 62 or older and received at least half of their financial support from the individual

The amount that family members could receive depends on the worker's earnings. These are examples of monthly payments:

- Widow or widower, full retirement age or older: 100 percent of your benefit amount
- Widow or widower, age 60 to full retirement age: 71.5 to 99 percent of your basic amount
- Widow or widower with a disability, age 50 through 59: 71.5 percent
- Widow or widower, any age, caring for a child under age 16: 75 percent
- Children: 75 percent

---

70. SSA, Survivors Benefits (2024), https://www.ssa.gov/pubs/EN-05-10084.pdf.

- A parent who was dependent on you for at least half of their support, age 62 or older:
  - One surviving parent: 82.5 percent; two surviving parents: 75 percent to each parent

For more information about survivor benefits, visit https://www.ssa.gov/survivor.

### O. Death Benefits

A surviving spouse or child may also be entitled to a one-time death payment of $255 from the SSA, if the spouse or child meets certain rules. Generally, the surviving spouse who was living in the same house when the individual dies will receive the payment. If they were living apart, the surviving spouse can still receive this payment if, during the month the worker died, they were already receiving benefits on the worker's record or became eligible for benefits upon the worker's death. If there is no eligible surviving spouse, the child (or children) will receive the payment if, during the month the worker died, the child was already receiving benefits on the worker's record or became eligible for benefits upon the worker's death. If the eligible surviving spouse or child is not currently receiving benefits, the spouse or child must apply for this payment within two years of the worker's death.

## V. Conclusion

While studies have shown that many individuals want to continue working after a cancer diagnosis,[71] it is often not possible, at least for a period of time. Maintaining some level of income is necessary to help individuals coping with cancer avoid losing their homes and their possessions, and ultimately to avoid bankruptcy. Disability insurance is one option to help bridge the financial gap that is created by being unable to work. There are multiple types of disability insurance, and while they can work together, it can be a challenging maze to navigate. Understanding the landscape of disability insurance is vital for individuals coping with cancer, their caregivers, advocates, and health care professionals.

## VI. Resources

SSA: https://www.ssa.gov

Triage Cancer Resources: Disability Insurance Resource Hub: https://triagecancer.org/disabilityinsurance

---

71. *2023 Cancer and Careers/The Harris Poll Survey: Work Motivation, Disclosure & Need for Support*, CANCER & CAREERS (Dec. 2023), https://www.cancerandcareers.org/newsfeed/research/posts/2023/12/2023-cancer-and-careers-the-ha.

Legal Assistance:

Triage Cancer—Cancer Finances Module on Legal Assistance: https://triagecancer.org/cancer-finances-legal-assistance

LawHelp: https://www.lawhelp.org

American Bar Association Lawyer Referral Directory: https://www.americanbar.org/groups/lawyer_referral/resources/lawyer-referral-directory/

# VII. Exercises and Discussion Topics

## A. Case Studies

1. Mary is a 62-year-old nurse who was diagnosed with cancer early last year. When she had her surgery, she took six weeks off under the FMLA and was paid a portion of her salary through an employer-sponsored short-term disability policy. A co-worker recommended that she retire early, but Mary really loves her job. As a result of her treatment, she is suffering from depression and chemo brain (short-term memory loss, inability to focus, etc.) as well as a tremor in her left hand. These side effects of treatment make her feel like she cannot continue to do her nursing job. The hospital pays for her health insurance coverage and has a rule that they will pay 100 percent of her premiums while receiving employer-sponsored disability benefits, but does not cover health insurance for retirees. She has some other benefits through her job at the hospital and as a union member, but she has not looked at that binder of paperwork in several years. She has some savings but is concerned about how she is going to pay her bills after her savings are exhausted. She is also concerned that if she applies for disability benefits, she would never be able to go back to work. *What are Mary's options?*

   **Answer.** One of the first steps Mary should take is to gather some additional information. For example, does she have a private LTD insurance policy through her employer and what does her union contract say about disability and retirement? If Mary has an LTD policy through her employer, she should contact the administrator and get information about whether she qualifies and how to submit a claim.

   If Mary's union contract required that she pay into the Social Security system, she may have the option to elect early retirement through the SSA and begin receiving partial retirement payments. Before electing early retirement, Mary should weigh her options carefully, because if she elects early retirement and subsequently files for SSDI, she will be denied. However, if Mary decides to first apply for SSDI, then elects early retirement, she may fare better. The reason is that if the SSA finds Mary to have a DOD prior to her electing early retirement, the SSA will retroactively pay the difference between Mary's partial

SSA retirement benefits and the full disability amount for the months she was disabled but collecting early retirement. Additionally, when Mary turns 67, she will be able to collect full retirement benefits, as if she never elected to retire early. Additionally, Mary's employer will pay 100 percent of her health insurance premiums while she is collecting employer-sponsored disability benefits, but they will not cover health insurance for retirees. Therefore, it may be in Mary's best interest to forgo early retirement and maintain her employer-sponsored health insurance for as long as possible to bridge the gap between that coverage and when she becomes eligible for Medicare.

Mary also has the option to forgo early retirement altogether and apply for SSDI. This option may be feasible especially if she has a private LTD policy to help her pay her bills during the five-month waiting period. Mary would likely meet the SSA's definition of "disability" in that she can no longer do her job as a nurse and the fact that her diagnosis is included in the CAL. The burden would then shift to the SSA to prove that there was an alternative job for Mary given her extensive disabilities. Mary should be cognizant of the fact that the private LTD payments will be reduced if she is awarded SSDI and she may have to repay to the LTD company any retroactive or back payments she receives from SSDI.

Depending on Mary's income and asset level once she stops working, she may also be eligible for SSI. However, if she does have a private LTD policy, it is likely that those payments would push her income over the SSI income limit.

Mary may also be able to apply for SSDI even if she is currently working, as long as she is not earning more than the current SGA amount ($1,550 in 2023).

Mary has indicated that finances are not the sole reason she works. For Mary, her job is her passion and a large part of her identity; therefore, if it is possible, she would like to work in some capacity after completing her cancer treatment. If Mary receives SSDI or SSI, there are multiple return-to-work programs that could be useful, including the trial work period when she can attempt to return to work while maintaining her disability and health insurance benefits.

2. Margaret started treatment for her cancer on March 1, 2023. As a result of the side effects from treatment she could not work and began using her LTD policy through her employer, which pays 80 percent of her income. She began receiving LTD benefits March 1, 2023. In July 2023, the LTD policy sent Margaret a letter saying she had to apply for SSDI. She applied for SSDI on September 1, 2023. Her SSDI application was approved on December 1, 2023, and the SSA agreed that her DOD was March 1, 2023. Margaret's SSDI benefit amount equals 60 percent of her income when working. *When would Margaret receive her first SSDI check and how much would it be for? What percentage will the*

*LTD policy continue paying? Does Margaret have to pay anything back to the LTD policy? If so, how much?*

## B. Discussion Topics

1. Individuals receiving SSI are immediately eligible for Medicaid, whereas individuals receiving SSDI must wait 24 months before they become eligible for Medicare. Should that be amended to provide immediate access to Medicare? Why or why not?
2. There is a wide discrepancy between ALJ decisions in the appeals process. Is there a way to standardize the process so that it is less subjective or are these disparities an inevitable result of judicial discretion?
3. Many advocates have called for the elimination of the five-month waiting period for SSDI benefits. Is this a sound public policy decision? Why or why not?
4. What are the practical challenges facing individuals diagnosed with cancer in getting access to Social Security disability benefits?

## C. Multimedia Sources

Triage Cancer Webinar Series: Cancer & Disability Insurance: https://triagecancer.org/webinar-disability

Triage Cancer Explains: How to Take Time Off & Pay for It: https://triagecancer.org/video-takingtimeoff

How to Triage Cancer Podcast—Understanding Disability Insurance: https://triagecancer.org/podcast

# CHAPTER FOUR

# Biomarkers and Genetics

## *Case Study: Jenny*

*Jenny, 39, was a five-year employee of a small company with 16 employees.*[1] *Jenny consistently received outstanding performance reviews and was even promoted twice. During Jenny's time at the company, two of her sisters were diagnosed with breast cancer. Jenny grew concerned that she would also be diagnosed with breast cancer, and she decided to take a genetic test to determine her risk level. The genetic test revealed that Jenny did have a genetic mutation that significantly increased her risk of developing breast cancer. Based on the test findings, Jenny decided to undergo a preventive bilateral mastectomy to reduce her risk of developing breast cancer.*[2] *Jenny spoke with her employer about her decision to get the operation and requested one month off of work for the surgery and recovery. A few days after that meeting, Jenny was terminated and was told it was because the company was downsizing. Upset and concerned about her future, Jenny shared this information with her social worker at her next appointment and asked for advice.*

1. This case study is loosely based on *Fink v. MX Energy* (2010), where Pamela Fink filed a genetic discrimination complaint against her employer, MX Energy, when it discharged her after she revealed her genetic susceptibility to breast cancer. *See* Steven Greenhouse, *Ex-Worker Says Her Firing Was Based on Genetic Test*, N.Y. Times (Apr. 30, 2010), http://www.nytimes.com/2010/05/01/us/01gene.html.

2. A preventive, or prophylactic, bilateral mastectomy is a surgical procedure whereby an individual who does not currently have breast cancer has both breasts removed in order to lessen their risk of developing the disease.

# I. Introduction

The field of biomarkers is a prime example of where the law cannot always keep up with advances in science and technology.

A biomarker is a gene, protein, or other substance that is in your blood, bodily fluids, tumors, or cells.

Biomarker testing is a way to look for those biomarkers that can provide information about an individual's cancer. Biomarker testing can be called different names, including genomic testing or profiling, tumor testing or subtyping, tumor genetic testing, somatic testing, or companion diagnostic testing (when paired with a specific treatment).

Some biomarker tests can test a solid tumor, and some can test your blood and other fluids for biomarkers (i.e., liquid biopsies).

Scientific advancements in the field of biomarker testing have created new ways for health care professionals to target therapies for specific patients, ultimately improving health outcomes. This is often called personalized or precision medicine. Biomarker testing is a key part of getting access to precision medicine. For example, some targeted therapies may only work if an individual has certain biomarkers.

Biomarker testing is different from hereditary genetic testing, which can provide information about an individual's risk for developing cancer. The increased availability of, and access to, biomarker and genetic testing has brought about some challenges with respect to privacy and discrimination issues, while providing useful information to individuals and their health care teams. For example, it may be useful for individuals to know that they have tested positive for an inherited genetic mutation that increases their likelihood of developing cancer, because they could make certain decisions to manage their health, such as request cancer screening tests, make lifestyle changes, or undergo preventive surgery. However, they may also be worried that the results of their genetic tests could lead to them being unable to access insurance or being discriminated against in some other way. This chapter focuses on genetic testing, and how the law addresses genetic discrimination.

## A. What Is Genetic Information?

Genetic information is information about an individual's chromosomes, genes, or proteins.[3] Some laws define "genetic information" only as information that comes from a genetic test, while others treat genetic information more broadly, including all information about an individual's family medical history as part of their genetic information.

3. *Genetic Testing for Inherited Cancer Risk*, NAT'L CANCER INST., https://www.cancer.gov/about-cancer/causes-prevention/genetics/genetic-testing-fact-sheet (last reviewed Apr. 18, 2024).

## B. What Is Genetic Counseling?

Genetic counseling is a process to help individuals understand how their genetic characteristics might impact their health or the health of their family and a way to help manage the medical, psychological, and familial implications of learning about their genetic characteristics. Genetic counseling can include:

- Interpretation of family and medical histories to assess the chance of disease occurrence or recurrence
- Education about genetic testing, health management, prevention, resources, and research
- Counseling to promote informed choices and adaptation to the risk or condition[4]

Genetic counseling is typically conducted by genetic counselors, who are health care professionals with specialized graduate degrees and experience in the areas of medical genetics and counseling.[5] The decision to undergo genetic testing or to learn more about one's medical family history can be incredibly challenging and emotional. These are very personal decisions and genetic counselors can be an excellent source of information and support.

## C. What Is Genetic Testing?

Genetic testing is designed to identify individuals who carry a genetic mutation for a particular disorder or that causes a higher risk of developing a particular disorder.[6] In some more rare circumstances, carrying a genetic mutation confirms that the individual will develop a particular disorder. Genetic mutations can have a beneficial, neutral, or harmful effect on an individual's health, but genetic mutations play a role in the development of all cancers.[7] Most mutations occur during a person's lifetime, but some mutations, including those that are associated with hereditary cancer syndromes, can be inherited from an individual's parents. To date, more than 50 hereditary cancer syndromes have been identified, and there are genetic tests for many of these syndromes.[8] Although some individuals have strong family histories of cancer, the cancer may not be caused by an inherited mutation. It is estimated that only approximately 5–10 percent of all cancers are hereditary.[9]

---

4. *Who Are Genetic Counselors?*, Nat'l Soc'y Genetic Counselors, https://www.aboutgeneticcounselors.com/Who-Are-Genetic-Counselors/Who-Are-Genetic-Counselors (last visited Nov. 18, 2024).

5. To find a genetic counselor, see *Find a Genetic Counselor*, Nat'l Soc'y Genetic Counselors, https://findageneticcounselor.nsgc.org (last visited Nov. 18, 2024).

6. *NCI Dictionary of Genetics Terms*, Nat'l Cancer Inst., https://www.cancer.gov/publications/dictionaries/genetics-dictionary (last visited Nov. 18, 2024).

7. *Genetic Testing for Inherited Cancer Risk*, *supra* note 3.

8. *Id.*

9. *Id.*

Insurance may or may not cover the cost of genetic testing. Some private health insurers and some state Medicaid programs will cover genetic tests for certain medical conditions, such as breast and ovarian cancer.[10] Under the Patient Protection and Affordable Care Act of 2010 (ACA), for individuals who meet the U.S. Preventive Services Task Force's definition of being at high risk for the BRCA1 or BRCA2 genetic mutations, most private insurance companies are required to cover the entire cost of genetic testing and genetic counseling.[11] This means that those individuals do not have to pay a co-payment, a coinsurance amount, or a deductible to access genetic testing and counseling. For more information about insurance coverage of genetic testing, see Chapter 1, Health Insurance.

## D. What Is Genetic Discrimination?

Genetic discrimination occurs when an individual is treated differently than other similarly situated individuals because of their genetic information, including family medical history.

According to the U.S. Equal Employment Opportunity Commission (EEOC), 3,648 genetic discrimination complaints were filed between 2010 and 2022.[12] Although many agree that genetic information should be a highly confidential matter between individuals and their health care providers, employers and insurance companies have financial motivations to obtain such information and potentially use it adversely. Employers might discriminate against current or prospective employees based on genetic information because they assume that people with a higher risk of developing cancer will eventually miss work, require accommodations, or in some way be less of an ideal employee. Furthermore, employers and insurance companies share a concern that individuals with a higher risk of developing cancer will be more expensive to insure. As a consequence, some individuals may be less likely to pursue genetic testing because they fear such discrimination.

In 1998, a case was brought challenging Lawrence Berkeley Laboratory's use of genetic tests to screen employees for syphilis, pregnancy, and sickle cell traits.[13] The laboratory defended the testing on the grounds that the tests were part of generally accepted medical practice; however, the court held that such tests violated the

---

10. *Medicare & Medicaid*, FORCE, https://www.facingourrisk.org/support/insurance-paying-for-care/genetic-services/medicare-medicaid (last visited Nov. 18, 2024).

11. *BRCA-Related Cancer: Risk Assessment, Genetic Counseling, and Genetic Testing*, U.S. Preventive Servs. Task Force, https://www.uspreventiveservicestaskforce.org/uspstf/draft-update-summary/brca-related-cancer-risk-assessment-genetic-counseling-testing (last updated Apr. 5, 2024).

12. *Table E7a. Genetic Information Nondiscrimination Act Charge Receipts and Resolutions by Type FY 2010–FY 2023*, EEOC, https://www.eeoc.gov/sites/default/files/2024-05/Table%20E7a.%20Genetic%20Information%20Nondiscrimination%20Act%20Charge%20Receipts%20and%20Resolutions%20by%20Type%20FY%202010%20-%20FY%202023.csv (last visited Nov. 18, 2024).

13. Norman-Bloodsaw v. Lawrence Berkeley Lab'y, 135 F.3d 1260, 1269 (9th Cir. 1998).

employees' constitutionally guaranteed rights to privacy.[14] Although cases like *Lawrence Berkeley Laboratory* were uncommon, Congress and many state legislatures foresaw the potential for widespread misuse of genetic information and enacted several laws that may protect individuals in specific circumstances.

## II. Genetic Discrimination Laws in Employment

There are three key federal laws and directives that address genetic discrimination in the employment context: the Americans with Disabilities Act (ADA), Executive Order No. 13145, and the Genetic Information Nondiscrimination Act of 2008 (GINA).

### A. ADA

The ADA is a federal law that prohibits discrimination in employment, accommodations, and public services based on an individual's disability. The ADA defines "disability" as a physical or mental impairment that substantially limits a major life activity.[15] The determination of whether or not an individual has a disability is made on a case-by-case basis. In other words, the law will not assume that all individuals with cancer or those with a higher risk of developing cancer have a disability.

In 1995, the EEOC declared that the ADA prohibits discrimination based on genetic information regarding disease or other illness.[16] Similarly, in 2000, EEOC Commissioner Paul Miller emphasized that "the ADA can be interpreted to prohibit employment discrimination based on genetic information."[17] Miller reasoned that employers that discriminate against employees on the basis of genetic information are regarding their employees as having a disability; therefore, the ADA protects those employees. Although these statements were significant, they were not legally binding. On September 25, 2008, the ADA Amendments Act (ADAAA) was signed into law. The main purpose of the ADAAA was to overturn a series of U.S. Supreme Court decisions narrowly interpreting the ADA as applying only to individuals with severely disabling impairments.[18] For more information about the ADA, see Chapter 2, Employment.

The ADA's goal is to prohibit employment discrimination based on a person's medical condition. As such, the ADA clearly prohibits certain conduct by employers.

---

14. *Id.* at 1264.
15. 42 U.S.C. §§ 12111–12117.
16. 2 EEOC, EEOC Compliance Manual, EEOC Order 915.002, Definition of the Term "Disability" 902–45 (1995).
17. Statement of Commissioner Paul Steven Miller, EEOC, before the Senate Committee on Health, Education, Labor, and Pensions (July 20, 2000).
18. *ADAAA* § 2(b)(2)–(b)(5). Among the restrictive decisions mentioned by Congress are *Sutton v. United Air Lines, Inc.*, 527 U.S. 471 (1999); *Murphy v. United Parcel Service, Inc.*, 527 U.S. 516 (1999); *Albertson's, Inc. v. Kirkingburg*, 527 U.S. 555 (1999); and *Toyota Motor Manufacturing, Kentucky, Inc. v. Williams*, 534 U.S. 184 (2002).

For example, the ADA forbids employers from asking questions about a job applicant's medical history or requiring an applicant to have a medical examination prior to making a conditional employment offer. An employer is also prohibited from taking adverse employment actions against an employee who is regarded as having a disability because the employee has a genetic predisposition to cancer.[19] A person's genetic predisposition to cancer may be a disability under the ADA when others regard it as substantially limiting one or more major life activities.[20]

For example, if John has a family history of cancer, and John's boss treats him differently based on that history and fear that he may be diagnosed at some point, then John's genetic predisposition to cancer may qualify him for protection under the ADA. Similarly, if Emily is never given substantial responsibility or a promotion at work because it is widely known that her three sisters have cancer and her bosses are afraid that she will have to take too much time off from work for preventive screenings, Emily's genetic condition could qualify her for protection under the ADA. In both instances, John and Emily may have a valid claim of discrimination under the ADA.

## 1. Using the ADA to Fight Genetic Discrimination

The ADA has been successfully used to challenge an employer's genetic testing practices. In *EEOC v. Burlington Northern Santa Fe Railroad*,[21] defendant Burlington Northern Santa Fe Railroad (BNSF) was secretly conducting genetic tests on employees to detect a rare genetic condition that causes carpal tunnel syndrome (CTS). The defendant ordered company-paid doctors to screen employees for hereditary neuropathy with liability to pressure palsy (HNPP) and several other disorders, including diabetes and alcoholism. The defendant alleged the testing was intended to determine whether high instances of repetitive-stress injuries among its employees were work related. Ultimately, BNSF settled, in 2002, for $2.2 million. The settlement agreement stated:

> BNSF, its officers, agents, employees will not, directly or indirectly, alone or in concert with others: a) require or request its current or former employees to submit to genetic testing; b) submit blood samples previously obtained from current or former employees to any process of genetic testing; c) analyze genetic samples previously extracted from blood samples from current or former employees of BNSF; d) use (including without limitation, evaluate, analyze or consider) any genetic test analysis previously performed on any of its current or former employees; or e) threaten or take any adverse employment

19. 42 U.S.C. §§ 12111–12117.

20. *Id. See also Cancer in the Workplace and the ADA*, EEOC, https://www.eeoc.gov/laws/types/cancer.cfm (last visited Nov. 18, 2024).

21. No. 02-C-0456, 2002 WL 32155386 (E.D. Wis. May 8, 2002).

actions of any kind because of an employee's or former employee's participation in EEOC proceedings challenging the legality of genetic testing or opposition to genetic testing.[22]

Therefore, it could be extrapolated from the outcome in *EEOC v. Burlington Northern Santa Fe Railroad* that the ADA might be a useful tool for fighting genetic discrimination in employment contexts.

## B. Executive Order No. 13145

President William Clinton issued Executive Order No. 13145 on February 8, 2000.[23] Executive Order No. 13145 prohibits discrimination in federal employment based on genetic information. Pursuant to Executive Order No. 13145, federal executive departments and agencies cannot require or request genetic information from their applicants, employees, or former employees, nor can they use such information to make employment decisions.[24]

## C. GINA

GINA is, perhaps, the most significant law to protect an individual against discrimination based on genetic information. GINA prohibits employers and health insurance companies from making "predictive assessments concerning an individual's propensity to get an inheritable genetic disease or disorder based on the occurrence of an inheritable disease or disorder in a family member."[25] GINA has two parts: title I, which prohibits genetic discrimination in health insurance, and title II, which prohibits genetic discrimination in employment.

### 1. Definitions

Under GINA, genetic information cannot be considered a preexisting medical condition.[26] GINA defines "genetic information" as any information about an individual's genetic tests or the genetic tests of a family member, request for and use of genetic services (e.g., genetic testing, counseling, or education), and the manifestation of a disease or disorder in a person's family members (otherwise known as "family medical history").[27] EEOC regulations specifically note that the phrase "manifestation of a disease or disorder in family members" includes a person's "family medical history"

---

22. *See id.*
23. Exec. Order No. 13145, To Prohibit Discrimination in Federal Employment Based on Genetic Information (Feb. 8, 2000), https://www.eeoc.gov/history/executive-order-13145-prohibit-discrimination-federal-employment-based-genetic-information (last visited Nov. 18, 2024).
24. To read the entire order, see *id.*
25. H.R. Rep. No. 110-28, pt. 3, at 70 (2007).
26. 42 U.S.C.A. § 300gg-53(c).
27. *Id.* § 2000ff(4).

as interpreted by medical providers. This is significant because previously genetic information was only considered genetic test results.

Under GINA, a family member includes any relative within four degrees of an individual. Second-degree relatives include grandparents, grandchildren, aunts, uncles, nieces, and nephews. Third-degree relatives include great-grandparents, great-grandchildren, great aunts, great uncles, and first cousins.[28]

It is worth noting, however, that for individuals diagnosed with cancer, their diagnosis is not considered genetic information.[29] If they were to get a positive genetic test result, then that would be considered genetic information. This distinction has practical importance, because it determines which law would protect an individual from discrimination in the workplace. For example, individuals who are being discriminated against at work because of their cancer diagnosis would look to the ADA for protection.

Similarly, an employee who is terminated because of a spouse's cancer diagnosis would also look to the ADA for protection against discrimination rather than GINA. Otherwise, the employee would need to show that the employer used a spouse's cancer diagnosis to predict the employee's likelihood of being diagnosed with cancer, and that the employer fired the employee based on that prediction.[30] Because spouses do not typically share genetic information, that would be a difficult claim to make.

## 2. Title II of GINA

Title II of GINA deals with genetic discrimination in employment settings. GINA covers job applicants, current employees, and former employees. GINA applies to private employers with 15 or more employees, as well as employment agencies, labor organizations, joint labor-management committees, and the federal government.[31] In 2010, the EEOC issued regulations specifically stating that GINA does apply to state and local governments.[32] Indian tribes and bona fide private clubs are not employers under GINA. Under title II, it is unlawful for employers "to fail or refuse to hire, or to discharge, any employee, or otherwise to discriminate against any employee . . . because of *genetic information with respect to the employee*."[33] It is also illegal for employers to do the following:

- Harass an employee based on genetic information
- Attempt to acquire a current or prospective employee's genetic information
- Disclose an employee's genetic information without their consent

28. *Id.* § 2000ff(3).

29. H.R. Rep. No. 110-28, pt. 2, at 27 (2007).

30. *See* Poore v. Peterbilt of Bristol, LLC, 852 F. Supp. 2d 727 (W.D. Va. 2012).

31. 42 U.S.C.A. § 2000ff(2)(B); *see also Background Information for EEOC Final Rule on Title II of the Genetic Information Nondiscrimination Act of 2008*, EEOC, http://www.eeoc.gov/laws/regulations/gina-background.cfm (last visited Nov. 18, 2024).

32. *Background Information for EEOC Final Rule on Title II of the Genetic Information Nondiscrimination Act of 2008*, *supra* note 31.

33. 42 U.S.C.A. § 2000ff-1(a) (emphasis added).

Harassment includes offensive or derogatory comments about an employee's genetic information or the genetic information of an employee's family member. Title II comes into play where the "harassment is so severe or pervasive that it creates a hostile or offensive work environment or when it results in an adverse employment decision." Teasing or isolated incidents, however, are generally not serious enough to assert a successful GINA claim. The employee bears the burden of establishing an actionable harassment case under GINA. The harasser under GINA can be the employee's supervisor, a supervisor in another department, a co-worker, or a nonemployee (i.e., a client).

Under title II, employers are also prohibited from attempting to acquire an employee's genetic information. Generally, employers are not allowed to ask questions related to genetic information, nor are they allowed to conduct independent research that would lead them to such information. There are six narrow exceptions where an employer will not be seen as violating GINA if they acquire an employee's genetic information:

- **Inadvertent acquisition.** An inadvertent acquisition might occur if an employer accidently overhears a discussion where an employee reveals details about their genetic information.
- **Part of a voluntary health service.** Under certain circumstances, the employer can obtain genetic information as part of a health service that the employer offers and for which participation in that service by employees is voluntary (e.g., a voluntary workplace wellness program).
- **Family and Medical Leave Act (FMLA) certification.** An employer can obtain genetic information as part of FMLA certification where an employee requests time off to care for a family member who is sick. For more information about medical certification, see Chapter 2, Employment.
- **Publicly available documents.** If an employee's genetic information is part of publicly available documents, as long as the employer is not searching those documents for the purpose of obtaining the employee's genetic information.
- **Monitoring program.** Employers can obtain genetic information under a legally required genetic monitoring program that measures the effects of toxins in the workplace.
- **DNA testing.** If employees participate in DNA testing for law enforcement purposes or to identify human remains. However, this genetic information can only be used to analyze DNA markers for quality control to uncover sample contamination.[34]

34. *Id.* § 2000ff-4(b).

Even if employers were to legally obtain an employee's genetic information, they are prohibited from disclosing that information without consent from the employee.[35] The disclosure need not be intentional to be actionable under GINA; the mere failure to adequately safeguard genetic information can be a violation of GINA. Employers that possess employees' genetic information are obligated to take measures to protect that information by keeping it in a separate medical file.[36] Employers can, however, distribute the information without consent if it is necessary for a government official's investigation, or if release of such information is required by court order.[37]

## D. Reporting an ADA or GINA Violation

### 1. Against Private-Sector Employers and State and Local Governments

An individual who feels that their rights under the ADA or GINA have been violated should file a complaint with the EEOC. Complaints should be filed within 180 calendar days from the day the discrimination took place. There are a few exceptions to this deadline:

- Individuals who live where a state or local agency also has a relevant fair employment law (300 days)
- Individuals who feel they were discriminated against during the job application process (45 days)
- Individuals who are employees of the federal government (45 days) (see following section)

It is generally in an individual's best interest to file the complaint as soon as possible. An individual can start the process of filing a complaint in person, over the phone, or by mail. While the EEOC does not accept online complaints, they do have an online assessment tool that may be useful for someone who is unsure if they should file a complaint. This tool can be found at https://publicportal.eeoc.gov/. The site will first ask general questions about an individual's complaint to determine whether or not the EEOC can provide assistance. Next, an individual will need to fill out a questionnaire regarding specifics about their employment situation. After an individual fills out the questionnaire, they should bring the questionnaire to the nearest EEOC office to begin filing a charge.[38]

Once the charge is filed, the EEOC will notify the employer and provide the employer with the charge investigator's contact information. The employee and the employer may elect to resolve the dispute through a settlement or mediation. If

35. *Id.* § 2000ff-5.
36. *Id.* § 2000ff-5(a).
37. *Id.* § 2000ff-5(b).
38. To find the closest EEOC office, visit *EEOC Field Offices*, EEOC, https://www.eeoc.gov/field/index.cfm (last visited Nov. 18, 2024).

the parties do not resolve the conflict voluntarily, the investigator will ask both parties for information. The employer may need to supply a statement of its position and copies of policies, files, and other evidence, and the employer may also need to allow on-site investigations and employee interviews.

Once the EEOC has completed its investigation, it will determine whether or not there is "reasonable cause" to believe that discrimination occurred. If there is not enough evidence to support a finding of reasonable cause, the EEOC will distribute a dismissal and notice of rights stating that the employee or job applicant has the right to file a lawsuit against the employer in federal court within 90 days of receipt of notice. Conversely, if the EEOC finds reasonable cause it will issue a letter of determination and try to reconcile the charge. When the charge cannot be resolved through conciliation, the EEOC will either file a lawsuit on behalf of the employee or job applicant or it will issue a notice of right to sue to the employee or job applicant, stating that the employee or job applicant is entitled to file a lawsuit against the employer within 90 days of receipt of the notice. If the process is taking a long time, the employee or job applicant may also request a notice of right to sue from the EEOC if 180 days have passed since originally filing the charge with the EEOC.[39]

For more information about filing a complaint on the basis of genetic discrimination, visit https://www.eeoc.gov/how-file-charge-employment-discrimination.

## 2. Against Federal Agencies

An employee, or job applicant, of the federal government who feels that their GINA rights were violated has 45 days from the date the discrimination occurred to contact an Equal Employment Opportunity (EEO) counselor at the agency where the employee works or applied for a job. The EEO representative will try to resolve the dispute through counseling or alternative dispute resolution (ADR). Usually, counseling concludes within 30 days and ADR concludes within 90 days.

If counseling and ADR are unsuccessful, the charging party may file a complaint with the agency and the agency must investigate the complaint unless it is dismissed. Once the agency concludes its investigation, the employee or job applicant may request an immediate final decision from the agency or a hearing from an EEOC judge. Where a hearing is requested, the administrative judge decides the outcome of the case and issues a notice of that decision to both parties. If the agency does not issue a final order within 40 days of receiving the judge's decision, the judge's decision becomes the agency's final action. Both parties are also entitled to appeal the judge's final decision. The employee or job applicant has 30 days and the federal agency has 40 days to file an appeal.[40]

---

39. For more information on this procedure, visit *What You Can Expect after a Charge Is Filed*, EEOC, https://www.eeoc.gov/employers/process.cfm (last visited Nov. 18, 2024).

40. For more information, see *Background Information for EEOC Final Rule on Title II of the Genetic Information Nondiscrimination Act of 2008*, *supra* note 31.

For more information about the process of filing a complaint as a federal employee, visit https://www.eeoc.gov/federal-sector/overview-federal-sector-eeo-complaint-process.

## III. Genetic Discrimination Laws in Health Insurance

There are three key laws that address discrimination on the basis of genetic information in the context of health insurance: the Health Insurance Portability and Accountability Act (HIPAA), GINA, and the ACA.

### A. HIPAA

When individuals undergo genetic testing, they may be concerned that if they test positive for a genetic mutation, they will not be able to get health insurance in the open market and, therefore, will not be able to leave their jobs because their jobs provide them with health insurance. However, HIPAA was the first federal law that created a protection against genetic discrimination in health insurance and allowed individuals to change jobs without fear of being denied health insurance at their new jobs due to the presence of an asymptomatic genetic mutation. Signed into law in 1996, HIPAA prohibits employer-based health insurance from determining eligibility for coverage, in limited circumstances, based on an individual's past or present medical conditions, including genetic predispositions to a disease. However, HIPAA's prohibition on discrimination only applies in the group market context (e.g., when moving from one employer's group health plan to another). So, while HIPAA did protect some individuals from being discriminated against based on their genetic information, others were still left unprotected (i.e., people with individual health insurance policies).

### B. GINA

As discussed in Section II, GINA is the federal law addressing discrimination based on genetic information.

#### 1. Title I of GINA

Title I of GINA prohibits health insurance companies and employers with self-funded health plans ("health insurers" for the purposes of this section) from discriminating against individuals on the basis of genetic information. Health insurers are not permitted to use genetic information to make eligibility, premium rating, underwriting, or coverage decisions. Additionally, health insurers cannot require individuals or their family members to take genetic tests or provide other genetic information. Under GINA, if a health insurer sends a request for medical records to a doctor or facility, they must include a notice that states that no genetic information should be included in the records.

Title I of GINA applies to group health plans, individual health insurance policies, and Medigap policies (Medicare supplemental policies).[41] However, GINA does not apply to the Indian Health Service, military and veterans' health coverage, or to the Federal Employees Health Benefits Program.[42]

It is also worth noting that GINA does not apply to life insurance, disability insurance, or long-term care insurance.[43] Each of those types of coverage "requires a time-limited substantial payout that could be tremendously variable depending upon an individual's medical risk."[44] Therefore, having prior knowledge about one's genetic risk for disease could motivate people to purchase more coverage, and closer to their time of need, than they normally would.[45] These circumstances could skew the risk pool and impact insurer viability.[46] On the other hand, consumers tend to use health care incrementally over long periods of time. For that reason, GINA drafters decided to focus on health insurers and employers and leave the subject of discrimination in other forms of insurance open as a possible topic for future legislation.[47] Some states have opted to address these other forms of insurance through state legislation.[48] (See Section IV.)

## 2. Enforcement of Title I of GINA

Several federal agencies are responsible for enforcing title I of GINA. The U.S. Department of Labor has jurisdiction over employer-sponsored health plans, and handles questions of genetic discrimination in job-based health insurance coverage.[49] The U.S. Secretary of Labor has the authority to fine employer-sponsored health plans that violate GINA. The Internal Revenue Service also has the power to impose tax penalties on employer-sponsored health plans that do not comply with GINA's requirements.

The U.S. Department of Health and Human Services (HHS) has jurisdiction over health insurance companies and policies that they sell to employers and individuals. HHS also has authority over Medigap supplemental policies sold to individuals with

41. 42 U.S.C. § 300gg-4(a)(6).

42. Note: Other laws may apply to these other types of health insurance coverage.

43. Life insurance is a contract between an individual and an insurance company, wherein the insurance company promises to pay a named beneficiary a sum of money upon the death of the individual policyholder. Disability insurance guarantees the beneficiary's earned income against a risk that a disability prevents the beneficiary from fulfilling the essential functions of their job. Long-term care insurance provides for the long-term care of a person beyond a predetermined period. Individuals who require long-term care are generally unable to perform day-to-day tasks such as dressing, bathing, eating, and walking.

44. Louise Slaughter, *Genetic Information Non-Discrimination Act*, 50 Harv. J. on Legis. 41 (2013).

45. *Id.*

46. *Id.*

47. *Id.*

48. For information about a state's law, visit *Genetic Information State Laws*, Triage Cancer, https://triagecancer.org/state-laws/genetic-information-laws (last visited Nov. 18, 2024).

49. To file a complaint with the U.S. Department of Labor, a person should contact their state's Department of Labor and submit the complaint in writing via mail, email, or fax. Certain states also allow complainants to submit complaints via an online complaint portal located on the state's Department of Labor website.

Medicare coverage. However, states are allowed to adopt standards that are more protective than those established by GINA. HHS will enforce those standards if the states fail to do so.

To report a GINA title I violation with HHS, individuals should file a complaint with the Office for Civil Rights (OCR).[50] The complaint must be in writing and submitted within 180 days of when an individual originally learns of the alleged GINA violation. The individual may submit their complaint via the OCR online complaint portal, or alternatively via mail, fax, or email.[51] After the complaint is submitted, the OCR will investigate the matter and determine whether or not a violation has occurred. In the event a violation has taken place, the individual may be entitled to various remedies, including reinstatement and monetary awards.

### C. ACA

The ACA prohibits health insurance companies selling insurance in either the group or individual markets from denying someone a policy based on health status. The law specifically lists genetic information as part of an individual's health status.[52] The ACA provides additional safeguards for individuals by mandating that health insurers may only base the cost of monthly premiums on a few factors (geographic area, age, and tobacco use), thereby prohibiting insurers from charging individuals more for their health insurance coverage based on their genetic information.[53] By including these provisions in the ACA, Congress reaffirmed its dedication to protecting individuals from discrimination based on genetic information. For a more in-depth discussion of the ACA, see Chapter 1, Health Insurance.

## IV. State Authority on Genetic Discrimination

Even prior to GINA's enactment, many states had laws in place to protect individuals against discrimination based on their genetic information. Some of those laws are less protective than GINA, but others provide greater protection than GINA. GINA does not preempt state laws that provide stronger protections against genetic discrimination. State laws may prohibit discrimination in disability insurance, life insurance, and long-term care insurance, all of which are not covered by GINA.[54]

---

50. The OCR is a department of HHS that investigates certain civil rights violations, including those falling under title I of GINA.

51. The OCR online complaint portal can be found at https://ocrportal.hhs.gov/ocr/cp/complaint_frontpage.jsf (last visited Nov. 18, 2024). Complaints may also be emailed to OCRcomplaint@hhs.gov.

52. 42 U.S.C. § 300gg-4(a)(6).

53. *Id.*

54. *See supra* note 48.

## V. Case Law

Often times, even after a law is passed, there are still questions about how the law will be applied in real-life situations. As a result, people must rely on court interpretations of the law to gain a better understanding of their rights. Court interpretations of the ADA, GINA, and other antidiscrimination laws paint a clearer picture of protections against genetic discrimination.

### A. *EEOC v. Fabricut*

On May 7, 2013, the EEOC filed suit against fabric distributor Fabricut,[55] claiming that Fabricut violated GINA. This was the EEOC's first lawsuit challenging an alleged act of genetic discrimination. The EEOC argued that Fabricut violated GINA when it asked for an employee's family medical history in its post-job offer medical examination. Rhonda Jones was offered a permanent position after serving as a temporary employee for Fabricut. After Fabricut offered Jones permanent employment, it requested that she submit to a medical examination with its contract medical examiner, Knox Laboratory. Knox Laboratory asked Jones about her family medical history and determined that further evaluation was necessary to determine whether Jones had CTS. Fabricut subsequently ordered Jones to report to her private physician to get tested for CTS. The physician's tests reported that Jones did not have CTS; however, Fabricut fired Jones despite those test results because Knox Laboratory indicated that Jones was predisposed to getting CTS.

GINA prohibits employers from discriminating against employees based on genetic information, and forbids employers from requesting, requiring, or purchasing such information. Fabricut's conduct violated GINA because it required Jones to provide genetic information regarding her potential CTS and terminated her based on that information. GINA forbids employers from requesting employees' genetic information, even through an affiliated third-party medical examiner.

The *Fabricut* case settled for $50,000 soon after the EEOC filed suit. In addition to the payment, Fabricut agreed to take further action to prevent discrimination in the workplace, including posting an antidiscrimination notice to employees, disseminating of antidiscrimination policies to employees, and providing antidiscrimination training to employees with hiring power.

*Fabricut* underscores the fact that GINA protects family medical history as a form of genetic information, and it is illegal for employers to request such information either directly or through mandatory medical examinations.

55. EEOC v. Fabricut, No. 13-CV-248-CVE-PJC (N.D. Okla. 2013).

### B. *EEOC v. Dolgencorp, LLC*

In 2023, the EEOC filed suit against retailer Dolgencorp, LLC,[56] doing business as Dollar General, for violating the ADA and GINA. "The EEOC sued on behalf of a class of 498 applicants who were required to divulge family medical history during the hiring process and on behalf of another class of qualified applicants whose job offers were rescinded based on their impairments."[57] According to the lawsuit, Dollar General required applicants to pass a pre-employment medical exam that included a request for past and present medical conditions of family members, such as for cancer, diabetes, and heart disease. The EEOC also alleged that qualified individuals with disabilities were screened out by Dollar General who rescinded job offers based on their impairments, even when those impairments would not prevent the applicants from safely performing their jobs. Dollar General agreed to settle the lawsuit, pay a dollar settlement, and change their hiring practices to comply with the ADA and GINA.

## VI. Conclusion

The science behind genetic information is constantly expanding, revolutionizing biomedical research, and transforming health care. Thousands of genetic tests are available to help health care professionals diagnose and treat many medical conditions.[58] With most of these tests available in clinics and some even direct-to-consumers, legal safeguards are necessary to ensure privacy.

Congress saw a potential for employers and health insurance providers to misuse genetic information and responded with a series of laws that protect employees and consumers from genetic discrimination. Among those laws are HIPAA and the ADA, but GINA was the first law passed that directly focused on genetic discrimination. GINA defends genetic privacy rights in workplace and health insurance settings and proclaims that employers and health insurers shall not discriminate based on an individual's genetic information.

GINA lets people confidently participate in genetic studies and, in doing so, enables scientists to collect a broader range of data about genetic information. With more data, scientists can make new scientific discoveries about the prevention and treatment of genetic diseases. GINA also protects individuals who face genetic discrimination based on a family member's cancer diagnosis.

Unfortunately, as with most laws, GINA has several shortcomings. GINA does not protect consumers from genetic discrimination in the areas of life insurance, disability insurance, and long-term care insurance. And, GINA does not apply to

---

56. EEOC v. Dolgencorp, LLC, No. 2:17-cv-01649-MHH (N.D. Ala. 2023).

57. Press Release, EEOC, Dollar General to Pay $1 Million to Settle EEOC Disability and GINA Lawsuit (Oct. 19, 2023), https://www.eeoc.gov/newsroom/dollar-general-pay-1-million-settle-eeoc-disability-and-gina-lawsuit.

58. *Genetic Testing*, Am. Med. Ass'n, https://www.ama-assn.org/delivering-care/precision-medicine/genetic-testing (last visited Nov. 18, 2024).

individuals who have already been diagnosed with a disease or disorder. The ADA protects eligible individuals who already have a cancer diagnosis from workplace discrimination. Likewise, HIPAA and the ACA protect those with an existing cancer diagnosis from discrimination by health insurers. Therefore, although GINA has some gaps, other federal and state laws can work together to address genetic discrimination in health insurance and employment.

Overall, consumers should feel comfortable taking advantage of the benefits of genetic testing, knowing that employers and health insurance companies cannot discriminate against them based on the test results. However, as there are no federal laws that protect individuals in the areas of life, disability, and long-term care insurance, it is important for individuals to consider the impact of genetic test results on their ability to access those benefits. GINA empowers people to learn about their genetic makeup and to take preventative action to address genetic disorders before they manifest themselves. In that respect, GINA is a valuable law for individuals with genetic predispositions for cancer because they can increase early detection screenings or get preventive surgeries and other prophylactic treatments without having to fear that their jobs and health insurance are at risk.

## VII. Resources

For information about hereditary cancers and genetic testing:

National Cancer Institute: https://www.cancer.gov/about-cancer/causes-prevention/genetics

HHS: https://healthfinder.gov/HealthTopics/Category/health-conditions-and-diseases/cancer/talk-with-a-doctor-if-breast-or-ovarian-cancer-runs-in-your-family#the-basics_1

U.S. Preventive Services Task Force: https://www.uspreventiveservicestaskforce.org/uspstf/draft-update-summary/brca-related-cancer-risk-assessment-genetic-counseling-testing

Triage Cancer—Cancer Finances Module on Understanding Genetics: https://triagecancer.org/cancer-finances-genetics

Triage Cancer Quick Guide to Genetic Discrimination: https://triagecancer.org/quick-guides/genetic-discrimination

Triage Cancer—Checklist to Understanding Biomarker Testing: https://triagecancer.org/checklist-biomarkertesting

Triage Cancer—Genetic Information State Laws: https://triagecancer.org/state-laws/genetic-information-laws

For information about finding support for cancer-related genetic conditions:

Facing Our Risk of Cancer Empowered (FORCE): http://www.facingourrisk.org

National Society of Genetic Counselors: https://www.nsgc.org

For information about GINA and the ADA in employment contexts:

EEOC: https://www.eeoc.gov

For information about GINA, HIPAA, and the ACA in health insurance contexts:

HHS: https://www.hhs.gov

## VIII. Exercises and Discussion Topics

### A. Case Studies

1. Jenny, 39, was a five-year employee of a small company with 16 employees.[59] Jenny consistently received outstanding performance reviews and was even promoted twice. During Jenny's time at the company, two of her sisters were diagnosed with breast cancer. Jenny grew concerned that she would also be diagnosed with breast cancer, and she decided to take a genetic test to determine her risk level. The genetic test revealed that Jenny did have a genetic mutation that significantly increased her risk of developing breast cancer. Based on the test findings, Jenny decided to undergo a preventive bilateral mastectomy to reduce her risk of developing breast cancer.[60] Jenny spoke with her employer about her decision to get the operation and requested one month off of work for the surgery and recovery. A few days after that meeting, Jenny was terminated and was told it was because the company was downsizing. Upset and concerned about her future, Jenny shared this information with her social worker at her next appointment and asked for advice. *What are Jenny's options?*

   **Answer.** GINA states that employers with 15 or more employees are prohibited from discriminating against individuals based on genetic information. Genetic information is information about a person's genetic tests or the genetic tests of that person's family members, as well as the manifestation of a disease or disorder in a person's family members. At first glance, it seems that Jenny may have a viable GINA claim. First, her employer is covered by GINA because it has more than 15 employees. Second, Jenny can argue that her employer discriminated against her based on genetic information. Jenny's two sisters have breast cancer, and a manifestation of a disease in family members counts as one's own genetic information. Furthermore, Jenny's test results showing that she has a high risk of contracting cancer also counts as genetic information.

---

59. This case study is loosely based on *Fink v. MX Energy* (2010), where Pamela Fink filed a genetic discrimination complaint against her employer, MX Energy, when it discharged her after she revealed her genetic susceptibility to breast cancer. *See* Greenhouse, *supra* note 1.

60. A preventive bilateral mastectomy is a surgical procedure whereby an individual who does not currently have breast cancer has both breasts removed in order to lessen their risk of developing the disease.

However, Jenny may struggle to establish that her employer made its decision to fire her based on such information rather than on their claim that they were downsizing. Although the facts state that Jenny spoke with her employer about her decision to get the mastectomy, the facts do not provide that Jenny told her employer about her sisters' cancer or about the details of her genetic tests. Therefore, it is unclear whether or not her employer fired her based on knowledge of Jenny's predisposition to developing cancer.

Furthermore, even assuming her employer did have knowledge of Jenny's genetic predisposition to cancer, there are other possible reasons that her employer may have let Jenny go. Generally, absent an employment contract, an employer may terminate an employee for any legitimate nondiscriminatory reason. It is possible that Jenny's month of leave from work was a substantial financial burden on her employer. Alternatively, her employer might have fired Jenny because she has a negative work attitude. The onus is on Jenny to establish that any nondiscriminatory reason that her employer provides for Jenny's termination is a pretext to a true discriminatory motive. In order to meet her burden, Jenny can point to any evidence that may suggest that she was the only one laid off at the time, or perhaps they hired someone for her position after she was let go. Jenny can also argue that she has consistently received positive performance evaluations, and, furthermore, she even received a promotion during her third year with her employer. However, overall, Jenny will struggle to make a successful GINA claim because her employer will likely claim that they had a legitimate nondiscriminatory reason for her termination.

2. Marie, 45, is a former at-will employee of Orange a Day dentistry depot, a dentistry equipment supplier with 40 employees. Orange recently discharged Marie from her management position after she shared with her employer that her sister has colon cancer. Marie fears that she may be a victim of genetic discrimination and she is considering filing an employment discrimination lawsuit against Orange. Marie would like your help to evaluate the legal strengths and weaknesses of her complaint. She has provided the following facts to aid your analysis:
   - Prior to her career as a marketing associate with Orange, Marie attended Northwest University. Marie graduated from Northwest with honors and received her bachelor's degree in marketing. After college, Marie accepted a lucrative marketing position with a kitchenware company. Marie advertised and sold kitchenware for five years until she began her career with Orange.
   - Marie held a superior reputation at Orange. She consistently received stellar performance reviews, and she only had one unexcused absence throughout her employment period. Orange's chief executive officer, Thomas, gave Marie a promotion to marketing supervisor during her third year at Orange. After Marie had been with the company for seven years, Thomas promoted

her to director of marketing. Orange named Marie "employee of the year" the same year that Marie received her second promotion.

- Shortly after her promotion, she learned that her sister, Celia, had been diagnosed with stage 2 colon cancer. Marie was devastated to learn about her sister's condition, particularly because Marie's mother had passed away from colon cancer 15 years prior.
- One day, Marie was in the lunchroom talking with Regina, a trusted coworker, about Celia's cancer diagnosis. While Marie was discussing Celia's condition with Regina, Thomas was getting his regular morning coffee and overheard Marie's conversation. Marie acknowledged Thomas with a brief greeting but then continued talking with Regina.
- The day after Marie's conversation with Regina, Thomas approached Marie with his sympathies. Thomas explained that he had overheard Marie's conversation with Regina and that he was "deeply regretful" to learn that Celia had cancer. Marie, unaware that Thomas had overheard her, was slightly taken aback by Thomas's condolences, but she was appreciative of his support.
- Thomas subsequently proceeded to ask Marie questions about Celia's prognosis. Thomas asked Marie how far Celia's cancer had advanced, what kinds of treatment Celia was receiving, and whether or not Marie has a history of colon cancer in her family. Marie informed Thomas that Celia's colon cancer was at stage 2, that Celia was undergoing chemotherapy and radiation, and that Marie's mother had died from colon cancer years ago.
- Marie's relationship with Thomas seemed strained ever since Marie talked with him about her sister's cancer. Thomas, who was generally friendly with Marie, had become noticeably indifferent to Marie's presence. Marie blamed Thomas's new attitude on business-related pressures, but she was alarmed when her next performance review reflected poor scores. Marie had always received excellent performance reviews during her employment with Orange and she could not understand what she had done differently during the most recent evaluation period.
- Marie tried talking with Thomas to get a better understanding of her poor scores, but despite her efforts she still could not grasp what had gone wrong. Marie tried working longer hours, having a more positive attitude at work and even began an innovative new marketing project with her team; however, her efforts were to no avail. Thomas informed Marie soon after she received her poor performance evaluation that Orange was discharging her from the company. When Marie demanded an explanation, Thomas told her that Orange was downsizing. Nevertheless, Marie suspects that Thomas discharged her because of her family history of colon cancer. She has filed a complaint with the EEOC and has otherwise exhausted all other administrative remedies. She now plans to file an employment discrimination lawsuit against Thomas and Orange.

Please evaluate the potential strengths and weaknesses of her claims.

3. John, 36, is a famous football player for the Chicago Wind. Four years ago, John's older brother, Paul, was diagnosed with pancreatic cancer. Last year, John's cousin, Brady, was also diagnosed with pancreatic cancer. Both diagnoses received media attention.

   John has been fortunate to have no health problems, other than a few sprains and broken bones from playing football. However, John has decided to take a genetic test to determine whether or not he is at higher risk for developing pancreatic cancer. John's test revealed that he had an 85 percent chance of getting pancreatic cancer. Based on the test results, John decided to apply for better health insurance. After researching several insurance companies, John chose to apply for health insurance with Dollar Insurance Co. because Dollar is known for its comprehensive coverage plans and low premiums. John called Dollar and spoke with Maritza, a Dollar representative, about the coverage plans that Dollar provides. Maritza informed John that he would need to fill out an application and Dollar would notify John of his eligibility in a few days.

   After John and Maritza ended their conversation, Maritza researched John on the internet. Maritza typed John's name into the search engine and discovered several news stories about the pancreatic cancer in John's family. Maritza also found an article that reported on one of John's football-related injuries and contained John's doctor's name. Maritza called John's doctor's office and talked the office secretary into revealing information about John's medical history, including John's test results. The secretary told Maritza that according to a genetic test, John has a high risk of getting pancreatic cancer. Soon thereafter, Maritza informed John that Dollar was denying coverage. John filed suit against Dollar and Maritza, alleging discrimination in violation of GINA. *Will his claim prevail? Would the outcome of the lawsuit be different if Maritza had never contacted the doctor's office? Does another law apply to his situation?*
4. Julia, 50, is an employee of Best Bargain, an electronics store that employs more than 15 employees. Julia has worked for Best Bargain for three years as a technology consultant and, until recently, she has consistently had stellar performance reviews.

   Julia was a computer engineer for Mango, Inc. for 20 years prior to working with Best Bargain. Julia was a lead engineer with Mango and designed several lucrative computer systems that earned the company billions in revenue. Before her time at Mango, Julia earned an engineering degree from prestigious University of Blackacre, where she graduated with honors.

   Several years ago, Julia was forced to quit her job with Mango after her husband, Eric, was diagnosed with brain cancer. Julia resigned from Mango so that she could stay home with Eric and take him to doctor appointments. After Eric recovered from his cancer treatment, Julia decided to pick up a job with

Best Bargain so that she could begin making money again. Julia enjoyed working with Best Bargain and she was happy to be doing what she loved again.

Just when Eric's illness started to drift into the past, Julia and Eric received terrible news: Eric's cancer had metastasized. Julia and Eric were devastated. One day, Julia sent Eric an email from her work account that said: "Dear Eric, don't worry. We got through this once and we can get through it again. I'll be with you every step of the way. I love you."

Soon after Julia sent the email, her boss, Michael, happened to be going through his emails, when he inadvertently received the message. Julia was accustomed to including Michael as a recipient on her work-related emails and she forgot to remove him as a default recipient when she emailed Eric. Michael knew that Eric had cancer before Julia started working at Best Bargain and he quickly deduced from the email that Eric's cancer had returned.

When Julia saw Michael in the lunchroom later, he told her that he received the email and gave his sympathies. Michael then asked what Eric's prognosis was and which cancer treatments Eric was receiving. After their conversation, Julia noticed that Michael began treating her differently. In particular, Michael gave Julia her first negative performance evaluation and told her that she did not seem "focused on her work." Additionally, Julia was passed up for a promotion to the lead engineer position. Instead, the recipient was a younger employee with overwhelmingly less experience than Julia. Michael had told Julia for almost a year that he believed her to be well-suited for the lead engineer position, and his consistent encouragement led her to believe she was next in line for a promotion. Finally, Michael started assigning Julia to projects that were deeply inferior to her full potential. As a result, Julia no longer enjoys coming to work and she is considering resigning from Best Bargain. Julia suspects that Michael is discriminating against her based on Eric's diagnosis and she is considering filing a GINA complaint against Best Bargain. *Please evaluate the likely success of Julia's potential GINA claim. Are there other laws that may apply to Julia's situation?*

5. Elijah went to Dr. Smith's office for his yearly physical. Elijah indicated on the intake form that he has a family history of cancer. When Dr. Smith asked Elijah about the cancer, Elijah explained that his grandfather passed away from stomach cancer and that his father is also a stomach cancer survivor. Based on that information, Dr. Smith recommended that Elijah get a genetic test to determine Elijah's risk for developing cancer. Elijah told Dr. Smith that he is afraid to take genetic tests because he fears discrimination by health insurance companies. *How should Dr. Smith advise Elijah?*

## B. Class Exercises

1. **Mock interview.** Draft questions for a job interview that contain a mixture of permissible and impermissible questions. After you have completed your questionnaire, pair up with another classmate and interview them. When you finish the interview, ask your classmate which questions they think are impermissible and why. Then, practice the interview again and try to develop model responses to prohibited questions, with the understanding that just because they are impermissible does not mean that a job applicant will not face those questions in an interview. When the class is finished with mock interviews, each team should share their sample impermissible questions and model responses with the class.

## C. Discussion Topics

1. GINA's protections against discrimination in health insurance coverage do not apply to life, long-term care, and disability insurance policies. Should GINA be amended to include protections in these other areas of insurance coverage? Why or why not?
2. GINA does not protect individuals who have been diagnosed with a genetic disease. Rather, the law only protects individuals whose genetic information shows a susceptibility or predisposition to a disease. Should GINA be amended to include protections for people who have already been diagnosed with a genetic disease? What are the benefits and flaws of such an amendment?
3. GINA does not protect against discrimination based on a spouse's cancer diagnosis. However, a spouse's diagnosis can arouse concerns that would lead to discriminatory behavior. Employers and health insurance companies are motivated to discriminate based on genetic information because they fear that a person will need accommodations and miss time from work, and they will be more expensive to insure. Similarly, a person whose spouse has cancer might be more likely to miss work in order to care for their spouse. Should GINA be amended to protect people from discrimination based on a spouse's diagnosis or do other laws address this?

# CHAPTER FIVE

# Estate Planning and Medical Decision-Making

## *Case Study: Steven and Pam*

*Steven and Pam have always talked about the fact that they should have a will and name a guardian for their two young children, but they never got around to completing any documents. Steven was diagnosed with pancreatic cancer last week. The doctors do not know how Steven will respond to treatment, but have warned him that there may come a time when he is unable to verbalize his wishes or make medical decisions for himself. Are there steps that Steven and Pam can take now to protect themselves and their family?*

## I. Introduction

There is a general misconception that only wealthy or older individuals need an estate plan. However, almost everyone can benefit from having even the most basic plan in place. Even if they have never considered creating an estate plan before, a cancer diagnosis can motivate individuals to prepare for the future in new ways.[1] Some individuals may think about writing a will for the first time, or they may consider updating financial plans they have not recently reviewed.[2] Others become interested in

1. American Bar Association, Legal Guide for the Seriously Ill (2010); Michael A. Dalton & Thomas P. Langdon, Estate Planning for Financial Planners (5th ed. 2009).
2. American Bar Association, Legal Guide for the Seriously Ill (2010).

expressing their health care wishes should they become incapacitated at some point in the future.[3] Though estate planning plays a crucial role in financial and health care decisions, only 32 percent of Americans have a will, the most basic component of an estate plan.[4] There could be several reasons for this. Some may think that that they do not have enough money or property to warrant a will or a more in-depth estate plan, while others may think that they cannot afford to hire an attorney, so there is no way they could create an estate plan. And, finally, some may not want to face their mortality or even investigate the benefits of having an estate plan.

Waiting until being diagnosed with a serious medical condition, like cancer, can make estate planning more difficult, especially facing issues of mortality. But creating an estate plan allows an individual the opportunity to express deeply held values and key personal preferences. Preparing in advance can provide individuals with the peace of mind that loved ones will be aware of and carry out their wishes. An estate plan is an important part of preparing for the future, regardless of the size or complexity of an estate.

Estate planning can mean different things to different people. Perhaps the broadest definition is that it is the process to create a plan to ensure that individuals' wishes about the distribution of their property, their health care, and caring for their loved ones are carried out in the event of their incapacitation or death.

## II. Estate Planning Basics

It can feel incredibly overwhelming to even start the process of estate planning, especially when someone may also be coping with all of the other issues that can accompany a cancer diagnosis. Some big picture questions an individual can start with include:

- What do I own?
- How do I own it?
- What do I want to happen to what I own when I die?
- Are there people whom I am legally responsible for?
- Are there people whom I want to take care of?
- Whom would I want to make medical and financial decisions for me if I am unable?

In order to effectively answer these questions, an individual will likely have to do some fact-finding or gathering of information about their estate.

3. *Id.*
4. Rachel Lustbade, 2024 *Wills and Estate Planning Study*, Caring.com (July 30, 2024), https://www.caring.com/caregivers/estate-planning/wills-survey.

## A. Getting Started with Estate Planning

Before individuals can start creating the documents that will make up an estate plan, they may need to gather and organize the following items:

- Personal and family records
  - Social Security card, driver's license or state identification card, passport, and military discharge papers (DD214)
  - Birth certificates for themselves, spouse, and children
  - Marriage license and/or proof of divorce, if applicable
  - Contact information for current employer and/or supervisor
  - Health, dental, vision, personal property, and/or homeowner's or renter's insurance with contact information of insurance agent(s)
  - Usernames and passwords for computers, tablets, phones, online accounts, music sharing sites, and so on
  - List of close relatives, friends, neighbors, and the like, with their contact information
  - Instructions or other messages for surviving spouse or children
- Financial accounts and property records
  - Account information for checking, savings, credit cards, loans, stocks, bonds, other securities, other assets, accounts receivable, and so on
  - Safe-deposit box bank information, key, and box number
  - Proof of car (and/or motorcycle, boat, etc.) ownership, registration, and insurance
  - Real estate deeds, title policies, mortgages, record of payments, tax receipts, receipts for improvements, and so on
  - Income tax returns for past three years, and contact information for tax preparer
  - Receipts and appraisals for any personal property of substantial value (e.g., furniture, silver, art, jewelry)
  - Any business ownership and financial records (e.g., for sole proprietors or partnerships)

## B. What Is an Estate?

An estate includes all of the property an individual owns at the time of death. The components of the estate may be wide-ranging. For example, in addition to a home and other real estate, an individual's estate may include cars, furniture, jewelry, collections (e.g., baseball cards), and artwork.[5] Bank accounts, stocks, bonds,

---

5. American Bar Association, The American Bar Association Guide to Wills & Estates: Everything You Need to Know about Wills, Estates, Trusts & Taxes (2012).

securities, pensions, Social Security benefits, and life insurance policies are also part of an individual's estate.[6] Even payments owed to the individual, like a tax refund or an inheritance, are included in their estate.[7] Digital property like online bank accounts, electronic devices, files and photos on the devices, email accounts, social media accounts, blogs, and intellectual property are considered part of an individual's estate. An individual's debts are also part of the estate. Once individuals determine what they owe, they need to figure out if their family members would be responsible for paying their debts after they die. For example, adult children are generally not responsible for the unpaid medical bills of their parents.

Once an individual has determined what they own, it may also be useful to determine its value. Some items, like a car, may have a set value based on the model and age of the car. Some values, like those for real property, may fluctuate based on the market. Other items, like keepsakes or family heirlooms, may not have a large monetary value at all, but a substantial sentimental value. Gathering this information may help individuals devise a plan for how they want to distribute their property upon their death.

## C. How Does an Individual Own Property?

After individuals determine what they own and its worth, they need to determine how they own the property. There is more than one way to own property. Sometimes how individuals own property will be determined at the moment they acquire the property and others will be based on law. The following are the three most common ways to own property:

- **Individual ownership.** This is property that an individual owns outright, to which no one else has a legal claim. For example, if Steven buys a car and only his name is on the title, he owns that car individually. Therefore, he can make decisions about who will own that car upon his death.
- **Joint ownership.** There are two different ways that one can own property jointly:
  - **Joint tenancy with right of survivorship.** With this type of ownership, all of the owners hold an equal right to the property and do not need the other owners' permission to access or utilize that property. For example, if Steven and Pam own a bank account in joint tenancy with right of survivorship, each one could spend money from that account without the other's permission. If Steven were to die, Pam would become the sole owner of the entire account without having to go through probate. Many married couples own

6. *Id.*
7. *Id.*

their homes as joint tenants with right of survivorship, so their home would not go through probate if one spouse were to die.

- o **Tenancy in common.** With this type of joint ownership, each individual "tenant in common" owns a specific percentage of the property. Each is only free to withdraw/mortgage/sell their own portion of that property. When a tenant in common dies, their share of the property would pass to their beneficiaries and not to the surviving tenants in common. For example, Pam and Steven own an apartment building with four units as tenants in common, with each of them owning 50 percent of the building. When Steven dies, ownership of two of the units would transfer to his niece, as named in his will. Now Pam and Steven's niece own the apartment building as tenants in common.

- **By contract.** In some types of property like life insurance, retirement accounts, and living trusts, ownership is determined by the contract itself. With these types of property, the owner has full control over the property while alive, but after death, the property transfers to a beneficiary of the owner's choice. For example, Steven has a retirement account and Pam is the sole beneficiary listed. While he is alive, Steven has the full right to withdraw or add funds to that account as he sees fit. Upon his death, the balance of the account will go directly to Pam. Generally, all Pam will need to do is provide a death certificate to access the funds without going through probate.

The following table outlines property ownership considerations:

| Ownership Type | Included in Will? | Probate Required? | Percentage of Ownership |
|---|---|---|---|
| Individual ownership | Yes | Yes | 100% |
| Joint tenancy with right of survivorship | No | No | 100% |
| Tenancy in common | Yes | Yes | Established when property is acquired |
| By contract | No | No | 100% |

Once individuals have more information about what they own and how they own it, they can better determine how to move forward with an estate plan.

## D. What Makes Up an Estate Plan?

An estate plan can have multiple components and benefits. An estate plan can:

- Provide direction for what a person wants to happen to their property after death

- Allow an individual the opportunity to express deeply held values and key personal preferences
- Protect family and loved ones from having to make challenging decisions when they are grieving a loss
- Provide financial benefits, including:
  - Reduce taxes beneficiaries may be responsible for
  - Help to avoid the time and costs associated with the transfer of the property after death (e.g., probate)
- Ensure peace of mind that loved ones will know about an individual's wishes and that there are no loose ends
- Give directions about how an individual's legal and financial affairs should be managed during their lifetime, if for any reason the individual is incapable of doing so themself
- Ensure that health care wishes are respected if the individual is incapacitated[8]

There are multiple components that should be considered when creating an estate plan, including a will, a trust, a power of attorney for financial affairs, and various options for advance directives for health care. The following section will discuss each of these options in detail. Keep in mind that estate planning rules are often very specific to each state.

## III. Decisions about Property and Final Wishes

As discussed, there are different ways to own property. For property that is owned individually or as a tenant in common, it is up to the property holder to make a plan for what happens to that property when they die. The two main estate planning tools to consider are a will and a trust.

### A. Wills

A will is a legal document that provides instructions for what an individual would like to have happen to their property upon death. A will is also the place where parents can name a guardian for minor children as well as provide other directions (e.g., wishes for a funeral).

#### 1. Creating a Will

Each state has different rules about how to create a valid will. At a minimum, most states require that a will be in writing, that the testator be of "sound mind," that the testator sign the will, and that the will be witnessed by an uninterested party. Some

8. Linda Long, *What Is Estate Planning?*, FindLaw (Sept. 21, 2021), https://www.findlaw.com/estate/planning-an-estate/what-is-estate-planning.html.

states may require two witnesses, that the witnesses are physically present when the testator signs the will, or that the will be notarized. Some states allow for a will to be "self-proving." To make a will self-proving, the testator and witnesses sign an affidavit in front of a notary that proves the identity of the testator and that all parties had knowledge of the will. A self-proving will expedites probate because the court can accept the will without contacting the witnesses who signed it. Very few states allow for oral, or nuncupative, wills. Generally, oral wills are allowed in very limited and unusual circumstances (e.g., statements made on one's deathbed).

The following states allow for holographic (e.g., handwritten without witnesses) wills: Alaska, Arizona, Arkansas, California, Colorado, Idaho, Kentucky, Louisiana, Maine, Michigan, Mississippi, Montana, Nebraska, Nevada, New Jersey, North Carolina (if found after death in place intended for safekeeping), North Dakota, Oklahoma, Pennsylvania, South Dakota, Tennessee, Texas, Utah, Virginia, West Virginia, and Wyoming.[9] However, most estate planning experts do not recommend relying on holographic wills because it is more difficult to prove their validity in probate court.

A limited number of states have a statutory will. These are wills that are created by a state legislature in a law and provided to individuals to fill in the blanks with the particulars of their estate and wishes. The benefits of a statutory will are that they are generally free to complete, and individuals can complete them on their own (i.e., they do not need to hire an attorney). The downsides of a statutory will are that they cannot be customized and are, therefore, best for very simple estates.

There are also several do-it-yourself options available for people who either have a relatively simple estate, or cannot afford an attorney. There are online services, books, and computer software that can cost anywhere between $0 and $200.[10] Creating a will can feel daunting and if individuals have an especially complicated estate, they may want to consider hiring an estate planning attorney.

Other reasons that an individual may consider hiring an attorney include:

- Having an estate so large there are significant tax implications
- Complex plans for inheritance
- Complicated family structure
- Co-owning a small business and have questions as to the rights of surviving owners
- Wanting to make arrangements for long-term care of a beneficiary (e.g., an incapacitated adult child)
- Anticipating someone would contest the will on grounds of fraud, undue influence, or an individual's capacity

---

9. Mary Randolph, *Holographic Wills*, Nolo (Feb. 21, 2024), https://www.nolo.com/legal-encyclopedia/holographic-wills.html.

10. Some examples include GoodTrust and FreeWill.com.

When an attorney helps create a will, an individual (testator) will typically be billed for services either on a flat fee or an hourly basis.[11] The cost would be determined by factors like the size of the estate or the complexity of the testator's wishes.[12] However, some resources, like LawHelp.org, are specifically designed to connect people with low or moderate incomes to legal aid.[13] State requirements for valid wills can be found at https://triagecancer.org/state-laws/estate-planning-wills.

## 2. What to Include in a Will

A will should include almost all of the property owned by the grantor. The few exceptions include property for which, upon acquiring, a beneficiary was chosen (e.g., a life insurance policy). Additionally, property owned jointly with right of survivorship needs to be included in all owners' wills the same way.

A will should also designate what should happen to any property that is acquired after the will is created. This can easily be done through a clause in a will called a "residuary clause," which allows for any property owned at the time of death to be given to specific individuals. For example, Javier has a will with a residuary clause that designates any property not specifically included in his will to go to his best friend Martin. Javier buys a vintage guitar and then passes away before adding the guitar to his will; the residuary clause in his will means that Martin would receive the guitar.

## 3. Decisions That Need to Be Made When Creating a Will

In addition to decisions around distribution of property, there are a few other decisions that an individual must make in the process of creating a will. These include who will serve as the executor of the estate and who will act as guardians for minor children.

The executor of an estate is the person who will carry out the instructions in the will. While duties of executors will vary state by state, here is a general list of duties an executor can perform.

The executor is responsible for starting and overseeing the probate process by filing a petition in the proper court, along with a copy of the will. The court will officially appoint the executor. The executor may be tasked with notifying potential heirs, anyone who benefits from the will (called beneficiaries), and creditors that probate has begun.

The executor will then need to inventory any of the individual's assets. This can include property, bank accounts and investments, personal belongings, and more. The

---

11. Stephanie Rabiner, *How Do Attorneys Charge You for Legal Representation?*, FindLaw (Mar. 21, 2019), http://blogs.findlaw.com/law_and_life/2011/06/how-do-attorneys-charge-you-for-legal-representation.html.

12. *Id.*

13. LawHelp, https://www.lawhelp.org (last visited Nov. 19, 2024).

executor then determines the value of all of the property, which may require hiring professionals to provide fair market valuations.

The executor will then use the assets to pay off the debts. If the individual does not have enough assets to pay off their debts, there are various debt relief or forgiveness programs that may help.

The executor must also file the individual's taxes and uses the individual's assets to pay for any funeral and burial expenses.

After paying off debts, taxes, and expenses, the executor must then distribute the remaining assets to the beneficiaries, according to the instructions in the will. The executor may also have to help resolve any disagreements about the distribution of assets.

The executor is responsible for keeping a record of all financial transactions related to the will. The executor should keep records of debts and expenses paid, assets distributed, and any income received (e.g., a last Social Security benefits check). The executor should also keep record of any communications with beneficiaries, creditors, attorneys, or anyone else involved in the administration of the will. The executor will often have to file documents in court and may have to represent the individual's estate if any legal matters come up.

#### *a. Hiring an Executor*

While many people choose to have a trusted family member or friend serve as the executor of their will, some choose to hire a professional instead. A professional executor will be paid out of the assets in the will and generally receive 2–5 percent of the will's assets. Hiring a professional executor may be a good option for people who:

- Do not have family members or friends they want to execute their will
- Have a complicated or very large estate, which may be overwhelming for a family member or friend to handle
- Want to speed up the administration of their will and make sure it goes as smoothly as possible

Individuals considering hiring a professional executor can ask an estate planning attorney, trust company, bank, or estate administration firm if they provide this service or for recommendations.

#### *b. Guardianship for Minor Children*

In addition to deciding who the executor of the estate will be, parents of minor children will also need to pick at least one individual to act as guardian to the children in the event of the parents' death. There are many factors to consider when picking a guardian:

- Whom does the child currently feel comfortable around?
- Where does the potential guardian(s) live?
- Will the child have to move schools, cities, state, and so on?

- Would the guardian move to the child's location?
- What is the potential guardian's parenting style like?
- How was the guardian raised as a child?
- What is the potential guardian's lifestyle like?
- Do they already have children?
- How old are they?
- Does the potential guardian have a stable job and secure financial situation?
- Is this potential guardian also going to be your child's financial trustee?
- If not, who will be the child's financial trustee?

When choosing a guardian, parents should name a single person, then consider a secondary guardian, in case the first guardian is unavailable. This is true even if the individual is considering a couple (i.e., only one person in the couple is named as primary, and the second person in the couple is named as a secondary guardian). The "Checklist: Planning Ahead for Minor Children" worksheet may help parents in making this important decision: https://triagecancer.org/checklist-minorchildren-pdf.

Parents may want to document instructions about their wishes. For example:

- Write a letter to the child's guardian detailing wishes and desires for how the child is to be raised.
- Describe what type of school they want the child to attend, and if they want the child raised in a faith, or to visit with certain family members regularly.
- Write a letter to the child's trustee or guardian detailing wishes and desires for how the child is to be financially raised.
- Address the following: Does the parent want them to get a job and work their way through school or be able to focus solely on their studies? Would they want them to have a new car or a safe used car? How much would they want the estate to help with in paying for a wedding, starting a business, or buying a house?
- During the parents' life, if they are unable to make medical decisions for the minor child, they can designate an adult to make those decisions instead. Some states have a Health Care Consent for Minor Children form that can be used. Some parents write up their own document or contact an attorney to learn about their state's rules.

Other practical suggestions to prepare for a minor child include:

- Make a list of the child's health care providers, any current medications the child is taking, and any immunizations that the child has received.
- Create a list of contact information for important family members and friends.
- Create a list of important advisors such as the parents' estate planning attorney, accountant, or financial advisor.

### *c. Planning Ahead for Pets*

Individuals with pets may also want to consider including instructions for their long-term care in their estate plans. These instructions could include informal agreements, adding instructions into a will, or creating a pet trust.

#### *i. Informal Agreements*

If an individual is no longer able to care for a pet, and has a trusted family member, relative, or friend who is willing to care for the pet, a simple agreement with them can be made. This can be oral or written, and a lawyer is not needed. However, these agreements are not legally binding. So, if the caretaker changes their mind later, the caretaker is not legally obligated. Also, if the individual wants to leave money for the pet's care, making a will or setting up a pet trust, discussed in the following subsections, can be better options. If an individual decides to use an informal agreement, it is important to

- choose a reliable person as the caretaker;
- talk to them to ensure they are committed to caring for the pets; and
- have a backup plan with different caretakers in case the first caretaker is not available.

#### *ii. A Will*

In a will, money or other assets cannot be left to pets because, legally, pets are seen as "property" and cannot own anything. However, an individual could name one or more caretakers of pets in a will, and leave the caretaker(s) money to look after the pets. But it is important to know that even if money is left for a caretaker, they are not legally required to care for the pets.

For example, Amy made a will stating that she leaves her dog, Dolly, to her friend, Bill, and $1,000 to Bill for taking care of Dolly. After Amy's death, Bill becomes the owner of Dolly and receives $1,000. But, if Bill gives Dolly away and keeps the $1,000, Bill would not be legally liable for not caring for Dolly.

If an individual is considering using a will to plan ahead for pets, there are some important things to think about:

- Name backup caretakers in case the first caretaker is not available.
- Be specific, mentioning each pet's name, breed, and the full name of the caretaker chosen for each pet.
- Set aside a reasonable amount of money for pet care.
- Consider having a third person oversee the money to make sure it is used properly.
- Give the caretaker copies of any pet directives. While not legally binding, they can be helpful.
- Also, given that probate can take time, an individual will need a plan for the pet's care until the probate process is complete.

*iii. A Pet Trust*

A pet trust is a legal document, where an individual picks a person, known as a trustee, to manage money for the pet's care. A trust can start as soon as it is created, or when the individual dies. With a pet trust:

1. Money can be put aside money for a pet's care and the trustee will manage that money for the benefit of the pet.
2. One or more caretakers can be chosen for the pets. The trustee and caretaker can be the same person or different ones. It may be helpful to name alternates, in case the first trustee or caretaker is not available.
3. Specific instructions for the pet's care can be listed.
4. A charity can be chosen to donate any leftover money, after the pets pass away.

A pet trust gives stronger protection for pets, because it legally requires the caretaker to follow the instructions outlined. If the caretaker does not, they can be held accountable. However, setting up a pet trust can be more complicated and expensive.

*iv. Rescue Groups or Animal Shelters*

If an individual cannot find someone to take care of a pet, some rescue groups and shelters might help by finding them a new home or caring for them. They might charge a fee or ask for a donation. Before an individual gives a pet to one of these organizations, the individual should gather information (e.g., visit the organization to see how they treat the animals, learn about their background and reputation, and understand the adoption process in case someone wants to adopt a pet from them).

## 4. Making Changes to a Will

It is important to remember that wills can be revoked or changed at any time as long as the testator is of sound mind. A codicil is a legal document that amends, rather than replaces, a previously executed will, and can be used for minor changes. Minor changes might include adding or removing a particular gift (like a car an individual no longer owns) or updating the legal name of someone after a marriage who receives property granted by the will.[14] Codicils must be executed in the same way that wills must be executed in that state. For example, if a state requires that a will be signed by two witnesses, the codicil must also be signed by two witnesses. On the other hand, revoking a current will and making a new one should be considered for major changes, such as completely removing a beneficiary or adding a new child as a beneficiary.[15] Generally, if an individual creates a new will, it is wise to destroy all old wills as to avoid any confusion or doubt as to which is the valid will.

Once a will is created, it should be kept in a safe, but accessible, location. The executor or a close loved one should be made aware of the location of the will and have

14. Julie Garber, *What Is a Codicil?*, BALANCE (Oct. 5, 2021), https://www.thebalance.com/what-is-a-codicil-3505182.

15. *Id.*

access. For example, it can cause a problem for an executor if the only copy of a will is in a safe deposit box that only the decedent can access. Regularly reviewing and updating a will in order to make necessary changes is an important part of estate planning.

## B. Probate

When an individual dies, the estate must be probated. Probate is the process through which a court supervises the gathering and distribution of the decedent's property. Each state has a slightly different probate process; however, they generally fall into two categories: Uniform Probate Code (UPC) and non-UPC.

The main benefit of the UPC is a transition from mandatory court proceedings for probate to less formal, paper-driven processes. In states that have adopted the UPC there are three kinds of probate: informal, unsupervised formal, and supervised formal.[16]

- **Informal.** This probate is conducted purely through paperwork and no court proceeding occurs. Generally, the executor files with the court to ask for informal administration from the probate court. If there is no will naming an executor, generally the application will be filed by a family member of the decedent. If the application is approved, then the executor is responsible for:
  - Sending formal notices informing heirs, beneficiaries, and creditors
  - Publishing a notice to creditors in a local newspaper
  - Preparing an inventory and appraisal of the deceased's estate
  - Paying all debts and taxes
  - Distributing the remaining property to heirs and beneficiaries
- **Unsupervised formal probate.** In certain situations, a slightly more traditional court proceeding is necessary, for example:
  - There is no will and the court must determine beneficiaries
  - The decedent has more debts than assets
  - Inheritors or creditors need the court to resolve a disagreement
  - The executor feels it necessary to avoid criticism or suspicion during estate administration
  - Minors inherit substantial property and need help protecting their interests
- **Supervised formal probate.** Generally, this process is very similar to the unsupervised version of probate, except that here a judge has the authority to order the executor to take specific steps to ensure that the estate is properly transferred to its rightful beneficiaries.

If someone has a will, the estate must first pay the decedent's debts and funeral and estate administration expenses, then any remaining property is distributed according to

---

16. Mary Randolph, *How the Probate Process Works: Information for Executors*, Nolo (Mar. 5, 2024), http://www.nolo.com/legal-encyclopedia/how-probate-process-works-information-32438.html.

the terms of the individual's will. The executor named in the will distributes property. The executor must be approved by the probate court before the executor has authority to handle the affairs of the estate and property distribution.

If someone dies without a will, their property will be distributed according to the state's intestacy statute. The intestacy statute is a ranking system of family members who inherit from the decedent's estate. Each state has a different set of rules with respect to intestacy. Once the estate has paid all of the decedent's debts, funeral, and estate administration expenses, then the probate court follows the state's intestacy statute to determine how the property should be distributed.[17]

Intestacy laws vary greatly from state to state.[18] Typically, there is a ranking system where the decedent's surviving spouse and/or children have priority over any other surviving relatives.[19] The following table offers a general intestacy distribution.[20]

**Example of Intestacy Succession (Indiana)[21]**

| If an individual dies with: | Here is what happens: |
|---|---|
| children but no spouse | children inherit everything |
| spouse but no descendants or parents | spouse inherits everything |
| spouse and descendants from individual and that spouse | spouse inherits 1/2 of the intestate property<br><br>descendants inherit 1/2 of the intestate property |
| spouse and at least one descendant from a previous spouse | spouse inherits 1/2 of the intestate personal property and 1/4 of the fair market value of real estate, minus the value of any liens or encumbrances on that real estate<br><br>descendants inherit everything else |
| spouse and parents | spouse inherits 3/4 of the intestate property<br><br>parents inherit 1/4 of the intestate property |
| parents but no spouse or descendants | parents inherit everything |
| siblings but no spouse, descendants, or parents | siblings inherit everything |

17. *Wills: An Overview*, FindLaw, http://estate.findlaw.com/wills/wills-an-overview.html (last reviewed May 30, 2023).

18. *Id.*

19. *Id.*

20. See examples of more state intestacy laws at Nolo, https://www.nolo.com (last visited Nov. 19, 2024).

21. Jeff Burtka, *Intestate Succession in Indiana*, Nolo (Dec. 30, 2023), http://www.nolo.com/legal-encyclopedia/intestate-succession-indiana.html.

If an individual has homes in more than one state, it may bring up questions of which state's law applies. The state's statute to be applied is the state where the individual resided at time of death. The probate court will appoint an administrator to manage affairs of the estate. Surviving family members may petition to serve as administrator or the probate court may appoint a public administrator. As state intestacy laws only recognize immediate relatives as beneficiaries, close friends or charities that the deceased favored will likely not receive anything.[22] If no relatives are found, any remaining property is held by the state government in escrow until someone comes forward to claim the property. Therefore, intestacy may often mean that the intentions of the deceased individual will not be fulfilled, further justifying the value for an individual diagnosed with cancer to complete an estate plan.

Keep in mind that even a valid will is not immune to legal challenges. Claims for undue influence, forgery, fraud, or duress could be brought to contest a will. And a court may not honor certain provisions of a will when a will is unclear or does not follow the rules of state law. However, generally, a will is presumed to be valid unless proven otherwise because it represents the final wishes of the testator. Therefore, in addition to eliminating most of the problems of intestacy, testators are able to select an executor to serve as their personal representative; set aside funds for the care of minor children, family members with disabilities, and pets; recommend a guardian for minor children or other dependents; and choose nonfamily member beneficiaries, including close friends and charities. Preparing a will can help loved ones avoid long and expensive proceedings in probate court, and also allows the testator to minimize taxes on the property left to others.

## C. Non-Probate Transfers

In some circumstances, individuals may choose to use a non-probate transfer to transfer ownership of property outside of the probate process in order to expedite the distribution of assets. There are several different types of non-probate transfers, and the tool used will depend on the type of asset being transferred:

- Payable-on-death accounts can be used to transfer money immediately upon death. The beneficiary must present the grantor's death certificate to the financial institution. The financial institution then transfers legal ownership and full control of the money to the beneficiary.[23]
- Transfer-on-death registrations can be used to transfer securities (e.g., stocks) to a beneficiary upon the death of the owner without having to go through

22. *Supra* note 5.

23. Jeff Burtka, *Payable-on-Death (POD) Accounts: The Basics*, Nolo (Oct. 4, 2024), https://www.nolo.com/legal-encyclopedia/free-books/avoid-probate-book/chapter1-1.html.

probate.[24] Beneficiaries of the securities must reregister the securities in their names once they have possession by sending a copy of the death certificate and an application for reregistration to the security issuer.

- A Lady Bird deed, also known as an "enhanced life estate deed" or a "transfer-on-death deed," is a way to transfer real property (e.g., a home) outside of probate, but maintain a life estate (i.e., control over the property while an individual is still alive).[25] A Lady Bird deed can also be useful for individuals who receive Medicaid and have had to leave their home for care on a permanent basis (e.g., nursing home or hospice). Typically, when that happens, the property is no longer considered the primary residence for the individual and the value can be counted against them for Medicaid eligibility. By executing a Lady Bird deed, an individual can keep their interest in the property while alive, but also maintain Medicaid benefits. In some circumstances, this also protects the property from being sold, after one's death, to repay the cost of Medicaid long-term care benefits that were received. A Lady Bird deed is only explicitly allowed in three states (Florida, Michigan, and Texas). However, transfer-on-death deeds that accomplish the same objectives are allowed in any state that has enacted the Uniform Real Property Transfer on Death Act. As of 2024, the following states have some version of a transfer-on-death dead: Alaska, Arizona, Arkansas, California, Colorado, District of Columbia, Hawaii, Illinois, Indiana, Kansas, Maine, Michigan (a Ladybird Deed, formerly called an enhanced life estate, achieves similar), Minnesota, Mississippi, Missouri, Montana, Nebraska, Nevada, New Mexico, North Dakota, Ohio, Oklahoma, Oregon, South Dakota, Texas, Utah, Virginia, Washington, West Virginia, Wisconsin, and Wyoming.

Other types of non-probate transfers include life insurance policies, deferred compensation plans, and pension plans. In these instances, the owner of the policy or account names a beneficiary. Upon an individual's death, the beneficiary typically only needs to present a death certificate to gain access to the funds.

These types of non-probate transfers are not going to be appropriate for all circumstances, but could be a very useful tool for some, especially those with smaller or less complicated estates.

## D. Life Insurance

Life insurance is insurance that individuals can buy to provide a preset amount of money to a beneficiary (or beneficiaries) of their choosing, in the event of their death.

---

24. Jennie Lin, *States That Allow Transfer-on-Death Deeds for Real Estate*, Nolo (Oct. 8, 2024), https://www.nolo.com/legal-encyclopedia/free-books/avoid-probate-book/chapter5-1.html.

25. *What Is a "Lady Bird Deed"?*, ElderLawAnswers (Mar. 6, 2015), https://www.elderlawanswers.com/what-is-a-lady-bird-deed--14653.

The overarching idea behind life insurance is that an individual pays during their lifetime to ensure that loved ones are taken care of financially when the individual passes away. Life insurance companies typically go through a process called medical underwriting to determine what they will charge an individual for a policy. Medical underwriting could entail a written questionnaire, a verbal survey, medical exams, and a review of medical records. Typically, the healthier an individual, the more affordable the policy.

## 1. Types of Life Insurance

There are different types of policies: term, permanent, universal, and variable. Term life insurance is the most straightforward policy; an individual pays a premium and should the person die during the term of the policy (e.g., one to 30 years), the beneficiary will get a payment. Permanent life insurance is also referred to as whole life insurance. These policies will pay the stated policy amount to an individual's beneficiary regardless of when the individual dies. Generally, term life insurance is less expensive, but the downside is that individuals will need to get a new policy once the term is over. Permanent life insurance tends to be a bit more expensive based on the ability to accumulate a cash value over time. Within permanent life insurance there are a few other variations, as follows:

- **Whole life insurance policies.** These policies have fixed premiums that an individual will pay every month. There are different ways an individual may pay the premiums (e.g., paying monthly until age 100, or paying monthly for 20 years, or a single lump-sum payment).
- **Variable life insurance policies.** These policies allow individuals to put the cash value of an insurance policy in an investment account managed by the insurance company. Once in the account, earnings can be used toward premiums or to add to a beneficiary's death benefit. The danger of these policies is that if the investments do not do well, beneficiaries may receive a limited amount. However, most companies typically guarantee a minimum death benefit.
- **Universal life insurance policies.** These policies have flexible premiums so that an individual can choose how to pay each month (e.g., an individual may be able to skip some payments). However, individuals must maintain a minimum level of premium payment over the year. These policies will also accumulate a cash value over time that may be used to skip a premium payment, or be maintained to increase the value of the policy.
- **Variable universal life insurance policies.** These policies feature a combination of variable life and universal life policies. Like with universal life policies, an individual can pay premiums at any point as long as the individual maintains the minimum level. Like with variable life insurance policies, the underlying cash value of the policy is subject to fluctuations in the chosen investments. Individuals can typically choose a death benefit that is equal to face value or

face value plus cash value. This is the most complicated type of permanent life insurance policy.

To understand the full range of life insurance options, individuals can consider speaking with a financial planner or life insurance agent.

## 2. Additional Life Insurance Benefits

Some insurance companies offer additional benefits that can be included in their policies for an added fee. These added benefits are called "riders." Common riders that may be particularly useful for people coping with cancer include:

- **Waiver of premium.** If an individual has a total disability and cannot work, the individual will not have to pay the monthly premium (these waivers usually expire around age 60).
- **Guaranteed insurability.** This allows an individual to purchase additional coverage in the future without going through medical underwriting.
- **Accelerated death benefit.** This allows individuals to collect a portion of the policy's death benefit if they become terminally ill and are expected to die within a year. This has become a very common rider and some companies offer it for little or no additional cost. The accelerated benefits are usually capped somewhere between $250,000 to $500,000, depending on the total value of the policy.
- **Critical illness.** This rider provides an individual with a lump-sum payment if they are diagnosed with a critical illness, specified in the policy, like cancer. These funds can be used for any purpose.

Individuals who are interested in additional life insurance benefits should discuss these and other possible riders when they first purchase their policy.

## 3. Purchasing Life Insurance after a Cancer Diagnosis

It can be difficult to purchase life insurance after an individual has been diagnosed with cancer, but not impossible. Life insurance companies are permitted to refuse to sell policies to people with preexisting medical conditions. Because life insurance consumers do not have the same protections that are now available in the health insurance arena, it is left up to each insurance company to decide the parameters for if, or when, they would be willing to insure someone who has been diagnosed with cancer. For example, some companies have a rule that they will insure an individual if it has been ten years since their cancer diagnosis. Other companies have a policy that they will insure an individual if it has been at least five years since they completed active treatment, depending on the type and stage of diagnosis. Finally, some companies have a policy to not provide coverage at all if an individual has ever had a cancer diagnosis.

Individuals who are considering purchasing life insurance after a cancer diagnosis should contact their state insurance agency to find a list of insurance companies that offer life insurance policies in their state. Then, individuals need to contact each insurance company to ask about specific rules related to selling policies after a cancer diagnosis and any potential costs. If an individual has difficulty purchasing an affordable life insurance policy directly from an insurance company, an individual may be able to buy coverage from a group policy through an employer or a professional association, where they may not ask medical questions and do not impose preexisting condition exclusions.

### 4. Cash Value of a Life Insurance Policy

In addition to providing financial security for loved ones after an individual dies, life insurance may also be a source of income while the individual is still living. For more information about using life insurance as a source of income, see Chapter 6, Finances.

### 5. Naming a Beneficiary

When an individual purchases a life insurance policy, the individual must name at least one person they wish to receive the proceeds of the policy (a beneficiary). Some common beneficiaries include:

- Spouse
- Children
- A trust
- A nonprofit organization or other charity

If the person or persons named in the policy are no longer living when the individual dies, the individual's estate will receive the proceeds of the life insurance policy.

### 6. Unclaimed Life Insurance Policies

If an individual purchases a life insurance policy, it is recommended that the beneficiaries be notified. However, beneficiaries often do not know they are supposed to receive money and never pursue a claim. According to Consumer Reports, nearly $1 billion in life insurance benefits remains unclaimed.[26] The National Association of Insurance Commissioners (NAIC) has an online tool called the Life Insurance Policy Locator: https://eapps.naic.org/life-policy-locator/#/welcome. This free tool allows consumers to search for possible life insurance policy or annuity proceeds anywhere in the nation. One of the problems consumers had in the past is that they may have suspected they or a family member was the beneficiary of a life insurance policy or annuity, but did not have key information like the policy number or the name of the insurance company. With the Life Insurance Policy Locator, beneficiaries can simply start with the individual's name.

---

26. *How to Claim an Unclaimed Life-Insurance Policy*, CONSUMER REPS. (Feb. 2013), https://www.consumerreports.org/cro/magazine/2013/02/how-to-find-lost-life-insurance-policies/index.htm.

The process for using the Life Insurance Policy Locator is as follows:

- A suspected beneficiary submits a request.
- NAIC will then ask participating companies to search their records to determine whether they have a life insurance policy or annuity contract in the name of the deceased.
- If there is a policy and the person searching is a beneficiary or authorized to receive information, companies will respond directly to the individual searching.
- It may take up to 90 business days to be contacted. The insurance company may require additional information from the individual searching, like a notarized death certificate and documentation of legal authority to request or obtain information about the deceased.

When purchasing life insurance, individuals should investigate several different companies and types of policies. Life insurance is another estate planning tool that individuals should take into consideration as they are planning their estate. For more information on life insurance visit https://triagecancer.org/cancer-finances-life-insurance.

## E. Trusts

A trust is another tool for estate planning. Unlike wills that express the testators' wishes for what will happen to their property after they die, a trust is a legal entity that will actually own the property. The person placing the property into the trust is known as the *grantor*. The person the grantor chooses to oversee the property in the trust is known as the *trustee*. Finally, the person who receives the benefit of the property in the trust is known as the *beneficiary*. Property that can be held in a trust includes land, buildings, bank accounts, stocks, artwork, cars, jewelry, and other personal property. To set up a trust, the grantor lists the purposes of the trust and makes the trust property available to the trustee. When property is put into a trust, legal ownership is transferred from the grantor to the trust itself. The trustee then has a legal responsibility to handle the property within the trust the way the grantor has specified in the written trust agreement.

Some of the benefits of establishing a trust include:

- **Control.** Trusts allow an individual to include specific terms providing more control as to when and to whom distributions may be made. For example, Steven's daughter only receives her portion of the trust if she has obtained a college degree by the age of 26.
- **Protection.** Trusts allow an individual to provide for heirs who may not be adept at money management. For example, Bill's daughter Pat has a gambling problem. Bill can establish a trust where Pat will only receive her living expenses each month, rather than a lump sum upon Bill's death.

- **Privacy and probate savings.** Some individuals prefer to establish a trust to avoid probate, both to reduce potential court fees and taxes, but also because they prefer to keep their financial matters private and probate is a matter of public record.

People set up trusts for a variety of reasons and there are different types of trusts depending on an individual's needs. The most common types of trusts are:

- **Living trust.** This type of trust is also referred to as an *inter vivos* trust. It is created while the individual is still alive and is generally revocable until one dies. The most common way to create these trusts is for the grantors to appoint themselves as trustees and as long as they remain mentally competent, they can change or dissolve the trust at any time, for any reason. Typically, a living trust becomes irrevocable when the grantor dies.
- **Irrevocable trust.** Unlike a living trust, an irrevocable trust cannot be changed or revoked by the grantor once created by the grantor. These types of trusts may provide some tax benefits and protection from legal action or creditors. However, one should not create this type of trust lightly since they will no longer have full control over the property once established, even if they name themselves trustee.
- **Testamentary trust.** These types of trusts are established, in a will, to provide for individuals who need help managing their assets. These types of trusts do not go into effect until the grantor dies. Testamentary trusts can be especially useful to parents who have young children and want to provide for future education, health care, or general support. They may also be helpful in meeting ongoing expenses for dependent adults with special needs while safeguarding their government benefits (e.g., Medicaid).
- **Special needs trust.** Sometimes referred to as supplemental needs trusts, these trusts allow individuals with a disability to hold an unlimited amount of assets in a trust for their benefit. The advantage of these trusts is that assets included in the trust are not considered "countable assets" for certain government benefits that are based on certain income and resource levels (e.g., Supplemental Security Income or Medicaid). A special needs trust may supplement care the government provides. For example, the trust may pay for hours of home health care in addition to those paid for by Medicaid. There are very specific requirements[27] that must be met in order to establish a valid special needs trust, including:
  - The beneficiary must be younger than 65 at the time the trust is established.
  - The trust is irrevocable.

27. Omnibus Budget Reconciliation Act of 1993, Pub. L. No. 103-66, 107 Stat. 312 (42 U.S.C. § 1396p(d)).

- o The trustee has sole and absolute discretion over the use of the trust funds for the sole benefit of the recipient of government benefits (i.e., the trustee cannot be required to pay the beneficiary directly from the trust).
- o The trust includes a provision that states that any funds remaining in the trust at the death of the beneficiary are available to reimburse the state for any Medicaid costs the beneficiary received.

Tax savings may be a benefit to establishing a trust. For example, a grantor may make annual tax-free gifts to trusts, in an amount allowed by law, to children or grandchildren. This practice reduces the taxable estate and so will help to save on taxes at the grantor's death. As a result, more of the grantor's assets will pass to the grantor's beneficiaries. Unlike a simple will, establishing a trust can be complicated and has serious implications because the grantor is giving up ownership of the property held in the trust. Therefore, it may be in an individual's best interest to hire an estate planning attorney who is well-versed in the state's trust and tax laws to ensure that the trust is set up in the proper manner.

Once a trust is established, it is important to let relevant parties know of its existence and of the location of all pertinent documents. Many people opt to keep their trusts with the attorney who drafted the trust. In that case, the trustee should be given the contact information for the attorney, at a minimum.

## IV. Decisions about Medical Care

There may come a time in an individual's cancer experience when they are unable to make medical or financial decisions. However, there are tools that individuals can use to ensure that their wishes are honored with respect to their medical care and financial affairs.

Advance directives emerged toward the end of the 20th century when concern grew about the power of new medical technologies to keep individuals with serious medical conditions alive. More generally, apprehension developed that medical decisions might be made without regard to the wishes and welfare of incapacitated individuals or their families.

Highly publicized court cases prompted many to consider leaving written instructions about treatment preferences where an individual might become unable to make medical decisions. For example, in 1976, the case of Karen Quinlan, whose father sought to be appointed guardian of his 21-year-old daughter and discontinue the ventilator sustaining her vital processes, garnered national attention.[28] In the 1990s, Nancy Cruzan's parents sought court approval to end artificial hydration and nutrition for their daughter who remained in a state hospital where she exhibited motor

28. *In re* Quinlan, 355 A.2d 647 (N.J. 1976).

reflexes but no indication of significant intelligence.[29] Then, in 2005, the parents of Terri Schiavo asked a Florida court to rule that their incapacitated daughter's rights were violated when another court ordered her food, fluids, and medical treatment to be withheld at the request of her husband.[30]

Despite these very public court cases, which demonstrated the need for advance end-of-life care planning, only about a third of U.S. adults have plans.[31] In an effort to increase access, in January 2016, Medicare began reimbursing physicians for counseling patients about advance care planning.

Each state has a specific set of rules for each of these medical decision-making documents. Therefore, the following sections only speak generally about each type of document. Individuals should check their state's requirements at https://triagecancer.org/estate-planning-toolkit.

## A. Advance Health Care Directives

There may come a time when an individual is unable to express their wishes about medical care. Fortunately, there are steps individuals can take to plan ahead in the event they become incapacitated. While laws vary from state to state, every state and the District of Columbia allows for some kind of advance health care directive.

Generally speaking, an advance health care directive is a legal document in which individuals can provide written instructions, or state preferences, about their medical care should they become unable to communicate. Advance health care directives are commonly seen as a method of directing the withholding or withdrawal of medical treatment at a future time when treatment may not be useful (e.g., stopping chemotherapy once doctors have determined it has become ineffective). However, they can also be used to ensure the start or continuation of treatment at a future time when individuals may not be able to verbalize their consent (e.g., starting artificial hydration).

Though terminology varies from state to state, advance health care directives come in two basic forms.[32] First, an advance directive may be an *instruction directive* that gives health care instructions for future care, but does not appoint another person (e.g., agent, surrogate, or proxy) to carry out the instructions. Second, an *appointment directive* specifies another person (e.g., proxy, surrogate, or agent) to make health care decisions if the individual becomes unable to do so. In some states, a hybrid version of the two forms of advance directives may be used. This version

---

29. Cruzan v. Dir., Mo. Dep't of Health, 497 U.S. 261 (1990); Tamar Lewin, *Nancy Cruzan Dies, Outlived by a Debate over the Right to Die*, N.Y. Times (Dec. 27, 1990), http://www.nytimes.com/1990/12/27/us/nancy-cruzan-dies-outlived-by-a-debate-over-the-right-to-die.html.

30. Schiavo *ex rel.* Schindler v. Schiavo, 403 F.3d 1289 (11th Cir. 2005).

31. Kuldeep N. Yadav et al., *Approximately One in Three US Adults Completes Any Type of Advance Directive for End-of-Life Care*, 36 Health Affs. 1244 (2017).

32. *Id.*

combines written instructions with the naming of a person to carry them out or to make decisions for the individual executing the document. Whether advance health care directives give instructions or make proxy appointments, it is important that they conform to state requirements if they are to be honored.

## 1. Power of Attorney for Health Care

The power of attorney for health care is known by a variety of names that differ from state to state.[33] Generally, this document is where an individual names an agent to make medical decisions if the individual is unable to express their wishes in the future. Some states allow for a broadly written power of attorney for health care that gives the named agent power to make any and all health care decisions the patient would have made. For example, the agent may consent to or refuse any aggressive medical procedures. Other powers that the agent may have include hiring or firing medical personnel, decisions about sharing medical records, or approving blood transfusions. Even in states that allow for this very broad power of attorney for health care, individuals have the opportunity to limit their agent's power and can include specific instructions or preferences about their health care.

Individuals can name an agent and an alternate agent in the event that one of them cannot be reached. However, it is never recommended to appoint co-agents. The rational for this is that having two people with equal decision-making power could lead to great conflict and confusion, thereby thwarting the very reason most people establish advance directives.

Some states have restricted the power of an agent. For example, in New York, an agent cannot make decisions about artificial nutrition or hydration unless the individual's wishes about artificial hydration or nutrition are specifically communicated in the document or the individual has stated that the agent is aware of their wishes. Thus, the power of attorney for health care may be a better option for individuals who are able to state at least some health care preferences, in addition to naming an agent.

## 2. Living Wills

The living will, possibly the most recognized type of advance directive, can often be confused with a power of attorney for health care. Unlike the power of attorney for health care, a living will allows an individual to express their wishes about medical care but typically does not name an agent. Generally, a living will is for more narrow circumstances than a power of attorney for health care. Typically, a living will would only apply to life-prolonging procedures (not routine care) for an individual unable to make their own health care decisions. However, it is important to remember that

33. *Health Care Power of Attorney*, FindLaw, http://estate.findlaw.com/living-will/healthcare-power-of-attorney.html (last updated Mar. 11, 2024).

not all states recognize stand-alone living wills as valid documents. If someone lives in a state like New York, for example, their best option would likely be to have both a power of attorney for health care that names an agent and a living will that lists specific wishes related to health care.

## 3. Specific Advance Health Care Directives

Most states have advance health care directive forms individuals can complete. For links to each state's health care power of attorney statutes, visit http://triagecancer.org/estateplanning. Hospital staff or a social worker may be able to help individuals prepare and complete these forms. There are also entities that provide information and tools that can help individuals start to think about medical decision-making.

### *a. Five Wishes*

The Five Wishes advance directive is a step-by-step, standardized form to help individuals express their preferences for end-of-life care.[34] In addition to conveying the seriously ill individual's desires about medical treatment, the Five Wishes document allows for the appointment of an agent.[35] A Five Wishes form meets the legal requirements for advance directives in a majority of states, if completed according to the document's instructions.[36] In states where a Five Wishes document is not accepted as a legal advance directive, it may still be a helpful tool for individuals who are evaluating their end-of-life choices.[37] More information about Five Wishes can be found at https://agingwithdignity.org/programs/five-wishes/.

### *b. Compassion and Choices*

Compassion and Choices is a national, nonprofit organization that works towards helping people make end-of-life decisions. There is a myriad of free resources available at https://compassionandchoices.org.

### *c. The Conversation Project*

The Conversation Project is an organization that is dedicated to helping people talk about their wishes for end-of-life care, particularly with loved ones. It provides useful information about having difficult conversations, including a toolkit that can be downloaded at https://www.theconversationproject.org.

## 4. Do-Not-Resuscitate Orders

A do-not-resuscitate (DNR) order is an advance directive written by a physician that tells medical professionals not to resuscitate an individual who goes into cardiac or

---

34. *Five Wishes*, Aging with Dignity, https://agingwithdignity.org/programs/five-wishes/ (last visited Nov. 19, 2024).
35. *Id.*
36. *Id.*
37. *Id.*

respiratory distress.[38] A DNR is used only when individuals decide that is what they want and they should work with their health care team to complete the form. A DNR order may allow natural death for someone whose heart is not beating or who is not breathing. For this reason, the order is sometimes called an "allow natural death" order.[39] Traditionally, the DNR order is placed in a patient's chart during a hospital stay. But some states now allow for a special DNR order or a do-not-attempt-resuscitation (DNAR) order for use outside of the hospital. To be sure that a DNR or DNAR is honored, it is important for medical professionals to know that one exists. Copies should be placed in an individual's medical file and perhaps even carried on the individual's person or posted in a prominent location where the individual is likely to be (e.g., on the nightstand in their bedroom or on the fridge in the kitchen).

All patients, but especially those at high risk of cardiopulmonary arrest, should be encouraged to express, in advance, their preferences regarding the extent of treatment if cardiopulmonary arrest occurs. During discussions about patients' preferences, physicians might include a description of cardiopulmonary resuscitation (CPR) or other resuscitation procedures.[40]

DNR and DNAR orders are very limited types of advance directives and do not cover any other kinds of life-prolonging medical treatment.

## 5. POLST and MOLST Forms

A physician order for life-sustaining treatment (POLST) and a medical order for life-sustaining treatment (MOLST) are medical orders completed by a seriously ill individual and signed by a physician.[41] POLST and MOLST forms include directions about using CPR to revive a person who has stopped breathing or whose heart has stopped beating. In addition, these forms may include instructions about other types of treatment, including antibiotics, artificial nutrition, hydration, mechanical ventilation, emergency transport, and placement in the intensive care unit of a hospital.

To prepare a valid POLST or MOLST, individuals with a life expectancy of less than one year may be required to consult with a physician or other health care professional. These orders are recorded on brightly colored papers that travel with the patient. In the states that recognize POLST and MOLST forms, they are designed to indicate what health care treatments emergency personnel and other medical professionals may use. As with a DNR, to ensure that a POLST/MOLST form is honored, copies should be placed in an individual's medical file and perhaps even carried

38. *Do-Not-Resuscitate Order*, MedlinePlus, https://medlineplus.gov/ency/patientinstructions/000473.htm (last reviewed Feb. 3, 2024).

39. *Quick Guide to Advance Health Care Directives*, Triage Cancer, https://triagecancer.org/quick-guides/advance-health-care-directive (last visited Nov. 19, 2024).

40. Council on Ethical and Judicial Affairs, American Medical Association, *Guidelines for the Appropriate Use of Do-Not-Resuscitate Orders*, 265 JAMA 1868 (1991).

41. *Id.*

on the individual's person or posted in a prominent location where the individual is likely to be (e.g., on the nightstand in the bedroom or on a fridge in the kitchen).

For more information about POLST or MOLST by state, visit https://polst.org/programs-in-your-state/.

## 6. Duty to Follow Advance Directives

Generally, medical providers have a duty to honor clearly written advance directives that comply with state law.[42] In addition, where the directive names an agent to make health care choices, medical providers are under a duty to follow the agent's decisions. However, there are a few instances when medical providers can refuse to comply with an advance directive. For example, a directive need not be honored when it goes against the conscience of the medical professional or the policies of an institution providing medical treatment. Also, if a directive contains choices that do not reflect standard medical practices, the health care provider may not have an obligation to honor it. Finally, terms of an advance directive may not be followed if a woman is pregnant, as the interests of the fetus must also be taken into account.[43] Although these exceptions allow medical personnel to refuse to administer treatment in compliance with an advance directive (e.g., withholding artificial hydration from a pregnant woman), the providers may still not be able to administer treatment in conflict with a valid advance directive (e.g., providing a blood transfusion). Rather, the provider might be obligated to transfer the patient to another health care provider who will honor the advance directive's terms.[44]

### *a. Federal Laws*

There are a few federal laws and model laws that deal with advance directives: the Patient Self-Determination Act (PSDA), the Uniform Health-Care Decisions Act, and the Health Insurance Portability and Accountability Act of 1996 (HIPAA).

The federal government first endorsed the idea of advance directives when it passed the PSDA in 1990.[45] The PSDA was based on the premise that widespread use of advance directives would help incapacitated individuals near the end of their lives. Congressional rationale was that the directives would ensure individuals received medical treatment that conformed to their treatment preferences.[46] Some said if these preferences were made known in advance, the country would be less likely to suffer

---

42. Rebecca Rosefelt, *Does My Medical Provider Need to Follow My Health Care Directives?*, FindLaw (Mar. 8, 2024), http://estate.findlaw.com/living-will/health-care-directives-is-there-a-duty-to-follow-them.html.

43. *Id.*

44. *Frequently Asked Questions about Advance Directives*, Am. Cancer Soc'y, https://www.cancer.org/treatment/finding-and-paying-for-treatment/understanding-financial-and-legal-matters/advance-directives/faqs.html (last revised May 13, 2019).

45. 42 U.S.C. §§ 1395i-3, 1395l, 1395cc, 1395mm, 1395bbb, 1396a, 1396b, 1396r.

46. President's Council on Bioethics, Taking Care: Ethical Caregiving in Our Aging Society ch. 2 (2005), https://bioethicsarchive.georgetown.edu/pcbe/reports/taking_care/chapter2.html.

from "wrenching decisions, bitter court battles, and national drama"[47] that occur when technology can sustain life indefinitely.

As the President's Council on Bioethics pointed out, advance directives were also recommended in cases where individuals may experience a gradual decline in physical or mental capacity (e.g., dementia).[48] The PSDA requires that hospitals, nursing homes, and other health care providers participating in Medicare and Medicaid inform patients about advance directives that comply with state law.[49] Upon admission to these facilities, patients have to be told about their rights to accept or reject medical care, and to make or submit advance directives for health care. In addition, health care facilities are allowed to provide advance directive forms.[50] Importantly, these facilities are prohibited from discriminatory treatment of patients based on whether or not they have advance directives.[51] And, finally, the PSDA requires that health care facilities receiving Medicare and Medicaid funding educate staff and community members about advance directives.[52]

Generally, HIPAA requires that health care providers, plans, and information clearinghouses protect against the misuse of health information.[53] But HIPAA permits disclosure of protected health information to a personal representative who has authority to make health care decisions for another (i.e., an agent).[54] To guarantee the agent's access to information, the authorization must be signed and dated by the patient.[55] Also, it must identify the information to be disclosed, the purpose of the disclosure, the recipients of the information, and an expiration date.[56] Therefore, any advance directives should be clear about the scope of the agent's authority to receive protected health care information.[57]

***b. State Laws***

Each state has its own laws about advance directives. Individuals can find information about the rules in their state at https://triagecancer.org/estateplanning.

---

47. *Id.*
48. *Id.*
49. *Law for Older Americans—Health Care Advance Directives*, A.B.A. (Mar. 18, 2013), https://www.americanbar.org/groups/public_education/resources/law_issues_for_consumers/patient_self_determination_act.html.
50. *Id.*
51. *Id.*
52. *Id.*
53. *Individuals' Right under HIPAA to Access Their Health Information 45 CFR § 164.524*, U.S. Dep't Health & Hum. Servs., https://www.hhs.gov/hipaa/for-professionals/privacy/guidance/access/index.html (last reviewed Jan. 5, 2024).
54. *Id.*
55. *Id.*
56. *Id.*
57. *Id.*

### 7. HIPAA Forms

While HIPAA protects the privacy of an individual's health information, it does allow protected health information to be shared with an individual's personal representative who has authority to make health care decisions for them (i.e., the health care agent or proxy). To guarantee the agent's access to information, a HIPAA authorization form must be signed and dated by the authorizing individual. Also, it must identify the information to be disclosed, the purpose of the disclosure, the recipients of the information, and an expiration date. This means that any advance health care directives should be clear about the scope of the agent's authority to receive protected health care information.

There are some other key reasons why it can be helpful to have a HIPAA authorization form. For example, if an individual is in a relationship with a person who is not their spouse, and the individual would like that person to have access to medical information, they should have a HIPAA form. Or, perhaps an individual would like a best friend to be able to communicate with the health care team. In that case, the HIPAA form should give that person that ability. Sample HIPAA authorization forms can be found in the Triage Cancer State-Specific Estate Planning Toolkit: https://triagecancer.org/estate-planning-toolkit.

### 8. Hospital Visitation Directives

Most hospitals are required by federal law to have written rules that give patients the right to choose their own visitors. However, in a crisis, or at a moment when an individual is not able to communicate decisions, it can be helpful to document their wishes about who the individual would like to visit them in a hospital. A hospital visitation directive is a document that tells a health care provider to allow chosen visitors access. It can be a separate document or part of another document, like an advance health care directive. This document can also exclude certain individuals if that is the individual's choice.

## V. Decisions about Finances

### A. Power of Attorney for Financial Affairs

If an individual is incapacitated, there may also be a need to have someone who can handle nonmedical decisions. A power of attorney for financial affairs is a legal document where an individual (the principal) names a trusted adult (the agent) who is authorized to make financial decisions on behalf of the principal. There are two types of powers of attorney for financial affairs: durable and springing. A durable power of attorney for financial affairs goes into effect as soon as the document is signed, whereas a springing power of attorney for financial affairs goes into effect if, and only if, the principal becomes incapacitated. If no specific end date is expressed, the power of attorney for financial affairs will end upon the death of the principal, or when the principal revokes the power. Some of the duties that the principal can grant an agent may include depositing or withdrawing funds from a bank account, or handling the principal's personal matters, such as receiving mail, making travel arrangements, or dealing with a health insurance company.

A power of attorney for financial affairs can be very useful in situations where someone with a cancer diagnosis could use help managing their finances, or if the side effects of treatment might lead to incapacitation. By having a power of attorney for financial affairs in place, the need for a court-appointed guardian to make financial decisions for the incapacitated individual is eliminated.

A properly created power of attorney for financial affairs can save caregivers considerable time and frustration. However, it is important to remember that this document will likely grant a large amount of the principal's decision-making power to an agent. Therefore, principals must be careful to create clearly defined conditions for the power of attorney for financial affairs. Where an agent is untrustworthy or a document fails to carefully articulate the principal's needs and desires, the power of attorney for financial affairs can be abused. To guard against misuse of the power, the principal must choose their agent or agents with great care. Often when people think about who to choose as their agent, they only think about family members. However, if an individual is having a hard time finding a trusted family member to act as an agent, it may be useful to think outside of the family to a trusted friend or business partner. An individual may appoint both an agent and an alternate agent in the event that one is unavailable. However, just like with powers of attorney for health care, it is never recommended to appoint co-agents. Having two or more agents with equal power could lead to conflict and confusion. Finally, as a precautionary measure, the principal should be sure to include any desired restrictions in the document itself. For example, the principal could only want the agent to have the power to write checks out of one bank account. While it is true that a power of attorney for financial affairs potentially gives an agent great power, it can also provide great peace of mind and security for an individual coping with cancer who may, at some point, become incapacitated.

## VI. Consequences of Not Planning Ahead

If individuals do not have advance directives or powers of attorney and become incapacitated, it may fall to a court to appoint a representative to oversee their medical and financial affairs. Many states have statutes that outline the priority of family members to act as surrogates (e.g., first the individual's spouse, then an adult child, then a parent).

A guardianship is a legal relationship that is established and monitored by a state court where someone (the guardian) is appointed to act in the best interest of an incapacitated individual (the ward).

There are two main types of guardianships: guardian of the person and guardian of the estate. However, terminology and rules will differ slightly state to state. For example, Oregon recognizes both guardians and conservators, and treats them as separate entities. Washington uses the terms "guardian of the person" and "guardian of the estate." California and Connecticut use "conservator of the person" and "conservator of the estate." For the purposes of this chapter, the term "guardian" will be used.

A guardian of the person may take actions and make decisions about a ward's care and well-being, such as:

- Discuss treatment options with a ward's health care team
- Make medical decisions to withhold or administer treatment
- Place a ward in hospice care if appropriate

A guardian of the estate, also known as a conservator of the estate, is responsible for decisions about the ward's property and financial affairs. A guardian of the estate may take actions on behalf of the ward, such as:

- Paying bills on behalf of the ward
- Selling property
- Investing money
- Selling assets
- Initiating legal proceedings

The guardian bears heavy responsibilities that vary based on state laws and must be fully accountable to the court that made the appointment. Some states require the guardian to make regular reports to the court about the ward's mental or physical well-being and the ward's finances, depending on the scope of the guardianship.

An individual who is deemed to be incompetent presents an exception to standard informed consent requirements.[58] Incompetency for the purposes of medical decision-making arises from factors such as an unawareness of different options for meeting health care needs; an inability to express preferences about those alternatives; and a failure to understand the risks and benefits of choosing whether or not to undergo treatment.[59] Even where the individual is unable to meet competency standards, though, the right of self-determination in making health care decisions is not foreclosed.[60] Instead, the right to determine one's own medical treatment is exercised on behalf of the incompetent individual by a surrogate decision maker.[61] And, to

58. President's Council on Bioethics, *supra* note 46.
59. *Id.*
60. *Id.*
61. *Id.*

protect the rights of incompetent individuals whose health care decisions are made by surrogates, the state may require safeguards be put in place.[62]

Courts do not create guardianships until making a judgment about the capabilities of the prospective ward.[63] First, the court must find some limitation in the ward that affects decision-making. Perhaps the prospective ward is a minor, has a mental or physical disability, or is entirely incapacitated.[64] Then, the incapacity or incompetency must be determined to be so severe that it affects the ability to manage affairs or make decisions that a court-appointed guardian is necessary.[65] However, where a guardianship proceeding is voluntary, the need for showing some type of incapacity is not necessary. Rather, those individuals who want to withdraw from actively participating in the management of their personal financial affairs may do so without meeting the incapacity requirement. These voluntary guardianships are very rare. Most attorneys would recommend that if someone feels they may become incapacitated in the future, that the individual establish advance directives or a power of attorney for financial affairs rather than rely on the guardianship process.

Despite the safeguards built into the guardianship system, there are still significant disadvantages. Sensitive details about the prospective ward's situation become a matter of public record, leading to a considerable loss of privacy and independence experienced by the ward. Also, as with most court proceedings, there can be significant costs and delay in establishing the guardianship. Depending on the nature of the incapacitation, this could leave the ward unprotected for a long period of time. And, not infrequently, when health care, financial, and other personal matters are not settled by family members and friends prior to incapacity or incompetency, conflict is likely to develop, even among the individuals who care very much about the ward. The Terri Schiavo[66] case is a prime example. Not surprisingly then, guardianships are typically only recommended when there is no alternative. Instead, the individual with cancer should consider other methods of maintaining decision-making power, like powers of attorney and advance directives.

The Uniform Adult Guardianship and Protective Proceedings and Jurisdiction Act allows for a guardianship order to be followed from another state without starting an entirely new proceeding. For example, if the ward and guardian move from New York to California, California will follow New York's guardianship order. The new law eliminates the stress, cost, and time of starting a new guardianship proceeding in another state.

---

62. American Bar Association Commission on Law and Aging & American Psychological Association, Assessment of Older Adults with Diminished Capacity: A Handbook for Psychologists (2008), https://www.apa.org/pi/aging/programs/assessment/capacity-psychologist-handbook.pdf.

63. *Id.*

64. *Id.*

65. *Id.*

66. President's Council on Bioethics, *supra* note 46.

## VII. Practical Estate Planning Topics to Consider

A comprehensive estate plan should also include decisions and wishes about some of the more practical aspects of life.

### A. When a Child Turns 18

Once someone is legally an adult, usually at 18 years old, parents' legal rights to access the child's medical, financial, and educational records are limited. Before a child turns 18, parents should talk to their children about the information they may still need to access. This can be especially important if a child is still receiving cancer treatment. Read Triage Cancer's "Checklist: When Children Turn 18" at https://triagecancer.org/quick-guides/child-turns-18 for information parents can use to start the conversation.

### B. Planning Ahead for Pets

If something unexpected happens, like an accident, illness, or emergency, pets might be forgotten. For example, if an individual were to be in a car accident on the way to work, and they were taken to the hospital unconscious, would someone be able to take care of the individual's dog? Planning ahead for pets could enable family, friends, or even emergency professionals to help. Individuals should consider the following steps:

1. **Identify a person or people they trust.** Individuals who might unexpectedly be away from their pets, like for a hospital stay, should make a list of people who could look after their pets, like trusted family members, friends, or neighbors. Before adding someone to the list, individuals should be sure to communicate and ensure the designated caregivers are willing and able to take care of any pets, and the parameters (e.g., if someone was unavailable for a few days, where would the pet be cared for?).
2. **Create a pet directive for each pet.** Individuals should write down all the important details about each of their pets and keep this document in a place that is easy to find. Copies should also be given to any caretakers who have been chosen.
   a. A pet directive should contain:
      i. Basic details, including the pet's name, any nicknames, breed, birthday, gender, and photo
      ii. Medical information such as health condition and records
      iii. Vet details like the hospital's address, phone number, and vet's name
      iv. Dietary information, such as brand/type of food and any supplements
      v. Information on the pet's habits, behavior around others, and training rules

b. Care instructions could include:
   i. How often to feed, water, and walk the pet each day
   ii. Any grooming needs the pet has and how often to clean the litter box
   iii. Where items like food, medicine, and accessories are kept
   iv. Any other important information or special instruction the caretaker should know

3. **Individuals can carry a pet alert card.** A pet alert card is a useful tool to have in case of an emergency that results in an individual being unable to communicate. It lets the police or emergency responders know that the individual has pets at home. The card should include a home address, and the emergency caretaker's name and phone number, so they can quickly reach out to the person identified to take care of pets.
4. **Post an emergency contact note in the pet's home.** Make an emergency contact note with the name(s) and phone number(s) of the pet's emergency caretaker(s), along with a note about where the pet directive is located. Individuals should put this note somewhere easy to spot in their home, like on the fridge or by the front door.
5. **Arrange for the caretaker to have access to the home.** Individuals should pre-arrange how the caretaker would access their home to care for pets (e.g., spare key, code lock, permission from apartment building manager).
6. **Check pet boarding facilities or shelters.** Individuals who do not have anyone who could care for their pets in an emergency could consider pet boarding facilities (like pet hotels), shelters, or charities that may be able to provide short-term care for pets. Some facilities allow one to pre-arrange care in the event of an emergency. That information could be added to a pet directive and pet alert card.

## C. Digital Afterlife

Thinking about an individual's email and social media accounts may seem trivial when dealing with a cancer diagnosis. However, in this day and age, when so much of an individual's life may take place in the electronic space, it can be useful for individuals to think about how they want to handle these accounts and create a digital estate plan.

The process of creating a digital estate plan is similar to that of creating a will. Individuals should start by collecting information about what they own. That may include:

- Information or data that is stored electronically (e.g., in the cloud, on a thumb drive)
- Online accounts, such as email, digital voicemail, social media, shopping, photo and video sharing, music, video gaming, online storage, rewards, and so on

- Domain names, blogs, and websites owned
- Intellectual property (e.g., copyrighted materials, trademarks)

In creating a list or catalog of digital assets, individuals should also document the login and password information for each account. There are password managing services with a master password that can be shared, or the information can simply be written down in a safe place, accessible to the executor of the estate. Executors should also be made aware of an individual's wishes about how each asset should be handled. For example, should accounts be closed, how should any monetary value be dealt with (e.g., rewards that can be turned in for merchandise), or if assets will continue to generate income (e.g., a copyrighted song), who will receive that income?

When thinking specifically about dealing with social media after one's death, each platform has a different process. For example, Facebook and Instagram gives users the option to elect whether they would like their accounts to be memorialized or permanently deleted when they die. Memorialized accounts will allow a user's friends to continue posting, and all of the existing content remains. Facebook also allows users to name a "legacy contact" who is authorized to manage the account after the user dies. Upon the user's death, the legacy contact should complete the online form and submit a death certificate. X and LinkedIn require that the user's agent notify the platform of the death and request that the account be deactivated.

It is important to go through each platform's terms of service to determine the proper procedure for dealing with the account. Agents should not automatically log on to another user's account to delete it, as that may be a legal violation.

Various email platforms also have procedures to deal with an individual's accounts after death. For example, Gmail, Outlook, and Yahoo have strict procedures to allow the authorized representative of the deceased person to access the content of an email account. Gmail also gives users the option to set an "inactive account manager," wherein after a set amount of inactivity an account is either shared or deleted.

Another significant area of personal property that can live in a digital account is music (e.g., iTunes). Apple specifically states that there is no right of survivorship for an Apple ID, and upon a user's death, the account, and all content within, will be deleted. So, if music is being stored in an iTunes account, individuals may want to make sure to have an electronic backup that they can share with their beneficiaries.

It may seem inconsequential to think about social media, music, and shopping accounts in the big picture of estate planning. However, planning ahead can simplify the process for loved ones, and ensure that all assets are accounted for and protected.

## D. Storing Documents

As discussed throughout this chapter, once an estate plan is completed, it is critical for people involved to know of the plan's existence and to have access. Documents should be kept organized and account information listed clearly. Triage Cancer's

"Financial Big Picture" document is one way to organize this information (https://triagecancer.org/FinancialBigPicture). Saving documents outside of the home can also be useful if an individual is traveling and experiences a medical emergency, or in the event of disaster (e.g., fire, earthquake, flood).

One option is to save electronic copies of the documents on an online drive or cloud storage. There are free services (e.g., Google Drive, iCloud, Dropbox) as well as paid options (e.g., GoodTrust, Everplans) that can be accessed from any computer. If those options seem too complicated, another option may be for individuals to simply email the documents to themselves. Anyone can sign up for a free email address from providers like Gmail, Yahoo, or Microsoft. These email accounts can be accessed on any computer or mobile device around the world that has internet access. Individuals may also consider giving the passwords to those accounts to their agents for easy access.

If individuals choose to keep these documents in a safe deposit box, they should be sure that the executor of their estate also has access to the box. If the documents are kept in a home safe, individuals should ensure that their executor or a loved one has the code or key. An estate plan that cannot be found or accessed is effectively the same thing as not having a plan.

## VIII. End of Life

### A. Legacy Planning

Another idea that may appeal to individuals coping with cancer is legacy planning. This is a way to communicate with loved ones throughout their lives. For example, individuals can leave videos, cards, letters, and presents for milestones in the lives of their loved ones, such as birthdays, graduations, and weddings. MyWonderfulLife.com is a practical resource for funeral and legacy planning.

### B. Palliative and Hospice Care

Palliative care, also called supportive care, is care designed to provide relief from the symptoms and stress of a serious illness, but not to cure the illness itself. Generally, palliative care is discussed in the context of a serious illness, like cancer. For example, an individual is receiving chemotherapy to treat colon cancer, but their doctor also prescribes medication to deal with nausea and pain. The medication for the nausea and pain would be considered palliative. There is a misconception that if an individual is receiving palliative care, they will not receive treatment for cancer. The goal of palliative care is to improve the quality of life for the individual coping with cancer. Typically, insurance coverage for palliative care is handled similarly to coverage for any other prescription drug or specialist (e.g., a referral to a cardiologist).

Hospice care is sometimes referred to as end-of-life care and "focuses on caring, not curing."[67] The overarching philosophy of hospice is to provide compassionate care for people in the last phases of incurable disease. Typically, hospice care is received at an individual's home or hospice residences, nursing homes, assisted living facilities, and veterans' facilities. Hospice care is typically covered by insurance for individuals with a terminal cancer diagnosis. Hospice care costs are covered by Medicare (through the Medicare hospice benefit), Medicaid (in most states), and the Veterans Health Administration. Many private health insurance companies also provide some coverage for hospice care; however, the coverage will vary by policy.

If individuals have wishes about palliative and hospice care, they should be sure to include them in their advance health care directives. For more information about palliative and hospice care, visit the National Hospice and Palliative Care Organization at https://www.nhpco.org.

## C. Appointment of Agent to Control Disposition of Remains (aka Funeral Agent)

Some states have a form that allows individuals to specify their funeral arrangements and any funeral insurance policies, and to choose an agent to handle their funeral arrangements and/or burial. In some states, like New York, an individual can prepare a document naming an agent to handle funeral and burial arrangements. A person can provide the agent with instructions about their funeral and burial wishes as well as inform loved ones about a prepaid funeral arrangement or a burial plot. In other states, individuals can add their funeral and burial wishes to their wills. To see more about funeral designations in each state, visit https://triagecancer.org/state-laws/estate-planning-funeral-designations.

## D. Funeral Arrangements

A sometimes-overlooked aspect of estate planning includes making funeral and/or burial arrangements in advance. By planning ahead, individuals can help avoid putting loved ones in the position of making additional decisions during a difficult time of loss. Some questions an individual can start with are:

- Where and how do I want to be laid to rest (burial, cremation, burial at sea, etc.)?
- Are there cultural and religious customs that I would like to abide by?
- Do my loved ones have any preferences?

---

67. *Hospice Care*, CaringInfo, https://www.caringinfo.org/types-of-care/hospice-care/ (last visited Nov. 19, 2024).

- Do I want a memorial service, a wake, or some other type of celebration of my life?
- Do I need to buy funeral insurance to help pay for these expenses in the future?

Funeral arrangements can be expensive, so an individual should also consider how to cover these costs. There are three main cost categories in funeral planning: costs related to the funeral home, the cemetery, and the grave marker. These costs can range from $3,000 to $15,000, and can vary greatly depending on where individuals live and what they choose. Some of the most common expenses include:

- Funeral home:
  - o Funeral director's basic services fee
  - o Embalming and body preparation
  - o Casket
  - o Funeral ceremony and viewing
  - o Miscellaneous (e.g., hearse or other transportation, death certificates, obituary, memorial services, flowers, music, prayer cards, motorcycle officers to escort a funeral procession between a memorial and burial site, and other custom features)
- Cemetery:
  - o Grave site (plot)
  - o Open/close fee for digging and placing the casket in the grave
  - o Fee to place the grave marker
- Grave marker (also called a headstone): The price of a headstone is generally calculated by weight, so the larger the headstone, the more expensive it will be. Features such as an engraved photo or image will be an additional cost. If the headstone is purchased from a retailer other than the cemetery, there may be an additional shipping fee.

Some individuals may also consider cremation. Cremation can be less expensive, averaging around $3,200 plus the cost of an urn, which starts at $20. Some funeral homes and cemeteries will not accept credit cards or payment plans, but require payment in cash and up front. Some funeral homes and cemeteries will allow individuals to set up a payment plan, if they chose to preplan a funeral. There are several options to purchase funeral or "final expense" insurance, to cover the cost of expenses.

Tools exist to help individuals preplan and document their wishes around funeral planning. For more information, visit http://triagecancer.org/estateplanning.

## E. Funeral Designation Forms

Some states have laws related to naming an individual to make funeral-related decisions on another person's behalf, or to document their own funeral preferences. To see more about the laws in each state, visit https://triagecancer.org/state-laws/estate-planning-funeral-designations.

## F. Death with Dignity Laws

Death with dignity laws are also referred to as physician-assisted dying or aid-in-dying laws. These terms generally refer to a practice in which a doctor provides mentally competent, terminally ill individuals with prescriptions for a lethal dose of medication, which individuals intend to use to end their own lives. The concept stems from the idea that a terminally ill individual should have the ability to make their own end-of-life decisions. As of April 2024, 11 states have death with dignity statutes, and several others are considering legislation.[68] In Montana, physician-assisted dying is legal by state supreme court ruling.[69] One of the most important assertions made by advocates for death with dignity laws is that those who assist individuals in these limited circumstances, and those who take the drugs to aid in their own death, are not considered engaging in suicide, homicide, or assisted suicide.[70] This distinction is particularly important to ensure that participating individuals do not face criminal charges and that individuals who chose to end their lives within these parameters will still be eligible for insurance benefits (i.e., life insurance).[71]

This is still an evolving area of law. For up-to-date information on death with dignity state laws, visit https://triagecancer.org/state-laws.

## G. When a Loved One Dies

When a family member passes away it can be difficult to focus on logistics, such as funerals and paperwork, but there are some practical steps that need to be taken, some of which are time sensitive. Being aware of these steps ahead of time can help make the process a little less stressful during a time of grief.

1. **Organ/body donation.** If a family member wanted their organs or body donated for transplant or research, inform the doctor immediately following the family member's death.
2. **Obtain a legal pronouncement of death.** Depending on where an individual dies, there may be a different process, for example:
   - If an individual unexpectedly passes away at home, 911 should be called to have them transported to the emergency room by emergency medical services (EMS) and legally declared deceased by a health care professional.

68. For an updated list, visit *Estate Planning State Laws: Death with Dignity*, TRIAGE CANCER, https://triagecancer.org/state-laws/death-with-dignity (last visited Nov. 19, 2024).

69. Baxter v. Montana, 224 P.3d 1211 (Mont. 2009).

70. Pamela S. Kaufmann, *Aid-in-Dying Laws Present New Challenges for Health Care Providers*, 13 A.B.A. HEALTH ESOURCE (2017).

71. *Id.*

- In some places, the local emergency medical technicians (EMTs) or fire department that arrives can make that declaration and they will not have to go to the emergency room.
- If an individual dies at a hospice facility or while receiving in-home hospice care, typically a hospice nurse can legally declare them as deceased.

3. **Immediate practical steps.** There will likely be some necessary practical things to do immediately following an individual's death. For example:
   - If the individual had any dependents and/or minor children, someone should ensure their immediate needs are being met (e.g., picked up from school, fed).
   - Ensure any pets are taken care of until a permanent home can be found for them.
   - Lock the windows and doors in the individual's home and car. Take care of housekeeping tasks such as bringing in the mail, throwing out food in the kitchen, and taking out the trash. Secure any valuables.
   - Locate the individual's estate planning documents, including the will. Ideally, the executor of the individual's estate knows where the will is located. If not, the document may be locked in a desk, safe, or other area of safekeeping. The executor of the estate should be contacted immediately. If there is no will, someone from the individual's life will have to go to a probate court judge to have an administrator named.
4. **Funeral, burial, or cremation arrangements.** Once an individual has been legally declared deceased, then the individual will need to be transported to a funeral home or cremation organization. The executor should check to see if the individual made any specific plans or prepayments for a funeral, burial, or cremation. This may be found in a will, funeral designation form, or other paperwork completed by the individual.
   - If there is no paperwork that describes the individual's preferences or plans, then a funeral home or cremation organization must be chosen. Other decisions will also need to be made, including whether and where to hold a funeral or memorial service, whether to use cremation and where the ashes will go, or where the individual will be buried and what type of casket and tombstone to order.
   - Typically, with information gathered from the hospital and family members, the funeral home or cremation organization will prepare and file the death certificate with the state's vital records office. The death certificate will be necessary for many other steps in this process.
   - If the individual was a military veteran or was part of a specific fraternal or religious group, the Veterans Health Administration or the specific organization should be contacted to determine if they offer benefits to help manage the costs of funerals and burials or provide other services, such as pallbearers or flags.

- o Decide who will help plan and participate in the services, and who will be invited.

5. **Make notifications.** When an individual dies there are a number of people and organizations that may need to be notified. For example, family, friends, coworkers, professional relationships, and other acquaintances may need to be notified. It should be decided if an obituary will be included in a local newspaper or on social media. The individual's employer should be contacted and information obtained about any paychecks that may be due to the individual and other benefits, such as an employer-sponsored life insurance policy. The Social Security Administration should also be notified. Finally, the U.S. Postal Service can forward the individual's mail, which will help the executor to identify if there are any subscriptions that must be canceled or bills to be paid.
6. **Complete/find necessary paperwork.** The executor should obtain multiple original copies of the individual's death certificate. These are needed to close bank accounts, file insurance claims, and notify government agencies. They can be obtained through the funeral home or the vital statistics office in the place where the individual died. These typically take about three to ten days to receive. If the individual had a life insurance policy or retirement account, notify the company of the death, and arrange payout details for the beneficiary (e.g., direct deposit, check). If the individual had a trust, those trust documents will need to be found and the trustee contacted.
7. **Initiate the probate process.** The executor will have to file a petition to start the probate process with the probate court in the county where the individual lived. Further, a notice that the estate is in probate must be mailed to all beneficiaries under the will and to creditors. Some states also require a notice to be published in the newspaper. As part of the probate process all assets, such as personal property, house, bank accounts, car, furniture, brokerage accounts, and other valuables, will need to be inventoried. These items may also need to be appraised. In addition to inventorying property, money owed to the individual, such as loans and paychecks, will need to be collected. While the probate process is ongoing, the executor will need to pay expenses like the mortgage, taxes, and utilities. If there are not enough assets in the estate to cover all debts, the court will prioritize payments made to creditors. Once probate is complete, the executor will likely have to distribute remaining assets, close the estate, and hire an accountant to file a tax return on behalf of the estate.
8. **Other practical steps.** After a person passes away, there are a number of practical things that need to be taken care of, including:
   - o Cancel services and accounts on auto-billing (e.g., prescriptions, streaming services).
   - o Cancel upcoming appointments (e.g., dentist, doctor, landscaping, cleaning services).

- o Close or forward email accounts. It can be useful to keep the account open for a period of time as to not miss any notifications (e.g., electronic bills). It is recommended that any electronic property associated with the email account be downloaded before closing (e.g., documents, pictures, or music stored in a cloud).
- o Cancel their driver's license by contacting the local Department of Motor Vehicles. This usually requires a copy of a death certificate.
- o Close credit card accounts. This usually requires a copy of the death certificate. The executor should be made aware of any outstanding balances on the cards.
- o Cancel insurance policies (e.g., health, dental, disability, long-term care, supplemental).
- o Contact any financial advisors, stockbrokers, and/or credit agencies that need to be notified.

9. **Seek out emotional support.** Grieving the loss of a family member is difficult, but there are some resources that may be helpful, including mental health care professionals, in-person or online grief support groups, religious leaders or organizations, and mobile apps (e.g., Talkspace.com).

## IX. Conclusion

Estate planning can be daunting, emotional, difficult, and yet rewarding. When individuals are coping with cancer, they may find great comfort in exercising some control at a time when much feels out of their control. Open dialogue with one's loved ones and health care team about the realities of health care and what is most appropriate for the individual should be encouraged. No one should feel that they are alone in this process. There are many resources out there to help individuals and families establish a comprehensive and cohesive estate plan.

## X. Resources

Triage Cancer Estate Planning Resources: http://triagecancer.org/estateplanning

The National Guardianship Network is a collaborative group of organizations dedicated to adult guardianship: https://www.naela.org/NGN-New/NGN New/Home.aspx

Good Trust is a platform that allows individuals to create a will-based estate plan, as well as securely organize digital life and assets: https://mygoodtrust.com/. For a 30 percent discount on a subscription, use code: TRIAGE30.

The Digital Beyond is a compilation of services that allow people to create a plan for their "digital life" after they die (e.g., posthumous email services and online memorials): https://www.thedigitalbeyond.com

Special Needs Alliance (SNA) is a national organization comprising attorneys committed to the practice of disability and public benefits law. Individuals with disabilities, their families, and their advisors rely on the SNA to connect them with nearby attorneys who focus their practices in the disability law arena: https://www.specialneedsalliance.org

## XI. Exercises and Discussion Topics

### A. Case Study

Steven and Pam have always talked about the fact that they should have a will and name a guardian for their two young children, but they never got around to completing an estate plan. Steven was diagnosed with pancreatic cancer last week. The doctors do not know how Steven will respond to treatment, but have warned him that there may come a time when he is unable to verbalize his wishes or make medical decisions for himself. *Are there steps that Steven and Pam can take now to protect themselves and their family?*

**Answer.** Fortunately, it is not too late for Steven and Pam to do some planning. At bare minimum, they should both draft wills that designate people to receive their property and a guardian for their minor children. They may also want to consider creating a trust to benefit their children. Depending on how complicated their estate is (e.g., number of houses, accounts), they may or may not feel comfortable creating their estate planning documents on their own. They could use software or an online service to create a will, and power of attorney for financial affairs. However, if their estate is complicated or they would feel more comfortable, there are many estate planning attorneys that are reasonably priced. Steven and Pam may also want to take stock of their digital assets and consider preplanning their funerals. During the estate planning process, Steven and Pam should speak openly and honestly about what kind of health care treatment each of them wants if they ever become incapable of making their own health care decisions, as well as complete advance health care directives.

### B. Class Exercises

1. Draft a will compliant with your state's requirements for your client.
2. Help someone complete an advance health care directive and power of attorney for financial affairs. What are some types of things to consider when drafting medical decision-making documents (e.g., who your agent should be, alternate agent)?
3. Read the long and complex will of Elvis Presley (available at http://www.ibiblio.org/elvis/elvwill.html). Then read the short and simple will of Warren Burger, a former Chief Justice of the U.S. Supreme Court.

**LAST WILL AND TESTAMENT of WARREN E. BURGER**

I hereby make and declare the following to be my last will and testament.

1. My executors will first pay all claims against my estate;
2. The remainder of my estate will be distributed as follows: one-third to my daughter, Margaret Elizabeth Burger Rose and two-thirds to my son, Wade A. Burger;
3. I designate and appoint as executors of this will, Wade A. Burger and J. Michael Luttig.

IN WITNESS WHEREOF, I have hereunto set my hand to this my Last Will and Testament this 9th day of June, 1994.

/s/ Warren E. Burger

We hereby certify that in our presence on the date written above WARREN E. BURGER signed the foregoing instrument and declared it to be his Last Will and Testament and that at this request in his presence and in the presence of each other we have signed our names below as witnesses.

/s/ Nathaniel E. Brady residing at 120 F St., NW, Washington, DC

/s/ Alice M. Khu residing at 3041 Meeting St., Falls Church, VA

Note how the two documents are different and list the different goals of the testators based on these documents. Decide which approach you think is better and explain why.

## C. Discussion Topics

1. Even people who are rich or famous have died without wills. For example, Pablo Picasso, Sonny Bono, Michael Jackson, Chadwick Boseman, Howard Hughes, and Aretha Franklin did not execute wills before they died. Surprisingly, Abraham Lincoln, himself a lawyer, was the first president to die intestate. What are some of the reasons people die intestate? What can be done to encourage people who do not have wills to make thorough estate plans that include the execution of a will?
2. Sometimes an agent or health care provider strongly disagrees on ethical grounds with instructions provided by a principal. How should such problems be dealt with? Should the agents or providers be required to follow the instructions? Or should the agents or health care providers be allowed to find a replacement to take over their responsibilities?
3. Should a chronically depressed person be allowed to refuse life-sustaining treatment in their advance directives? Should consultation with a mental health

professional be required before the advance directives are filled out? What safeguards should be implemented to protect depressed people from others who might exploit their mental condition?

4. As an attorney, what is your role to work with your client's health care team to make sure that an advance health care directive is appropriate for their situation?
5. What is the role of the health care professional in estate planning?
6. How can physicians, nurses, social workers, and patient navigators help patients start to think about estate planning issues? Should they be talking to patients about these issues? What are the potential pitfalls health care professionals should be aware of?
7. National Healthcare Decisions Day is designed to inspire, educate, and empower the public and providers about advance health care directives. Watch the video at https://www.nhdd.org and then discuss what impact it has on a viewer who never heard of advance directives.

# CHAPTER SIX
# Finances

## *Case Study: William*

*William is 32 years old and just had his last chemotherapy appointment. He has been in treatment, which included surgery, for more than a year. He will also need physical therapy to help with some of the side effects from his treatment. During treatment, William had to stop working completely, but is now working part-time. After exhausting his savings, he paid some of his utility bills and health insurance premiums by credit card and is now having a hard time keeping up with the minimum payments. As a result of the missed payments on those credit cards and the fact that he returned his leased car early, William's credit score is considerably lower than it was prior to his diagnosis. Because he is only able to work part-time, his resources are limited, and he is falling behind on paying his mortgage, student loan payments, and other bills. He has been offered a full-time job, but would need access to a car. He is concerned he will not qualify for a car loan because of his low credit score and that he will not be able to afford the monthly payments even if he can get the loan. Also, William received a bill from the hospital last week for a chemotherapy treatment that was double what he had paid for similar treatments in the past. Yesterday, a collection agent showed up at his job demanding payment for an overdue bill, which was incredibly embarrassing for William, and he is worried it will impact his full-time job offer. William wants to do the right thing and move past this part of his life, but feels overwhelmed and hopeless. He wonders if he should sell his home to pay off his bills, and, if so, what the tax implications might be, or if bankruptcy is his best option. But he is also concerned that if he sells his home, he will not be able to get an apartment with his low credit score. What are William's options?*

## I. Introduction to Cancer-Related Financial and Consumer Issues

Cancer care is one of the costliest health care specialties in the United States.[1] Cancer treatments are expensive, insurance coverage is often inadequate, and compared to individuals without a cancer history, cancer survivors have higher out-of-pocket health care costs, even years after an initial diagnosis.[2] According to the Institute of Medicine, "rising costs are making cancer care less affordable for patients and their families and are creating disparities in patients' access to high-quality cancer care."[3] By 2030, the cost of cancer care is expected to reach more than $240 billion.[4]

In 2013, researchers coined the term "financial toxicity" to refer to the financial side effects of cancer treatment.[5] Since then, numerous studies have shown a direct correlation between financial stress and a cancer diagnosis. In a study of patients participating in a phase 1 clinical trial and their spousal caregivers, 82 percent of patients reported medical cost concerns and 79 percent reported financial stress. In the same study, 83 percent of employed spousal caregivers reported wage concerns. These financial concerns significantly contributed to a decrease in quality of life among cancer patients and their caregivers.[6] Furthermore, the physical, psychological, and financial impacts of cancer do not necessarily end when active treatment does. In a study of individuals who were at least six months post-diagnosis, 49 percent reported increased financial stress (e.g., impact of cancer diagnosis on their ability to make ends meet) and 32 percent reported an increased financial strain (e.g., depression, anxiety, and distress related to finances) due to cancer.[7] Another study concluded that the "increased financial burden as a result of cancer care costs is the strongest independent predictor of poor quality of life among cancer survivors."[8]

---

1. *Financial Toxicity and Cancer Treatment (PDQ®)—Health Professional Version*, NAT'L CANCER INST., https://www.cancer.gov/about-cancer/managing-care/track-care-costs/financial-toxicity-hp-pdq (last updated May 29, 2024).

2. *Id.*

3. INSTITUTE OF MEDICINE, DELIVERING HIGH-QUALITY CANCER CARE: CHARTING A NEW COURSE FOR A SYSTEM IN CRISIS (Laura A. Levit et al. eds., 2013).

4. Angelo B. Mariotto et al., *Medical Care Costs Associated with Cancer Survivorship in the United States*, 29 CANCER EPIDEMIOLOGY BIOMARKERS & PREVENTION 1304 (2020).

5. S. Yousuf Zafar & Amy P. Abernethy, *Financial Toxicity, Part I: A New Name for a Growing Problem*, 27 ONCOLOGY (WILLISTON PARK) 80 (2013), https://pmc.ncbi.nlm.nih.gov/articles/PMC4523887/.

6. Fay J. Hlubocky et al., *Financial Burdens (FB), Quality of Life, and Psychological Distress among Advanced Cancer Patients (ACP) in Phase I Trials and Their Spousal Caregivers (SC)*, 30 J. CLINICAL ONCOLOGY 6117 (2012).

7. Linda Sharp et al., *Associations between Cancer-Related Financial Stress and Strain and Psychological Well-Being among Individuals Living with Cancer*, 22 PSYCHO-ONCOLOGY 745 (2013); Scott Ramsey et al., *Washington State Cancer Patients Found to Be at Greater Risk for Bankruptcy Than People without a Cancer Diagnosis*, 32 HEALTH AFFS. 1143 (2013).

8. Kathleen Fenn et al., *Impact of Financial Burden of Cancer on Survivors' Quality of Life*, 10 J. ONCOLOGY PRAC. 1332 (2014).

While "financial toxicity" is a relatively new term, the problem itself is not new. Based on data from 2007, 62 percent of all bankruptcies in the United States were due to medical debt and 78 percent of those filing bankruptcy due to medical debt had health insurance coverage.[9] In 2013, a study found that cancer survivors are 2.65 times more likely to declare bankruptcy as those without a cancer diagnosis.[10] One study reported that bankrupt cancer patients are nearly 80 percent more likely to die than patients who do not file for bankruptcy.[11] A 2017 study found that more than one-third of cancer patients who have health insurance spend more out of pocket for their treatments than they expected having to pay; the median monthly out-of-pocket expenditure was $703.[12] There is also a new trend in hospitals asking for up-front payment even when a patient has health insurance.[13] This is especially true for individuals who have high deductible plans; health care providers may try to secure payments up front to maximize their collections.[14]

When individuals face a cancer diagnosis, there are a number of factors that could contribute to a challenging financial situation. Perhaps they were unable to work for a period of time due to treatment and recovery. Or, maybe they had inadequate health insurance and were unable to pay their high out-of-pocket medical expenses, ultimately resulting in damaged credit scores. It can often seem overwhelming for individuals coping with cancer and their caregivers to try to find their way out of that maze. Some survivors are able to tap into their savings. But, unfortunately, half of U.S. adults do not have enough "rainy day" savings for a $500 emergency.[15] As of 2022, more than 100 million Americans had medical debt.[16] And, that medical debt is impacting patients' ability to get care. Approximately one in seven people with medical debt say they have been denied access to medical care due to unpaid bills.[17]

Even if an individual is able to access quality cancer care, the financial burden can negatively affect a survivor's quality of life. Research has shown that individuals saddled with high out-of-pocket costs related to their cancer treatments "reduce their

---

9. David Himmelstein et al., *Medical Bankruptcy in the United States, 2007: Results of a National Study*, 122 Am. J. Med. 741 (2009).

10. Ramsey et al., *supra* note 7; Peter A. Ubel et al., *Full Disclosure—Out-of-Pocket Costs as Side Effects*, 369 New Eng. J. Med. 1484 (2013).

11. Scott D. Ramsey et al., *Financial Insolvency as a Risk Factor for Early Mortality among Patients with Cancer*, 34 J. Clinical Oncology 980 (2016).

12. Fumiko Chino et al., *Out-of-Pocket Costs, Financial Distress, and Underinsurance in Cancer Care*, 3 JAMA Oncology 1582 (2017), https://pmc.ncbi.nlm.nih.gov/articles/PMC5824215.

13. Michelle Andrews, *Doctors and Hospitals Say "Show Me the Money" before Treating Patients*, Cal. Healthline (Dec. 6, 2016), http://californiahealthline.org/news/doctors-and-hospitals-say-show-me-the-money-before-treating-patients/.

14. *Id.*

15. Noam N. Levey, *100 Million People in America Are Saddled with Health Care Debt*, KFF Health News (June 16, 2022), https://kffhealthnews.org/news/article/diagnosis-debt-investigation-100-million-americans-hidden-medical-debt.

16. *Diagnosis: Debt*, KFF Health News, https://kffhealthnews.org/diagnosis-debt/ (last visited Dec. 1, 2024).

17. *Id.*

spending on food and clothing to make ends meet or reduce the frequency in which they take prescribed medications."[18] Unfortunately, health care providers rarely have meaningful conversations with their patients about the costs prior to starting treatment.[19] Fifty percent of patients were interested in talking about the cost of care, but only 19 percent have had that cost discussion.[20] When financial issues were discussed, it was the patient who initiated the conversation 70 percent of the time.[21] Sometimes, this lack of communication between patients and health care providers leads to overlooking viable, less-expensive, yet equally effective treatments. The end result is that patients experience unnecessary financial distress.[22]

The research and conversations on the financial toxicity of cancer care have primarily focused on high out-of-pocket costs. One study found that "policies and practices that minimize cancer patient's out-of-pocket costs can improve survivors' health-related quality of life and psychological health."[23] The most effective way to reduce individuals' out-of-pocket costs is to ensure they have adequate health insurance. For more information on picking a health insurance plan, see Chapter 1, Health Insurance. Additionally, individuals coping with a cancer diagnosis should make certain their income is not negatively impacted because they are forced out of work. See Chapter 2, Employment. For individuals who need to take time off work, either for themselves or as a caregiver, maximizing disability insurance and paid family leave benefits can help to minimize the negative financial impact. See Chapter 3, Disability Insurance.

Finally, individuals should take four key steps to build a strong financial foundation after a cancer diagnosis: (1) understand how to manage medical bills; (2) leverage strategies for paying expenses; (3) adopt long-term financial strategies; and (4) understand their consumer rights.

## II. Dealing with Medical Bills

Medical debt is a leading contributor to financial burden after a cancer diagnosis, especially since medical bills may continue to arrive long after active cancer treatment has ended. It is important for individuals to stay diligent and verify the accuracy

---

18. Allen St. John, *How the Affordable Care Act Drove Down Personal Bankruptcy*, Consumer Rep. (May 2, 2017), https://www.consumerreports.org/personal-bankruptcy/how-the-aca-drove-down-personal-bankruptcy/.

19. Dennis Thompson, *Many Doctors Not Forthcoming about Cost of Cancer Care, Study Suggests*, UPI (June 21, 2017), https://www.upi.com/Health_News/2017/06/22/Many-doctors-not-forthcoming-about-cost-of-cancer-care-study-suggests/1741498140607/.

20. Kristen Chanley, *Avoiding the Toxicity of Cancer Care*, Conquer (Apr. 2016), https://conquer-magazine.com/issues/2016/vol-2-no-2-april-2016/240-avoiding-the-toxicity-of-cancer-care.

21. St. John, *supra* note 18.

22. *Id.*

23. Hrishikesh P. Kale & Norman V. Carroll, *Self-Reported Financial Burden of Cancer Care and Its Effect on Physical and Mental Health-Related Quality of Life among US Cancer Survivors*, 122 Cancer 283 (2016).

of bills. Individuals have the right to dispute bills if there are errors. If individuals believe a procedure or treatment should have been covered by their health insurance policy and it was not, they have the right to appeal that decision. (See Chapter 1, Health Insurance, for information about appealing a health insurance company's decision.) There are strategies to lower costs before receiving care, and ways to manage bills after receiving care.

## A. Avoiding Higher Medical Bills

While it is impossible to completely avoid incurring medical costs related to a cancer diagnosis, there are several steps individuals can take to avoid higher than necessary medical bills.

### 1. Have the Right Insurance

Ensuring individuals have appropriate health insurance coverage is imperative to avoid higher than necessary medical bills. Too often, individuals will only look at the monthly premium cost when choosing a health insurance policy. However, it is critical for individuals to also look at the deductibles, out-of-pocket maximums, networks of doctors and hospitals, and prescription drug coverage before picking a plan.

### 2. Discuss Costs with Health Care Team and Insurance Company before Treatment

Even if individuals have comprehensive health insurance, they will still likely be faced with some medical bills related to cancer treatment. Perhaps the most important thing that individuals can do when they are concerned about their medical bills is to talk to their health care team. Members of their health care team may have ideas about how to reduce costs and access financial assistance options. Occasionally, it may be possible for an individual to group health care appointments together, so that they are only paying one co-pay and one office visit fee. When calling to schedule appointments, individuals should ask if this is something they can do. Furthermore, there may be times when it is possible to take an equally effective generic prescription drug, instead of a brand-name prescription drug, which may be less expensive. Or, there may be an oral version of the prescribed chemotherapy that might allow the individual to keep working, rather than having to take unpaid medical leave. These treatment decisions should be thoroughly discussed with an individual's health care provider, as it is never advisable to take a less effective course of treatment for financial reasons.

Some questions individuals may consider asking of their health insurance company include:

- Are the treatment facility and providers in-network?
- Will there be a co-payment for each individual treatment and what amount is it?

- Does the plan require a pre-authorization for any of the prescribed services?
- What is/is not covered if an individual is admitted to a hospital?
- What is/is not covered if an individual is treated as an outpatient?
- Are there out-of-network benefits? If so, what is the cost-share?
- Does the plan require a referral to see a specialist?
- Does the insurance company provide a case manager to assist with claims?
- Is the prescription drug on the plan's formulary or preferred drug list? What is the co-pay?
- Does the state require similar out-of-pocket costs for oral chemotherapy as intravenous chemotherapy?
- Is it less expensive to receive prescription drugs via mail order versus at a retail pharmacy?

Some questions individuals may consider asking of their health care team include:

- Are there ways to change the prescribed treatment schedule to work around an individual's job or child care situation?
- Could the prescribed treatment impact the individual's fertility? If so, are there options to preserve fertility? How are those options typically paid for?
- Is there an appropriate clinical trial? If so, how will participating impact an individual's finances?
- Are there other costs individuals should be thinking about (e.g., transportation, loss of work, expenses for "cosmetic items" like wigs or prostheses)?
- Is there a less expensive prescription drug option (e.g., generic, over the counter, brand-name) that would be equally effective?

## 3. Pre-authorization

Many health insurance policies require that individuals obtain a pre-authorization before they receive a health care service or a prescription drug. If a pre-authorization is not obtained, the health insurance company may deny the claim. Individuals should work with their health care team to contact their health insurance company prior to treatment, testing, survey, or hospitalization to check if a pre-authorization is necessary. If a health insurance company denies the pre-authorization, that decision can be appealed.

## 4. Make Sure Health Care Providers Have Up-to-Date Insurance Information

Individuals should take their insurance cards with them to each doctor appointment and the pharmacy. Typically, providers will make a copy of individuals' cards and keep it on file; however, since an individual may change providers midyear, it is helpful to always have the card on hand. Furthermore, if individuals have two insurance policies, they should ensure that their providers have all relevant information for both policies. It may also be helpful for individuals to know which is the primary insurer, meaning which policy pays first, and which pays second. Ensuring that all health care providers have the correct health insurance information for an individual is another way to avoid unnecessary costs.

## 5. Be a Good Consumer

Individuals should consider their health care options as they would any other item or service they purchase. They should shop around and compare prices. For example, individuals do not typically have to use the lab a doctor recommends. Instead, they may be able to look for stand-alone facilities, or facilities in their insurance network, when they need certain tests or lab work. Not all labs charge the same amount and there can be a significant difference if the health care provider or lab is not in the individual's health insurance network. Individuals can ask their doctors for a list of tests that are going to be performed and shop around for the lowest prices. The cost of treatment can vary widely, so it can be useful to know the real cost of medical care received. Websites like New Choice Health (https://www.newchoicehealth.com/) and Healthcare Bluebook (https://www.healthcarebluebook.com/ui/home) provide some of this information.

Individuals should also pay attention to the quality of care being provided by their health care providers. Individuals can get referrals from family members, friends, or other people they trust, or they can check websites such as Medicare's https://www.medicare.gov/care-compare/ and https://ratings.leapfroggroup.org/.

When shopping around for procedures, individuals may consider asking the following questions:

- To the prescribing health care professional:
    - What is the exact name and five-digit Healthcare Common Procedure Coding System code for the procedure?
    - Is there a specific time frame in which this test/procedure needs to occur?
- To the potential health care professional providing the test/procedure:
    - Is a consultation needed? If so, is there an added charge?
    - Is there an additional fee for reading the results of the test?
    - Is there a way to confirm if all of the providers, including the anesthesiologist, are in-network?
    - Are there any other fees to be aware of?[24]

Individuals may consider asking for signed and dated quotes in writing.

24. *Cracking the Code: 10 Questions to Find What That Medical Procedure Will Cost You*, Times-Picayune (May 9, 2017), http://www.nola.com/health/index.ssf/2017/05/10_questions_to_find_out_what.html.

### 6. Negotiate with Health Care Providers

Individuals should ask for up-front pricing for all non-emergency tests and procedures. If shopping around for lower cost providers is not an option, individuals may be able to negotiate their medical bill, before they get care. Individuals should also ask if there are any discounts available. For instance, providers may offer a discount for paying in cash, rather than by credit card. Some individuals may qualify for "charity care" at a health care facility.

## B. Charity Care

Nonprofit hospitals are required to offer free or discounted health care to patients with certain incomes.[25] This is called charity care, but could also be called patient financial assistance or ability-to-pay programs. Charity care can include inpatient and emergency room services. Nonprofit hospitals are required to post their financial assistance policy online and in the hospital.[26] Hospitals must also pause sending a bill to collections while they are reviewing a financial assistance application. Some for-profit hospitals also offer financial assistance programs.

Each hospital's charity care programs have different rules. Hospitals offer charity care to patients who are uninsured or underinsured, based on their household income level. These are the key things that an individual needs to find out:

- What are the income or other requirements to qualify?
- What is the deadline to apply? How does someone apply?
- Who should an individual call if they have questions?

Nonprofit hospitals are required to give patients 240 days to apply for financial assistance. The 240 days starts from the day the hospital sends a patient the first copy of the bill, not the day that the patient visits the hospital. Some hospitals will give even more time to apply. It is always worth calling the hospital to find out if they will accept a financial assistance application, even if the deadline has passed.

If an individual has any questions about the financial assistance rules at the hospital, the best place to start is to call the hospital financial assistance department directly. The phone number is usually on the financial assistance website or in the financial assistance policy. This number may be different from the hospital's billing office. When calling, make sure to ask for the financial assistance department.

---

25. *Requirements for 501(c)(3) Hospitals under the Affordable Care Act—Section 501(r)*, INTERNAL REVENUE SERV., https://www.irs.gov/charities-non-profits/charitable-organizations/requirements-for-501c3-hospitals-under-the-affordable-care-act-section-501r (last updated Aug. 19, 2024).

26. *Financial Assistance Policy and Emergency Medical Care Policy—Section 501(r)(4)*, INTERNAL REVENUE SERV., https://www.irs.gov/charities-non-profits/financial-assistance-policy-and-emergency-medical-care-policy-section-501r4 (last updated Aug. 20, 2024).

Each hospital has different rules for how to submit the application, so make sure to read their instructions. Include copies of all the documents requested. It can be helpful to keep a copy of what is sent to the hospital for an individual's own records. This can also be helpful if the hospital loses the application and an individual needs to resubmit it. An individual can call the hospital a few days after sending in the application, to make sure it was received. If the hospital asks for more documents, make sure to send them within a few days.

If the hospital denies an application, it is important to find out why. The hospital must send the patient a letter with the final charity care decision and reason. An individual may be able to reapply or appeal the decision. Ask the hospital if they will consider an appeal.

Dollar For is a nonprofit organization that can check eligibility for charity care at an individual's hospital, provide tips on applying, or even submit an application to the hospital on an individual's behalf. For medical bills that have already been received, Dollar For can help negotiate the bills for patient's eligible for charity care. For more information about Dollar For, visit https://DollarFor.org/TriageCancer.

## C. Communications about Medical Bills

The amount of paperwork generated each time an individual receives medical care can be overwhelming. Individuals can expect to receive some, or all, of the following items in the mail, by email, or posted in an individual's online insurance account, after each visit:

- From the health insurance company:
  - A letter indicating it has received a claim from the health care provider
  - A letter saying the insurance company is processing the claim
  - An explanation of benefits (EOB), which details the claim received and how much the provider charged for the particular service (e.g., an x-ray), what the health insurance company is going to pay, and what the patient may owe the provider (often called the "patient responsibility"); generally, EOBs are identified by the statement "THIS IS NOT A BILL" somewhere on the page
- From the health care provider:
  - The bill with an amount that the patient is responsible for paying ("patient responsibility")

Individuals may not receive all of these communications, but at a minimum, they should get an EOB from their insurance company and a bill from their health care provider, assuming there was an amount owed. This sounds straightforward, but the reality can often be more complicated. Occasionally, the bill from the provider comes before the EOB. Or, the bill comes from the provider and it says that the patient is responsible for 100 percent of the cost of the medical care. This can happen when the provider has not gotten a timely response from the insurance company and they send the bill directly to the patient without waiting for the insurance company to provide payment. In all cases, individuals should wait to send in a payment until they receive their EOB, to ensure that the bill and the amount of their patient responsibility is correct. If individuals are concerned about missing the due date on the bill while waiting for their EOB, they should contact their provider to inform them of the situation. Most providers will be understanding and will not impose a penalty for missing the due date in this circumstance.

## D. Review Medical Bills

Once individuals have both the EOB and provider's bill it is imperative to review them for accuracy. Individuals should not be afraid to ask their providers to clarify codes or descriptions of services, to make sure that they actually received all of the services for which they are being charged.

There are sometimes mistakes or discrepancies that, if corrected, could significantly reduce the amount owed. For example, the billing code for an office visit is 12345 and would cost an individual $250. The billing code for a mastectomy is 12346 and would cost an individual $5,000. Or, perhaps a number was added, so that one round of chemotherapy becomes ten rounds. It would only take a health care provider entering in one number incorrectly for the individual to be significantly overcharged.

Individuals can request a copy of their medical records and pharmacy ledgers to ensure that everything matches and there are no mistakes and subsequent overcharges. Individuals may be able to challenge charges that result from the following:

- Procedures that may have been ordered and then cancelled
- Medications that were ordered but never administered
- Extended operating room times that were not needed
- Hospital error (e.g., lab results were lost so the test had to be redone)
- Hospital delays (e.g., an extra night's stay in the hospital because of an unavailable surgical suite)

Occasionally, hospitals publish standard charges for all of their products and services. Individuals can compare their bills to those standard charges if available, and potentially negotiate a reduction in their bills.

Also, individuals may reach their deductible or out-of-pocket maximum with a particular bill; in doing so, the amount that they owe would be reduced. Take Phoebe for example. Phoebe has a plan with an 80/20 coinsurance, a $500 deductible, and a $1,000 out-of-pocket maximum. As of January 10, 2023, she has paid $700 out of pocket. She recently had three medical appointments:

- January 15, 2024, Appointment #1: Oncologist bills $300
- January 17, 2024, Appointment #2: Chemotherapy infusion center bills $1,000
- January 29, 2024, Appointment #3: Cardiologist bills $500

If the infusion center sends its bill to Phoebe's insurance company first, she will not have reached her out-of-pocket maximum and would have to pay 20 percent of the $1,000 bill ($200). However, if Phoebe waits until the insurance company processes the claim from the oncologist, she will have met her out-of-pocket maximum and would not have to pay the coinsurance amounts for the chemotherapy infusion or cardiologist bills. For a more in-depth discussion of out-of-pocket maximums, see Chapter 1, Health Insurance.

Some insurance companies provide their customers with a case manager to help individuals navigate their medical care, health insurance policy, and bills. Enlisting the help of a case manager can be useful in that individuals can speak to the same person each time they call, which avoids explaining and re-explaining their situation. Furthermore, case managers become familiar with the individual and their health care needs. While these case managers can be very helpful, it is important to remember that they work for the insurance company. It is still important for individuals to keep track of every conversation, names, dates, and what was discussed.

To help keep track of all of this paperwork, staying organized can be helpful. Triage Cancer offers a free Medical Bill Tracker to help individuals keep track of their out-of-pocket costs (https://triagecancer.org/medical-bill-tracker). Some individuals use a simple three-ring notebook or an accordion file folder, and some scan everything and carry around electronic records on a smartphone, tablet, computer, or USB drive. The best system is one that an individual will commit to using!

If individuals have a large number of providers and bills of substantial size, they may want to consider enlisting the help of a professional bill reviewer or medical claims organization. In addition to helping individuals negotiate payment plans, bill reviewers can check diagnosis codes for upcharges (i.e., when a medical condition is documented as being more serious than it is); if itemized charges are also included in any bundled charges; and to ensure that everything is meeting the industry standard. The Alliance of Claims Assistance Professionals may be able to provide references to a local claims assistance professional.

Individuals should also consider engaging their health care team if they need help dealing with bills. After a cancer diagnosis, many individuals hear from loved ones, "How can I help?" Individuals are often at a loss and do not know what they need. Dealing with the paperwork is an opportunity for individuals to enlist the support of family and friends. Loved ones can be tasked with opening the mail, matching EOBs to provider bills, and perhaps even putting due dates onto the individual's calendar. A relatively simple task for friends and family may significantly reduce an individual's stress levels. Furthermore, if mistakes are found, individuals should contact their health care providers and insurance company. If a claim was denied, individuals have the right to appeal the decision. See Chapter 1, Health Insurance, for more information about appealing a claim denial.

In addition to medical bills and EOBs, individuals should keep track of preauthorization documents, other communications with insurers and providers, non-reimbursed medical costs (e.g., over-the-counter medications, out-of-network care, etc.), meals, lodging, and travel expenses (including gas and parking) related to medical care, and any long-distance phone calls related to medical care. Some of these expenses can be paid for using a flexible spending account (FSA). FSAs are discussed in Chapter 1, Health Insurance. These expenses may also be tax-deductible.[27]

Individuals should be careful when considering paying medical bills with a credit card. Most credit cards have high interest rates, and individuals will likely end up spending more than necessary. It is also not recommended to deal with medical bills by taking out a home loan (e.g., a second mortgage or a home equity line of credit (HELOC)) because doing so converts unsecured debt into secured debt. Individuals risk losing their home if they cannot make the payments. Some health care providers may be willing to discount medical bills or set up payment plans without interest, so it can be worthwhile to ask.

The key is not to ignore medical bills, as there may be significant consequences for the individual. Unpaid medical bills can be sent to collection agencies, ultimately impacting an individual's credit rating; individuals' wages may be garnished; and health care providers can refuse to provide further treatment. Medical bills after a cancer diagnosis are unavoidable, but utilizing these techniques can help make them manageable.

## E. Negotiating Bills

Individuals should contact their creditors before unpaid medical bills get sent to collection agencies. Once a creditor sends a bill to collections, it can impact an individual's credit score. If individuals cannot make a payment, they should ask for more time, or check to see if a creditor would be willing to negotiate a payment plan or accept a lower lump-sum payment. Other options a creditor might offer include:

- Suspending payments for a few months in exchange for paying a higher amount later
- Converting payments to interest-only repayments for a specific period of time
- Extending the terms of a loan
- Allowing payment by installments
- Reducing the total amount owed

When speaking with creditors, individuals should ask for a payment plan that they can actually afford. Once an individual reaches an agreement with a creditor, the individual should get the agreement in writing, either formally (e.g., a signed contract) or informally (e.g., a thank-you email that also outlines what an individual understands is the agreement).

This strategy also applies to landlords, student loan companies, and other creditors.

27. *Topic No. 502, Medical and Dental Expenses*, Internal Revenue Serv., https://www.irs.gov/taxtopics/tc502 (last updated Sept. 26, 2024).

## F. Balance and Surprise Billing

In order for an individual to avoid unexpected medical bills, it is important to know how their health plan works. Most plans have a specific network of doctors and facilities that their members can use for their medical care. To be a part of a plan's network, these doctors and facilities contract with the plan and agree to accept a specific rate for their services under the plan. These doctors and facilities are considered "in-network." Doctors and facilities that do not have a contracted relationship with an insurer are considered "out-of-network."

The main difference between in-network and out-of-network health care providers is that in-network health care providers work with an insurance company to provide negotiated (discounted) rates, while out-of-network providers do not agree to discounted rates. The rate the in-network providers agree to is called the "allowed amount." For example:

> Janet visits an in-network doctor and the total charge is $250. The doctor and Janet's plan have negotiated an allowed amount of $175. Based on the cost-share, the plan pays the doctor $140 and Janet is responsible for paying the remaining $35.
>
> But, if Janet visits an out-of-network doctor, there is not a negotiated discount, and the total charge is $250. The plan does have some coverage for out-of-network providers and pays the doctor $140. Janet is responsible for paying the entire balance of the original bill, $110.

This is an example of "balance billing." Balance billing occurs when out-of-network doctors and facilities bill patients for the difference between a billed charge and a health plan's allowed amount. However, this type of balance billing is typically not allowed when:

- Individuals have Medicare and they use a health care provider that accepts Medicare
- Individuals have Medicaid and their provider has an agreement with Medicaid
- Individuals' doctors or facilities have a contract with their health plan (they are in-network) and are billing individuals more than the plan's contract allows

Individuals may face larger than expected bills when they receive care from a provider they did not know was out-of-network. For example:

> Ron is having surgery at a hospital. Both the surgeon and the hospital are in Ron's plan's network. But during the surgery, Ron needs anesthesia so that he is not awake. The person who gives Ron the anesthesia, the anesthesiologist, whom he did not choose, is not in-network. A few weeks later, Ron receives a large bill from the anesthesiologist, who was not covered by his plan.

This is an example of "surprise billing." Individuals who think that they are being careful to only visit in-network providers are often surprised by these bills from an unexpected out-of-network provider on their health care team. Another example of when this happens is when an in-network doctor sends blood to an out-of-network lab for testing. Individuals can avoid this by asking their doctor to make sure they are using an in-network lab for their plan.

These situations can leave individuals with huge medical bills that they are unable to pay, and can even lead to bankruptcy. Before making an appointment to see a health care professional or receiving tests, individuals should confirm that the provider and facility are in their plan's network. Many insurance companies have websites that allow individuals to search for providers in their network, or individuals can call the insurance company to ask about specific providers and their network.

About half of states have passed laws that protect patients from surprise medical bills; however, the details vary from state to state, and do not usually apply to self-insured employer-sponsored plans. For example, a California law protects consumers who have a non-emergency service and visit an in-network facility (e.g., hospital or lab), by only requiring them to pay the in-network share of the cost even if they are seen by an out-of-network provider. For more information about state balance billing laws, visit https://triagecancer.org/state-laws. As of January 1, 2022, a federal law, the No Surprises Act (NSA), protects patients who have private insurance from surprise medical bills.[28] The NSA requires private insurers to treat unexpected out-of-network providers as if they are in-network providers. This requirement applies to emergency medical services and non-emergency medical services. It also includes air ambulances; however, it does not apply to ground ambulances. When a patient sees an out-of-network provider for non-emergency care, the provider is allowed to ask the patients to waive their NSA rights. If the patient refuses, the provider can refuse care. But, asking patients to waive their NSA rights is not allowed for services such as anesthesiology, pathology, diagnostic services, or in situations where an out-of-network provider is the only option. The NSA also provides some protections for patients who are uninsured or choose not to use insurance. In these cases, providers must provide a good-faith estimate of the cost of care. If the actual cost exceeds the estimate by more than $400, the patient can file a dispute with the U.S. Department of Health and Human Services (HHS).

Individuals who receive a surprise medical bill can contact the HHS—No Surprises Help Desk ((800) 985-3059) or file a complaint online (https://www.cms.gov/medical-bill-rights/help/submit-a-complaint).[29]

---

28. *Medical Bill Rights*, Ctrs. for Medicare & Medicaid Servs., https://www.cms.gov/medical-bill-rights (last modified Nov. 5, 2024).

29. Centers for Medicare and Medicaid Services, No Surprises Act: How to Get Help and File a Complaint (2023), https://www.cms.gov/files/document/nsa-helpdesk.pdf.

## G. Managing Taxes

The Internal Revenue Service (IRS) allows individuals to reduce their tax burden by claiming certain itemized deductions, such as medical and dental expenses. The following are some things to think about if an individual is considering deducting medical expenses:

- Taxes must be itemized on the federal tax return. If individuals take the standard deduction, they cannot claim medical expenses.
- Generally, most medical and dental expenses paid for by individuals, their spouses, and their dependents can be claimed. Exceptions and special rules apply. Costs reimbursed by insurance or other sources do not qualify for a deduction.
- The following medical costs can be claimed:
  - Costs associated with diagnosing, treating, easing, or preventing disease
  - Payments for prescription drugs and insulin
  - Insurance premiums for policies that cover medical care
  - Some long-term care insurance costs
- Costs related to traveling to and from receiving medical care may be deductible. Individuals may be able to claim travel costs such as public transportation, ambulance service, tolls, and parking fees. If a personal vehicle is used, individuals may deduct either the actual costs or the standard mileage rate for medical travel.

Individuals are entitled to include all the qualified medical and dental costs they incurred during the year. However, they can only deduct the amount that is more than 7.5 percent of their adjusted gross income (AGI).[30] The IRS has an online tool called the Interactive Tax Assistant (https://www.irs.gov/help/ita) that can help an individual determine if they can deduct medical and dental expenses. The IRS requires that individuals keep records of any expenses claimed on taxes for a minimum of three years.[31] An individual can access tax records online, by creating an account here: https://www.irs.gov/individuals/get-transcript.

The IRS offers tax repayment plans for individuals who are unable to pay their entire tax debt at once. Individuals can apply online for an installment agreement to make monthly payments, provided they owe less than $50,000 in individual income tax, penalties, and interest, combined, and have filed all required returns.[32]

30. *Topic No. 502, Medical and Dental Expenses*, *supra* note 27.

31. For a full list of the IRS requirements on how long individuals should keep tax records, visit *How Long Should I Keep Records?*, IRS, https://www.irs.gov/businesses/small-businesses-self-employed/how-long-should-i-keep-records (last updated Aug. 20, 2024).

32. *Apply Online for a Payment Plan*, IRS, https://www.irs.gov/individuals/payment-plans-installment-agreements (last updated Nov. 25, 2024).

The IRS has programs to provide certain individuals with tax assistance. The Volunteer Income Tax Assistance (VITA) program offers free tax help to people who generally make $54,000 or less per year, persons with disabilities, and limited English speaking taxpayers who need assistance in preparing their own tax returns.[33] IRS-certified volunteers provide free basic income tax return preparation with electronic filing to qualified individuals.

In addition to VITA, the Tax Counseling for the Elderly (TCE) program offers free tax help for all taxpayers, specializing in questions about pensions and retirement-related issues unique to seniors.[34]

Before going to a VITA or TCE location, individuals should review the "Services Provided"[35] and "What to Bring"[36] pages to ensure they have all the required documents and information.

It may be worthwhile for an individual to consult an accountant or tax attorney if they are interested in claiming medical and dental expenses on federal and state taxes.

Individuals should think about their federal and state income tax preparations throughout the year, rather than waiting until April 15.[37] Some of the practical steps individuals can take include:

- Ensure that they have a good accounting for what they have earned and spent during the year. Software options, like QuickBooks or many of the available free apps, can be helpful to record payments and receipts. Individuals should also reconcile bank and credit card accounts, mileage logs, medical bills, and unreimbursed business expenses.
- Make any necessary medical and dental appointments before the end of the year, if an individual has already met health or dental insurance deductibles. Individuals should keep records of any payments made for these appointments.

If an individual runs their own business, the individual should:

- Take inventory of the business's fixed assets (i.e., furniture, fixtures, equipment, vehicles) and purchase any additional needed assets before the end of the year.
- If a business vehicle is needed, it should be purchased well before year-end. This is necessary to establish adequate business use of a vehicle (i.e., 50 percent

---

33. *IRS VITA Grant Program*, IRS, https://www.irs.gov/individuals/irs-vita-grant-program (last updated Nov. 1, 2024).

34. *Tax Counseling for the Elderly*, IRS, https://www.irs.gov/individuals/tax-counseling-for-the-elderly (last updated Nov. 1, 2024).

35. IRS, IRS Certified Volunteers Providing Free Tax Preparation (2022), https://www.irs.gov/pub/irs-pdf/p3676bsp.pdf.

36. *What to Bring to Your Local VITA or TCE Site*, IRS, https://www.irs.gov/individuals/checklist-for-free-tax-return-preparation (last updated Nov. 15, 2024).

37. Some years the IRS tax filing deadline falls on a different date.

or more of the vehicle's use is for business) and to get the maximum amount of depreciation deductions.

- Donate to a charity, including churches, schools, or other 501(c)(3) public charities. Individuals are also able to donate up to $100,000 directly from an individual retirement account (IRA) to a charity of their choice.[38] Such a donation would be applied towards a required minimum distribution for the year and would not be included in one's annual AGI. Doing so has the potential to be a significant tax benefit.

Individuals should talk with an accountant or financial planner to fully maximize their tax return or minimize their tax liability.

## H. Unexpected Financial Expenses

A cancer diagnosis can bring with it a number of unexpected financial expenses. This poses a significant challenge because more than half of Americans earning more than $75,000 a year said they would not be able to handle a $500 surprise bill.[39]

Individuals will likely incur new expenses directly related to their cancer treatment. Some common treatment-related expenses include:

- Deductibles, co-payments, and coinsurance amounts
- Comfort for cosmetic side effects (e.g., wigs, skincare products, prosthetics, compression garments, specialty clothing)
- Caregiving costs
- Long-term or home health care costs
- Psychosocial care
- Complementary therapies (e.g., yoga, massage, Reiki, meditation)
- Transportation costs related to traveling to and from treatment
- Child care above normal expenses due to time away for treatment

Other costs may be less obvious. A cancer diagnosis and subsequent treatment may require individuals to take time off work, making it challenging to pay for basic daily living expenses such as food, rent, mortgage, utilities, and car payments. The physical impact of treatment may make daily tasks challenging and require an individual to pay for help with tasks such as meal preparation and household chores. Individuals may also need to hire professional services related to employment, legal assistance, and finances.

---

38. *Qualified Charitable Distributions Allow Eligible IRA Owners Up to $100,000 in Tax-Free Gifts to Charity*, IRS, https://www.irs.gov/newsroom/qualified-charitable-distributions-allow-eligible-ira-owners-up-to-100000-in-tax-free-gifts-to-charity (last updated Oct. 15, 2024).

39. Aimee Picchi, *A $500 Surprise Expense Would Put Most Americans into Debt*, CBS News (Jan. 12, 2017), https://www.cbsnews.com/news/most-americans-cant-afford-a-500-emergency-expense.

Talking about financial concerns with others can be challenging and uncomfortable, especially if individuals do not know what questions to ask or what to say. Individuals who are trying to navigate their finances after cancer should remember they are not alone. Individuals may consider speaking with one, or many, of the following people about the expenses they are facing:

- Doctors
- Nurses
- Social workers
- Case managers
- Navigators
- Financial counselors
- Patient advocacy organizations
- Employer's human resources department
- Insurance company
- Family
- Friends
- Spiritual advisors
- Community leaders

Some of these individuals may be able to provide information about finances, others may provide emotional support, and some may be able to provide practical help, such as sorting medical bills and filling out financial assistance applications. Certainly, the questions that could be asked will differ depending on the audience; however, one way to start a conversation is simply to say, "I am worried about costs associated with my cancer treatment. Can we please discuss my concerns?"

It is key to individuals to talk with their health care team about finances, even if it is uncomfortable. Health care professionals can help individuals understand their insurance coverage, prepare them for any unexpected expenses, and identify possible financial assistance options. Individuals can work together with their health care team to develop a plan to reduce or limit the financial burden of cancer treatment.

## III. Strategies for Paying Expenses

There are some key strategies that can be used to pay for expenses, whether an individual is in treatment or even after cancer treatment has been completed, as there may still be medications or other medical care needed to help manage side effects from treatment or other long-term medical conditions.

### A. Review Current Financial Picture

Even if individuals had a viable financial plan prior to their cancer diagnosis, it can be helpful for them to review where they are financially after completing treatment.

Figuring out what their finances look like *now* can help them decide which of the following steps they should take, if any. It can also help them identify their priorities. For example, do they need to find a job immediately or can they wait until the right job presents itself? Do they have a stack of bills that they have been too afraid to open? Or are they ready to start thinking about saving for a home or contributing to a retirement plan? Figuring out what the appropriate path is after treatment will be personal to each individual's situation.

For individuals to get a clear picture of their financial status after a cancer diagnosis, they should consider the following questions:

- What is the current status of their finances? For example, are they living paycheck to paycheck, do they still have savings, or are they in danger of losing assets (like a care or home)?
- Do they have health insurance? If so, is the policy adequate? Is the policy going to cover the cost of their treatment and follow-up care? Are there other options that would reduce their out-of-pocket costs?
- Were they able to keep working through treatment or did they need to take time off? How did that affect their financial situation?
- If they are finished with treatment, are they back at work; are they able to go back to the same job or type of work; or do they need to look for another career path because of side effects?
- Do they have a stable source of income (e.g., paycheck, disability insurance, unemployment benefits)?
- What are their recurring and potential expenses?
- What assets do they have (e.g., homes, savings bonds, retirement plans)?
- What secured and unsecured debt do they have?
- Where might they be able to reduce their ongoing expenses and debt?

## B. Track Assets and Debts

One way to organize the answers to some of these questions is to create a "financial big picture" spreadsheet. This document should keep track of any assets, liabilities, and overall net worth. Compiling all of this information may take some time initially, but once the spreadsheet has been created, it can be updated just once or twice a year to keep everything current. There are many ways to go about creating a financial big picture document and special software is not necessary. There are free programs available such as Google Sheets that are accessible to anyone that has a free Gmail account. Individuals can figure out their net worth by completing a simple math problem:

Assets – Liabilities = Net Worth

The customizable Financial Big Picture spreadsheet, available at https://triagecancer.org/FinancialBigPicture, is an example of how to organize this information.

Using a system like this spreadsheet can be beneficial for many reasons: it can help keep the family organized, it can be helpful for estate planning purposes (see Chapter 5, Estate Planning and Medical Decision-Making, for more information), and it can also be very satisfying as individuals pay down debt to see it reflected in the black and white of the spreadsheet. Once an individual has considered these questions, the individual should have, at a minimum, a big picture assessment of their current financial status.

There are different types of debt and it is important for individuals to understand the types of debt they may have. Debt will either be considered secured or unsecured. Secured debt is secured against an asset. For example, when an individual obtains a mortgage, they are receiving a loan secured by a house. If the individual stops making payments on that loan, the lender can take the house and sell it to recover the amount the individual owes. Mortgages, car loans, and HELOCs are examples of secured debt. Conversely, unsecured debt is a loan that is not secured by property. Credit cards and personal loans are typically unsecured debt. For example, if an individual purchases goods using a credit card, they are taking an unsecured loan. If the individual stops making repayments on that loan, the credit card company cannot take anything away from the individual. However, there are other consequences if individuals stop making payments. Creditors of unsecured debt can get a court order to compel an individual to repay the debt. If individuals do not repay their debts, their creditors will report their debts to the credit bureaus, which in turn will lower their credit scores.

## C. Create a Current Budget

The first step individuals can take to repair their financial situation is to create a budget that reflects their current income and expenses, including any expenses they might have remaining related to medical care. To start creating a budget, individuals should write down all of their income and expenses. Income may include paychecks, bonuses, child support, repayments from people who owe them money, interest on accounts, or any other type of income. Expenses may include housing costs, loan payments (e.g., student loans), medical bills, insurance (e.g., home, dental, health, life, disability), education or child care costs, utilities, food, transportation, clothes, personal care (e.g., gym memberships, haircuts), entertainment, travel, and incidentals (e.g., pocket cash). Tracking expenses can be difficult. Some experts suggest keeping a daily spending diary for a few weeks. Some banks and credit card companies allow individuals to see their spending by category (e.g., gas, groceries, entertainment). Once individuals understand what money is coming in and what is being spent, they should also decide if their budget will be weekly, biweekly, monthly, or yearly. Many people choose to match their budget to their pay periods. It can be challenging to create a budget if individuals do not have a steady paycheck. One method is to budget expecting the lowest income amount possible. For months in which income is higher, the excess can be used to pay down debt or build savings.

There are multiple ways to go about creating a budget: creating one from scratch, using a free template, purchasing software, or hiring a professional. There are literally thousands of free templates available online that individuals can download and customize to best fit their situation. Alternatively, individuals could purchase software such as Quicken,[40] MoneyWell,[41] and You Need a Budget[42] to help keep track of expenses and debt. The advantage of software is that it will generally provide users with questions to answer and then automatically do the calculations. Similarly, if individuals use smartphones, there are a myriad of smartphone applications available for free and for a nominal fee. For instance, iPhone users could use the free Credit Karma app from Intuit. This app boasts the ability to "gather all your financial information into one place, giving you the whole picture in a way that's easy to understand."[43] However, creating a budget, even with the assistance of software, can feel like a daunting task. Individuals who are overwhelmed or do not know how to start creating a budget may want to consider talking with a financial planner. The Financial Planning Association (http://www.plannersearch.org) has an online tool to find local financial planners. Financial planners work with people of all income levels, so those coping with cancer should not be deterred by a feeling that they do not have a lot of money.

A consumer credit counseling agency can also provide individuals with practical tools, such as financial calculators, budget worksheets, and other resources. The agency also may be able to help individuals negotiate payment plans or settlements with their creditors.[44]

Debt solutions, while useful for some, may negatively affect an individual's credit score.[45] However, individuals with a challenging financial picture may be less concerned about a drop in their credit score that might result from working with a debt solutions agency or even filing for bankruptcy. These decisions are personal to each individual and should not be taken lightly because, as discussed earlier, creditworthiness is important for multiple reasons. Individuals should also be aware that there are many debt solution scams in existence. Before an individual works with a credit counseling agency, it is prudent to check with the state attorney general[46] or the local consumer protection office[47] to ensure that the company is legitimate. The Federal

40. Quicken, https://www.quicken.com (last visited Dec. 1, 2024).

41. MoneyWell, https://moneywellapp.com (last visited Dec. 1, 2024).

42. You Need a Budget, https://www.ynab.com/ (last visited Dec. 1, 2024).

43. Credit Karma, https://www.creditkarma.com/ (last visited Dec. 1, 2024).

44. National Foundation for Credit Counseling, https://www.nfcc.org (last visited Dec. 1, 2024).

45. *How to Get Out of Debt*, Fed. Trade Comm'n (Apr. 2022), https://consumer.ftc.gov/articles/how-get-out-debt.

46. The National Association of Attorneys General has the contact information for each state's attorney general at https://www.naag.org (last visited Dec. 1, 2024).

47. Find state consumer protection offices at https://www.usa.gov/state-consumer (last visited Dec. 1, 2024).

Trade Commission also warns consumers to be aware of the following when considering using a debt solution company:

- Many programs often require that clients deposit money in a special savings account for three or more years, before debts will be settled. Individuals should be sure they can meet those payments, for the designated time period, before they agree to a program.
- Creditors are not required to negotiate a settlement, so there is a chance that these companies may not be able to solve the issue.
- These programs often suggest that individuals stop sending payments to their creditors, which can damage an individual's credit further, and late fees and penalties can create even more debt. Furthermore, creditors may be successful in lawsuits against individuals resulting in wages being garnished or liens being placed on homes.[48]

It is also important for individuals to realize that if they are able to negotiate with creditors to have a portion of their debt forgiven, the IRS could consider the amount that is written off to be taxable income.[49] Individuals should consult with a tax advisor, accountant, or attorney to determine how debt forgiveness will affect their income taxes.

## D. Identify Expenses That Can Be Reduced

Individuals who have a comprehensive picture of their financial status can start to identify areas where they can reduce expenses. Certainly, the tried-and-true methods of reducing expenses are relevant here. For example, if individuals have a daily $8 coffee habit or pay for an expensive cable package subscription, they may be able to reduce spending in those areas. If individuals have multiple insurance policies (e.g., car, homeowner's, and life insurance), they may be able to bundle their policies with one company for a discount, or even do some comparison shopping to see if switching companies can lower the cost of their coverage. Individuals may also consider making small lifestyle changes to help reduce expenses—for example, checking out books and movies from the local library instead of purchasing them; packing a lunch rather than eating out; and carpooling or ridesharing to save on transportation costs. Simple changes can have a large impact on an individual's budget.

Additionally, there may be some options that are available to individuals because of their health status. For instance, some life and disability insurance policies include a clause that waives the monthly premiums for policyholders who experience a disability that keeps them from working. Insurance companies may charge a higher

---

48. *How to Get Out of Debt*, FED. TRADE COMM'N CONSUMER ADVICE (Apr. 2022), https://consumer.ftc.gov/articles/how-get-out-debt.

49. *Topic No. 431, Canceled Debt—Is It Taxable or Not?*, IRS, https://www.irs.gov/taxtopics/tc431 (last visited Sept. 26, 2024).

premium to include this type of waiver in the policy and each policy will have a different definition of disability and length of time the payments will be suspended. Similarly, some home mortgages, credit cards, or other types of loans may include this kind of premium waiver. Even if a policy does not specifically contain this type of language, it may still be worthwhile for individuals to call their creditors and ask for some sort of payment plan or exception to be made.

Individuals should always use credit cards carefully due to their high interest rates and the ease in which debt can rapidly accumulate. However, there are some strategies that can be used to an individual's financial benefit. Perhaps a balance transfer can be made to a card that has a 0 percent interest rate for a period of time so that individuals can pay off their debt faster. One thing to note is that most of these offers will include a fee for the transfer; typically, it is 1–5 percent of the amount being transferred or a flat $50 fee, whichever is more. This type of transfer is typically only advisable if the individual is confident that they can pay off the entire balance before the 0 percent financing period is over and the internet rate increases. Another strategy for intelligently using credit cards is to shop around to find a card with the lowest interest rate available. Some cards that offer miles or cash back may seem attractive, but if individuals are carrying a balance month after month at a higher interest rate, those privileges may not be worthwhile in the long run. Some individuals may even be able to reduce the interest rate on their credit cards by calling the credit card companies and asking them to reduce their rates.

## E. Leverage Out-of-Pocket Maximums

Out-of-pocket maximums will vary by health insurance policy; however, understanding what is included in a policy is imperative. Individuals can save a significant amount of money by leveraging their policy's out-of-pocket maximum. If individuals have reached their maximum for the year, they should consider if they have any other health care needs for the year. For example, as a result of her cancer treatment, Serena has reached her out-of-pocket maximum in August. She also needs an MRI for her sore knee, and would like to see a dermatologist about a skin rash. To leverage the fact that she has already met her deductible and reached her out-of-pocket maximum for the year, Serena should make those appointments this year, rather than waiting until a new plan year when she will have to meet her annual deductible and out-of-pocket maximum again. Individuals should not attempt to receive unnecessary services, but they should be aware of their out-of-pocket maximums to get the most out of their health insurance coverage.

## F. Deal with Student Loans

Repaying student loans might be challenging for individuals facing a cancer diagnosis, which may bring with it a loss of income or increased expenses. It is important for individuals to have accurate information about their loan and understand their options to change payment plans or postpone payments through a loan deferment or forbearance process.

If individuals have a student loan, a first step is to figure out how much money is still owed and to whom it is owed.

- Are the loans from federal government lenders, private lenders, or both?
- If the loans are federal loans, individuals can look up their information in the National Student Loan Data System (https://nsldsfap.ed.gov/login). There are two types of federal loans—direct loans from the U.S. Department of Education and loans serviced by a private company. Individuals can find contact information for who services their loan here: https://studentaid.gov/manage-loans/repayment/servicers.
- If the individual has private loans, they will need to contact the specific loan provider.
- What is the interest rate on each loan?

If individuals are having trouble making payments on their student loans, in order to protect their credit, they should communicate with lenders before they stop making payments. There may be options to lower monthly payments or reschedule payments to make it easier to stay current on bills. For example, some options include:

- Signing up for automatic payments, to get an interest rate deduction
- Asking to change the payment due date
- Asking to move to an income-driven repayment (IDR) plan, which bases monthly payments on an individual's current income level (for more information about IDR plan options, visit: https://studentaid.gov/idr)
- Using a student loan repayment simulator (e.g., https://studentaid.gov/loan-simulator/) to see if it is possible to lower payments through refinancing, consolidating, or other financial options
- Speaking with a loan counselor to learn about options for payment plans, refinancing loans, consolidating loans, deferring loans, forbearing loans, or even discharging loans

There are a number of ways to make changes to student loans:

- **Deferment.** This is when an eligible individual can temporarily stop making payments or reduce the monthly payment owed for a certain amount of time. If an individual is done with school, and is not in a situation to start paying on student loans, they may have the right to defer the loans.
- **Forbearance.** Forbearance is similar to deferment; however, an individual may be responsible for paying the interest that has accrued on certain types of loans while in forbearance.

- **Loan forgiveness.** An individual may be eligible for loan forgiveness (aka cancellation), which means that the individual no longer needs to repay part or all of the loan. For example, some loans may be eligible for forgiveness if the individual has a job in public service. These different repayment programs apply to the federal Direct Loan program, Federal Family Education Loan (FFEL) Program, and Perkins loans.
- **Disability discharge.** If eligible, an individual may also be able to get a loan discharged (aka forgiven) as a result of their disability.

There are a number of ways to defer (or delay) paying student loans. These are some of the most common situations:

- Enrolled in at least a half-time eligible college or career school; also, if an individual is in a graduate or professional program, and received a direct PLUS loan or FFEL PLUS loan
- Enrolled in an approved rehabilitation program for people with disabilities
- Unemployed or not able to find a full-time position for up to three years
- Experiencing an economic hardship, or serving in the Peace Corps for up to three years
- Active member of the military in connection with war, military operations, or a national emergency

In addition to these options, if an individual has a cancer diagnosis, they may qualify for a cancer treatment deferment for their federal direct loan, FFEL, or federal Perkins loan. This means that individuals are given permission to not make student loan payments while in treatment and up to six months following the end of treatment. This applies to loans made on or after September 18, 2018, or that entered repayment on or before September 28, 2018. For more information, see the Cancer Treatment Deferment Request form at https://studentaid.gov/sites/default/files/CancerTreatmentDeferment.pdf.

There are two different types of forbearance that an individual can be granted; general or mandatory. General forbearance can be requested when an individual is temporarily not able to make a scheduled monthly loan payment, for the following reasons: financial difficulties, medical expenses, change in employment, or other reasons that a loan servicer finds to be appropriate. Mandatory forbearance is when an individual is eligible for forbearance and the loan servicer is required to grant a forbearance.

There are a number of ways to discharge student loans, meaning that an individual no longer has to make payments on a loan.[50] This could be because of a job,

50. *Student Loan Forgiveness*, Fed. Student Aid, https://studentaid.gov/manage-loans/forgiveness-cancellation (last visited Dec. 1, 2024).

closure of the school where an individual received the loans, or having a disability. Discharge of student loans can also be called "forgiveness" or "cancellation."

- **Forgiveness and cancellation.** There are different types of programs available to forgive or cancel a part or all of a loan.
- **Total and permanent disability (TPD) discharge.** TPD discharge allows qualified individuals with disabilities to discharge their loans through the Direct Loan Program, FFEL Program, Perkins Loan Program, and Teacher Education Assistance for College and Higher Education (TEACH) grants.[51] To be eligible, an individual must prove that they are
    - a veteran with a service-connected disability;
    - receiving Social Security Disability Insurance (SSDI) or Supplemental Security Income (SSI); or
    - totally and permanently disabled, according to a licensed doctor. The doctor must provide certification that the individual is unable to engage in any substantial gainful activity. This must be supported by a medical reason, and that TPD can be expected to last for a continuous period of not less than 60 months, has lasted for a continuous period of 60 months or more, or can be expected to result in death. If an individual is receiving SSI or SSDI, the individual will automatically receive TPD discharge; they do not have to complete an application for discharge. As of January 1, 2018, if a student loan is forgiven, an individual does not have to pay federal income tax on the amount of the loan forgiven.

Some private lenders also offer disability discharge options for individuals with disabilities. These lenders may have different rules, so it is important to contact lenders directly for more information.

- **Death discharge.** When someone with a federal student loan dies, their loan will be discharged. If an individual has a private loan, details vary. See https://studentaid.gov/manage-loans/forgiveness-cancellation/death.

## G. Consider Financial Assistance Programs

There are a number of different types of financial assistance programs. Some financial assistance programs may help with medical expenses, and some may help with insurance premiums. Additionally, organizations or pharmaceutical companies may have programs to help individuals who are having financial difficulties with paying for their medications. There are cancer-specific and health care organizations that

---

51. *Frequently Asked Questions (FAQs) about Total and Permanent Disability Discharge*, Total & Permanent Disability (TPD) Discharge, https://www.disabilitydischarge.com/faqs (last visited Dec. 1, 2024).

may provide financial assistance, or organizations that may help with specific types of expenses such as fertility preservation, or college scholarships for individuals diagnosed with cancer. To find financial assistance resources, visit https://triagecancer.org/cancer-finances.

## H. Fundraise Online

An individual's family, friends, neighbors, and co-workers may also be sources of financial help. However, they may not realize that financial assistance is needed, especially if an individual has completed active cancer treatment. Crowdfunding (asking for donations from others) may be an effective way to help pay for medical and other expenses. While crowdfunding can be done in person, it is most often done online. Individuals can create their own crowdfunding campaign, or create one to help someone else. Generally, crowdfunding campaigns include information about the person who will benefit from the fundraiser and why the person needs financial help. That personal story can help motivate people to give. Once a fundraiser has been created, it can be shared electronically (e.g., via email or on social media) to help increase the number of potential donors.

With the increased cost of cancer care, crowdfunding for medical expenses has become more popular. Funds raised through crowdfunding are classified as gifts by the IRS, so they typically are not considered taxable income and are considered "unrestricted" funds. This means that the funds raised can be used for any expenses an individual might have. Each platform has its own set of rules and fees. Some entities do not charge a fee to the fundraiser's beneficiary; however, their payment processor does charge a fee of a certain percentage plus a certain amount of every donation to manage the transfer of funds from the accounts of donors.[52]

If individuals set up a fundraiser, or have money donated to them, they must understand all of the implications. For example, would the IRS consider the donations to be taxable income? Does this lump-sum payment affect eligibility for other government benefits (e.g., Medicaid, Marketplace financial assistance, food stamps, SSI)? One way to avoid any potential issues is to set up a special needs trust. See Chapter 5, Estate Planning and Medical Decision-Making. Another option is to use an Achieving a Better Life Experience (ABLE) account.

ABLE accounts are savings accounts for individuals with disabilities and their families. The beneficiary of an ABLE savings account is the account owner, and contributions can be made by anyone (including family and friends) using post-tax dollars. The most significant impact of ABLE accounts is that the funds will not be counted against individuals for the purpose of determining eligibility for governmental programs. In order to be eligible to open an ABLE account, the disability must

---

52. *Quick Guide to Crowdfunding*, Triage Cancer, https://triagecancer.org/quick-guides/crowdfunding (last visited Dec. 1, 2024).

have begun prior to the individual turning 26, and the medical condition must meet the Social Security Administration's (SSA's) definition of "disability." Starting in 2026, people who had a disability prior to turning 46, and meet the other requirements, will be able to open an ABLE account.

- In 2024, annual contributions were limited to $18,000; however, accounts can generally hold a balance of up to $100,000. Under the ABLE to Work Act, individuals who are working may be eligible to contribute more than $18,000. The additional ABLE contribution is up to the lesser of
    - o the federal poverty level for a one-person household ($15,060 in 2024) or
    - o the account owner's compensation for the taxable year.[53]
- Funds included in ABLE accounts must be used for "qualified disability expenses," which are any expenses, transportation, assistive technology, personal support services, education, and other expenses to enhance the beneficiary's quality of life.
- An ABLE account can be opened by a beneficiary, parent, guardian/conserva tor, or agent designated through a power of attorney for financial affairs. ABLE accounts are established through the state, and each state has slightly different procedures.

Individuals should also thoroughly consider privacy issues before setting up an online fundraiser. Disclosure of a cancer diagnosis and medical information is a very personal decision and all of the ramifications should be thought through. See Chapter 2, Employment, for a discussion of disclosure decisions.

For more information about financial resources, visit http://triagecancer.org/financial.

## I. Assess Other Potential Sources of Income

When assessing potential sources of income, it can be necessary to think creatively. Many times, when dealing with a cancer diagnosis, an individual may just need immediate access to cash to compensate for the lack of wages or a particularly large medical bill.

### 1. Insurance as a Source of Income

There are different types of insurance coverage that individuals may already have through an employer or that they purchased on their own, which can provide some financial assistance. Disability insurance is a way to replace wages if individuals need to take time off from work. See Chapter 3, Disability Insurance. In addition to disability insurance, an individual might also consider life or disease-specific or

53. *About ABLE Accounts*, ABLE Nat'l Res. Ctr., https://www.ablenrc.org/what-is-able/what-are-able-acounts (last visited Dec. 1, 2024).

supplemental insurance (e.g., cancer insurance). Supplemental insurance policies can help cover gaps in a regular health insurance policy (e.g., help paying for deductibles, co-payments, and additional expenses not covered by regular health insurance such as needing to travel to treatment). Supplemental health insurance policies can be purchased from private insurance companies or offered as part of an employer-sponsored benefits package (e.g., Aflac, MetLife).

Caregivers may also have options for replacing lost wages if taking time off work to care for a loved one, called paid family leave. Additionally, some states have programs within Medicaid through which caregivers can be paid for acting as an in-home caregiver for a family member. The availability of these options differs by state. See Triage Cancer's Chart of State Laws for the specifics of each state's paid leave (https://triagecancer.org/state-laws) and the state resources for information on the Medicaid in-home services programs (https://triagecancer.org/stateresources). For details about these options for caregivers, see Chapter 7.

**Types of Insurance to Consider**

Disability insurance

Life insurance

Supplemental insurance

Disease-specific insurance

Long-term care insurance

If an individual already has a life insurance policy and needs an influx of cash, the person could consider the following:

- Does the policy allow for borrowing money from the policy, if the policyholder has a disability?
- Does the policy contain a waiver that suspends the monthly premiums while the policyholder is unable to work because of a disability?
- Could the life insurance policy be used as collateral for a loan? For example, an individual with metastatic cancer, who has a life insurance policy with a built-up cash value, may be able to take a loan out from their life insurance policy to help meet immediate financial needs. The loan can be up to 70 percent of the death benefit.
- Does the policy have an accelerated death benefit (ADB) rider? An ADB rider allows an individual who is diagnosed with a terminal illness resulting in a life expectancy of less than six to 24 months to receive up to 50 percent of the policy's death benefit paid in a lump-sum payment or in monthly payments.

- Could a viatical settlement be beneficial? A viatical, or life, settlement is when the policyholder sells the life insurance policy to a third party, typically for less than the full policy amount. This may be a useful option because the policyholder gets access to needed funds; however, the original beneficiary will not receive anything from the life insurance policy.

For more information on life insurance, see Chapter 5, Estate Planning and Medical Decision-Making.

## 2. Other Assets as a Source of Income

If individuals own a vacation home or even a primary home that they can no longer afford, they may want to consider selling that property. However, they should speak with an accountant or tax attorney to ensure they understand all of the financial ramifications. For instance, selling a home may result in a large tax bill that negates any potential financial benefit.

Some individuals may be eligible for a reverse mortgage. A reverse mortgage is a loan in which an individual borrows against the equity in the home to stop making mortgage payments. These types of mortgages are only available to individuals who are 62 or older. Typically, the income received from a reverse mortgage is not taxable and does not affect the homeowner's Social Security or Medicare benefits. For more information about reverse mortgages, visit https://consumer.ftc.gov/articles/reverse-mortgages.

Some individuals may also consider their retirement accounts as a potential source of income. There are different types of retirement accounts and the options around taking out loans from these accounts vary. An IRA is a retirement account that individuals contribute to throughout their working years. One cannot withdraw the money from these accounts before the age of 59.5 without paying a 10 percent penalty. Some individuals may want to use these accounts as collateral for a personal loan; however, it is generally frowned upon to use an IRA as loan collateral because the IRS can impose a 10 percent tax on the entire amount of the IRA. An alternative to using an IRA as collateral is doing a transfer from an IRA to a 401(k). If, and only if, an individual has a 401(k) with an employer and the employer agrees, an individual can transfer the funds in an IRA to the 401(k) and use that account as collateral for a loan. In these circumstances, the individual would have to repay the loan within five years, with interest.

Some retirement or pension plans also allow individuals to take out loans directly from these plans or to cash them out entirely, which is likely to have significant tax implications. As with all of the suggestions made in this chapter, individuals should make sure they understand the ramifications these solutions may have on their taxes and government benefits, and talk with a financial planner and/or accountant.

## IV. Long-Term Financial Strategies

Given that the number of cancer survivors in the United States continues to rise, it is critical that discussions around cancer and financial health do not start and end at solving the immediate financial crises (e.g., dealing with a single looming medical bill). Individuals also need support in thinking about, and dealing with, their financial future for themselves and their families.

### A. Financial Goals Identification

Goals are personal, so it is up to each individual to figure out how to prioritize financial goals. Potential goals may include:

- Paying off medical debt
- Paying off a credit card
- Paying off school loans
- Buying a car
- Buying a house
- Building a savings account/emergency fund
- Saving for retirement
- Saving for a child's education
- Taking a vacation

### B. Credit Score and Report

To fully assess individuals' financial standing, they must understand their credit score and know what is included in their credit report. Having good credit is imperative in today's world. Credit may be checked when individuals try to rent an apartment, lease or buy a car, buy a home, or even get cable television. In addition, in some states, during the job application process, employers can conduct background checks that include looking at an applicant's credit score or full credit report and may make character judgments based on information in the report.[54] Therefore, it is important for individuals to keep track of their credit score and check their credit report on a regular basis.

A credit score is a three-digit number determined by looking at five main categories of financial history: debts owed, new credit, length of credit history, type of credit used, and payment history.[55] The score is then used by lenders to predict an individu-

54. *See State Laws*, Triage Cancer, https://triagecancer.org/state-laws (last visited Dec. 1, 2024).
55. *What's in My FICO Scores?*, myFico, https://www.myfico.com/credit-education/whats-in-your-credit-score/ (last visited Dec. 1, 2024).

al's financial risk. The most widely used credit score is the FICO© score. FICO scores range from 300 to 850; a higher number indicates an individual is more creditworthy and less risky. If individuals are seeking a loan, they will likely be offered a lower interest rate if they have a high credit score. The rationale is that if an individual has a high credit score, they have demonstrated financial responsibility and are, therefore, more likely to repay the loan.

The three largest national credit bureaus are Equifax, Experian, and TransUnion. An individual's FICO score may differ among the three credit bureaus. There are smaller credit reporting agencies that provide specialized consumer reporting services that report payment data for utility services such as phone, electricity, and cable.[56] Periodically, FICO releases new versions of its scoring that calculate various types of debt differently. The most recent version is FICO 10©, but FICO 8© and FICO 9© are more commonly used. For example, FICO 8© weighs high credit card limits more negatively than the sporadic late payment. FICO 9© puts less emphasis on unpaid debt due to medical bills as compared with other types of unpaid debt, and does not take into consideration accounts in collections that have been paid in full. For more information about FICO scores, visit https://www.myFICO.com.

## C. Steps to Rebuilding Credit

It can be challenging to raise a credit score, but it is possible. Moreover, just because individuals have a low credit score does not mean that they cannot get credit. Each creditor sets its own standards, and some may look only at recent credit history. If bill-paying history has improved, the creditor may decide to offer an individual credit. Therefore, it may be worthwhile to informally contact potential creditors to discuss their credit standards.

Demonstrating general fiscal responsibility is key to building a better credit report. Here are some tips to improve a credit score:

- **Pay at least the minimum due of every bill, on time.**
- **Maintain an appropriate debt-to-credit ratio.** Generally, experts agree that it is most beneficial to keep your debt utilization below 30 percent of all available credit. For example, if an individual has two credit cards each with a limit of $5,000, they should not carry a balance on both together more than $3,000.
- **File taxes.** Even if individuals cannot pay the whole amount that is due, they should file their federal and state income tax returns and request a payment plan with their state tax entity and the IRS. See Section II.G, Managing Taxes.

---

56. Darryl Getter, Congressional Research Service, Consumer and Credit Reporting, Scoring, and Related Policy Issues (2015).

- **Reduce overall debt** (e.g., by using either the snowball or avalanche methods of debt reduction, discussed in detail in Section IV.D, Strategies for Paying Down Debt).
- **Look into secured credit cards.** Secured credit cards require a consumer to put a certain amount of money into an account and then the creditor will give the consumer a credit card with that spending limit. Avoid credit card scams by going to a reputable institution, such as a large bank or a local credit union, and getting all of the information before acquiring a secured card. Individuals should avoid cards with fees or ones that require them to buy insurance.
- **Contribute to savings even if it is a small amount each month.** It has been routinely recommended by financial experts that individuals should have three to six months' worth of their expenses saved. While this is a worthy goal, it can be discouraging, if not impossible, for individuals who have been diagnosed with cancer and are feeling the resulting financial impact. The important message here is to start with whatever individuals can manage; if it is $10 a paycheck or $500 a month, savings will grow over time.
- **Plan for retirement.** Retirement also might seem far off in the future, but building retirement assets is important, especially if individuals had to dip into their retirement plan to help pay bills. If their employer matches contributions to a 401(k) plan or another type of retirement plan, they should not leave this "free" money on the table. Individuals should try to contribute the maximum amount that their employer will match, to maximize this opportunity to save for retirement.

## D. Strategies for Paying Down Debt

In order to effectively pay down debt, individuals must prioritize their debt. There are many schools of thought on how best to eliminate debt; however, the reality is that there is no one-size-fits-all approach. Many experts suggest prioritizing secured debt (e.g., mortgage, car loan) to ensure that individuals do not lose their homes or cars while trying to regain financial stability. However, since these types of loans typically have the lowest interest rates, another school of thought is to simply pay the minimum due to keep the accounts current, and use any additional funds to pay any legal obligations (e.g., child support or court-ordered payments) and unsecured debt (e.g., medical bills, personal or student loans, or credit cards).

Individuals should think very seriously before converting unsecured debt, like credit cards, to secured debt, like a HELOC. It may be appealing to individuals to consolidate all of their high-interest credit card debt into one HELOC. However, if they are unable to make the payments on the HELOC, they risk losing their homes.

Once individuals have prioritized how they want to pay their debt, they next need to decide on a debt reduction strategy. There are two main strategies for paying down debt: snowball and avalanche. With the snowball approach, individuals focus on paying down the smallest debt first "to create the greatest momentum" in reducing debt.[57] Alternatively, the avalanche approach focuses on paying down the debt with the highest interest rate first. In both approaches, individuals must continue to pay the minimum amounts due on all debts, and put any remaining funds towards the debt they choose to pay off first. While the avalanche method always results in a lower amount of interest being paid, the argument for the snowball method is that people are motivated by seeing the number of debts diminish faster (i.e., paying off an entire account sooner). Each method has its pros and cons, so the bottom line is that individuals should choose a method that they are going to be able to stick with, as both will have the end result of reducing debt. See the "Math Matters" text box for an example of how this can work. There are also many free calculators online, such as https://unbury.me, which individuals can use to help them do the math and see how the methods differ when applied to their individual financial situations.

### Math Matters

Billy has the following debts:

Student loan: $5,000 balance, 4.5 percent interest rate

Credit card: $8,000 balance, 29.99 percent interest rate

Medical debt: $25,000 balance, 10 percent interest rate

Assuming Billy has an extra $2,000 a month that he can put towards paying off his debt, here are how the two methods differ:

#### Debt Snowball

Billy would focus on paying off his student loan first (with the lowest balance), then the credit card, and, finally, the medical debt (with the highest balance).

Billy would be debt free in 18 months. Total interest paid: $4,449.14

#### Debt Avalanche

Billy would focus on paying off the credit card first (with the highest interest rate), then the medical debt, and, finally, the student loan (with the lowest interest rate).

Billy would be debt free in 18 months. Total interest paid: $3,506.25

This method would save Billy $942.89 in interest.

57. *How to Get Out of Debt with the Debt Snowball Plan*, Ramsey Sols. (May 31, 2024), https://www.daveramsey.com/blog/get-out-of-debt-with-the-debt-snowball-plan.

## E. Wise Use of Credit Cards

Credit cards can be a useful financial tool, if used wisely. Having credit cards can help improve an individual's credit scores, as well as provide additional benefits. There are literally hundreds of different options for cards. Some have an annual fee, some provide benefits for using the cards (e.g., rewards cards), and each card will have a different interest rate. For the week of December 1, 2024, the national average for credit card interest rates was 28.75 percent.[58] Individuals should be sure to pick the right credit card for their needs.

*Standard credit cards* are the most common type of credit card and are offered by most banks and credit unions. These are unsecured credit cards, which means individuals do not have to provide collateral or a security deposit to obtain one. Two variations of standard credit cards are:

- **Balance transfer credit cards.** These cards allow individuals to transfer a credit card balance (typically with a higher interest rate) onto another credit card with a lower interest rate. It is very common for credit card companies to encourage an individual to make a balance transfer by offering an introductory annual percentage rate (APR) of 0 percent for a certain period of time (e.g., 18 months), then the interest rate will go up. Some of these cards are "deferred interest," which means that individuals will not have to pay interest during that initial period, but if any amount remains after that period, they will be charged an interest rate retroactively. Balance transfers can be very useful for individuals who are trying to pay off credit card debt and just need additional time, interest free. However, if individuals do not have the means to pay the balance during that introductory period, or they plan on making additional purchases using that card, they should avoid these balance transfer cards. Typically, the 0 percent APR is only for the transfer and does not apply to new purchases. Additionally, there is often a fee for transferring the balance (e.g., 3 percent of the amount transferred). The terms of balance transfer credit cards vary between offers, so be sure to thoroughly read the terms and conditions for each card offer.
- **Low-interest credit cards.** These cards offer individuals a low introductory APR that increases to a higher rate after a certain period, or a single low fixed-rate APR. Low-interest cards can be helpful for individuals who need to make a large purchase (e.g., a new appliance) because they provide several months to pay it off with little to no interest. However, individuals should use these types of credit cards wisely, and read all the terms and conditions of the introductory rate to not be surprised by fees or accumulated interest.

---

58. Michelle Black & Clint Proctor, *What Is the Average Credit Card Interest Rate This Week? December 1, 2024*, FORBES (Nov. 25, 2024), https://www.forbes.com/advisor/credit-cards/average-credit-card-interest-rate.

*Rewards credit cards* have become increasingly popular. These credit cards allow individuals to earn benefits when using the cards for purchases. Typically, points accumulate for each dollar charged on the card, and individuals can redeem these points for various rewards. Reward cards usually require good credit for approval. Details vary widely among programs, but some examples of rewards credit cards are:

- **Cash back credit cards.** With these cards, individuals earn cash back when they make a purchase. The percentage of cash back ranges from 1–5 percent of the purchase price. Typically, these cards have an annual fee (e.g., $50 to $100). This type of card is best for individuals who pay off the balance each month. If used appropriately, individuals can earn a significant amount of money over time.
- **Universal rewards credit cards.** With these cards, individuals earn points based on amount of use. Rewards can typically be exchanged for items like gift cards, merchandise, hotel stays, plane tickets, and so on. Reward programs and promotional offers often change and individuals should review a card's terms and conditions before applying. Many rewards cards do not have an annual fee, which may depend on an individual's credit score.
- **Hotel, airline, or travel points credit cards.** Often co-branded with hotels or airlines, these cards allow individuals to earn points for dollars spent that can be redeemed for hotel stays, flights, or other travel expenses. Many of these cards come with an annual fee. For individuals who do not travel often, the annual fee may outweigh the benefits of the rewards earned.
- **Retail rewards credit cards.** Co-branded with a retailer (e.g., Amazon.com), these cards allow individuals to earn points for dollars spent. When used at the co-branded retailer, individuals are usually offered additional discounts or double points. Individuals should try not to carry a balance on these cards, as they generally have high interest rates.
- **Gas credit cards with points or rebates.** General gas cards can be used at any station, while brand-specific cards only provide benefits at one company. Benefits are earned for using the card to purchase gas. For individuals who tend to be loyal to a certain gas company, a brand-specific card may be beneficial.

When individuals are thinking about a new credit card, they should weigh their options carefully to determine which rewards they would benefit from the most. For example, if they do not travel, then an airline card is not the best option. For others, having a card without an annual fee may outweigh the benefit of getting 1 percent cash back.

Once individuals have a card, they should also think carefully about maximizing the benefits. For example, perhaps instead of trading in rewards for merchandise, they can choose a gift card to purchase needed items from online retailers. Occasionally, credit card companies will offer the option to use rewards to pay down a balance. Individuals should also pay attention to cards with specific spending categories to maximize benefits (e.g., gas, groceries). Credit cards can be a highly useful financial tool if used strategically and responsibly.

When considering the future and an individual's financial health, other sources of income, and taxes, meeting with a financial professional can be extremely beneficial. Individuals should consider working with financial planners or credit counseling agencies to get assistance with achieving their long-term financial goals.

## V. Understanding Consumer Rights

To effectively maintain or rebuild financial health, individuals should understand what legal rights they have as a consumer, and the various entities with which they may interact.

The Consumer Financial Protection Bureau (CFPB) is responsible for enforcing laws that protect consumers. They have announced that they will improve the educational tools on their website to help those with medical debt understand the rules about medical billing and help people find financial assistance. The CFPB also investigates the credit reporting agencies and bill collectors who violate patients' rights.

### A. Medical Debt and Credit Reports

As of July 2022, the three main credit reporting companies began changing how medical debt in collections affects credit reports. For individuals who have paid off their medical debt after it was sent to a collection agency, the debt will no longer appear on their credit report. Also, for individuals who have new medical bills sent to a collection agency, those bills will not be added to their credit report until the bill has been in collections for one year. As of April 2023, medical debts of less than $500 will no longer appear on credit reports.[59]

In 2022, the Biden Administration announced some new ways the federal government plans to help people manage medical debt. The federal government backs many of the loans taken out by homebuyers each year through the Federal Housing Administration (FHA), the U.S. Department of Agriculture's (USDA's) Rural Development program, and the Federal Housing Finance Authority (FHFA). These agencies have made changes to decrease the impact of medical debt on an individual's chances of getting a loan.

- FHA will no longer take medical debt into consideration when making a decision about a loan application.

59. *Have Medical Debt? Anything Already Paid or under $500 Should No Longer Be on Your Credit Report*, CFPB (May 8, 2023), https://www.consumerfinance.gov/about-us/blog/medical-debt-anything-already-paid-or-under-500-should-no-longer-be-on-your-credit-report.

- USDA will not include recurring medical debt in an individual's debt-to-income ratio, which increases the amount individuals can borrow.
- FHFA will be reviewing how they use medical debt in their processes to improve an individual's chances of getting a loan.

With these steps, potential homebuyers with medical debt will be more likely to get mortgages than in the past.[60]

In addition, the U.S. Department of Veterans Affairs (VA) will stop reporting medical debt to credit agencies altogether. Additionally, the VA is working to create an easier process to request the forgiveness of medical debt, including an online form and a simple income requirement. The current process has been so difficult that many who would benefit from forgiveness are deterred from applying.

## B. Dealing with Discrepancies on Credit Reports

While an individual's overall credit score is important, it is only part of the equation. Consumers should also know what is listed in their actual credit reports.

The Fair Credit Reporting Act (FCRA)[61] is a federal law that provides consumers with various protections. Under the FCRA, individuals must be told when information in their credit report is used against them (e.g., a loan was denied because of history of past late payments).[62]

Each of the three federal credit bureaus is required to provide individuals with a free copy of their credit report once every 12 months. However, individuals must proactively request a report. Copies of credit reports can be ordered online at https://www.annualcreditreport.com or by calling (877) 322-8228. Credit scores will not be affected by the consumer requesting an annual credit report. It may be beneficial for individuals to spread out their requests of credit reports throughout the year, depending on their motivations. If individuals are simply checking their report to ensure accurate information, it might be most useful to spread out their requests from each bureau—for instance, request their report from Equifax in January, from Experian in May, and TransUnion in October. However, if an individual is trying to use their credit to obtain a loan, it may be most useful to check all three bureaus' reports at once. However, these reports will not include the corresponding three-digit credit score. These bureaus are permitted to charge consumers a nominal fee for providing a score. Individuals should be wary of services that require them to input credit card information before they provide a report or score because these are not truly "free."

---

60. Fact Sheet, The White House, The Biden Administration Announces New Actions to Lessen the Burden of Medical Debt and Increase Consumer Protection (Apr. 11, 2022), https://www.whitehouse.gov/briefing-room/statements-releases/2022/04/11/fact-sheet-the-biden-administration-announces-new-actions-to-lessen-the-burden-of-medical-debt-and-increase-consumer-protection.

61. 15 U.S.C. § 1681.

62. *Credit Reporting*, FED. TRADE COMM'N, https://www.ftc.gov/news-events/media-resources/consumer-finance/credit-reporting (last visited Dec. 1, 2024).

that trial period is over, they will start charging monthly fees.

Typically, they will provide a service for free for an initial amount of time and after that trial period is over, they will start charging monthly fees.

Another reason for individuals to check their credit is to protect against identity theft. After receiving their credit report, individuals should check to make sure that the information is correct. A credit bureau is permitted to report the most accurate negative information (e.g., a late payment on a credit card bill) for seven years and bankruptcy information for ten years. If individuals see inaccurate information on their report, they are entitled to ask the credit bureaus to fix the information. Individuals who have an issue with their credit report can submit a complaint with the CFPB online at https://www.consumerfinance.gov/complaint/#credit-reporting or by calling (855) 411-CFPB (2372).

For more information about credit scores and reporting, visit the Federal Trade Commission at https://consumer.ftc.gov/credit-loans-debt and the CFPB at https://www.consumerfinance.gov/consumer-tools/credit-reports-and-scores/.

## C. Creditor versus Debt Collector

The entity from which individuals receive a loan or services is referred to as a creditor. For example, if an individual receives medical care at a hospital, the hospital is owed money for those services and is the creditor. Similarly, if a bank loans an individual money, the bank is a creditor. The individual who owes the money is referred to as the debtor. If an individual does not pay a creditor, the creditor is entitled to contract with a debt collection agency to recoup money owed to them. If an individual has a secured loan, the creditor may also contact a repossession agency to repossess the property (e.g., car, mortgage, bike).

## D. Debt Collection

While it is permissible for creditors to turn unpaid bills over to a collection or repossession agency, debtors still have rights and protections. There are both federal and state laws that limit what debt collectors are allowed to do to collect debts. The main federal law that protects consumers is the Fair Debt Collection Practices Act (FDCPA).[63] The FDCPA prohibits debt collection companies from using "abusive, unfair or deceptive practices" to collect past due debts.[64] It is important to note that the FDCPA does not apply to original creditors (e.g., a hospital where an individual received care).

Debt collectors cannot harass individuals, meaning individuals cannot be contacted at inconvenient times or places (e.g., before 8:00 a.m. or after 9:00 p.m., walking out of work) and collectors cannot use threatening or profane language in their

63. 15 U.S.C. § 1692.
64. *Id.*

communications.[65] Furthermore, they cannot tell individuals they will be imprisoned for unpaid debt, threaten to include their names in a published list of debtors, or erroneously threaten to sue. If the debt collector contacted a third party (e.g., an employer) to locate the individual, they can only ask for the individual's contact information (i.e., address, phone number, and place of employment). They cannot disclose that the individual owes money or contact the third-party multiple times, unless there is a reasonable belief that the third party was untruthful.[66]

A debt collector is required to send an initial notice to the debtor describing the amount of debt and the name of the creditor. The individual then has 30 days to dispute the validity of the debt or pay the amount. If a creditor contacts an individual via phone, the individual may ask for the creditor's contact information and inform them to expect a response by mail. Sample response letters can be found at https://www.consumerfinance.gov/ask-cfpb/what-should-i-do-when-a-debt-collector-contacts-me-en-1695. Also, if an individual believes that the debt collector has made a mistake (e.g., the bill has already been paid, or it was not submitted to the insurance company correctly), the individual should inform the collection agency that the bill is being disputed. In this circumstance, it is also advisable to follow up with the health care provider to get clarification on why the bill was sent to collections.

Individuals are never required to give a debt collector their credit card number over the phone to satisfy a debt. In fact, most financial planners would warn against doing this, for a couple of reasons. First, there are some debt collection scams out there, so it is important to make sure that the collector is a legitimate entity. Second, as discussed previously, it is generally inadvisable to pay medical bills by credit card due to the high interest rates.

For more information about the limits placed on debt collectors, visit https://consumer.ftc.gov/articles/debt-collection-faqs. If an individual believes that a debt collector has violated their rights, a report can be filed with the CFPB (https://www.consumerfinance.gov/complaint/#debt-collection). Also, many states have their own debt collection laws that are different from the federal FDCPA. Contact each state's attorney general's office (https://www.naag.org) for more information.

## E. Bankruptcy

If an individual has already worked with a credit counseling agency and is still unable to pay or negotiate a payment plan for medical or other bills, the individual may want to consider bankruptcy and talking with a bankruptcy attorney. It is critical for individuals to be informed about the bankruptcy process and its impact on their credit.

---

65. *Id.* § 1692c(A)(1).
66. *Id.* § 1692(c).

### Tips When Considering Bankruptcy

1. **Assess current financial situation.**
2. **Pull free credit report and check for accuracy.** If creditors are excluded from bankruptcy filings, individuals may go through the entire process and still owe other creditors.
3. **Inform all debt collectors and creditors.** Bankruptcy law requires that all debt collection calls, letters, and efforts to reach debtors cease once a bankruptcy petition is successfully filed in court.
4. **Get a credit counseling certificate.** Before an individual can file for bankruptcy, they must obtain a certificate of successful completion of credit counseling with a government-certified counseling agency (https://www.nfcc.org).
5. **Get an attorney.** Bankruptcy laws have become so complex that most experts agree individuals should not attempt to file by themselves.

## 1. Types of Bankruptcy

There are different types of bankruptcy. Chapter 13 and Chapter 7 may be the most relevant to individuals coping with cancer.

In a Chapter 13 bankruptcy, often called "reorganization," individuals use their income to pay some or all of what they owe to creditors over time. Typically, the payment plans range from three to five years, depending on the size of debts and income. In return, individuals may keep their property. The repayment plan describes in detail how (and how much) the individual will pay for each debt. For example, homeowners who have defaulted on their mortgages may be given extra time to catch up on their payments. Unsecured debts, like credit cards, may be paid in full or a percentage of the amount owed over time, without facing late charges and interest rates. In order for the Chapter 13 bankruptcy to proceed, the court must approve a repayment plan and agree that an individual has enough income to meet the payment obligations under the plan.

Chapter 7 bankruptcy, also called "straight" or "liquidation" bankruptcy, discharges most types of debt, and, in return, individuals sell (liquidate) any nonexempt property in order to pay their creditors.

The types of debt that can be discharged under Chapter 7 include:

- **Credit card debt.** Since credit card debt is considered nonpriority unsecured debt, any outstanding balance remaining after individuals complete their repayment plan is discharged.
- **Medical bills.** Medical debt is one of the main reasons people file for bankruptcy. If individuals coping with cancer incur debt because their medical care

was not fully covered by insurance, they may be able to discharge outstanding medical bills.

- **Personal loans.** Similar to credit card debt, any personal loans an individual has may also be discharged at the end of bankruptcy. However, individuals should keep in mind that if they pledged an asset as collateral for the loan, bankruptcy may discharge an individual's personal liability on the loan but the creditor can usually repossess the collateral.
- **Older tax obligations.** Most tax obligations are "nondischargeable priority debts," which means they will not be discharged through the bankruptcy process. However, certain taxes (such as older income taxes) may be considered nonpriority debts and get discharged if individuals filed returns on time and did not commit fraud.

## 2. Bankruptcy Limitations

There are also limits to bankruptcy.

Bankruptcy cannot:

- **Prevent a secured creditor from repossessing property.** A bankruptcy discharge does not eliminate liens. So, if individuals have secured debts (i.e., a debt where the creditor has a lien on property and can repossess it if the individuals do not pay the debt), bankruptcy can eliminate the debt, but the creditor can still repossess the property (e.g., a car loan).
- **Eliminate child support and alimony obligations.** Child support and alimony obligations survive bankruptcy. Individuals will continue to owe these debts in full, just as if they had never filed for bankruptcy. If individuals file for Chapter 13 bankruptcy, their plan will provide for these debts to be paid in full.
- **Eliminate student loans, except in very limited circumstances.** Student loans can be discharged in bankruptcy only if an individual can show that repaying the loan would cause "undue hardship," a very high standard to meet. An individual must be able to show not only that they cannot afford to pay the loans now, but also that the individual has very little likelihood of being able to pay the loans in the future. For example, if a young adult who has been diagnosed with a brain tumor and due to the resulting cognitive deficits is unable to maintain employment and earn an income, the young adult may be able to discharge student loans.
- **Eliminate most tax debts.** Eliminating tax debt in bankruptcy is challenging; however, some older debts for unpaid income taxes may be discharged.
- **Eliminate other "nondischargeable" debts.** Nondischargeable debts, under either Chapter 7 or Chapter 13 bankruptcy, include:

    - o Debts not listed in bankruptcy filings
    - o Debts for personal injury or death caused by intoxicated driving
    - o Fines and penalties imposed for violating the law, such as traffic tickets and criminal restitution

## 3. Requirements Prior to Filing Bankruptcy

Over the past decade, laws have been enacted that have made it more difficult to completely eliminate medical debt through the bankruptcy process than it was in the past. The Bankruptcy Abuse Prevention and Consumer Protection Act (BAPCPA) of 2005[67] created additional requirements and limitations around bankruptcy filings.

The BAPCPA requires individuals to complete credit counseling prior to filing for bankruptcy.[68] The purpose of credit counseling is to help individuals determine if there are other options for dealing with their debt, or if bankruptcy truly is the most appropriate option. A credit counseling "briefing" can be conducted in-person, by telephone, online, or in another individual or group setting. The credit counseling briefing should be received from an approved agency within the 180 days before an individual files a bankruptcy case.[69] Most approved credit counseling agencies charge between $5 and $35 for the prefiling counseling, but if individuals cannot afford the fee, the agency may provide counseling for free or at a discount. Courts may waive the requirement that the debtor complete credit counseling if they are disabled, incapacitated, or on active military duty in a combat zone. Courts may also defer the counseling requirement for 30 days after the bankruptcy is filed if there are "exigent circumstances," and the debtor requests counseling from an approved agency but was not able to obtain services within five days.[70]

For a list of approved providers, visit https://www.justice.gov/ust/list-credit-counseling-agencies-approved-pursuant-11-usc-111. In Alabama and North Carolina, visit https://www.uscourts.gov/services-forms/bankruptcy/credit-counseling-and-debtor-education-courses. Once individuals complete the briefing, they will receive a certificate that is necessary to file a bankruptcy case.

## 4. Bankruptcy Eligibility

Prior to 2005, bankruptcy judges had significant discretion to decide if an individual met the bankruptcy requirements. Since the BAPCPA was enacted, if an individual does not meet certain requirements for Chapter 7 bankruptcy, the court may opt to convert the case to a Chapter 13 bankruptcy,[71] which restructures, but does not eliminate, most debt.

To be eligible for Chapter 7 "liquidation" bankruptcy, an individual must pass a "means test," certifying they have a household income below the state's median

---

67. Pub. L. No. 109-8, 119 Stat. 23 (as codified in scattered sections of 11 U.S.C.).

68. 11 U.S.C. § 109(h).

69. *Frequently Asked Questions (FAQs)—Credit Counseling*, U.S. Dep't Just. U.S. Tr. Program, https://www.justice.gov/ust/frequently-asked-questions-faqs-credit-counseling (last updated May 1, 2024).

70. Victoria L. VanZandt, *The Exigent Circumstances Exception to the Pre-Petition Credit Counseling Requirement under the Bankruptcy Abuse Prevention and Consumer Protection Act of 2005: Exigent or Extreme?*, 6 DePaul Bus. & Com. L.J. 265 (2008), http://via.library.depaul.edu/bclj/vol6/iss2/5.

71. 11 U.S.C. § 109(b).

family income.[72] In 2023, the national median family annual income for an individual ranged from $48,603 in Mississippi to $86,370 in Washington, D.C. There are a series of forms that individuals seeking bankruptcy must complete. The first is Form 122A-1, which is designed to help individuals collect the information necessary for a bankruptcy judge to determine if they satisfy the means test. Individuals should include the following when considering their household income:

- Wages, salary, tips, bonuses, overtime, and commissions
- Gross income from a business or a farm
- Interest, dividends, and royalties
- Rent and other real property income
- Child or spousal support
- Unemployment payments
- Pension and retirement income
- Workers' compensation
- State disability insurance

An individual does not have to include income tax refunds or Social Security benefits. If an individual's income is below the state's median household income, then it is possible to file for Chapter 7. There are limited exemptions to the means test for business debts and individuals with recent military service. Form 122A-1 Supp is designed to help individuals determine if they are exempt from the means test, and, therefore, would not need to complete Form 122A-1.

If an individual does not qualify for an exemption or satisfy the means test, the court will look at how much disposable income remains after the individual has paid for allowed monthly expenses, such as rent and food. Individuals in this situation will need to complete Form 122A-2, Chapter 7 Means Test Calculation. This form helps a court determine if the individual has enough money to pay some unsecured creditors through a Chapter 13 repayment plan. If the court determines that the individual does have enough money, it will typically convert the Chapter 7 filing to a Chapter 13 filing.

For more information about the Chapter 7 means test and to download the relevant forms, visit https://www.uscourts.gov/forms/bankruptcy-forms.

## 5. Costs of Filing Bankruptcy

Many individuals are surprised to learn that bankruptcy is not free. In fact, the BAPCPA made it more expensive to file for bankruptcy. The filing fee for Chapter 7 bankruptcy is $338 and the filing fee for Chapter 13 is $313.[73] In addition, the individual

---

72. *Means Testing*, U.S. Dep't Just. U.S. Tr. Program, https://www.justice.gov/ust/means-testing (last visited Dec. 1, 2024).

73. *Bankruptcy Court Miscellaneous Fee Schedule*, U.S. Cts., http://www.uscourts.gov/services-forms/fees/bankruptcy-court-miscellaneous-fee-schedule (last visited Dec. 1, 2024).

will likely have to pay for the credit counseling briefing and approximately $50 for an education course that is required after the case is filed. Many individuals also hire a bankruptcy attorney if they are not eligible for low-cost legal services or pro bono legal assistance. Attorney's fees to file bankruptcy can range anywhere from $500–$6,000.

### 6. Bankruptcy Timing

The bankruptcy process can take anywhere from three to six months. There are also limitations on how often individuals can file bankruptcy:

- Individuals who have received a bankruptcy discharge under Chapter 7 must wait at least eight years before filing for another Chapter 7 bankruptcy.
- Individuals who have filed Chapter 13 cannot file for another Chapter 13 bankruptcy for at least two years.
- Individuals who first received a Chapter 7 bankruptcy may be entitled to receive a Chapter 13 bankruptcy after four years.
- Individuals who received a Chapter 13 bankruptcy must typically wait a minimum of six years before filing a Chapter 7 bankruptcy. However, they may be able to file Chapter 7 bankruptcy sooner if, during the previous Chapter 13 bankruptcy, they paid back all of the unsecured debts or paid at least 70 percent of the unsecured debts, the plan was proposed in good faith, and they made their best effort.[74]

### 7. Bankruptcy's Impact

Bankruptcy can be included on an individual's credit report for up to ten years. It is often the case that bankruptcy does not make an individual's credit record any worse in the short term if there have already been numerous defaults. However, bankruptcy should not be seen as a quick fix to financial challenges, but rather a last resort.

The American Bar Association's *Guide to Credit and Bankruptcy* can be purchased at https://www.americanbar.org or at https://www.amazon.com/American-Association-Credit-Bankruptcy-Second/dp/0375723005. For more information, see Triage Cancer's Quick Guide to Bankruptcy (https://triagecancer.org/quick-guides/bankruptcy).

## VI. Conclusion

The financial impact of a cancer diagnosis can be debilitating for many. As the costs of cancer care and other medical care continues to rise, and the cost of insurance

74. Cara O'Neill, *Multiple Bankruptcy Filings: When Can You File Again?*, Nolo (Feb. 1, 2024), https://www.nolo.com/legal-encyclopedia/multiple-bankruptcy-filings-when-file-again.html.

coverage also continues to rise, it is becoming increasingly difficult to avoid the financial toxicity of a cancer diagnosis.

For individuals who have just been diagnosed or are still in treatment, there are ways to minimize expenses and to access financial assistance options. For individuals who have completed the bulk of their cancer care, they may be most concerned with how to manage their medical bills and rebuild their credit. For individuals who have already triaged most of the financial impact of their diagnosis and treatment, they may be more focused on adopting long-term financial strategies.

One way individuals can ensure a healthy financial future is by making sure that they are properly insured. This includes having adequate health insurance that covers follow-up care and future screenings, a disability insurance policy should they ever have a period of time they cannot work due to a medical condition, and a life insurance policy to help care for their loved ones. These are policies that can be purchased from an insurance company, or they may also be offered as part of an employer-sponsored benefits package. If individuals are looking for a new job, it can be beneficial to identify whether or not these benefits are available.

If individuals leave their job after a cancer diagnosis, they should be sure to explore all of their options with respect to their benefits. For example, they should consider rolling over their retirement accounts into an IRA, seeing if they can convert their employer-sponsored supplemental insurance, disability insurance, or life insurance policies to individual policies, and determine what they are going to do for health insurance coverage (e.g., Consolidated Omnibus Budget Reconciliation Act (COBRA), Marketplace coverage, Medicaid). See the other chapters in this book for more information on these options.

## VII. Resources

General financial resources:

CancerFinances.org: A Toolkit for Navigating Finances after Cancer: https://cancerfinances.org
Triage Cancer Financial Resources: http://triagecancer.org/financial

Education resources:

CancerFinances.org: Education: https://triagecancer.org/cancer-finances-education
FinAid, Cancer Scholarships: https://finaid.org/scholarships/cancer/
Scholarships.com, Cancer Scholarships: https:www.scholarships.com/financial-aid/college-scholarships/scholarships-by-type/cancer-scholarships

Consumer rights and bankruptcy resources:

The Alliance of Claims Assistance Professionals: https://www.claims.org
IRS: https://www.irs.gov

CFPB: https://www.consumerfinance.gov
National Foundation for Credit Counseling: https://www.nfcc.org/
To find a local bankruptcy court: https://www.uscourts.gov/federal-court-finder/search
The American Bankruptcy Institute's bankruptcy attorney directory: http://bankruptcyresources.org/choose-a-state
National Association of Consumer Bankruptcy Attorneys: https://nacba.org

## VIII. Exercises and Discussion Topics

### A. Case Study

William is 32 years old and just had his last chemotherapy appointment. He has been in treatment, which included surgery, for more than a year. He will also need physical therapy to help with some of the side effects from his treatment. During treatment, William had to stop working completely, but is now working part-time. After exhausting his savings, he paid some of his utility bills and health insurance premiums by credit card and is now having a hard time keeping up with the minimum payments. As a result of the missed payments on those credit cards and the fact that he returned his leased car early, William's credit score is considerably lower than it was prior to his diagnosis. Because he is only able to work part-time, his resources are limited and he is falling behind on paying his mortgage, student loan payments, and other bills. He has been offered a full-time job, but would need access to a car. He is concerned he will not qualify for a car loan because of his low credit score and that he will not be able to afford the monthly payments even if he can get the loan. Also, William received a bill from the hospital last week for a chemotherapy treatment that was double what he had paid for similar treatments in the past. Yesterday, a collection agent showed up at his job demanding payment for an overdue bill, which was incredibly embarrassing for William, and he is worried it will impact his full-time job offer. William wants to do the right thing and move past this part of his life, but feels overwhelmed and hopeless. He wonders if he should sell his home to pay off his bills, and, if so, what the tax implications might be, or if bankruptcy is his best option. But he is also concerned that if he sells his home, he will not be able to get an apartment with his low credit score. *What are William's options?*

**Answer.** William should start by assessing his financial big picture, perhaps using a spreadsheet to track all of his assets and debts. Next, he should complete a budget for his current financial situation. William can do it himself, perhaps with the help of an online template, or he can contact a consumer credit counseling agency for help. He should consider contacting his credit card companies to see if they are willing to negotiate a payment plan with him, either by allowing him to pay a lower lump sum to discharge the total debt, or to have more time to pay back the debt. He may also want to consider contacting his mortgage and student loan companies to see if they offer any disability waivers, or could negotiate a plan. While his credit score may be low, he can shop around for a low-interest loan, perhaps from a credit union of which he is a member. William should think creatively about his financial resources. Does he have any type of insurance he can use as collateral for a loan until he gets back on his feet? He should check https://www.cancerfinances.org to see if he can access any of the available cancer community financial assistance resources, or if he is eligible for utility assistance or other financial aid. Perhaps he can set up an online fundraiser since he is not concerned about disclosure and he is not receiving any means-based government aid.

William may also consider contacting the Federal Trade Commission to file a complaint against the collection agent's harassing practices. Before William sells his home, he should speak with a consumer credit counseling agency, a financial planner, or accountant to understand the full financial ramifications. They can also talk with him about bankruptcy and his eligibility.

## B. Discussion Topics

1. More attention is being paid to the cost of cancer care and its financial toxicity for patients. How can costs be reduced? Who should be reducing their costs, picking up the expense of caring for people diagnosed with cancer and/or other serious medical conditions? Health care providers? Insurers? Pharmaceutical companies and device manufacturers? The government?
2. Do health care providers have a responsibility to discuss finances with their patients? Should health care providers be reimbursed for the time it takes to have that financial discussion?
3. Should private health insurance companies be required to provide unbiased, third-party case managers to assist consumers in navigating medical bills? Why or why not?
4. Should there be different bankruptcy rules for individuals facing financial devastation after a serious illness like cancer? Why or why not?

# CHAPTER SEVEN

# Conclusion

## I. Other Cancer-Related Legal Issues

This book addresses the most common issues that arise for individuals diagnosed with cancer and their caregivers. However, we acknowledge that there are many other topics that could be included.

For example, a cancer diagnosis may disrupt the education of children, adolescents, and young adults, who may need to take time off from, or delay entering, school. Students may also experience cancer-related medical and nonmedical complications in school, when attending school during treatment, or returning to school after treatment. Students may also experience long-term or late-term side effects that impact their education. Therefore, parents, teachers, and students should be aware of the educational issues related to cancer, and the legal protections available, in order to meet their needs. For information about cancer-related education issues and resources, visit the module on Education Rights at https://www.cancerfinances.org.

Another area of law is family law, which includes divorce, dissolution of marital property, alimony, child custody, and child support. These family law issues may already be present in a family when an individual is diagnosed with cancer, or they may be brought up by the numerous psychosocial and financial stressors of a cancer diagnosis. There are also legal issues around family building, such as access to fertility preservation, in vitro fertilization, surrogacy, and adoption. For information about cancer-related family building issues and resources, visit the module on Family Building at https://www.cancerfinances.org.

There are also cancer-related legal issues that relate to certain populations. For example, veterans and their family members may have been exposed to toxins, contaminated drinking water, and other hazards that makes them eligible for certain benefits. Veterans may also qualify for a variety of benefits if they served in active

U.S. military service and were released under any condition other than dishonorable.[1] The U.S. Department of Veterans Affairs (VA) is the federal agency that assists veterans with disability compensation, disability pensions, health care, employment, education, and housing. There are also support programs for caregivers and family members. For more information about benefits available, visit https://triagecancer.org/military-veterans-cancer.

Navigating these issues can feel overwhelming and cause stress and anxiety. Staying organized can be very helpful, not only to successfully navigate these issues, but also to help lessen stress and anxiety. There are also many opportunities to get help from your support system. That may include family and friends, your health care team, neighbors, co-workers, or communities of faith. But, sometimes, you actually need a lawyer. And, it is important to understand when it is helpful to get legal assistance and where you can find legal help.

## II. Staying Organized

A cancer diagnosis can come with a never-ending influx of health records, medical bills, correspondence, and legal and other important documents that, over time, can get difficult to keep track of, especially on top of daily clutter. To effectively navigate many of the legal issues discussed in this book, it can be extremely helpful to stay organized. But it can take some time and effort to get organized. Organization may be something that family and friends can help with, especially sorting through mail and medical bills. Here are some organizational tips that might help:

- Keep it together.
  - If things are left scattered, there is a higher chance of losing something important. Consider creating a workspace (e.g., a desk, counter, computer, storage rack, or even a basket) that is dedicated to keeping paperwork organized. Maybe start with an inbox for mail and other paperwork that is waiting to be opened, processed, or filed. Perhaps there could be one file for health care items and one for everything else. Color coding files could make it easier to find files. There are also a number of cancer-specific and other resources to help manage medical bills and other paperwork. See Chapter 6, Finances.
- Streamline a wallet and save money.
  - CardStar is a smartphone app that collects store rewards or discount cards in one place on a smartphone. After downloading the app, an individual can take a picture of the barcode on each card using a smartphone, to save the card. At checkout, the store scans the barcode straight from the smartphone.
- Get rid of junk mail.

1. 38 U.S.C. § 1701 *et seq.*

  - o DMAchoice is an online tool developed by the Direct Marketing Association to help people manage mail. Through this website, an individual can request to stop receiving entire categories of mail, such as catalogs or credit offers, or to unsubscribe from specific companies.
  - o unroll.me is a service to unsubscribe from unwanted emails and helps organize the emails an individual may want to keep.
  - o PaperKarma is an app that helps eliminate unwanted paper mail with a smartphone. By taking a picture of the unwanted mail through the smartphone app, an individual can be unsubscribed from that mailing list.
- Organize electronic files.
  - o Scan paper copies to electronic files to reduce clutter. There are scanning machines that can be purchased as well as applications for smartphones and tablets to act as a scanner.
  - o Utilize a filing system for electronic files with clearly named and dated folders.
- For other practical tips on how to stay organized, watch the recording of the Triage Cancer webinar "Getting Organized" at https://triagecancer.org/webinar-gettingorganized.

## III. Managing Stress

Dealing with cancer-related legal issues can be stressful. Navigating these legal systems can require significant patience and persistence. Here are some practical tips to manage stress:

- **Sleep.** Sleep can be restorative in a variety of ways.
- **Go outside.** Taking a break and getting some fresh air is proven to boost a person's mood.
- **Exercise.** In addition to improving physical health, staying active releases endorphins in the brain, relieves stress, and boosts self-esteem.
- **Engage in a hobby or find a new one.** A hobby that an individual enjoys and that demands complete attention provides an outlet that can improve patience, focus, relaxation, and well-being.
- **Spend time with family and friends.** With the support, love, and company of others, those positive relationships can significantly improve well-being.
- **Do a good deed.** Giving back allows an individual to make a positive difference in the lives of others, which can be very rewarding.

For more extensive information on identifying sources of stress and stress management techniques, visit https://triagecancer.org/stressmanagement.

For information on resiliency, watch the recording of the Triage Cancer webinar "Resilience: Thriving Not Just Surviving" at https://vimeo.com/triagecancer/resiliencewebinar.

Individuals may also consider seeking psychosocial care from a licensed psychologist, psychiatrist, or other mental health provider. Mental health services are covered by almost all health insurance policies. For more information on accessing mental health care services, visit https://triagecancer.org/quick-guides/mental-health-care.

## IV. Accessing Legal Assistance

We strongly believe that gaining a greater understanding of the law, and how to navigate systems related to the law, may be the key to resolving many of the issues discussed in this book. And, while we hope that this book provides a greater understanding of the law and serves as a tool to help people exercise their legal rights, we recognize that accessing legal assistance may be appropriate and necessary.

### A. Finding Legal Assistance

One of the most common ways that people access legal assistance is through referrals from family, friends, and co-workers. Getting a recommendation from a trustworthy source can be a convenient way to find an attorney, but there are other options:

- Certified lawyer referral services
  - Most state and local bar associations have lawyer referral services, which can provide referrals to attorneys who practice in a specific area of the law and geographic location. Some services provide referrals to attorneys who provide an initial free consultation. Some attorneys will provide an initial consultation for a small fee. One of the benefits of using this type of service is that they may be able to provide an attorney at a reduced rate. Lawyer referral services are required to make arrangements to serve people with limited means. Furthermore, some of these programs provide discounted services to people who have been diagnosed with a serious medical condition, such as cancer.
  - The American Bar Association has complied lawyer referral programs by state: https://www.americanbar.org/groups/lawyer_referral/resources/lawyer-referral-directory.
- Legal aid
  - Civil legal aid is legal assistance for people living at or near poverty, for legal issues outside of the criminal justice system. In many cases, without access to such legal assistance, legal justice would be outside the reach of these individuals. Legal aid programs across the country vary in their services, but provide free or low-cost legal assistance in areas such as housing, consumer rights, family law, education, and employment. The Legal Services Corporation (LSC) is a federally funded nonprofit corporation that provides legal services grants to legal aid programs. To view a list of LSC grantees, visit https://www.lsc.gov/grants/our-grantees.

- LawHelp.org
  - LawHelp.org is also a useful resource to locate legal aid and public interest law offices, as well as to access basic information about legal rights, court forms, self-help information, court information, and links to social service agencies.
- LawHelpInteractive.org
  - For individuals who choose to represent themselves, LawHelpInteractive .org provides online legal forms.
- Medical-legal partnerships
  - Medical-legal partnerships are partnerships between lawyers or legal service organizations and health care organizations to improve patient access to legal assistance. For instance, a hospital can offer its patients a legal clinic to complete estate planning documents. To find medical-legal partnerships by state, visit https://medical-legalpartnership.org/partnerships.
- Law school legal clinics
  - Some law schools offer legal clinics, which provide their communities with access to legal assistance and provide students with clinical learning opportunities. These clinics may be a useful way to access pro bono (free) legal services.
- Prepaid legal services
  - Prepaid legal services may be another lower cost way to access legal assistance with a variety of legal topics. An individual can purchase a service directly from a company, but it is important to beware of scams. Individuals may have access to prepaid legal services through an employer or labor union, or through an employee assistance program. Some credit unions and banks also offer access to prepaid legal services.

## B. Cost of Legal Representation

Legal aid organizations, legal clinics, medical-legal partnerships, and other public interest law programs may provide free or low-cost legal services. However, hiring a private attorney could be significantly more expensive. Each attorney operates differently, but, generally, for issues like employment discrimination or disability claims, attorneys work on contingency. This means the attorney will get a percentage of the settlement if the case is won. If the case is lost, then the attorney is usually only reimbursed for expenses. For most attorneys (e.g., employment attorneys), there is usually not a cap on a contingency fee. For other types of attorneys (e.g., attorneys handling Social Security disability appeals cases), attorney's fees may be capped by law. For other types of cases (e.g., estate planning), attorneys may charge an hourly rate or a flat fee for a specific project, such as drafting a will. It is always important to get a fee agreement in writing, including an agreed-upon contingency percentage, if applicable. Individuals should be comfortable asking questions about fees and expected legal services before signing a contract for representation.

For more information about legal representation, visit the Finding Legal Assistance module at https://triagecancer.org/cancer-finances-legal-assistance.

## V. Conclusion

As the number of cancer survivors continues to increase, the need for addressing cancer-related legal issues will only continue to grow, as well. When individuals with cancer and their caregivers have a better understanding of how to obtain and use insurance coverage, appeal denials of coverage, take time off work if needed, access workplace protections and accommodations, protect their estates, and manage other financial stressors associated with cancer care, their quality of life and cancer survivorship outcomes improve.

### A. Case Study: Maria

In an attempt to illustrate how one person coping with cancer can be forced to contend with all of the issues addressed in this book, we introduce Maria.

- *After college, Maria worked as an assistant at a large company for four years. At the age of 42, she was diagnosed with cancer. After talking with her health care team, she decided her best course of action was to initially take four months off work to undergo treatment. When she shared her diagnosis with her employer, and expressed a need to take time off, she was told that she would be let go. At the time, she felt like she was being treated unfairly, but she could only focus on getting through her treatment.*
- *Before Maria was let go from her job, her co-worker, and close personal friend, set up an online fundraiser for her and promoted the fundraiser through various social media platforms, tagging Maria in the posts.*
- *Maria took Consolidated Omnibus Budget Reconciliation Act (COBRA) coverage to keep her health insurance, but her 18 months are up and she is concerned about how to get health insurance coverage with a preexisting condition.*
- *Maria is now 44 and is ready to get back into the workforce, especially since she has student loans to pay back, and a pile of outstanding medical bills. She also has a large amount of debt, as she used credit cards to pay some bills, and feels weighed down by her financial situation.*
- *She is not sure how to deal with the gap on her resume, and how to address it in an interview. Or if she even needs to discuss it.*
- *Maria also has monthly medical appointments and has been experiencing "chemo brain." She is worried this will keep her from getting a job.*
- *At the time of her diagnosis, she was told she may have a hereditary cancer, but she opted not to take a genetic test. Now that her cancer treatment is behind her, she is considering getting tested but is concerned about her privacy and whether or not her health insurance will cover the test.*

- *Maria is particularly worried about disclosing her diagnosis to any future employers because she does not want it to affect her ability to get a job or to affect her two sisters who work in the same field.*
- *Maria has also not made any estate planning or medical decision-making arrangements. When she went through her initial treatment, she experienced a complication and was admitted to the hospital for two weeks while in a medically induced coma. During that time, her rent was due, but she had not given financial power of attorney to her sisters to access her bank account, so they were unable to pay her rent for her. Fortunately, her landlord was understanding, but Maria wants to make sure that things are taken care of if she is unable to care for or make decisions for herself in the future.*
- *Finally, while Maria does not have any significant assets, she does have a few family heirlooms that she wants to make sure are passed to her family members in the event of her death.*

**Answer.** Many of the cancer-related legal issues facing Maria have been discussed in this book.

Maria may have had some legal options at the time that her employer let her go, but she has likely missed her window to pursue an employment discrimination claim.

If Maria is concerned about disclosure, she can learn about her privacy rights related to disclosing a medical condition to a potential or current employer, under the Americans with Disabilities Act (ADA) and state fair employment laws. She should also take into consideration her online footprint and possible inadvertent disclosures that she may have made online (e.g., the online fundraiser in her name). She can take steps to remove any disclosures if possible or think about how she might proactively address any possible disclosures during the job search process.

Because Maria has exhausted her COBRA coverage, she is eligible for a special enrollment period of 60 days to purchase an individual health insurance policy in the State Health Insurance Marketplace. Depending on her income level, she may also be eligible for Medicaid in her state. If she gets a job, then she may have up to a 90-day waiting period before she is eligible for health insurance benefits, so she can keep the Marketplace plan until her employer-sponsored health insurance coverage begins.

There are many steps that Maria can take to address her medical and other debt, such as negotiate with her creditors, access financial assistance programs, and rebuild her credit, to establish a foundation for financial health.

As Maria is still experiencing side effects, such as chemo brain, and she is concerned that those side effects might impact her ability to get or keep a job, then she may be able to access reasonable accommodations under the ADA or state fair employment laws to get help at work.

Maria can learn about her privacy rights under the Genetic Information Nondiscrimination Act (GINA) to protect her family history, as well as any genetic test results, from being used by an employer or a health insurance company. Whether or not her insurance will cover the genetic tests depends on whether or not she is at high risk for a hereditary cancer, such as BRCA1 or BRCA2.

Maria's sisters are also protected against genetic discrimination, based on Maria's cancer history or on her genetic test results, in the employment and health insurance arenas, under GINA.

Maria can complete a power of attorney for financial affairs, and designate a sister as the person who will make financial decisions for Maria if Maria cannot make them for herself. She should also think about other estate planning and medical decision-making documents such as an advance health care directive.

Even if Maria does not have any significant assets, she does have some family heirlooms that she wants to pass to her family members. The best way for her to do that is do document her wishes in an estate planning document. She can choose to use a will or a trust if Maria has family, but if she has an uncomplicated estate, she may be able to use a simple will form, depending on the state in which she lives.

## B. Final Thoughts

This book has highlighted some of the most common legal issues that can arise after a cancer diagnosis, to share practical information to navigate those issues, and to provide useful resources to assist in addressing them. One of the greatest failures of the cancer community would be to not connect people to information and resources that exist to help them navigate cancer-related legal issues, mitigate financial toxicity, address social determinants of health, lessen health disparities, and improve access to care and quality of life. We hope that this book will encourage professionals across cancer-related disciplines to not only share information on these topics, but to advocate for educational opportunities and resources on these topics.

*"Never doubt that a small group of thoughtful, committed citizens can change the world; indeed, it's the only thing that ever has."*

—Margaret Mead

# Index